FEAR OF
ABANDONMENT

FEAR OF ABANDONMENT

AUSTRALIA IN THE WORLD SINCE 1942

ALLAN GYNGELL

LA TROBE
UNIVERSITY PRESS

IN CONJUNCTION WITH BLACK INC.

Published by La Trobe University Press
in conjunction with Black Inc.
Level 1, 221 Drummond Street
Carlton VIC 3053, Australia
enquiries@blackincbooks.com
www.blackincbooks.com
www.latrobeuniversitypress.com.au

National Library of Australia Cataloguing-in-Publication entry:
Gyngell, Allan, author.
Fear of abandonment: Australia in the world since 1942 / Allan Gyngell.
9781863959186 (paperback)
9781925435559 (ebook)
Australia—Foreign relations—21st century.
Australia—Foreign relations administration—History.

Cover design by Peter Long
Text design and typesetting by Tristan Main

Printed in Australia by McPhersons Printing Group

MIX
Paper from
responsible sources
FSC
www.fsc.org
FSC® C001695

For Sebastian, Xavier, Max, Heidi and Annabel

CONTENTS

7 A 'POST'-WORLD: THE 1990s   192

INTRODUCTION

US AND THEM

If we plod along with only the feeble lantern of our vision of contemporary events, unaided by history, we see – to be sure – a little of the past just under our feet; but the shadows are grotesque and misleading, the darkness closes in again behind us as we move along, and none can be sure of direction or of pace or of the trueness of action.

GEORGE F. KENNAN, 1957

The story Australians know best of their country's engagement with the world is one of wars and battles. From Gallipoli and the Western Front, to Kokoda and Vietnam, right through to Afghanistan, war is central to Australians' image of their nation in the world. There is no denying the importance of that history or the valour of those involved, but by focusing on it Australians have neglected another story – one that has been even more important in building their world. This is a much quieter chronicle, of statecraft and diplomacy; of the creation of the institutions that frame Australia's international activities, from the US alliance to the United Nations; and of how the country learnt to live in a region with very different neighbours and to project its own interests and values onto a wider international stage.

This process – foreign policy – has shaped, sometimes decisively, the world Australians now know: a world in which Australia is a close ally of the United States and where Japan is seen as a good friend, where Australians find easy familiarity in Singapore or Bali, in which Australia seeks United Nations Security Council help to investigate a plane shot down over Ukraine, and where it is unsurprising that Australia should host a meeting of leaders from the world's twenty largest economies.

The story of foreign policy – the way Australians and their governments have thought about, and acted in, the world since the end of World War II – is the subject of this book.

Historians debate exactly when and how Australia developed a foreign policy, and that debate forms a background to the first chapter. But however you look at it, the indisputable moment when Australia had full sovereignty over its international policy was when its parliament said it did, in 1942, by ratifying the Statute of Westminster – legislation enacted by the British parliament in 1931 that established beyond debate the international standing of the overseas dominions of the British Crown. So it is in 1942 that our story begins.

Of course, not even the greatest of superpowers can determine outcomes in the world by itself. Foreign policy always involves others. The world is a messy, contingent place and foreign policy is an unceasing cycle of action and reaction in response to an inconceivably complex set of variables. For most of the period covered by this book, the 'others' we are talking about were foreign governments, and Australia learnt to deal with them in traditional ways, by setting up a diplomatic service and working in newly developed forums such as the United Nations. Towards the end of the twentieth century, driven by the technological changes of the information revolution, a new element was added to the mix – the groups international relations scholars call 'non-state actors'. By attacking the Pentagon and New York's Twin Towers in 2001, a small group of Islamist terrorists moved armies and changed the national security priorities of governments all over the world. These groups, too, form part of the story of Australian foreign policy.

Foreign policy is not just a government's response to events outside its borders, but also an effort to anticipate and shape them in ways that advance the country's interests and values. Together with diplomacy, which is its operating system, foreign policy requires imagination and effort. First, a government has to determine how it wants the world to look – a vision – then what it can do to bring about that outcome – a strategy – and finally – tactics – how to use skilful advocacy and negotiation to bring it into being.

Contrary to its favourite myth about itself, Australia is an old country: old geologically, old in terms of the civilisation of its original inhabitants, and an old democracy. But it is surprisingly young at foreign policy. There is something about foreign policy that has always made Australians a little uncomfortable.

That's not to say Australia hasn't developed effective, in some ways distinctive, traditions of diplomacy. It has had creative foreign ministers and made its mark on the world. But the ceaselessly interactive processes of foreign policy, the adjustments and compromises it requires, the close attention it demands, its backroom dimensions, its unheroic nature: these don't sit easily with Australians. In part, that is why defence and security policy has been much more central to their sense of themselves in the world. But if, as the great nineteenth-century Prussian strategic thinker Carl von Clausewitz wrote, war is the continuation of politics by other means, then foreign policy is the politics whose failure means conflict. Its success matters deeply.

This book is not intended to be – and could not be – an account of Australia's response to everything that happened in the world over the past seventy years. For a country with Australia's population size and economic weight, located where it is, many important international issues will arise to which its responses will be essentially rhetorical. It can express its views, throw what weight it has behind one side or the other in debates in the United Nations or elsewhere, alleviate some suffering through aid, but it will not be able to shape the results in any significant way. The unravelling of the Balkans in the 1990s and the collapse of Syria twenty years later are just two of many examples.

There's nothing wrong with declaratory and symbolic policy. It helps shape global values and is important to the way a country thinks about itself. But this book is mostly concerned with those areas of the world and issues on the international agenda that have required complex policy responses from Australia, and where its actions have shaped outcomes. For obvious reasons of where Australia's interests lie and where its influence can be most effectively deployed, this is often Asia and the Pacific. But not always. We will look at the role of the Fraser and Hawke governments in ending apartheid in South Africa, and of Gareth Evans in securing passage of a major international arms control initiative, the Chemical Weapons Convention. Inevitably, though, Australian activities in many parts of the world can receive only cursory coverage in a book of this length.

Most Australian prime ministers take to international policy questions with a sense of exhilaration and relief. The exhilaration comes from the subject matter – the world – which is important and interesting. The relief stems from the fact that, for the most part, this area of government policy is free of the grinding slog of developing and passing legislation and the frustration of dealing with state governments and domestic stakeholders. The constitution is refreshingly unambiguous regarding the Commonwealth government's responsibility for external affairs, providing prime ministers and their foreign ministers with an opportunity to play on a large stage and to influence great causes.

It is important to remember that foreign policy is domestic politics too. All Australian governments use foreign policy to signal to the electorate

their own values and priorities. They are conscious of the impact of decisions on particular groups of voters and on their own political interests. That
will be clear in this story.

One familiar way of analysing Australian foreign policy is to see it
through the prism of two separate 'traditions' – a liberal internationalist
Labor tradition that has put most weight on collective security and international institutions, and a Coalition tradition that has emphasised power and
alliances. There is obviously some truth in this division, as we will see in the
chapters that follow. But if we think about the story of Australia in the world
predominantly in that way, we miss more important elements of continuity.

Of course, some governments have been better at managing Australia's
foreign relations than others, and some ministers have seen further into the
future than others or been more astute and tactically clever. To assert that
there is an essential bipartisanship about Australian foreign policy is not
the same as saying that its path has been preordained or that distinctions
are impossible.

Australians have always been a journeying people, and throughout the
period covered by this book they were travelling, conducting business, falling in love and engaging with the outside world quite independently of their
governments. The people who were Australians changed too. By 2015 there
were more than three times as many of them (16.5 million more) than in
1942, and they looked very different. They had arrived from new places and
brought with them knowledge of and views about other parts of the world.
But this isn't a history of people-to-people relations, although it acknowl-
edges that in areas such as relations with Japan these have been important.
Nor is it a diplomatic history. The development and work of the institutions
of foreign affairs – the Department of Foreign Affairs and Trade and its predecessors – have been covered well by others. This book pays less attention
to the engine room of the ship of state than to the bridge.

It all began, however, in uncharted waters.

1

FEAR OF ABANDONMENT

The fear of abandonment lies deep in the history of European settlement in Australia. 'Here on the summit of the hill, every morning from daylight until the sun sunk did we sweep the horizon, in the hope of seeing a sail,' wrote Watkin Tench, a young British officer who arrived in Port Jackson with the First Fleet in 1788. The colonists and convicts in the struggling British settlement 'on the shores of this vast ocean' had no fresh supplies and no information about the world outside. For Tench, 'The misery and horror of such a situation cannot be imparted, even by those who have suffered under it.'[1] It would be two and a half years before relief arrived.

This book is in many ways the story of how Australia has responded to that fear. For the early settlers in this new land (new, at least, to them; home for millennia to those who were already here), this was the dilemma: how could this small group of people protect an audacious claim to a vast continent far from the places from which most of them had come and from the markets for their products?

For a century and a half after Tench scanned the horizon, only one response was conceivable for most of the people who lived here. They thought of themselves as just as much part of the great British Empire as residents of London or Manchester. They were, in the image they used so often, children of the mother country – scattered perhaps, but bound as family. Australia's security and Britain's were, they knew, inseparable.

The ambitions and rivalries of European imperialism moulded Australia's modern identity. It was why the continent was explored and settled. And those imperial ambitions also shaped large expanses of Asia. India, Burma, Singapore, the Malayan peninsula and Hong Kong were all part of the British Empire. The Dutch controlled the Netherlands East Indies (NEI), the French ran Indochina. Weak and impoverished, China had been carved up, first by the European powers and later by Japan. Japan was the exception to this story of European control in Asia, and the more threatening for it.

Australia had a Minister for External Affairs from the beginning of the federation. The title 'External Affairs' was important. Foreign policy was still conceived of as the responsibility of Britain, which was not, of course, foreign. As late as 1949, Richard Gardiner Casey, the Australian diplomat and future minister, would still be talking of Australia as 'a member of a great cooperative society: the British race, of which the senior partner is our mother country'.[2] And twenty years after that, the department I joined as a young diplomatic trainee in 1969 was still called External Affairs, and relations with Britain were formally handled by the prime minister's department.

Although neither London nor the new Australian government in Melbourne thought in terms of Australia's conducting an independent foreign policy, the Commonwealth needed its own means of dealing with a range of practical issues that came with nationhood. These included relations with Papua – Australia's own colony – and the Pacific, and the control of passports and immigration. The *Immigration Restriction Act* of December 1901 had entrenched the White Australia policy, and the protection of that policy became one of the main external policy aims of Australian governments.

At Imperial Conferences held every four years or so, Australia was given an opportunity – with Canada, South Africa, New Zealand and the other self-governing dominions of the Empire – to discuss imperial foreign policy, but none of the participants was in any doubt that it was set by London.

Even at this early stage, however, Australians were conscious of differences between Australian and British priorities. Australian apprehension about Japan's naval ambitions, reinforced by its startling defeat of the Russian navy in the Russo–Japanese War of 1904–05, would continue to grow throughout the following decades, notwithstanding the alliance agreement signed by Britain and Japan in 1902.

But when war with Germany broke out in 1914, Australians were united in their support for Britain and the Empire. Labor leader Andrew Fisher promised that Australians would join the fight to 'our last man and our last shilling'. Drawn from a population of five million, 330,000 members of the Australian Imperial Force would serve overseas in the Middle East and on the Western Front.

The national unity did not last. The carnage of the war, the experiences of the troops and the deep sectarian and political divisions revealed during the 1916 and 1917 referendums on conscription for overseas service split the country and the governing Labor Party. Labor prime minister Billy Hughes, who had replaced Fisher, broke away to form a new party.

It was Hughes who went to the Versailles Peace Conference at the end of the war. Like the other dominion leaders, he was in an ambiguous position, partly a member of the British Empire delegation, partly representing Australia. He made his mark, declaring, 'I speak for 60,000 [Australian] dead.' Unfortunately, his aims were narrow and short-term: support for tough German reparations, demands for the transfer of German colonies to Australian control, and vigorous opposition to Japanese efforts to include a commitment to racial equality in the covenant of the new League of Nations – for fear that it might lead to criticism of the White Australia policy.

With the war's end, pressure began to build from the other dominions, especially Canada and South Africa, for greater control over their own relations with other countries. The lesson they had drawn from the war was that they needed the right to act internationally and to sign treaties independently of Britain. The term 'Commonwealth' began to replace 'Empire'. The move towards greater dominion autonomy began at the 1923 Imperial Conference in London and developed during the 1920s. A report by the former British prime minister Arthur Balfour to the 1926 Imperial Conference set out the terms of the new relationship, which eventually found legislative form in the 1931 Statute of Westminster. This Act of the British parliament declared the dominions to be 'autonomous Communities within the British Empire, equal in status, in no way subordinate one to another in any aspect of their domestic or external affairs, though united by a common allegiance to the Crown'. For the first time, the dominions' assertion of rights outside their own territory was fully legitimised.

The other dominions took advantage of these changes to appoint overseas diplomatic representatives. But Australia was reluctant. The nation seemed drained and inward-looking as it tended the wounds of war. The conservative parties did not want to have to think about the world and found it more comfortable to defer to London. The Labor Party, traumatised by its split, embraced something closer to isolationism than Australia has seen from one of its major political parties before or since. Both sides believed in the preservation of the White Australia policy and tariff protection for industry, and both expressed their loyalty to the Empire and Britain.

The political uncertainty facing the Labor government of James Scullin (1929–32), as it wrestled with the economic disasters of the Depression and fears that the Statute of Westminster might threaten the unity of the Empire, led the Australian parliament to pass legislation stating that the statute would not apply to Australia until it was specifically adopted. It would be eleven years before that happened.

Even so, from immediately after World War I, tentative steps were taken to expand Australia's engagement with the world. The Covenant of the League of Nations permitted membership by dominions and non-self-governing territories, so Australia took its seat at the table. This became an additional external affairs responsibility, although not one that received much high-level attention.

Formally, information about the world flowed to the Australian prime minister through the conduit of the governor-general, who was still at that time the representative of the British government, rather than the Crown. Stanley Melbourne Bruce, who replaced Billy Hughes as prime minister in 1923, was keen to strengthen Australian links with imperial foreign policy and to secure his own insights into it. So in 1924 a position of London Liaison Officer was established outside the formal channel of the Australian High Commission, to liaise with the foreign office and report directly to Bruce in Melbourne. Casey was the first appointee and held the position successfully until 1931.

In 1933 the Minister for Commerce, F.H. Stewart, convened a conference on Eastern trade in Sydney, announcing that the Depression had taught Australia that 'external trade can no longer be left to look after itself'[3], and parliament passed the *Trade Commissioners Act*, which led to the opening of trade posts in Japan, the NEI and China.

In early 1934 John Latham, the Minister for External Affairs, was sent by Prime Minister Joseph Lyons on an extensive 'mission of friendship and goodwill distinct from a trade mission' around Asia. This visit to the NEI, Japan, China, Hong Kong, Malaya, Singapore, French Indochina and the Philippines was the first of its kind. Latham returned to report to parliament that although this region was 'the "Far East" to Europe, to the old centres of civilisation . . . we must realise it is the "Near East" to Australia'.[4] But Latham's visit had no lasting impact on Australian policy. Requests to Latham from the Japanese foreign minister for the establishment of diplomatic relations were, like other approaches from China and the United States, rebuffed.[5]

Most Australians, carrying memories of the war and facing tough times, did not think much about the outside world. The country was an insular and self-absorbed place. It was difficult, the future external affairs minister, Percy Spender, wrote later, 'to recapture the degree of ignorance of and indifference to foreign affairs which existed in Australia, even in its parliament – before the outbreak of hostilities in 1939, indeed right up to the time when the Japanese swept like a torrent almost to the shores of Australia.'[6]

Nevertheless, a small group of individuals like Latham himself, the lawyer and politician Frederic Eggleston and the public servant Robert Garran, who would go on to influence the development of Australian connections with the Pacific and Asia, tried to generate greater Australian interest in international affairs through organisations like the Round Table movement, the League of Nations Union and the Australian Institute of International Affairs (AIIA). Their numbers were tiny but they began to write for the first time about something called Australian foreign policy, the title of the proceedings of a 1934 conference of the Queensland branch of the AIIA.[7]

And throughout the 1930s the world kept reminding Australians that it could not be ignored. With the Japanese invasion of Manchuria in 1931, the rise of the European dictatorships of Hitler and Mussolini, the outbreak of the Spanish Civil War, the Italian invasion of Abyssinia, and the Second Sino–Japanese War, the hopes of the early supporters of the League of Nations foundered.

From 1935 onwards, the Department of External Affairs was given independent status within the public service, as a separate department with its own minister. It was becoming clearer that Australia needed its own sources of information about the world. In 1937 an Australian liaison officer was posted to work out of the British embassy in Washington. But that was not enough. With the international situation deteriorating, the United Australia Party prime minister Joseph Lyons decided that Australia had to appoint its own diplomatic representatives in the Pacific. He was opposed in this both by his external affairs minister, Billy Hughes, and by Attorney-General Robert Menzies, who saw the proposal as a threat to British unity that would 'lead to nothing but chaos and disaster'.[8]

But although Menzies was out of the government in March 1939 when the decision was taken, it fell to him a month later, as the incoming prime minister, to announce the appointments of new Australian representatives to Washington, Ottawa and Tokyo. As he told the Australian people: 'In the Pacific we have primary responsibilities and primary risks ... What Great Britain calls the Far East is to us the near north. Little given as I am to encouraging the exaggerated ideas of dominion independence and separatism ... I have become convinced that in the Pacific Australia must regard herself as a principal providing herself with her own information and maintaining her own diplomatic contacts with foreign powers.' Even so, he was emphatic that 'I do not mean by this that we are to act as if we were a completely separate power; we must, of course, act as an integral part of the British Empire.'[9]

The first diplomatic appointment was that of Casey, who had entered parliament on his return from London, to head the Australian Legation in Washington. In 1940 Latham was sent to Tokyo and in 1941 Eggleston arrived in China.

In many respects Australia shuffled its way into a foreign policy. Several potential starting points for the history of that policy present themselves, but none would have seemed so to the people who were involved in them. The one indisputable marker of the nation's sovereignty as a full member of the international community was the ratification of the Statute of Westminster in 1942 by John Curtin's Labor government, which had taken office just before the outbreak of the Pacific War. That was the point at which Australia was legally free from any residual formal constraints by London. Not that you would have known it from the parliamentary debate about its ratification. Opposition members worried that, whatever the merits of the bill, even debating it in this atmosphere of wartime crisis would 'inflame public opinion'; it would be seized on by 'the high priest of propaganda, Dr. Goebbels ... as evidence of the disintegration of the empire.'[10]

As attorney-general (and also external affairs minister), H.V. Evatt was equally insistent that there was nothing to see here: the bill would simply tidy up some regulatory loose ends – 'a few dry technical questions of law that have been thrashed out over a long period of years.'[11] Nothing else would change. 'Another question which has been asked ... is: "Will the adoption of the statute weaken the Imperial ties?" My answer is unhesitatingly "No". I go further. I say that the tie between Britain and Australia will be confirmed and strengthened.'[12]

But the changes would come, and it is from this unexceptional beginning that the following chapters proceed. The mounting international crises of the 1930s had shown that a policy of isolationism would not protect

Australia. And the idea that Australian interests could be addressed solely or primarily by trying to influence a single imperial policy set in London seemed increasingly fanciful.

In quite a short period it would become clear that an emerging Australian foreign policy would have to embrace three broad responses to address the nation's fear of abandonment. First, Australia could continue – as it had from the beginning – to embed itself with what Robert Menzies famously called 'our great and powerful friends'. Second, it could seek to shape the region around it to create a more benign environment. Another prime minister, Paul Keating, would explain that as seeking Australia's security 'in and not from Asia'. Finally, as a state with weight in the world but not enough of it to determine outcomes through its own power, it could support and try to influence, in its own interests, the organisations, rules and norms – the generally accepted standards of behaviour that most states apply to themselves and others – which together made up a rules-based international order.

Although the origins of these approaches were seldom acknowledged, the Coalition's ideas about that order rested on traditions drawn from the seventeenth-century Dutch philosopher Hugo Grotius, who argued that the international system requires rules if order is to be maintained. Labor's commitment to liberal internationalism, most clearly seen in the views of ministers such as Evatt and Gareth Evans, was more heavily drawn from the philosophy of the eighteenth-century German thinker Immanuel Kant, who sought to extend individual and national rights to the international arena.[13] But for each of them, the core was the recognition that Australia was better off in a world in which dependable rules – whether governing trade, shipping, civil aviation or warfare – were cooperatively developed and consistently applied.

Elements of all three responses have been woven into the fabric of the foreign policies of every Australian government since. For example, in setting out the principles of Australian foreign policy for parliament in April 1955, Menzies listed support for the United Nations charter, support for close cooperation within the British Commonwealth and between the Commonwealth and the United States, the pursuit of 'good neighbour' policies towards Asian countries, the encouragement of peaceful trade, and our own acceptance of obligations in order to justify the cooperation of other nations.[14]

One more thing was required to achieve these objectives: a seat at the global table where decisions were made. If you weren't in the room, you were too easy to ignore. Sometimes Australia sought better access to existing or proposed organisations, such as imperial forums or the United Nations. At other times, as with the creation of APEC, it helped build the table itself.

In a country like Australia – occupying a continent for itself and without land borders with its neighbours – foreign policy does not register highly with the public. Nevertheless, no government can operate a policy at odds with the general consensus of voters on these questions. On the whole, any Australian government since 1942 that has looked as if it could not handle competently each of those three broad responses has felt the sting of public reaction. Both the major parties have developed narratives – origin stories – that attest to that political need. Labor sources the US alliance in Curtin's 'turn to America' in December 1941; the Coalition in Spender and the creation of ANZUS. The Coalition begins its account of engagement with Asia with Menzies' speech about Australia's 'near north' in 1939; Labor with Ben Chifley's support for Indonesian independence. Labor claims Evatt's contribution to the establishment of the United Nations; the Coalition asserts its support for the global rules-based order. None of these narratives tells the full story, but they each reflect a political need as well as a policy desire.

Over the next three decades, as we will see in the following chapters, those three responses – embedding with strong allies, support for a rules-based order, and engagement with Asia – would shape the emerging Australian foreign policy. But Asia, changing faster than anyone expected, was the region with which Australia most urgently had to come to terms.

2

ASIA AND DECOLONISATION: THE 1940s TO THE 1960s

When the young West Australian Paul Hasluck, freshly recruited from a career in journalism to join the Department of External Affairs, entered Canberra's West Block offices in 1941, he found a handful of professional staff (all male), a couple of dogs lying under desks, and a filing system so chaotic that papers on the Middle East had been misplaced by a part-time filing clerk who thought Syria was a town in Tasmania.[1] By the time he retired as Minister for External Affairs in 1969, twenty-eight years later, Australia had learnt difficult lessons about how to make its way in the world. And no issue so dominated Australian foreign policy during that time as the consequences of the unravelling of European colonialism in Asia.

In 1941 war was no longer a European affair, but at Australia's doorstep. Japanese forces had struck easily through a region whose security, in the hands of European powers, Australia had taken for granted. As the tide of war shifted and the Japanese forces were turned back – on the land in New Guinea and at sea in the battles of the Coral Sea and Midway – the Australian government of John Curtin began to shift its thinking from survival to what sort of world would emerge from the conflict. A general view began to form that Australia would need to be able to think and act for itself internationally, that the United States was going to remain the predominant Pacific power, and that the days of European colonialism in Asia were numbered. There were questions, certainly, about how long it might take for the colonial powers to depart, but it was clear to some that the familiar world in which Britain controlled the seas around India and Singapore, the Dutch held the Netherlands East Indies (NEI), the French occupied Indochina and a weak and divided China was dominated by outside powers was disappearing.

H.V. Evatt

The man charged with managing this new situation was the intellectually gifted, emotionally complicated Minister for External Affairs, Herbert Vere Evatt, known to all as 'Doc'. Evatt had been a brilliant high-school and university student, and while still in his twenties had had a successful legal career and become a NSW state parliamentarian. He was appointed as a Justice of the High Court in 1930 at the age of thirty-six, resigning ten years later to enter federal politics. He became attorney-general as well as external affairs minister in Curtin's government in 1941.

Evatt was one of those people about whom almost everything that everyone said was true. He was ferociously intelligent, ambitious and hard-working, but also prickly, vain and self-centred. 'What was the daemonic urge that drove him on?' asked Paul Hasluck, who worked with him extensively and was a critic. 'Ambition is too simple a reply. I could give six answers to the question and be uncertain about all of them.'[2] For another official, John Burton, who was closer to Evatt in temperament and policy views, he was 'exacting and difficult as a government minister. Many found it hard to work with him. He had little respect for the majority of his public servants. During the war he ignored them, and quickly took decisions with little consultation. He challenged advice and had little respect for those who were not prepared to defend their positions. He had little respect for those who bowed to his views.'[3]

But whatever his personal weaknesses, Evatt imposed a necessary structure and ambition on Australian foreign policy, and had a lasting impact on the way the country thought about itself. The external affairs department he inherited was not up to the task of supporting an independent foreign policy, and he built it up. In the three years from June 1946 staff numbers grew from 210 to 642, and the number of overseas diplomatic missions from nine to twenty-six.[4] He established a diplomatic cadet scheme to recruit university graduates to a public service that regarded them with suspicion. This cadre of clever, ambitious individuals (nearly all of them men; Evatt was thwarted in his efforts to recruit more women) would shape Australian diplomacy over the following thirty years.

Before his appointment, Evatt hadn't shown any great interest in international affairs, but a central element in his thinking was the view that Australia needed to have a seat at the table of allied councils and to be consulted on decisions that might affect it.[5] Evatt was not the first to pursue this aim, but he cemented it as a theme.

Irritated by the Cairo Declaration of November 1943, in which Churchill, Roosevelt and Chiang Kai-shek had agreed to terms of peace in the Pacific without consulting Australia, Evatt was instrumental in convening a conference in Canberra in January 1944 between the Australian and New Zealand prime ministers and ministers. The outcome was the negotiation of the ANZAC Pact – the first treaty-level agreement Australia had entered into without Britain – which committed the two governments to closer consultation and cooperation in the 'Southwest and South Pacific' and closer defence cooperation. The pact ambitiously asserted Australian and New Zealand rights to participate in decisions about the coming post-war settlement and in the new United Nations organisation foreshadowed by the great powers. It proposed the creation of a new South Seas Regional Commission and the convening by Australia of a conference with other powers – the United Kingdom, the United States and France – to discuss the future order of the region. It declared, provocatively, that powers that had built bases on Allied territories during the war (i.e. the United States) had no right to keep them at the end of the war.

The ANZAC Pact, which provoked irritation in London, was the first manifestation of Australia's new international identity after the passage of the Statute of Westminster legislation. It provided the foundation for what would continue to be the closest of Australia's international relationships over the following seventy years, despite differences in strategic outlook. 'I regard permanent collaboration between Australia and New Zealand as pivotal to a sound post-war Pacific policy,' said Evatt.[6]

In the Australia of the later 1940s there was no national issue more sensitive than the terms of the peace with Japan. Australians felt they had earned a right to have a say in what happened next, not least given the experiences of more than 22,000 prisoners of war. But in July 1945, at the Potsdam Conference, the Allied leaders set out the terms of the Japanese surrender – again without consultation with Australia. This reinforced Evatt's antagonism to the idea of a 'great power peace'. His resentment was deepened by the decision, later reversed, not to give Australia independent representation at the Japanese surrender ceremony after the atomic bombing of Hiroshima and Nagasaki brought the war to an end.[7]

By August 1945 the Australian government, now led by J.B. (Ben) Chifley, after Curtin's death in July, had set out for the British government a framework for policy towards Japan. Australia wanted 'radical changes in Japan's social, political and economic pattern'.[8] It sought the dethronement of the Japanese emperor and his punishment as a war criminal and the dismantling of the industrial conglomerates that dominated the Japanese economy. All this, it was assumed, would only be accomplished by a long occupation.

Britain made some small concessions to Australia's concerns. An Australian commander was appointed to lead a single British Commonwealth Occupation Force sent to Japan in the first half of 1946, responsible jointly to the Australian and British governments, and the Melbourne-based academic and journalist William Macmahon Ball represented the Commonwealth on the toothless Allied Council in Tokyo. But the Americans were firmly in control of policy, and by the middle of 1947 both they and the British had reached the conclusion that, with the dimensions of the emerging Cold War now clear, they needed to shift their focus from remaking Japan's society to rebuilding its economy as quickly as possible to counter Soviet expansionism in Asia.

This policy shift worried Australia. Both under Evatt and, more successfully, under his Liberal Party successor, Percy Spender, Australia would try to leverage the new Allied objectives to reshape its relationship with the United States. That is the story taken up in the next chapter.

In October 1943 Evatt, in a statement to parliament that Hasluck had a hand in drafting, had set out an Australian approach to the coming world:

> Whilst ... the time has passed when either the peace or prosperity of mankind can be regarded as divisible and one continent or one nation can be treated in isolation from another, we also feel that, because of our special geographical position and our growing responsibility and power, we can, and should, make a very special contribution towards the establishment and maintenance of the peace settlement in South East Asia and the Pacific ... Our regional approach will not be an isolationist approach. On the contrary, it can and should ensure that the post-war Pacific settlement will be practical and effective in operation, provided due regard is paid to those with special experience of the problems of the Pacific.[9]

The elements of this approach – acceptance that Australia had broad interests in global peace and security but a special role in Asia and the Pacific, and the assertion that others needed to pay 'due regard' to Australian experience and, by implication, interests – would echo through the foreign policies of future Australian governments of all shades.

Meanwhile, the challenge of learning how to manage its Asian neighbours was to confront Australian diplomacy sooner than expected – in a place, Indonesia, which most Australians did not yet know by that name.

Indonesian independence

The collapse of Dutch control in the NEI in 1942 in the face of the Japanese attack had reminded Australians how flimsy the colonial shield protecting their northern approaches was. Australian troops had to fight the Japanese in Ambor and Timor, diverting a whole Japanese division away from New Guinea. By the end of the war more than 50,000 Australian troops were stationed in the NEI, mostly in Balikpapan on the east coast of Borneo.

The Japanese occupation forces had provided some encouragement to the emerging Indonesian nationalist movement and on 17 August 1945, two days after Japan's unconditional surrender but before Allied forces had an opportunity to return, the leaders of that movement, Sukarno and Mohammad Hatta, proclaimed the independence of the Republic of Indonesia.

The British, under Lord Mountbatten, had been given Allied responsibility for the liberation of Southeast Asia, but the forces available to take back control of the NEI, many of them Indian troops, were few in number, and Mountbatten had higher priorities in Singapore and Indochina. British forces occupied enclaves in Java and Sumatra but were keen to avoid confronting the Indonesian nationalists.

Despite wartime promises from the Dutch government-in-exile of a new constitutional order for its colonies, access to the economic riches – rubber, oil and tin – of the East Indies was considered indispensable to the reconstruction of the war-devastated Netherlands. Dutch administrators, some of whom had been based in Brisbane during the war, returned with British forces in September, determined to resume control. They met a hostile reception.

In late October a British-Indian brigade was almost wiped out in intense fighting with republican forces in Surabaya. It took three weeks for the British to restore control. Although the British government supported the restoration of Dutch sovereignty, Mountbatten recognised that he needed to broker a deal between the Dutch and the Indonesian nationalists that would allow his forces to withdraw.

The US administration was politically and temperamentally in favour of decolonisation, but American interests in the NEI were limited. No American troops were involved, and recovery in Europe – including the Netherlands – was a higher priority than anything happening in Southeast Asia, so US officials understood the importance of the Dutch economic stake in its colony.

The Australian government had begun thinking about post-war arrangements in the NEI while the war was still being fought. It expected the Dutch to return, but under different arrangements, perhaps through some sort of international trusteeship agreement.

By 1945 the wartime experiences of Australian troops, and contact in Australia with Dutch evacuees and some of the Indonesian political prisoners and workers they had brought with them, deepened the familiarity of many Australians with the islands of Indonesia. Soon after the declaration of independence, Indonesian nationalists in Brisbane established a Central Committee of Indonesian Independence. An Australia–Indonesia Association was formed in Sydney in July 1945.

The 1945 declaration of independence and the circumstances of the transfer of power from the Japanese to the Allies raised immediate questions for the Australian government. Under the Allied arrangements, the 50,000-strong Australian forces in Indonesia when Japan surrendered were responsible for restoring order in the eastern areas of the archipelago until the Dutch could resume control. It suddenly became urgent to decide what Australian interests now were. What sort of Indonesia suited Australia best? And what was likely to happen there? How could these interests be registered with the other parties involved?

Australian trade unions and the Communist Party of Australia involved themselves in the issue. After the declaration of independence, the Seamen's Union of Australia encouraged its counterpart, the Indonesian Seamen's Union, to boycott Dutch shipping involved in assisting the Dutch to return. In September 1945 Indonesian merchant seamen in Brisbane, Sydney and Melbourne walked off Dutch ships, and later that month the Waterside Workers Federation of Australia imposed black bans on the loading of Dutch ships bound for the NEI. Nearly 4000 Indonesian republicans were transferred back to republican areas of Java in ships chartered by the Chifley government.[10]

The Opposition opposed these developments and they were unpopular with the public, who largely saw the boycott as a communist-inspired plan to deny supplies to loyal allies. Wanting to understand the situation on the ground, Chifley sent Ball, who had been one of the early thinkers about Australian foreign policy, as an Australian representative to the Allied forces in November 1945. This move was a clear sign that Australia had security interests in the future of the colony and reflected Chifley's personal belief that deep reform was needed in the NEI.[11] Ball was received with what he described as 'icy formality' by the Dutch, but was greeted warmly by the nationalist leaders, Sukarno and Hatta.[12]

Ball was impressed by the strength of support for the nationalists, and recommended that Australia support Sukarno's efforts to secure a United Nations inquiry into the situation in the NEI. Chifley was cautious, but Evatt saw an opportunity to advance Australian interests. Faced with the British desire to withdraw and the American disinclination to become involved, he proposed that Australia should intervene militarily in Java in order to hold the ring while negotiations were conducted between the Dutch and the nationalists. 'Our interest in the region lies in security and also in order, provided it is founded on justice, welfare, progress and the satisfaction of legitimate political aspirations,' he told Chifley.[13] Chifley agreed that Australia had an interest in a negotiated settlement but ruled out any Australian military commitments.

Throughout this period Australian diplomats, including Justice Richard Kirby of the New South Wales District Court, who had been sent by the government to Batavia in May 1946 to investigate the death of three Australian war crimes investigators, reported positively about the strength and ability of the nationalists, and more critically about the Dutch, who were dragging their feet in negotiations with the independence movement.

In August 1946 Australia decided to curtail support to the Dutch. The Australian government was influenced in this decision by 'the feeling the Dutch are not making a bona fide effort to negotiate a military settlement and that if Australia facilitated the building up of Dutch military strength under these conditions we might well stir up lasting resentment among the Indonesians'.[14]

Discussions between the Dutch and the republicans continued. In March 1947 they agreed to a complex arrangement under which the Netherlands would recognise the Republic's de facto control over Java, Sumatra and Madura, while the Republic would cooperate in the formation of a federal United States of Indonesia (USI), which would incorporate smaller Dutch-created states in the rest of the archipelago. A joint Netherlands–Indonesian Union would deal with defence and foreign affairs. Under the Linggadjati Agreement, Dutch troops would be withdrawn from the Republic and disputes not settled by negotiation would be submitted to arbitration. All sides had reason to want to secure this deal, but it left important issues unresolved. Even so, it was enough to allow the British forces to pull out at the end of November, leaving 92,000 Dutch troops in place. The target date for the USI's formation was 1 January 1949. Australia welcomed the outcome. Evatt declared: 'Our idea is that Dutch sovereignty should not be terminated, but that the people of Indonesia should obtain a substantial measure of self-government.'[15]

But the Dutch soon began trying to limit republican authority, and in July 1947 its forces initiated a 'police action' that seized back economically important areas in Java and Sumatra from the republicans. Strongly influenced by the newly appointed 32-year-old Secretary of the Department of External Affairs, John Burton, in close consultation with Chifley, Australia announced de facto recognition of the republican government on 9 July. It also took the radical and domestically risky decision of referring the situation to the United Nations Security Council as 'a threat to the peace' under Article 39 of the Charter, the first time the article had been invoked.[16]

On 30 July Australia and India asked the Council to intervene in the dispute. This decision was probably critical for the future of Indonesian independence. Australia's objective was to persuade the Security Council, of which it was a temporary member, to impose a ceasefire and instruct the Republic and the Netherlands to submit to the third-party arbitration mandated under the Linggadjati Agreement.

After US efforts to reach a compromise, the Security Council called for a ceasefire and established a tripartite Committee of Good Offices to help reach a settlement. Indonesia chose Australia as its representative. Australian military observers attached to the committee were the world's first UN peacekeepers.

Australia's actions in 1947, both at the United Nations and in its repatriation of prominent Indonesian republicans, severely tested relations with the Netherlands and irritated Washington and London. Britain had specifically asked Australia not to submit the matter to the United Nations. But the government saw distinctive Australian interests involved.

It did not carry all Australians with it. For Menzies, speaking in a parliamentary debate on international relations, the idea of supporting the nationalists against the Dutch colonists was 'the very ecstasy of suicide – that we, a country isolated in the world, with a handful of people, a white man's country with all the traditions of our race, should want to set ourselves apart by saying to our friends here and there, as in the case of the Dutch, who have been great colonists and our friends, "Out with you, we cannot support you."'[17]

In the following months, another agreement was reached. Named after the US warship on which the negotiators met, the Renville Agreement was a poor result for the republicans. It legitimised the extension of Dutch control over economically important parts of Java and Sumatra, while giving the Republic little except for a vague provision for plebiscites in republican territory seized by the Dutch.

During this period, Australia emerged as the Indonesian republic's most effective ally. Chifley, acting as external affairs minister for much of this time in Evatt's absence overseas, was central to the response, which reflected the distaste he felt for Dutch colonialism during a private visit to the NEI in the early 1930s.[18] Worried about the Dutch economic blockade of republican areas, Canberra contemplated sending direct assistance. Indonesian gratitude for Australian support was evident in the 'touchingly friendly' reception the Australian Goodwill Mission to East Asia, led by Ball, received in the republican capital of Yogyakarta in June 1948.[19]

Pressures from that economic blockade led to a coup attempt by communists in the republican territory, which was quickly suppressed by the Indonesian military. This action would prove important in later convincing the US administration that the nationalist government could be reliably anti-communist.

In December 1948 the Dutch terminated the Renville Agreement and launched a second military action, seizing the main republican towns, including Yogyakarta, and arresting the principal members of the republican cabinet. The response from the Security Council was weak. With the British and the Americans reluctant to break with the Netherlands, the Council called for a ceasefire, rather than a withdrawal of Dutch forces.

India convened a meeting of Middle Eastern and Asian countries in January 1949 to discuss the situation. Australia was represented by the secretary of the external affairs department, John Burton, rather than by a minister. Burton's notes for the New Delhi conference reflect the sense building among Australian policy-makers that Australia had its own interests in Asia: 'Australia believes its own security and prosperity is bound up with the security and prosperity of all Asian countries and that this depends on mutual cooperation and respect throughout the area.'[20]

Burton helped draft the conference resolutions, and this signal of Asian solidarity, together with increased American domestic concern about Dutch actions, stiffened Washington's response. The United States now moved in the United Nations for the return of the republican government to Yogyakarta, the early establishment of an interim government and the transfer of sovereignty to the USI no later than 1 July 1950. The Committee of Good Offices was reconstituted and given stronger powers to make recommendations. When the parties met in The Hague in August 1949, the path ahead was clear: full sovereignty would come.

A stumbling block remained in the future of Dutch New Guinea, the western half of the island of New Guinea, which had been part of the NEI. The Australian diplomat Thomas Kingston Critchley, who would be a central figure in Australia's Southeast Asian diplomacy for the next twenty years, broke the impasse by securing agreement to set aside its status for future negotiations.

On 27 December 1949 the Netherlands formally transferred sovereignty to the USI, with Sukarno as president. The following month, the new Australian foreign minister, Percy Spender, became the first official state visitor to Indonesia.

The unfinished business of West New Guinea, and other new sources of tension, would continue to bedevil the Australia–Indonesia relationship in the decades ahead. In August 1950 the USI was dissolved and replaced by the unitary Republic of Indonesia. But the policies on Indonesian independence driven by Chifley and Evatt, officials like Burton and Critchley and advisers like Ball and Kirby laid down a foundation which would make easier the management of the problems to come.

Australia's support for Indonesian independence had involved some uncomfortable decisions to break ranks with old friends. It was an early example of the successful crafting of an Australian foreign policy shaped around Australia's national interests.

Alarms and anxieties

By December 1949, when the Liberal Country Party took office under Robert Menzies following Labor's defeat, the confrontation between the United States and the Soviet Union had become the central feature of the international environment. Questions were being asked about what the 'great world struggle', as Menzies had described it during the election campaign, meant for Australian security. To what extent was that security still tied up with the broader defence of the Empire and the expectation that in the event of global war Australia would deploy its forces to protect British bases in the Middle East? How much could Australia still rely on a common Empire foreign policy of the sort Menzies was calling for in June 1950 to protect its interests?[21]

The Cold War may have been a global struggle but it was also playing out much closer to Australia and in a region that now looked very different. Even before World War II was over, Vietnam and Indonesia had declared their independence. The Philippines, India, Pakistan, Burma and Ceylon had all joined them by 1948. And, most dramatically, on 1 October 1949, at the Gate of Heavenly Peace in Beijing, Mao Zedong proclaimed the establishment of a new communist state in the world's most populous country.

The question dividing the Australian political parties was not so much the importance of Asia. Politicians on all sides agreed about that. As the incoming external affairs minister, Percy Spender, noted in January 1950, there had been 'a shift in the gravity of world affairs ... from the Atlantic to the Pacific'. His focus was regional: 'Europe has ceased to be of primary importance and ... it is possible for Australia to help fashion vitally the shape of things to come in the Pacific, Indonesian and Far Eastern regions, provided she adopts a vital and forceful foreign policy'.[22] The dividing issue was rather whether it was communism, linked to the ambitions of the Soviet Union, or nationalism that was primarily driving unrest in Asia. That debate would be a central question for Australian political leaders over the following twenty years.

The lesson Chifley and Labor had drawn from the experience of Indonesian independence was the centrality of nationalism to the changes in Asia. For Spender and Menzies, the driving force was anti-colonialist sentiment driven by communism. 'We are a handful of white people in a coloured sea,' Spender told parliament in 1948, 'and all the nations of the East – Burma, Malay, Indonesia, Indo-China – are coming more and more under the domination of the communist ideology. Does anyone in his senses think the events in those countries spring simply from some local national movement? We know very well that in every one of those countries the movement to destroy the constituted authority is activated or aided from one place, namely Moscow'.[23]

An era of what one of Spender's successors, Garfield Barwick, would describe as 'alarms and anxieties' had begun. Conflicts in Indonesia and now in Malaya were focusing Australia's attention back on its neighbourhood.

The Malayan Emergency

The British naval base in Singapore and its Malayan hinterland had always been central to the Australian idea of Southeast Asia. After the war, Britain, like the Netherlands, had to decide what to do with its Asian possessions. It had confirmed in 1943 that it intended to guide all its dependent territories to self-government.[24] The jewel in the Imperial crown, India, had become independent on 15 August 1947. But the administrative situation of the British possessions in Southeast Asia was complicated – a mishmash of nine Malay states whose rulers were in various relationships with the Crown, the Straits Settlements of Penang, Singapore and Malacca and the protectorates of Sarawak, North Borneo and the Brunei Sultanate. When the British returned to Singapore and Malaya in 1945 they moved to bring these states together. After protracted negotiation with anxious Malay rulers, the result was the establishment of the Federation of Malaya in February 1948.

Malaya remained important for Britain – and Australia too. In an era of currency blocs, in which free conversion into US dollars was impossible, Malaya's tin and rubber production was the largest earner of dollars for the sterling area (the countries that used the British pound or pegged their currencies to it). Singapore remained the base for future British military power in the region, whose continuation in some form all Australian governments wanted to see.

Those tin mines and rubber plantations were heavily dependent on Chinese immigrant workers. Chinese residents now represented 34 per cent of the population on the peninsula, many of them poor and politically marginalised. They provided a solid recruitment base for the revolutionary ambitions of the Malayan Communist Party (MCP), which had moved in 1948 from a strategy of peaceful resistance to one of armed revolt.

When three estate managers were murdered by MCP guerrillas in June that year, the British declared an Emergency. The Chifley government had already agreed the month before to send shipments of weapons and radio equipment to assist the British in outlying areas, although it resisted the dispatch of personnel. Soon after Menzies took over, and partly driven by criticism from Keith Murdoch in the Melbourne *Herald* that Australia was taking too little notice of communist threats in Southeast Asia, RAAF aircraft and military personnel were also sent to help.[25]

The outbreak of the Korean War in June 1950 deepened the sense that communism was on the march in Asia. Communist aggression, Menzies argued, linked what was happening in Korea to the insurgent movements in Indochina and Malaya. By sending bombers to Malaya, Australia would demonstrate to the communist movement internationally that there was 'no division among the British countries of the world'.[26]

Drawing on perhaps 4000 disaffected Chinese supporters, the MCP posed a real threat and managed to tie down an increasing number of troops and police. But the assassination of the British High Commissioner in October 1951 galvanised the British and Malayan response, and by 1955 the threat of the Emergency had been reduced by successful anti-insurgency operations and a more effective political strategy. Helped by economic growth in Malaya, the British slowly got on top of the insurgency and in 1957 the new Federation of Malaya achieved independence. In July 1960 the Emergency was formally declared over.

But the Emergency had generated a profound policy shift in Australia. Canberra had agreed in 1955 to the stationing of Australian and New Zealand military units in Malaya as part of a Commonwealth Strategic Reserve. This was the first peacetime commitment of Australian ground forces outside Australian territory, and it was to Asia, not the Middle East.[27] It was both a way of reinforcing a British commitment to Asia and a signal to the United States that Australia was prepared to carry some of the burden of its own defence. Labor and Evatt, now its leader, were strongly opposed to the use of Australian troops to 'bolster up imperialism in South-East Asia'.[28]

The government's argument for 'forward defence', a concept that would dominate Australian military planning for the next fifteen years, was simple: as Menzies explained it in April 1955, 'if there is to be a war for our existence, it should be carried on by us as far from our own soil as possible'.[29]

Richard Gardiner Casey

For almost the entire period of the Malayan Emergency, from Percy Spender's resignation as minister in 1951 right through to 1960, Australia's Minister for External Affairs was Richard Gardiner Casey. Few Australians could have brought wider international experience to the job. After studying engineering and science at Melbourne University and Cambridge, Casey served with distinction during World War I, at Gallipoli and on the Western Front, emerging with a Military Cross and a Distinguished Service Order. After the war he followed his father into business in Melbourne, but his friendship with Stanley Bruce, who became prime minister in 1923, led to his posting to London – in effect, as the prime minister's agent on foreign policy. He made an impact there and developed a large network of contacts, but returned to Australia in 1931 to enter politics. He served successfully, including as treasurer, but after losing a leadership competition with Menzies after Lyon's death he went back to diplomacy in 1940 as the first head of Australia's legation in Washington.

That led in turn to appointments from Churchill as UK minister of state based in Cairo in 1942 and then governor of Bengal in 1944, Casey's first extended exposure to Asia. These wartime appointments of an Australian as a senior representative of Britain seemed less unusual then than they would now. Casey returned to Australia in 1946 and re-entered parliament in 1949. He became minister in May 1951, and his first overseas visit, two months later, was an extensive trip through Jakarta, Singapore, Saigon, Bangkok, Tokyo, Manila, Hong Kong, Pusan and Seoul. Apart from Singapore, this was all new territory to Casey. While in Tokyo he confided in his diary that 'One thing (perhaps beyond others) that I've learned on this trip is the value of our Australian missions in the East and South-East Asia. I had not quite realised before that *we* have something positive and useful to contribute as well as the U.S.A. and the U.K. A great deal of thought and sympathetic attention has to be given to these parts if we're going to get anything like the right answer. And this means maintaining the sort of personal contact that this trip has started, for me at least.'[30]

The idea of 'personal contact' was central to Casey's approach to the job. As his biographer, W.J. Hudson, expressed it: 'His successes as a foreign minister were the successes of a diplomat; his failures were the failures of a politician.'[31] Casey was not a theoriser; he was always happier with the practical and with people. He valued personal connections and tended to see the world in terms of the personalities he encountered and his judgements about them. His department liked him. After the large egos and demanding personalities of Evatt and Spender, he was a relief: polite, solicitous of the welfare of his officers and a good administrator.

Like many of his generation and social class, Casey found no difficulty in being both patriotically Australian and proudly British. 'There is no prouder word than "British" in the world's vocabulary, nor do I believe there ever has been,' he wrote in 1959.[32] But he had a sharp sense of Australian interests. He wanted to align the interests of Britain and the United States and to support non-communist Asia against the challenges he saw from China.

Although his public pronouncements were conventional, Casey differed from his colleagues on some of the deep policy issues of the time – the recognition of China, Britain's role in Suez, the need for greater Australian defence expenditure and the degree of intimacy that Australia should seek with the United States. But he carried no-one with him. His greatest weaknesses were his indifferent parliamentary performance and his ineffectiveness in cabinet. 'I doubt whether there was any other minister during the time he was in Cabinet with me who lost so many submissions,' Hasluck wrote.[33] Casey was politically dependent on Menzies, but had no great influence over him.

Still, he was a frequent visitor to Asia, sympathetic to its people and cultures in a way that Menzies was not, and he argued effectively to the Australian public and to his own department the case for Australia's relations with Asia. 'It is not sufficient for us to be vaguely conscious of the existence of our near neighbours to the north,' he told parliament after that first visit. 'In fact it is necessary that we should get to know them, establish personal contacts, exchange visits and study their problems as well as our own.'[34]

West New Guinea

The problems for Australia's largest neighbour, Indonesia, included the unfinished business on the island of New Guinea. This issue would hang over Australia's relations with Indonesia for the two decades after independence.

From the beginning of the Menzies government, the views of Indonesia and Australia on the future of West New Guinea began to diverge. For Sukarno and Indonesia, the excision of the territory from the independence arrangements had been a ploy by the colonial power to prevent the unity of the new nation. Sukarno's rallying cry for independence had been 'From Sabang' – off the tip of Sumatra – 'to Merauke' – in West New Guinea. The idea that the Melanesian people were different from the rest of Indonesia was dismissed as irrelevant in what was already a multiethnic state whose motto was 'Unity in Diversity'. For Australia, with fresh memories of the Japanese threat in New Guinea, the dominant concern was how a land border with an Asian state, about whose stability and foreign policy there were increasing doubts, would affect its own security and the management of its territories in the east of the island.

During his goodwill mission to Jakarta in January 1950, Spender had been direct in expressing opposition to the Indonesian claim to Dutch New Guinea. Australian views had hardened with the victory of the communists in Beijing at virtually the same time as Indonesia became independent. Spender tried to encourage Washington to intervene in the negotiations between Indonesia and the Netherlands, but as in so many other aspects of Australia's Indonesia policy in those years, Washington had other economic and strategic interests to pursue and wanted to stay out of the dispute. On his own first visit to Jakarta in 1952, Casey had found Sukarno to be 'an attractive intelligent man'.[35] But the passage of time increased Australia's concern about the growing influence of the Communist Party of Indonesia (PKI) on Sukarno. Casey told the United States that Australia would not accept an Indonesian takeover of West New Guinea either by peaceful or military means.[36] Concerned not to increase the chances of a communist takeover in Jakarta, however, Washington steadily hardened its position against the Dutch.

Now in Opposition, Labor's position had also changed. From 1949 onwards it took the view that West New Guinea should not be handed over to Indonesia without reference to interested parties, including Australia and the inhabitants of the territory.

The political and diplomatic focus moved to the United Nations, where Sukarno tried to muster a two-thirds majority of votes in the General Assembly to demand that the Netherlands negotiate with Indonesia over sovereignty. But with the full flush of decolonisation still to come, the Indonesians could not attract the necessary votes. Australia was a leading advocate for the Dutch defence.

By the time of Indonesia's final attempt to secure UN endorsement of its position in 1957, the country's weak post-independence parliamentary democracy was in crisis. A succession of fragile Coalition governments replaced one another and policy swung wildly. In line with the mood of the army and much public opinion, Sukarno moved to contain political parties and strengthen presidential control through a process he called 'Guided Democracy'. His foreign policies became more radical. He established financial ties with Moscow and seized Dutch assets. Most of the remaining tens of thousands of Dutch residents were expelled. In 1957 rebellions broke out in Sumatra and Sulawesi, supported with American supplies funnelled through the CIA. The army was able to put down the revolts, but to balance his increasing dependence on the military Sukarno moved to strengthen his ties with the Communist Party.

These events heightened Australian fears that Indonesia had designs on the rest of New Guinea. It responded in November 1957 with a joint statement with the Netherlands envisaging administrative cooperation which would lead to a united New Guinea. The Dutch committed to self-determination for the western half. But this statement from two colonial powers angered not just Indonesia but other newly independent countries. In the following year the Dutch raised with Australia the possibility of military cooperation in West New Guinea. Casey and defence minister Philip McBride argued against this.

After the failure of the Sumatra and Sulawesi rebellions, the United States reviewed its policy and concluded that the Indonesian army was the most effective anti-communist force in the country and needed to be supported, and that Washington's interests would be best served by working with Sukarno rather than against him. So US aid and arms began to flow. With its interests in Malaya, Britain was also reluctant to keep backing the Dutch, and Australia again found itself with a position that was not supported by its main allies.[37]

When Indonesian foreign minister Subandrio visited Canberra in early 1959, Australian policy also began to shift. In a joint statement with the minister, Australia said it would not oppose a peaceful transfer of West New Guinea if Indonesia and the Netherlands reached agreement. As the secretary of the external affairs department, Arthur Tange, advised the Australian ambassador in Jakarta in October 1960, Australia's policy was: 'Basically … counting upon the Dutch sweating it out and the Indonesians refraining from force.'[38]

When US President John F. Kennedy and British Prime Minister Harold Macmillan met in Bermuda in December 1961, they agreed on the need to prevent military conflict in West New Guinea and to pressure the Dutch into accepting change. Recognising that Australian policy was becoming less tenable, Tange tried to prepare Menzies for the idea that the Dutch would go and that Australian policy had to be reappraised.[39]

Garfield Barwick

Menzies had taken on the additional responsibilities of external affairs in February 1960 when Casey resigned from parliament to become governor-general after being given a life peerage. At the end of 1961, however, he handed the portfolio to Garfield Barwick. It was Barwick who cut the cord on West New Guinea. Known as the 'Bradman of the bar', he was a highly successful lawyer who had made his mark in the legal fight against Chifley's proposed nationalisation of the banks and in the royal commission into the Petrov spy affair. He had only entered parliament in 1958, at the age of fifty-four. Feisty and self-confident, he represented a significant change from Casey.

Barwick said later he came to the job with 'no taste for the Dutch position' and had thought for some time that Australia 'was, at the very least, facing ridicule and enmity for its continued support for the Dutch'.[40] In a statement on 30 December 1961 he referred to Australia's 'great interest in the ability of the indigenous people of West New Guinea to have the ultimate choice of their own future, whether it be for integration with Indonesia or for independence'.[41] Meeting a few days later with Menzies, Barwick argued that further temporising could expose Australia to the risk of becoming involved in a colonial war, that neither the United States nor Britain would intervene on the Dutch side in any such crisis and that Sukarno might turn to the communist powers for help.

Menzies concurred and agreed to the release by Barwick on 4 January 1962 of a statement asserting that there was 'no evidence whatever of any present threat to Australia or to any Australian territorial interest' arising from the West New Guinea situation. Effectively, this signalled the end of Australia's support for the Dutch position.[42] As a cable to the Australian ambassador in Washington put it: 'We have been obliged to conclude from the past response of the United States and from our military knowledge of the probability that the United States will not give military assistance to the Dutch under attack, that Dutch withdrawal largely on Indonesian terms is inevitable'.[43]

On 12 January 1962 Barwick put the proposed changes in the Australian position to a somewhat resistant cabinet, acknowledging that the United States and Britain wouldn't support Australia and arguing that the Dutch position of self-determination could constitute an unstable power vacuum.[44] Cabinet accepted the long-term importance to Australia of 'friendly and cooperative' relations with Indonesia but would not come at Barwick's proposal to have Australia mediate between the parties.[45]

The Dutch knew the game was over. In September 1962 they negotiated an agreement with Indonesia providing for West New Guinea to pass to Indonesian administration in May 1963, after a short caretaker period under the control of the United Nations. An 'Act of Self-Determination' would be held in West New Guinea by the end of 1969, although Indonesia made it clear that it did not expect anything other than a decision in favour of integration to come from this.

The Indonesia–Malaysia Confrontation

But the difficulties with Indonesia were not over. Despite the end of the Emergency in Malaya, Britain still had some postcolonial tidying up to do with its territories in Southeast Asia.

Singapore had been self-governing since 1959, under the political control of the socialist People's Action Party of Lee Kuan Yew, then thought to be at the radical end of the anti-colonial spectrum. Britain remained responsible for foreign affairs and defence, but full independence was expected to come in 1963. Australia worried that an independent Singapore might turn to Beijing and that Britain's remaining small Borneo states looked very vulnerable on their own. So when the Malayan prime minister, Tunku Abdul Rahman, suggested in 1961 the formation of a federation including Malaya, Singapore, Sabah and Sarawak (North Borneo), plus the Sultanate of Brunei, Australia was sympathetic. Australia's principal goal, a continuing British presence in the region, seemed more likely to be served with the larger state.

The other proposed participants had their own interests in the scheme. Lee Kuan Yew saw union with Malaya as essential for the economic survival of his small island, while Tunku Abdul Rahman wanted the Borneo states as members to ensure that the Malay ethnic balance was not skewed by Singapore's Chinese majority population. Brunei dropped out of the negotiations at the end of 1962, after an internal popular revolt, which was repressed by British military forces.

The neighbours were hostile, however. Sukarno saw the federation of Malaysia, which would border Indonesia on the island of Borneo, as a 'neo-colonialist' plot by Britain to perpetuate its presence in Southeast Asia. He worried, too, about ethnic Chinese influence in the new federation. For its part, the Philippines had a historic claim to Sabah.

At first, Indonesia seemed to acquiesce in the new arrangements, but Sukarno's hostility steadily increased. In January 1963 his foreign minister, Subandrio, described Indonesia's attitude as one of 'confrontation'.[46] The Confrontation with Malaysia turned out to be a mixture of hostile rhetoric, trade embargoes, political manoeuvring and, after April 1963, raids and military incursions.

Britain asked Australia and the United States for help in establishing Malaysia. The Americans, whose focus was increasingly on Indochina, were worried about upsetting Sukarno, who held the unstable balance of power in Indonesia between the army, Muslim groups and the Communist Party. They made it clear that they would be staying out of anything beyond diplomatic help.

Despite the presence of Australian forces in Malaya, Garfield Barwick was cautious – due to the uncertainties of the plan, the hostility of Indonesia and the Philippines, and the ambivalence of the Americans. In February 1963 he got his cabinet colleagues to agree that Australia's objective should be to seek to improve relations with Indonesia 'wherever and in whatever ways possible'.[47] In March, however, cabinet agreed to continue supporting the creation of Malaysia, while managing the possible costs to relations with Indonesia through diplomacy 'directed toward maintaining a firm but friendly attitude towards this country'.[48]

In the first half of 1963 Barwick tried on his own initiative to reconcile Indonesia, Malaya and the Philippines. Although tensions were increasing as Indonesian 'volunteers' crossed into Sarawak, his efforts were rewarded when the three countries met in June and agreed to form a loose confederation called Maphilindo. Indonesia and the Philippines would agree to support the establishment of Malaysia if the UN secretary-general ascertained that it was endorsed by the people of Sabah and Sarawak. The three countries agreed that foreign bases should not be allowed in Southeast Asia and that they would 'abstain from the use of arrangements to serve the particular interests of any of the big powers'.[49]

Menzies was critical of Barwick's handling of the issue, believing that Sukarno had been the main beneficiary of his policies, given 'a lever to urge for a neutralist posture within [Maphilindo] and thus press for the winding up of bases'.[50] Menzies signalled his desire for firmer Australian support for Britain. Australia was facing growing difficulty reconciling the positions of Washington, whose focus was preserving a stable non-communist Indonesia, and Britain, which gave priority to defending Malaysia.[51]

Malaysia was formally established on 16 September 1963, but despite the earlier signs of compromise, it was soon clear that Indonesian confrontation would continue. Mobs in Jakarta attacked the British and Malaysian embassies. Sukarno declared he would 'gobble Malaysia raw'.[52]

On his way to the celebrations in Kuala Lumpur, Barwick had visited Jakarta and told an angry Sukarno that if Australia was forced to choose between Indonesia and Malaysia, it would choose Malaysia.[53] So when Macmillan asked for the help of Australian troops in defending Malaysia, Menzies announced, cautiously, that Australia would 'to the best of our powers and by such means as shall be agreed upon with the Government of Malaysia, add our military assistance to the efforts of Malaysia and the United Kingdom in the defence of Malaysia's territorial integrity and political independence'.[54]

By the end of 1963 Australia had committed itself to assisting Britain to defend Malaysia against Indonesia, despite Washington's continuing neutrality. It saw its main interest as maintaining a forward military position in a British-influenced state, despite the risk of conflict – even war – with Indonesia. Australia consulted the United States about the support it could expect under the ANZUS Treaty if Australian troops came under Indonesian attack. The response Barwick received was cautious. Any support from American ground forces, even in the case of direct Indonesian attack, was ruled out.

For the first half of 1964 relations with Indonesia were reasonably smooth, thanks in part to skilful diplomacy by the Australian ambassador in Jakarta, Keith ('Mick') Shann, and his staff. But from the middle of that year tensions deepened. By then, Barwick had resigned to become Chief Justice of the High Court, and Paul Hasluck had replaced him as minister.

On 17 August Indonesia landed armed groups at various points on the Malayan peninsula and Sukarno proclaimed his 'Year of Living Dangerously'. When Indonesian paratroops were dropped in northern Johore on 2 September, the United Kingdom assured Malaysia that it would help.

From late 1964 to early 1965 the danger of war was real. Indonesia withdrew from the United Nations in January 1965, and Sukarno talked about collaboration with China to lead the world's 'New Emerging Forces'. Indonesia built up its forces on the borders of Sarawak and Sabah, and in January 1965 Australia shifted its combat forces from peninsular Malaya to Borneo, where they were to remain until the end of the Confrontation. Australia approved the possible use of Darwin and Fremantle in British plans to retaliate against selected military targets in Indonesia,[55] and Australian and Indonesian forces engaged in sporadic hostilities on the Sarawak border.

It was a complex policy dilemma for Canberra. Australia shared Washington's concern that a direct conflict with Indonesia would tip the fragile internal political balance in favour of the Communist Party, and it was also conscious of the growing possibility that the United States would soon ask for assistance in Indochina. In fact, the commitment of an Australian battalion to Vietnam came less than three months later.

Australia managed the foreign policy test of Confrontation skilfully. It had a clear policy and expressed it consistently. It supported Malaysia's formation but wanted to maintain close relations with Indonesia. Menzies kept repeating that Australia and Indonesia had 'vital interests in common': this issue of Malaysia was the one thing preventing the development of that relationship. Ministers and diplomats adhered closely to those lines.[56] In Jakarta, the embassy maintained a dialogue with Sukarno throughout the period, and Australian aid continued.

Confrontation ended when the murder of six army generals on 30 September 1965, in circumstances still unclear today, generated a violent struggle for power between the Communist Party and the Indonesian army under the control of General Suharto, who was also supported by student groups. At least half a million and perhaps as many as a million people were killed throughout Java and Bali as alleged communists and their sympathisers were targeted by the military. The conflict ended with an army victory and Suharto's emergence as the country's pre-eminent force. Sukarno remained in office but was sidelined. By March 1966, when Suharto acquired emergency powers to re-establish order and security and dissolved the Communist Party, Sukarno had been effectively deposed.

The new Indonesian foreign minister, Adam Malik, and his Malaysian counterpart, Tun Abdul Razak, negotiated an end to Confrontation in May 1966, and a peace agreement followed in August. Thus, in the end there was an Asian solution to the problem, underlining the diminishing political role of the Western colonial powers in Southeast Asia.

That point was reinforced by developments in Singapore. Throughout 1965, political tension had been growing between Kuala Lumpur and Singapore as a result of racial tensions between Malays and Chinese, and of Kuala Lumpur's unwillingness to accommodate Singapore's interests. On 7 August 1965 these pressures culminated in Tunku Abdul Rahman and Lee Kuan Yew agreeing that Singapore should separate from Malaysia. A shocked United Kingdom and Australia were told about this agreement only hours before its announcement.

The region now looked very uncomfortable to Australia. The merger of Singapore and Malaya, which had brought Australia close to war with Indonesia, had failed, but in the process Australia had found itself with additional defence responsibilities in Sabah, where its troops were now stationed. Britain, whose continuing military presence in the region had been the underlying objective of Australian policy, was talking about getting out. Indonesia's future was deeply uncertain, and the United States was pulling Australia towards Indochina – a story taken up in Chapter 3.

Relations with the Indonesian New Order

As Suharto's power grew, Indonesian relations with Australia slowly improved. Hasluck paid three visits to Indonesia in the eighteen months after August 1966. In February 1967 Suharto was appointed as acting president and by mid-1967 his 'New Order' government was in control. He appointed pragmatic civilian advisers and streamlined the administration. In 1966 a group of Western-trained Indonesian economists, with the assistance of a visiting International Monetary Fund (IMF) mission, had worked out the economic strategy for the New Order. Australia became a core member of a new Inter-Governmental Group on Indonesia (IGGI) to coordinate aid.

John Gorton paid a prime ministerial visit in June 1968, and his successor, William McMahon, followed in June 1972. Suharto made the first visit to Australia by an Indonesian president at the beginning of 1972. Australian ministers and diplomats under this and subsequent governments would accord much greater weight to the strategic implications of these developments than to human rights concerns about the mass killings or the many tens of thousands of political prisoners being held by Suharto's government.

In July 1969, as agreed, an act of self-determination was held in West New Guinea: unsurprisingly, the decision to join Indonesia was ratified by the unanimous vote of a 'representative' assembly. The secretary-general, Australia and the Netherlands all endorsed the result. Asked to comment on the consultations, foreign minister Gordon Freeth referred elusively to the considerations facing 'any responsible government or person who has in mind both the interests of the people concerned and the intractable facts of history, geography, and economic and political development'.[57] It was those intractable facts that had in the end shaped Australian policy.

ASEAN

The end of Confrontation and the separation of Malaysia and Singapore made it possible for the countries of the region to think again about regional cooperation. Some rather anaemic efforts had been made in the past, such as Maphilindo and an earlier Association of Southeast Asia (ASA) comprising Malaya, Thailand and the Philippines. Australia itself had in 1966 joined an Asia Pacific Council (ASPAC) involving the non-communist states of South Korea, Taiwan, South Vietnam, the Philippines, Thailand, Malaysia and New Zealand.

But with the negotiated end of Confrontation in May 1966, the Thai foreign minister, Thanat Khoman, suggested the creation of a new regional organisation that would bring Thailand, Malaysia, Singapore, the Philippines, and Indonesia together in an Association of Southeast Asian Nations (ASEAN). This might eventually be extended to the rest of the region.

The new organisation was formed in August 1967. Its agenda was largely economic and social, but it also had a deeper strategic purpose: to embed Indonesia in a formal framework with its neighbours, and to provide solidarity for the non-communist states of the region as the war in Indochina intensified. Drawing on themes from the Bandung Conference of 1955, which had established the Non-Aligned Movement, the ASEAN members agreed, at Indonesia's insistence, that regional countries themselves had principal responsibility for preserving the region's stability, and that foreign bases were temporary.

The Australian government welcomed the new organisation but, especially because of the neutralist sentiments in the preamble, no serious thought was given to Australian membership. It was hard at that stage to see whether ASEAN would develop far, but it represented a new sort of home-grown Asian regionalism to which Australia would soon have to respond.

Papua New Guinea

Australia was not simply an observer of the process of European decolonisation; it had its own stake in the system. At the beginning of World War I, the Dutch held the western half of the island of New Guinea and the Germans the northeast, but the rest of the island, Papua, was an Australian colony. Ownership had been transferred to Australia from Britain soon after Federation; Britain had only annexed the territory in 1884–85 under pressure from Queensland. That pressure reflected a widespread Australian fear that the Southwest Pacific was a potential source of threats to its security.

At the Versailles Peace Conference after World War I, Billy Hughes had insisted that Australia should annex German New Guinea, as part of 'the defensive ramparts of Australia against naval attack' and to help preserve the White Australia policy.[58] When that idea was rejected by American president Woodrow Wilson, Hughes demanded the League of Nations mandate for the territory.

Another German territory in the Pacific, the phosphate-rich island of Nauru, was transferred to joint control by the United Kingdom, Australia and New Zealand. Australia became the administering power on behalf of the others in 1947.

Papua and New Guinea received little attention from Canberra in the interwar years, but views about the responsibilities of colonial powers were changing. The idea was growing that such possessions were held in trust for the indigenous people and that the objective of rule had to be the development of those people. This view was reflected in the ideals of the 1941 Atlantic Charter and the 1944 ANZAC Pact, in which Australia and New Zealand declared that 'the doctrine of "trusteeship" is applicable in broad principles to all colonial territories in the Pacific and elsewhere, and that the main purpose of the trust is the welfare of the native peoples and their social, economic and political development'.[59]

With the creation of the United Nations, Australia's Mandate for New Guinea became a UN Trusteeship, and from 1949 onwards both New Guinea and Papua were administered as one, under the assumption that they would be moved progressively towards self-government or independence together.

But progressively did not mean speedily. The early post-war idealism on trusteeship expressed by Evatt soon waned in the face of Australia's insistence in the United Nations that it should be allowed the free exercise of power to govern the trust territory as it thought fit. Spender was still asserting in 1950 that 'Australia is in New Guinea and must in all circumstances remain there'.[60]

The territory was deeply undeveloped. Its people mostly lived a subsistence life, education was limited, and it was the most linguistically diverse place on earth. And progress was slow. Until 1958 the public service contained not a single indigenous member.[61]

But the requirement to submit an annual report to the Trusteeship Council, and the criticisms of India and the other members of the Special Committee on Decolonisation (the Committee of 24), had an effect. Returning from the Commonwealth Prime Ministers' Conference in June 1960, Menzies conceded that, 'Whereas at one time many of us might have thought that it was better to go slowly in granting independence so that all the conditions existed for a wise exercise of self-government, I think the prevailing school of thought today is that if in doubt you should go sooner, not later. I belong to that school of thought myself now, though I didn't once'.[62]

Even so, Menzies was not contemplating early independence or even target dates, as Hasluck, who had been Minister for Territories since 1951, soon made clear. 'Before self-government can be effective in a country as primitive socially and as undeveloped economically as Papua-New Guinea is at present, considerable social changes and economic progress will be required', he told parliament in August.[63]

Hasluck's successor in 1963, the Country Party member C.E. Barnes, was even more cautious. Barnes did not think that independence need be 'the inevitable or predetermined result of political development'.[64]

But international pressure didn't abate. In 1963 a United Nations Visiting Mission led by the British diplomat Sir Hugh Foot recommended an economic survey by the World Bank, a new program of university and higher education, and the election of a representative parliament. The World Bank report that followed in 1964 was largely accepted by the Australian government as the basis for the development of Papua New Guinea (PNG). The University of Papua New Guinea was established in 1966 and produced its first graduate in 1970. A House of Assembly with a majority of indigenous members met in 1964, and by 1969 six indigenous ministerial members had been given budgetary control of some less politically sensitive areas of government.

Although the small indigenous PNG elite formed a political party, the Papua and New Guinea Union (PANGU) Party, in 1967, at no point was there any great internal pressure for movement towards self-government. The populous highlands regions resisted the idea, fearing domination by the more developed regions of Papua.

Even so, Australia was being reminded of the pressures on an administering power. From 1964 prospectors had been investigating rich deposits of copper, gold and zinc on the island of Bougainville. Revenues from the mine were expected to almost double the territory's export earnings, providing a potential economic base for self-government – an attractive prospect for Australia, which provided more than half PNG's budget.

But the Australian administration's crude handling of local landowners and its paternalistic approach to negotiations encouraged local sentiment in favour of Bougainville's secession or association with the neighbouring

Solomon Islands.[65] A deal was eventually reached in 1967 providing 5 per cent of royalties to landowners. The administration granted Bougainville Copper, a subsidiary of Conzinc Riotinto of Australia (CRA), a 42-year lease on the land. But a stock of future trouble had been laid in.

By July 1969 Prime Minister John Gorton was finally ruling out the notion of any special constitutional arrangements involving links to the Australian federation for PNG. 'We see the future of Papua and New Guinea as an intact, self-governing state in its own right and we are seeking to develop it towards that end,' he told an interviewer.[66] From the Opposition, Gough Whitlam was even stronger. He made it clear that any outcome other than independence was 'just not negotiable' and that if the ALP won the 1972 election, home rule would follow.[67] This was not, Whitlam made clear, simply a question for the people of PNG themselves.

The Southwest Pacific

Decolonisation was also changing Australia's environment elsewhere in the South Pacific. The region had been prominent in Evatt's thinking after the war. He wanted Australia and New Zealand to have a predominant interest in it and had contemplated the idea of Australia and New Zealand offering to take over the British-run Solomon Islands and the Anglo-French condominium of the New Hebrides (later Vanuatu). Australia had old and important commercial interests in the region through the trading companies Burns Philp and W.R. Carpenter, and the Colonial Sugar Refining Company in Suva.

In the ANZAC Pact Australia and New Zealand had proposed the establishment of a South Seas Regional Commission to develop common policies on social, economic and political developments.[68] The South Pacific Commission was established in 1947 with the six colonial powers of the region, including the United States, which took control of Japan's Pacific territories under strategic trusteeship arrangements. Australia's initiative, Evatt told parliament, reflected 'the growing realization that we must make positive efforts to direct and control developments in this part of the world'.[69]

The first of the island states, Western Samoa, became independent in 1962 and was admitted to the Commission in 1965. Nauru followed in 1968, then Tonga and Fiji in 1970.

China

But the country that loomed most menacingly in Australian policy discourse during the 1950s and '60s was China. It was seen as a direct threat to stability in Asia, as well as a manifestation of the broader global challenge of communism. Attitudes towards it had a direct impact on domestic politics as well.

Australia had established diplomatic relations with the Chinese nationalist government in 1941. A legation had been established in the wartime capital of Chongqing before being moved to Nanjing and then withdrawn in 1949.

China's long civil war came to an end when Mao Zedong proclaimed the People's Republic on 1 October 1949, and Chiang Kai-shek's nationalist forces fled to the offshore island of Taiwan, from which they continued to claim sovereignty over all China.

Chifley's inclination, as he told parliament, was to recognise the new communist government. But elections were just weeks away and his party was in trouble politically and divided on the issue of communist influence in Australia. So he did not move before Menzies took over on 10 December 1949.[70]

Just a week later, Menzies received a message from his British counterpart, Clement Attlee, advising him that Britain would recognise the inescapable reality that the new government was in control of China very early in the new year. 'We do not expect to carry the US with us on this question of recognition,' Atlee noted, but asked whether Australia would feel disposed to take parallel action.[71] Australia's main Asian Commonwealth partners – India, Pakistan and Ceylon – would also recognise the communist government.

But for the Menzies government the strong opposition of the United States, which Australia was trying to draw into a Pacific security pact, weighed against recognition. Domestic considerations also came into play: a government seeking to ban the Communist Party internally didn't want to send conflicting signals about its attitude to communism. Cabinet decided not to proceed.

Nevertheless, over the following year the Menzies government hovered over the question of recognition. Spender, and even Menzies, contemplated it.[72]

Spender's replacement as external affairs minister, Casey, came back from his trip to Southeast Asia in 1951 with a strong sense that although the new communist regime in Peking was a threat to Southeast Asia, it also had to be accommodated diplomatically. A 45-minute meeting with Zhou Enlai at the Geneva Conference in June 1954 reinforced this view. Casey told guests at a dinner in New York in September that 'Chiang Kai-shek would never be a millimetre more important than he was today and that Peking was unlikely to be a millimetre less important than they were today. To continue to regard Chiang Kai-shek as "China" was quite unreal.'[73]

In 1953, 1954 and 1955 Casey recommended to cabinet that Australia move on recognition. He tried without success to persuade Menzies that 'Peking's entry into normal world relationships is only a matter of time ... and our best interests are that she should. ... It is desirable for us to have a representative in Peking as soon as we can.'[74] But, as on so many occasions, Casey was unable to carry his colleagues with him. Cabinet only wanted to move if Washington approved, and that was not going to happen.

But whatever differences of emphasis Australian ministers may have had on the issue of establishing diplomatic relations, they were all fully persuaded that, as Menzies told parliament on 9 March 1950, Chinese communism was part of a global revolutionary movement subservient to Moscow and connected to communist movements in Southeast Asia.

The Cold War had become the central driver of global affairs, and the conviction that China was part of it was reinforced by the signature of the Treaty of Friendship and Alliance between China and the Soviet Union in February 1950 and by China's entry into the Korean War. Indeed, all the evidence now available shows the high degree of Chinese Communist Party compliance with Moscow's directions in the late 1940s.[75]

As time went on, China's own behaviour – its reaction to the Tibetan uprising of 1959, the limited war with India over their disputed border in 1962, and its first nuclear test in 1964 – caused even Casey to modify his position on recognition.

Even so, Australia took a harder view on these issues than other US allies such as Canada or Japan. In the United Nations, it co-sponsored the regular resolutions to keep Beijing out of the China seat, which was still held by Taiwan. Australian attitudes to China throughout this period were much closer to those of Washington than of London.

China continued to be a domestic political issue as well as a foreign policy problem. Attitudes towards it were one of the factors in the increasingly bitter divisions within the ALP over the activities of the staunchly anti-communist and largely Roman Catholic industrial groups. These led finally to a split in the party in 1955 and to the formation of the Democratic Labor Party (DLP) – a schism that would be central to Labor's political weakness in the following fifteen years or so.

After the split, the Labor Party supported recognising China and opposing troop deployments to Malaya, which led the government to attack Labor as pro-communist. On the government's side, growing dependence on the voting preferences of the DLP, as well as conservative views on its own backbench, kept its policies intact. And later in the 1960s, Mao's efforts to export revolution to Asia, Africa and Latin America and the anarchy of the Cultural Revolution made it hard to see what advantages recognition might offer. In any case, American pressure did not abate and Beijing refused to contemplate any two-China solution that might have softened the blow for Taiwan and saved face for Australia.

The government's position on China was also electorally popular. In April 1965, when announcing the dispatch of Australian troops to Vietnam, Menzies referred to the 'thrust of communist China between the Indian and Pacific Oceans' – an echo of the experience not much more than twenty years before with Japan. Such language tapped into deeper and older fears of a 'yellow peril' from Asia, which still lay not far beneath the surface for many Australians.

At the core of the government's policy failure in the latter part of the 1960s was its inability to understand the dynamics of Asian nationalism. For Hasluck, Asia's problems were largely the result of China's expansionary efforts to impose communism by aggression. Even so, he acknowledged that 'China cannot be ignored, China cannot be suppressed ... It is a problem of co-existence with China and that lies behind all that is happening in Asia.'[76]

On one matter Australia took a different view from the United States. Washington had placed a trade embargo on China, but by 1960–61 China had become Australia's main customer for wheat, which was vital to the Chinese Communist Party's efforts to alleviate the famine Mao's own policies had caused. Over the next decade, between 30 and 40 per cent of Australia's wheat harvest would be shipped to China.[77] Wool was also important, and by 1965 China ranked as Australia's fourth-largest export market, after the United Kingdom, Japan and the United States. The trade relationship was in the hands of the formidable Country Party trade minister John McEwen. In 1962 McEwen pushed again for recognition of China as part of a broad Asia trade strategy to compensate for the prospect of UK membership of the European Economic Community (EEC). This worried the Americans, but Menzies scuttled the proposal.[78]

After the Coalition's strong election win in 1966 under Harold Holt, its political strength began to fade when Holt drowned in the ocean off Portsea in December 1967. It survived narrowly in 1969, and the political support of the DLP became even more important. Meanwhile, China was emerging from the anarchy of the Cultural Revolution, and its tensions with the Soviet Union were reaching breaking point. Canada extended diplomatic recognition in 1970, and Australia paid a commercial price, as China began to discriminate against Australian wheat sales.

But the government seemed unable to move beyond its long-established policy positions. In June 1966, Holt had complicated any eventual decision to recognise the PRC by appointing an ambassador in Taipei, although such a step had not been taken in the preceding years.

The McMahon government rejected departmental advice that Australia should move towards recognition, even when it was advised that the United States and other allies were taking similar steps.[79] It was increasingly clear that Chinese membership of the United Nations was imminent. It was not until mid-May 1971, however, that McMahon announced that the 'government would seek normalisation as a long-term objective'.[80]

Australia, it was becoming apparent, trailed behind even its closest ally. The policy of non-recognition had run out of steam. A bold move by the Labor leader, Gough Whitlam, would make that clear.

White Australia

Clinging to the fabric of the emerging Australian foreign policy like a stale odour was the issue of race. The *Immigration Restriction Act 1901*, which gave legislative form to the White Australia policy, had been one of the first Acts passed by the new Commonwealth parliament. At the Versailles Peace Conference in 1919, Billy Hughes had been untiring in his efforts to prevent the Japanese from inserting a racial equality clause in the covenant of the new League of Nations. His cabinet colleagues were perplexed that Woodrow Wilson, who was standing in the way of Australia's annexation of German New Guinea, did not 'sympathise with a people isolated and adjacent to unnumbered coloured millions but resolutely facing its duty to keep this fertile continent and its intimately associated islands for the selected white races'.[81] Even for a man as experienced in the world as Casey, White Australia was at 'the heart of our being'.[82]

World War II had exposed more Australians to the realities of Asia, but the country itself was overwhelmingly European. Excluding Indigenous Australians (which Australians did both socially and in the census), non-Europeans made up just 0.3 per cent of the Australian population in 1947.[83]

For all the liberal aspirations set out in the 1942 ANZAC Pact, the two countries agreed that in the coming peace settlement Australia and New Zealand would fully support each other 'in maintaining the accepted principle that every government had the right to control immigration and emigration in regard to all territories within its jurisdiction'.

In the negotiations in San Francisco over the responsibilities of the new United Nations Organisation, Evatt argued vigorously that immigration was none of its business, a purely domestic issue. And his colleague Arthur Calwell, the Minister for Immigration, refused to let the Japanese wives and fiancées of Australian citizens come into the country,[84] while preparing to expel some 15,000 Asians who had come to Australia during the war as evacuees.

But things were different now. Australia's immigration policy had also become a dimension of its foreign policy. Cases like those of the American-Filipino Sergeant Lorenzo Gamboa and the Indonesian Annie O'Keefe were causing more Australians to reflect on the policies of their government and were attracting notice in Asia.

Gamboa, a Filipino serving with the US forces in the Philippines, had in 1942 been evacuated to Melbourne, where he met and married an Australian. On his return to Australia after further service in New Guinea and Japan, he was told by immigration authorities that he had to leave the country within three months. Believing his situation would be resolved if he took out US citizenship, he went to the United States and did so, only to find he was refused even a visitor's visa to return to Australia.

In 1942 Annie Maas Jacob, an Indonesian, was evacuated to Australia with her Dutch husband and their seven children. After her husband's death in an air crash on a mission in New Guinea, she married her Australian landlord, John William O'Keefe. But when Calwell refused to let her or her children remain in the country after the war, she challenged the action in the High Court, where her appeal was upheld.

There were signs within the community – from church groups, people who had served in Asia, parts of the press, academics and unionists – that these and other similar cases, if not the overall policy, required a more sensitive Australian response. And the cases also drew international attention. General Douglas MacArthur intervened unsuccessfully on behalf of Gamboa, who had served on his staff. Following the decision to deport fourteen Malay seamen who had been permitted to remain in Australia during the war and had married and had children, Ball found his goodwill mission to Kuala Lumpur 'faced with a storm of protest against Australian Immigration Acts'.[85]

But Calwell was implacable in his belief in the White Australia policy and the demands of absolute consistency in order to avoid establishing precedents. He responded to the High Court's decision in the O'Keefe case by introducing the *Wartime Refugees Removal Act*, designed to rectify the legal problems. While not rejecting the Act or the objectives of the White Australia policy, Opposition attacks on Calwell's uncompromising administration played a part in the election campaign of 1949.

A decade later the Labor frontbencher Fred Daly was still approvingly quoting as Labor's position Calwell's words that '[t]he evils of miscegenation always result in rioting and bloodshed. We have avoided them in this country, thanks to the foresight of our forebears and our own innate common-sense ... We will continue to avoid them if we are wise.'[86]

The new Liberal immigration minister, Harold Holt, reversed the Gamboa and O'Keefe decisions, but, whatever the foreign policy differences between Labor and the Coalition in the 1950s, the restricted immigration policy remained a matter of bipartisan agreement. Immigration issues were already beginning to impinge on Australia's reputation in the United Nations. Reflecting on the debate about the mistreatment of Indians in South Africa in November 1952, Casey recorded in his diary: 'In all these racial questions ... I have our immigration policy constantly in mind. It is certain to be brought before the U.N. some day.'[87]

Small adjustments were made to the policy in the 1950s and '60s, and community attitudes gradually relaxed. In 1954 a Gallup poll recorded 61 per cent of respondents agreeing that Australia should not permit the entry of even a few hundred Asian immigrants under a strict quota system. By 1961 this had fallen to 39 per cent.[88]

In 1956 non-Europeans already in the country were allowed to apply for permanent residence after fifteen years, compared with five years for Europeans. A notorious policy requiring applicants to pass a dictation test in any European language chosen by an immigration official was abandoned in 1958.

In 1965 the ALP dropped the words 'White Australia' from its platform but reassured voters that it still supported 'the avoidance of the difficult social and economic problems which may follow from an influx of peoples having different standards of living, traditions and cultures'.[89] It was mid-1971 before the Labor platform finally endorsed a non-discriminatory immigration policy.

Menzies had held off further changes while he was in office, but soon after his retirement, his successor, Harold Holt, introduced a cautious review in 1966, while promising Australians that 'the basic principles of the policy' were unchanged. Different requirements still applied to people of European and non-European descent, but the capacity to integrate readily (which had in practice a skin-colour dimension) as well as possession of qualifications positively useful to Australia were now factors to be taken into account. The length of time non-white residents on temporary visas had to wait until they were eligible for resident status was reduced from fifteen years to five.[90]

But in this shift, Australia was late. New Zealand had abandoned discriminatory entry policies in 1952. Canada did so in 1962. It remained for Whitlam's government to remove racial discrimination from Australian legislation.

Of course immigration policy was not simply concerned with restrictions. Another lesson Australians had taken from the war was that the country needed to 'populate or perish', and the large-scale European migration program introduced by Chifley and Calwell, and continued by their successors, would also have a foreign policy impact, diluting the sense of Britishness which had still been so central to Australians' identity in 1942.

3

GREAT AND POWERFUL
FRIENDS: THE 1940s
TO THE 1960s

Robert Menzies would repeat the sentiment many times: 'No country in the world more than ours needs great and powerful friends.' He was reflecting a conviction strongly shared by most Australians, one which ran much deeper than the country's developing sense that it needed to shape the region around it. Of course, Menzies had two relationships in mind – the deep old links with the British motherland, a term still in common use in those years, and the new dependence on the United States, so sharply etched by the recent experiences of the war.

In the 1940s and '50s Australians hoped that they would not have to choose between these two powers. In the end there was no choice at all: by the middle of the 1960s Australia's future had been aligned firmly to the United States, though not without trauma and regret.

It had become clear to Australians during the war that, whatever happened next in the Pacific, the dominant influence would be American. This was not an entirely new thought for them. Soon after Federation, the first Australian prime minister, Alfred Deakin, had invited the US Navy – President Theodore Roosevelt's Great White Fleet – to include Australian ports on its 1908 circumnavigation of the world. To bring the visit about, Deakin had effectively done an end run around the Secretary of State for the Colonies in London. The response from the Australian public was overwhelming. More than half a million people turned out in the streets of Sydney, the largest crowds the city had ever seen. When it was over, Deakin sent Roosevelt a message expressing the thanks of Australians to the sailors of the country 'whose glorious flag they hope to see always floating beside that of their motherland'.[1] Apprehension about a threat from Japan had been part of Deakin's consideration in extending the invitation.[2]

The United States was lodged in the Australian mind as a potential ally, but the traumatic circumstances under which American help was eventually needed were unexpected. Just twenty days after the Japanese attack on Pearl Harbor, John Curtin's famous call to America was published in the Melbourne *Herald* on 27 December 1941. 'The Australian government,' he wrote, 'regards the Pacific struggle as one in which the United States and Australia must have the fullest say in the direction of the democracies' fighting plan. Without inhibitions of any kind I make it quite clear that Australia looks to America, free of any pangs as to our traditional links or kinship with the United Kingdom. We know the problems that the United Kingdom faces. We know the constant threat of invasion. We know the dangers of dispersal of strength, but we know too that Australia can go and Britain can still hold on.'[3]

Curtin did not have in mind any profound rupturing of Australian ties with Britain when he expressed these understandable thoughts at a critical time. Menzies was nevertheless affronted: 'Mr Curtin has made a great blunder if he thinks that the ties between this country and Great Britain are merely traditional. They are real and indissoluble.' Curtin responded defensively, but almost certainly sincerely, by expressing his imperial bona fides. 'There is no part of the Empire more steadfast in loyalty to the British way of living and British institutions than Australia ... I do not consider Australia a segment of the British Empire. It is an organic part of the whole structure.'[4]

Two years later, in 1944, Curtin was still arguing – now at a Commonwealth Prime Ministers' Conference – for a British Commonwealth foreign policy that would be determined through regular conferences of prime ministers. But at the same time, his external affairs minister, Herbert Vere Evatt, was in the United States talking about the importance of future collaboration between the US and Australia.[5]

In the early post-war years, it was hard to see exactly what form a greater US role in the Pacific might take. The Australian diplomat and future external affairs minister Paul Hasluck, who participated in early discussions about these questions with Americans, noted that, unlike the situation at the end of World War I, the possibilities for the future 'did not lie in a difference between American collaboration in the world and American isolation, as though it were a difference between going out and staying home, but between one kind of American participation in world affairs and another kind of participation.[6]

For Australian policy-makers the question was how to keep the Americans engaged in the post-war world in the way Australia wanted. Hasluck reflected that the American voter 'would like to feel that he was collaborating with people worth helping. We had to do our share of fighting and working for victory. One of the gravest risks Australia ran from her geographical situation was that the war might be won without Australian troops sharing in the final victory and that, at the end, the war would pass us by. We had to show that we too were forthcoming in peace plans, that we were people with ideas and were ready to cooperate and to adjust our own life in order to form a new order.'[7]

Evatt wanted to keep the Americans engaged in the region by encouraging their continuing use of the defence installations at Manus Island in New Guinea. In April 1946 he told cabinet that Australia should seek a tripartite pact with Australia, New Zealand and the United States, although the cooperation he foresaw was predominantly limited to the Southwest Pacific.[8]

But the time wasn't right and Evatt wasn't the man to get such an agreement. The Americans and other foreign governments identified Curtin as more sympathetic to the American position than Evatt (although in some ways Curtin was simply the more sympathetic man).[9]

In any case, Manus was too far south of the Asian action to matter to the Americans. By 1946 or 1947 any interest on Washington's part had evaporated. Evatt's successor, and the man who did get the agreement, Percy Spender, noted later, 'I do not doubt that Evatt would have availed himself of every opportunity to advance the general idea of a Pacific Security Pact ... Evatt, I think, never abandoned hope even when it was plain there was no such basis for wishful thinking.'[10]

By now, American policy was being shaped by the intensifying Cold War. It was becoming clear that the Grand Alliance of the war years – between the United States, Britain and Stalin's Soviet Union – was over. In 1947 President Truman announced the commitment of American military and economic assistance to the struggling governments of Greece and Turkey, after Britain conceded it could no longer bear this burden. 'It must now be the policy of the United States,' Truman declared, 'to support free peoples who are resisting attempted subjugation by armed minorities or by outside pressures.'[11] In June, the Marshall Plan, named after Truman's secretary of state, provided the framework for a massive American commitment to the economic reconstruction of Europe. And the American diplomat George F. Kennan had in his famous 'long telegram' from Moscow in February 1946 framed the grand strategy of 'a long-term, patient, but firm, containment of Russian expansive tendencies' that would guide US policy throughout the Cold War.[12]

The Australian government adjusted to this new world. The Chifley government had already sent Australian aircraft to participate in the great airlift to relieve West Berlin after the Russians cut off its land access to the rest of West Germany in February 1948. 'Soviet Expansionism could not be permitted to continue,' Evatt told the Commonwealth Prime Ministers' Conference, where he was representing Chifley, in October 1948.[13]

The Cold War and the Petrov case

As a result of one of the Cold War's greatest secrets, the deciphering of Soviet intelligence codes in a program known as Venona, by 1947 the highest levels of the American and British governments were concerned about the presence of Soviet spies inside the Australian government and public service.[14] Consequently, Washington was reluctant to share secrets with Australia. In response to representations from the British, Chifley agreed to set up the Australian Security Intelligence Organisation (ASIO) in March 1949.

On 3 April 1954, Vladimir Petrov, a third secretary in the Soviet embassy, who was in fact the head in Australia of the MVD intelligence organisation (the forerunner of the KGB), defected to Australia, promising detailed information about Russian spy networks. Petrov's wife, also an intelligence officer, was offered asylum in dramatic circumstances as the plane taking her back to Moscow was being refuelled in Darwin. The defection helped the Menzies government win the election in May 1954.

Menzies then established a Royal Commission on Espionage to investigate the Petrov allegations. Two members of Evatt's staff were called before the royal commission and Evatt, now the leader of the Labor Party, decided to represent them himself, but the commissioners withdrew his right to appear, deciding that he could not properly dissociate his political interests from his role as an advocate for his clients.

Evatt became convinced that the timing of the whole affair had been politically motivated to damage him, although there is no evidence to support this.[15] In one of several serious errors of judgement, he read to parliament in October 1954 a letter he had sought from the Soviet foreign minister, Molotov, unsurprisingly denying that the Soviet Union had committed espionage in Australia.

The foreign policy implications of the Petrov defection were mostly indirect. In the immediate term the Australian embassy was expelled from Moscow and the Soviet embassy recalled from Canberra. Diplomatic representatives were not returned until 1959.

More significantly, the drama of the defection, the conclusions of the long-running royal commission, and Evatt's erratic behaviour and miscalculations all served to heighten community concern about the direction of Labor's policies and to sharpen divisions within the ALP. The resulting split within the party had a lasting impact on the politics of foreign policy in Australia.

Percy Spender: Getting to ANZUS

Evatt's replacement as minister, Percy Spender, later outlined the Australian dilemma in this uncertain time in familiar terms: 'Australia's geographical position in any major world conflict was one of isolation from her traditional sources of defence, equipment and assistance. For these she had, in the past, looked to Great Britain. The events of 1942–44 compelled us to look at our position of defence entirely afresh.'[16]

From a modest background, the 52-year-old Spender had become a successful barrister in Sydney, specialising in company law. He had already served as treasurer and then Minister for the Army in Menzies' early war government. Ambitious, quick-witted and highly competitive, he came to the foreign affairs post with experience and well-formed views. He had published 'Australian Foreign Policy: The Next Stage' in 1944. He was a committed Cold Warrior, but with a clear sense of Australian interests. He had been a strong advocate of greater Australian defence preparedness. Above all, he was bold in his self-belief and willingness to act quickly. Despite his brief tenure of just sixteen months, he would be one of the most consequential of all Australian foreign ministers.

In Opposition Spender had expressed the view that Australia needed to develop strategic links with the United States and had talked about a Pacific Pact with other nations in the Indian Ocean/Pacific area, as an eastern counterpart to NATO. In a speech to the House of Representatives on 9 March 1950 he went further:

What I envisage is a defensive military arrangement having as its basis a firm agreement between the countries that have a vital interest in the stability of Asia and the Pacific and which are at the same time capable of undertaking military commitments. I would like to hope that Australia, the United Kingdom, and I fervently hope other Commonwealth countries might form a nucleus and that such other countries as might wish to do so should be given the opportunity of associating themselves with it, providing, as I have said, that they are capable of contributing military commitments. I have in mind particularly the United States of America, whose participation would give such a pact a substance that it would otherwise lack. Indeed, it would be meaningless without her.[17]

This was an ambitious goal for Australia and quite new in its view of the centrality of the United States – 'it would be meaningless without her'.

The British were not enthusiastic about adding to their responsibilities in this way. The foreign secretary, Ernest Bevin, told Spender he didn't think a Pacific Pact necessary.[18] Neither was his own prime minister keen. Spender later recounted hearing that Menzies had described the idea of a Pacific Pact as 'a superstructure on a foundation of jelly'.[19] 'Menzies did not share my view that Asia was then the area of potential danger,' he wrote. 'His interests were focussed principally upon Europe and I have little doubt that he thought me overly concerned with the possibilities of threats to Australia's security developing in Asia.'[20] (Menzies' views seem to have changed in the course of 1950, however, and he would later claim the ANZUS Treaty as one of the greatest of his government's achievements.) But, most importantly, the Americans were not interested. In January 1950, after the communists had taken power in China, the US Secretary of State, Dean Acheson, had ruled out US defence of the Philippines, South Korea or Taiwan, adding that in other areas of the Pacific 'no person can guarantee ... against military attack. But it must also be clear that such a guarantee is hardly sensible or necessary.'[21] From early 1950 onwards it seemed that the Pacific Pact was not of much interest to any other country, apart from New Zealand.

At the end of the war, Korea, which had been annexed by Japan in 1910, was placed under a divided trusteeship between the United States in the south and the Soviet Union in the north, but as Cold War tensions grew, they were unable to agree on its future. The Americans were keen to leave. In August 1948, following the election of Syngman Rhee as president, the Republic of Korea was proclaimed in the south. A month later the Democratic People's Republic of Korea was declared in the north, with the communist guerrilla leader Kim Il-sung as premier.

Following the withdrawal of most American troops, tensions built up between north and south, and on 25 June 1950 full-scale fighting broke out as northern troops crossed the line of division, the thirty-eighth parallel. The report of two Australian military observers to the United Nations Commission on Korea (UNCOK), which had been formed to help moves towards unification and to observe military activities on the peninsula provided the evidence necessary for the United Nations to secure – in the absence of a Soviet veto, because Moscow was boycotting the Security Council – a UN commitment to support the south against a clear act of aggression.[22]

With the outbreak of war in Korea, American strategic responses to developments in Asia changed very quickly and the situation provided Spender with an opportunity to demonstrate to Washington Australia's value as an ally. Labor – comfortable with the UN's endorsement – supported action in Korea.

Spender argued in cabinet that Australia should send troops as well as aircraft and ships to the conflict, but Menzies overruled him. In part, this was because of concern, reinforced by a visit in June from the chief of the Imperial General Staff, Sir William Slim, that Australian troops would be needed to help Britain in the Middle East if war broke out with the Soviet Union. As a result, parliament agreed on 6 July to commit only the aircraft and ships then deployed in Japan as part of the occupation force to operate under the UN command.[23]

Three days later, Menzies left on a long overseas trip. On 14 July, after a further approach from the UN secretary-general for ground forces, Spender cabled him in London. The prime minister again restrained him: Britain was not sending troops and neither should Australia.[24]

But back in Canberra, on 26 July, a British diplomat told the Secretary of the Department of External Affairs, Alan Watt, that Britain had changed its mind and would now commit troops to the conflict. Watt contacted Spender, who was recuperating from illness outside Canberra. Spender was determined, Watt later recorded, not 'to allow the United Kingdom to cash in on American goodwill ahead of Australia, having restrained Australia from acting earlier'.[25] He persuaded the acting prime minister, Arthur Fadden, to make a public statement committing Australian ground forces, thereby pre-empting the British.

It is unclear just how important this confident action was in preparing the ground for the ANZUS Treaty, but Menzies received a warm reception when he arrived in Washington.[26] The action certainly distinguished

Spender, in the minds of American policy-makers from Evatt, whose abrasiveness they resented.

The outbreak of the Korean War strengthened Washington's determination that the peace treaty under negotiation should not prevent Japan from adding its industrial weight to the Western side in the Cold War as soon as possible.

Spender also recognised opportunity here. A determination that Japan should be restrained from future military aggression lay at the heart of a bipartisan Australian policy. Memories of the war remained very raw: of the 22,000 Australians captured by the Japanese, more than 8000 had died in captivity.

Spender understood, however, that America's desire for a 'soft' treaty made a punitive peace impossible and that the political future of the government would therefore depend on its ability to secure an alternative form of security for the Australian people – the long-sought Pacific Pact. He also saw such a pact as a sensible response to the growth of communist power in Asia. This was a concern he shared fully with Washington. In his March 1950 speech to the House of Representatives, he had explained that the communists' seizure of power in China had 'fundamentally changed the whole picture of Asia'.[27]

Although the Cold War was central to Spender's understanding of the security environment, his angle of view focused on Asia. He wanted Australians to understand the importance of Southeast Asia. And – like Evatt – he wanted to give Australia a voice in the strategic decision-making about it. Over the next six months Spender argued and cajoled in Canberra, Washington, New York and London. In September 1950 he put the arguments directly to Truman, Acheson and John Foster Dulles, who had been appointed to work on the Japanese Peace Treaty. Spender told Acheson that Australia 'would not subscribe to a treaty with Japan unless there were adequate assurances that Australia would be protected against Japanese aggression . . . a formal commitment by the US might go some way to allay our fears'. In Washington a month earlier Menzies had not raised the Pacific Pact.[28]

Spender instructed his officials to tell the Americans that 'unless the Australian government was satisfied with the security position arising out of a Japanese peace settlement we would not, under any circumstances, sign any peace treaty'.[29] He rejected a suggestion from the Assistant Secretary of State, Dean Rusk, that Australians might be sufficiently reassured if the American president simply made a statement that the United States could be relied upon to come to Australia's assistance if it was attacked. 'Presidents come and Presidents go,' he noted. But such a proposal also failed to offer 'machinery enabling Australia to play a constant part in the determination of such security'.[30] In a speech to parliament on 28 November, he talked of Australia's 'right to have a suitable voice in the determination of policy and the shaping of events which deeply affect Australia wherever they may take place'.[31]

What form a Pacific Pact might take was still unclear. Australia wanted Britain in it. The United States generally did not want to extend its commitments to the mainland of Asia or to agree to something that looked too much like a white man's club in Asia, but it was toying with ideas of Japanese or Philippine membership. Britain itself vacillated. It became clear to Spender that the simplest and neatest way of getting American agreement would be through a tripartite agreement with New Zealand.

In February 1951 Dulles, as Truman's envoy, arrived in Australia to pin down Australian support for the peace treaty with Japan. At a meeting in Canberra with Spender and his New Zealand counterpart, Frederick Doidge, the outline of the ANZUS Pact – which Spender had already asked his department to draft – was worked out.

Knowing that the US senate would not agree to another NATO-type automatic commitment (which it saw as an abrogation of Congressional power to declare war), Spender drew on the text of the Monroe Doctrine – the 1823 declaration by the United States that it would regard European intervention in its own hemisphere as 'dangerous to its own peace and safety'. So the operative article of the treaty, Article IV, read, 'Each Party recognizes that an armed attack in the Pacific Area on any of the Parties would be dangerous to its own peace and safety and declares that it would act to meet the common danger in accordance with its constitutional processes.'

The text needed to be tidied up and approvals secured. The US chiefs of staff were particularly unenthusiastic, and Australia needed to deal carefully with Britain, whose officials had expressed views ranging from agnosticism to antagonism towards the new pact.

Within a few weeks Australia received London's go-ahead, although Watt noted that reading between the lines of the response, 'it seemed clear that, at the political level, Britain found distasteful a security treaty between the United States and two Commonwealth countries to which she herself was not a party'.[32]

Spender signed the treaty in San Francisco on 1 September 1951, just before the Japanese peace conference opened. His energy, self-confidence and toughness in negotiations had borne fruit. For the first time in its history, Australia had entered into a foreign defence engagement to which the United Kingdom was not a party.

By that time, though, Spender had been sidelined to Washington as ambassador; he would be an assertive advocate there until 1958, when he was appointed to the International Court of Justice. The circumstances of his departure from the ministry are still unclear. Spender's public explanation was his health, but exile did not much diminish his active engagement in policy setting. Three months into his term in Washington, his successor, Richard Casey, noted in frustration that 'Percy seems to believe he is not only Ambassador to USA but Minister for External Affairs and the Cabinet as well'.[33]

The parliamentary debates on the ANZUS Treaty and the Peace Treaty with Japan took place at the same time, in February 1952. Labor supported the ANZUS Treaty, but a common refrain was that it provided insufficient compensation for the perceived leniency of the Japanese Peace Treaty, which Labor opposed.[34]

It was not clear at the beginning exactly what ANZUS was or how it would now develop. Reflecting Spender's aspirations, Casey told his parliamentary colleagues that the ANZUS Council 'gives Australia access to the thinking and planning of the American Administration at the highest political and military level'.[35] But in reality there was never quite enough of that for Australia's satisfaction. Privately, Casey criticised America's 'stubborn opposition to inner circle planning'.[36] Australia's efforts to secure greater access to such planning were deflected from Washington to the local branch office – the US Navy's Pacific Command in Honolulu.[37]

And it took time for the borders around ANZUS to set. Would Britain – where Churchill was back in Downing Street and miffed by the United Kingdom's exclusion – yet join? The matter was finally resolved when Dulles told Casey in September 1953 that 'efforts to enlarge ANZUS would end in its dissolution'.[38]

SEATO

The formation of the Southeast Asia Treaty Organization (SEATO) in 1954 seemed to address some of Australia's hopes of involving both its main partners in the collective defence of Southeast Asia.

In September 1954, just a few months after the Geneva Conference on Indochina, the nations of Australia, New Zealand, France, Britain, Pakistan, the Philippines, Thailand and the United States signed the South-East Asia Collective Defence Treaty at a conference in Manila. The treaty was part of the network of alliances Washington was constructing around the borders of the Soviet Union, as part of its grand strategy to contain communism. SEATO's area was defined to include Vietnam, Cambodia and Laos, although under the terms of the Geneva Accords, they could not join it. Other regional states such as Indonesia, Burma and India declined to participate.

Casey attended the Manila meeting with a brief to seek as part of the treaty a strong, automatic commitment from the United States and the formal military planning which had so long been the aim of Australian policy-makers. But the United States would not go beyond ANZUS-like words to 'act to meet the common danger' of attack or subversion 'in accordance with constitutional processes'.

It declared furthermore that it interpreted the treaty as applying only to communist aggression. Worried about the public response at home to Australia taking on broader responsibilities than the Americans, cabinet instructed Casey to apply an equal Australian reservation.[39] But faced with a strong American view that the United States should be the only member to limit its commitment in this way, and fearing that the treaty might then be unpicked completely, Casey deliberately disobeyed his instructions. Menzies cabled to express his outrage, but by that time Casey had already signed the treaty on Australia's behalf. It was another indication of the uncertain relationship between the prime minister and his external affairs minister.[40]

The Opposition was critical of the differential responsibilities of Australia and the United States under SEATO, but Labor didn't oppose the treaty.

Throughout the late 1950s and early '60s SEATO was a central element in any Australian government speech about Asia, but it never really lived up to the hopes policy-makers held for it. The deep engagement in planning with its allies that Australia always wanted didn't eventuate.

Over the early 1960s, as Pakistan sought China's support in its dispute with India, and French policy towards Vietnam diverged from that of the United States, SEATO grew weaker. It became clear to the Australian government that ANZUS was the only solid foundation for its links with the United States.

Perhaps SEATO's most significant legacy was its role in providing the putative legal basis for American involvement in the Vietnam War. It would not survive long after the war's end, and was formally disbanded in 1977.

Suez

A crisis over the nationalisation of the Suez Canal in 1956 became an unlikely turning point in Australia's efforts to engage both Britain and the United States in its post-war security.

From its opening in 1869, the canal had been a vital link between Australia and the United Kingdom, its most important trading partner, cutting weeks off shipping times. By 1956 around £900-million worth of Australian trade passed through the canal each year.[41]

Since the 1880s Britain had exercised effective power in Egypt. Control of the canal was one of the reasons Australian troops had fought in the Middle East during two world wars. It was why Australians saw their imperial defence responsibilities tied up with the Middle East. And why, as late as 1950, Australia and Britain were still discussing Australian participation in a proposed Middle East Command.

A charismatic young army colonel, Gamal Abdel Nasser, had led a nationalist coup which deposed the British-supported Egyptian monarchy in 1952, and by 1956 he had become president. Provoked in part by an American and British decision to withdraw funding from the huge Aswan Dam project, Nasser announced on 26 July 1956 the nationalisation of the Suez Canal Company, which ran the canal. Almost half the shares in the company were held by the British government.

Nasser offered compensation to shareholders and promised that free passage through the canal would be honoured, but London and Paris were outraged. Together with the United States, they invited twenty-four canal users, including Australia, to an international conference in London to consider the next steps. Menzies was in the US when the news came through. He decided to abandon a planned Asian trip and to represent Australia himself at the conference, although the other delegations were led by foreign ministers.

In a cabinet meeting back in Australia on 7 August, Casey and the defence minister, Philip McBride, the two ministers most directly involved, argued that Australia should warn Britain against the use of military force. 'If and when the first round is fired,' Casey wrote in his diary that day, 'the *merits* of the Suez Canal case will be forgotten, and the fact that a great Power has used force on a small Afro-Asian nation to deal with a political problem will dominate the minds of the majority of the countries of the world. World opinion would be overwhelmingly against the UK and inferentially against Australia.'[42] Again, however, he could not carry his colleagues. Cabinet supported Britain's position and condemned Egypt's actions.[43]

Arriving back in London, Menzies was publicly critical of Nasser, accusing him of 'creating the world's greatest crisis since 1945'.[44] The international conference developed a list of demands to put to Egypt, of which the most important was the creation of a new international authority to control the canal. Menzies was asked to lead a delegation to put the proposal to Nasser in Cairo.

He was an odd choice for such a diplomatic mission. In personal style Menzies was an advocate, not a conciliator. He didn't think much of either Nasser or Egyptians generally,[45] and he was closely associated with the British position. But London and Paris did not really want success. They had other plans in mind. They assumed Nasser would reject the compromise proposal and were secretly planning military action to take back the canal and get rid of Nasser. The evidence is unclear, but, despite his loyal support for Anthony Eden's position, it does not appear that Menzies was taken into the British prime minister's confidence. In Cairo, Menzies put the conference demands to Nasser, making it clear to him that the possibility of force remained open. The delegation made no progress.

Casey was still worried. He affronted his cabinet colleagues by suggesting that British ministers were acting on the basis of emotion rather than reason. They had their objection to this calumny informally recorded: 'The United Kingdom reaction could not possibly have been based on emotion. It must be accepted that a body having the experience and responsibility of the United Kingdom Cabinet could not base itself otherwise than on hard fact and reason.'[46]

Returning to Australia in September, Menzies vigorously defended the British position in a speech to the House of Representatives, describing Nasser as a tyrant. 'We must avoid the use of force if we can. But we should not, by theoretical reasoning in advance of the facts and circumstances, contract ourselves out of its use whatever those facts and circumstances might be.'[47]

Meanwhile, however, the United States was making its opposition to a military response clear. President Dwight Eisenhower told Eden directly that force would not work and that the US would not support Anglo-French action.

Against the wishes of the Americans, who suspected them of clearing away some diplomatic undergrowth so they could resort to force, Britain and France asked the UN Security Council to consider the situation. The Australian government, which in 1956 was occupying one of the temporary seats on the Council, was paralysed. It wanted to support the British position, but it didn't know what the British position was. It found itself having to make the choice it most wanted to avoid, between London and Washington. The Australian delegation in New York was limply instructed to find out what the British wanted to do and then support them.[48]

With nothing resolved, France put to Britain on 14 October a secret plan concocted with Israel, which had its own border problems with Egypt. Israeli forces would strike across the Sinai towards the canal, and France and Britain would would intervene militarily – ostensibly to keep the two sides apart, but with the real objective of seizing the canal and ousting Nasser. Most of Eden's own cabinet was kept in the dark, and Australia was told nothing, although Casey was in London at the time.

The Israelis struck on 29 October. France and the United Kingdom then issued an ultimatum to Israel and Egypt that each side must withdraw forces to ten miles either side of the canal and let UK and French forces establish themselves there. Nasser was never going to accept.

US anger was sharp. Anglo-American relations could hardly be worse, reported the Australian embassy in Washington.[49] The British and the French were ignoring Washington's clear advice and dissembling about their intentions. Suez was deflecting international attention from the Soviet Union's action in sending troops into Hungary to put down a revolution on 23 October.

A US resolution was put to the UN Security Council on 30 October calling on Israel to withdraw and for other UN members to refrain from intervention. Australia abstained from voting. But the British went ahead, bombing Egyptian airfields on 31 October. Eisenhower, in the last days of his election campaign, was furious. He publicly described the actions as 'not wise or proper'. 'How could we possibly support Britain and France if, in doing so, we lose the whole Arab world?' he asked.[50]

On the following day, at the General Assembly's first-ever emergency session, Australia joined Britain, France, Israel and New Zealand as the only countries to oppose a US resolution calling for a ceasefire and a halt to the movement of forces and arms. Menzies wrote reassuringly to Eden: 'You must never entertain any doubts about the British quality of this country.'[51]

The following day Canada proposed the formation of a United Nations Emergency Force to supervise a cessation of hostilities. Still, the British and the French ploughed on. Their paratroops landed outside Port Said on 5 November, and the city surrendered on 6 November. But it was all over. Faced with a run on the pound and a fear of US-backed sanctions, Britain and France announced a ceasefire at midnight. The US said it would only support a British application for help from the International Monetary Fund if a ceasefire was in force. For Casey, the divisions revealed between Britain and the United States were an 'unmitigated calamity'.[52] By 22 December all French and British troops were out. The invaders had gained nothing.

Australia was humiliated. Menzies' unswerving support for the British position had not been matched by London's willingness to take him into its confidence, and his judgements about the likely outcome of the crisis had been flawed. He remained unrepentant. A year later he told a Liberal Party gathering that 'Great Britain and France have lost prestige; they have been forced to look on the President of Egypt with bated breath and whispering humbleness. Is this a contribution to world peace? Of course it isn't.'[53] Even so, he would never again quite so unreservedly commit Australia to a British diplomatic cause.

Casey, who had seen it coming, or at least had seen something coming, found himself ignored by his colleagues and suffered politically, trounced in a vote for the position of Deputy Leader of the Liberal Party on 26 September, in part because of his caution. His fears for British prestige, his worries about divisions between London and Washington and his concern about Australia's reputation in Asia had all been borne out.

The immediate impact of the crisis in Australia was limited. Distracted by the opening of the Melbourne Olympic Games on 22 November, and the introduction of television to view them, Australians had other things on their minds. A Gallup poll in December showed 61 per cent of respondents, including a majority of Labor voters, thought the British and French actions had been justified. The economic impact of the temporary closing of the canal and its long-term administration by Egypt had none of the disastrous consequences first feared. When the Egyptians closed the canal at the beginning of the Six-Day War with Israel in 1967, the impact on Australia was minimal.

But for Australian foreign policy, the most important consequence of the crisis happened back in Britain.

The drift from Britain

The Suez crisis brought home to Britain its shrunken post-war power. Eden resigned, his reputation in tatters, and his replacement, Harold Macmillan, instituted a defence review. He set out to repair the damage with Washington in an important summit meeting with President Eisenhower in March 1957 in Bermuda. To preserve what it could of its great power status, Britain had to shift, with American assistance, to a defence strategy that gave priority to its nuclear capabilities. But the cost of maintaining the nuclear arsenal would eventually be retrenchment 'East of Suez' from the global network of garrison colonies that had girdled the Empire from Gibraltar to Hong Kong and driven so much of its past strategic interest in Asia.[54]

Suez had demonstrated painfully, too, Britain's eroding economic weight. After Germany, France and four other West European states signed the Treaty of Rome in 1957 establishing the European Economic Community (EEC), momentum grew for closer British association with Europe. Keen to strengthen the western alliance, Washington encouraged this.

These changes in Britain's position came as a shock to Australians. Notwithstanding the experiences of World War II, Australia still wanted Britain present in the region around it. And Britain remained Australia's largest export market, taking 26 per cent of its total exports in 1960, more than twice as much as its second-largest trading partner, Japan.[55] The Australian pound was pegged to sterling and most of the country's reserves were held in that currency.[56] Until 1958 all US dollars earned by members of the sterling area were pooled. Foreign investment in Australia was largely sourced from the London capital markets.

The critical years for the Australia–United Kingdom relationship were 1961 and 1962. In July 1961 Macmillan announced that Britain would apply to join the EEC. This was not unexpected, but that did not diminish Australia's alarm. For John Crawford, the veteran Secretary of the Department of Trade, 'our psychology has been changed. We will never be the same as we were before we were given a shake-up by Britain's application'.[57] Treasurer Harold Holt told Menzies, 'It is the biggest peace time problem ... Australia has had to face in the life of our Federation.'[58]

The most immediate economic threat for Australia was to the Commonwealth preferences it received on the agricultural products which accounted for more than 70 per cent of its exports to Britain.

But there was more to it than money. Many Australians experienced a sense of psychological abandonment by what Menzies called the 'Mother Nation'.[59] For Menzies himself, the economic implications of Britain's move were less important than the challenge to the ties of family. He feared that British membership of EEC would weaken the organic bonds that joined the Commonwealth. Although he knew that Australia could not blindly oppose the move, Britain's decision, he felt, was 'one of historic and almost revolutionary importance'.[60]

The 1962 Commonwealth Prime Ministers' Conference in London was the scene of bitter bargaining about the future, but the crisis passed when the French president, de Gaulle, vetoed British EEC membership four months later. Britain formally withdrew its application.

The incoming Labour government of Harold Wilson made an effort to revive a Commonwealth-centred approach to trade, but could get no real traction. In 1967 Wilson launched another bid for EEC membership. It was again vetoed by de Gaulle, on the grounds that Britain was not fully committed to Europe, but this time the bid application remained on the table. In 1970 Edward Heath's conservative government revived it again.

But something had changed in Australia's response between 1961 and the second bid in 1967. The shock had dissipated; the fears were diminished. With annual GDP growth rates throughout the 1960s averaging 5.3 per cent, the highest in the nation's history, Australia was growing more economically confident. The trade minister, John McEwen, a tenacious negotiator with the British, was fighting to find new markets, and the signs were promising. Australian policy-makers recognised that all they could do was negotiate the best possible terms for a phase-out of preferences in the British market.[61]

But weighing increasingly on the Australian response was its higher need to keep Britain militarily engaged in the region, especially in Malaysia and Singapore, where it had stationed two aircraft carriers, five submarines, more than 200 aircraft and 50,000 troops. That security interest, rather than the preservation of the economic relationship, was now Australia's priority.

When he became prime minister in October 1964, Wilson initiated his own defence review. Speaking to him in London the following year, Menzies listed as the first of Australia's defence commitments in Southeast Asia 'the almost instinctive obligation, unwritten but there nonetheless, to do all in [our] ... power to help Britain'. Only then did ANZUS, SEATO and the commitment to Malaysia follow.[62]

But whatever Australia might want, it was becoming increasingly clear that Britain could not continue to maintain its defence commitments east of Suez. In July 1966, with the pound under pressure, Wilson announced huge cuts in military expenditure, falling most heavily in Southeast Asia. This decision was made easier for London by the end of Confrontation, which meant that troops committed to Malaysia's defence could be pulled out.

In April 1967 British ministers concluded that all UK forces would have to be withdrawn from the region by 1975–76. Australian ministers were consulted before the final decision. Their shock at the magnitude of the plan was unfeigned.

Australia set about trying to devise strategies to keep Britain involved. 'The central objective of Australian policy,' ministers determined in May 1967, 'is to secure a continuing British commitment to the Malaysian region.'[63] But there were limits. British ministers floated the idea that Australia might itself offer to host future British bases but the government was unresponsive, reluctant to give the British an easy escape hatch.[64]

In June 1967 Wilson announced that the number of British forces in Malaysia and Singapore would be halved by 1970–71 and reaffirmed their complete withdrawal by the middle of the decade. In response, Holt wrote bitterly to Wilson that 'some of the basic assumptions on which the foreign policies of our two countries have been based – at least in relation to this area of the world – seem to us to have been destroyed and we must rethink our whole situation.'[65]

Privately, however, Australian ministers recognised that the situation was probably irreversible. The deputy prime minister, John McEwen, told the New Zealand prime minister that 'Britain would soon be out of Southeast Asia and we would be dependent on the United States for our security. Our attitude should be to bind ourselves to the United States and to induce the United States to accept a security responsibility towards us.'[66]

Australia had already been slowly shifting its defence posture to give more weight to the United States. In 1957 the government announced that it would standardise future defence purchases with the Americans. The most dramatic demonstration of this shift came with the 1963 choice of US F-111 fighter-bombers instead of the British contender to replace Australia's Canberra bombers. The Labor Party attacked the decision for its shabby treatment of Britain.[67]

The crises in the British economy kept coming. The pound was devalued in November 1967, requiring the date of the withdrawal to be brought forward again. Finally, on 16 January 1968, Wilson announced that all UK forces east of Suez, except those in Hong Kong, would be withdrawn, not by the mid-70s but by December 1971. It was the clear end of the British Empire in the east.

In June 1970 Heath and the Conservative Party came to power unexpectedly, promising to continue a British presence in Malaysia and Singapore through Five Power Defence Arrangements (FPDA). These would replace the automatic guarantees of the Anglo-Malayan Defence Agreement with promises from Britain, Australia, New Zealand, Malaysia and Singapore to consult in the event of a threat of attack on peninsular Malaysia or Singapore. The Heath government agreed to provide a modest force presence when the FPDA was concluded in April 1971.

Heath signed the Treaty of Accession to the EEC in January 1972, and a year later Britain finally joined Europe. By 1974, when the Whitlam government withdrew most Australian ground forces from Singapore, the British, too, had gone.

A profound shift had taken place in Australia's relationship with Britain over the preceding decade. The language changed, the attitudes altered, the interests of the two countries drifted apart. But looking back, the tone of the Australian response to the genuine dilemma in which Britain found itself often seemed graceless and self-absorbed.[68]

It wasn't just the economic and defence structures of the past that were being dismantled. Between 1953 and 1960 Australians had made up about 10 per cent of all immigrants to Britain.[69] Now new restrictions were introduced on Commonwealth immigration. More Australians asked themselves, if you couldn't go there, how could the UK be home?

The Vietnam War

The origins of the Vietnam War are firmly grounded in the struggles over European decolonisation in Asia, discussed in the last chapter. But its importance to Australian foreign policy lay less in Australia's direct interest in the conflict in Indochina than in its desire to keep its great and powerful friends engaged in Asia.

Since late 1946, when the French drove Ho Chi Minh and his followers from the communist-dominated Viet Minh out of Hanoi and resisted demands for Vietnamese independence, a violent but inconclusive war had been raging across the country. By 1954, however, the French position was crumbling. With China now in communist hands, the United States was worried about what the implications of a further communist victory in Vietnam would mean for the increasingly tense Cold War. It even considered a French request for military intervention to relieve the besieged French forces in the jungle at Dien Bien Phu. The British, fearful of nuclear escalation, opposed such an intervention, and Casey supported them. On 12 April 1954 he wrote in his diary, 'The first thing to get straight in our minds is the answer to the question – where does the menace come from in Indo-China.

My answer is – the Viet Minh, not Communist China ... I believe that getting into direct holts with Communist China is the most vitally important thing to avoid. Heaven knows where this would lead us, or what would be the end of it'.[70]

The focus of policy-making then turned to the international conference in Geneva, which was to consider both the Korean War armistice and the situation in Indochina. Formally, Australia was represented only for the discussions on Korea, but Casey also spoke to all the key participants about Indochina. On his way to Geneva, he visited Saigon, and a few days later reflected, 'A prominent Frenchman said to me a year ago that there was no military solution to [the] Indo-China problem but that the only solution was a political one ... I tend to believe it is largely true'.[71]

The outcome of the Geneva negotiations was ceasefire agreements in Cambodia, Laos and Vietnam. It was agreed that Cambodia and Laos should remain neutral and that Vietnam would be divided at the seventeenth parallel, on the understanding that the country would be reunified after internationally supervised elections.

Neither the United States nor South Vietnam accepted this Final Declaration, however. The US made it clear that it saw the temporary border as permanent and threw its strong support behind the government in the south – the Republic of Vietnam. That government was in the hands of Ngo Dinh Diem, a former senior civil servant from an aristocratic family. Diem was a Roman Catholic in a largely Buddhist country, ascetic and autocratic. The repression and corruption of his government generated a growing resistance movement in the south under the banner of the communist-supported National Liberation Front. Military support began to flow from North Vietnam to the southern fighters.

By 1961 the Kennedy administration had concluded that if Vietnam fell to communism the rest of Southeast Asia would either follow or be forced to accommodate it, a version of the 'domino theory' first enunciated by President Eisenhower. Military advisers were sent in to assist Diem.

In May 1962 the ANZUS Council meeting was to be held for the first time in Australia. One of the reasons the US secretary of state, Dean Rusk, was making the long journey to Canberra was to encourage Australia to send its own military advisers to Vietnam. The US administration wanted to be able to demonstrate international support for its involvement. The Australian ambassador in Washington, Howard Beale, a former Menzies cabinet member, had floated the idea a couple of months earlier.[72]

Casey had now been replaced by Barwick (following the period from February 1960 to December 1961 when Menzies held the portfolio himself), and Australian ministers shared the American assessment of what was happening in Vietnam. The Republic of Vietnam, Barwick thought, was fighting not a civil war but a 'grim war of survival' against communist aggression from the north.[73] In a judgement that went beyond any of their military advice, ministers characterised a victory for the Viet Cong as 'the greatest possible threat to Australia'.[74]

But the main reason for the Australian decision to support the United States was to encourage a direct American physical presence in the region. This would give substance to ANZUS, providing a warning to all around the Pacific, as Barwick put it, 'that we do not stand alone'.[75] The government decided before the ANZUS Council meeting that it should again use the opportunity to gain entry to 'the inner political thinking and defence planning' of the United States 'and especially its political thinking in relation to the Southeast Asian area'.[76]

Australian defence policy was based on the principle, as the chiefs of staff would express it in 1964, that the 'security of the Australian mainland and its island territories is best achieved by a forward defence strategy to hold South East Asia; thus providing defence in depth for Australia'. By participating in collective defence arrangements and contributing to the security of more-threatened parts of the region, Australia would, in turn, attract 'the support of powerful allies, particularly the United States'.[77] The idea of the payment of the premium on an insurance policy became the most powerful metaphor in Australian public life.

So cabinet agreed on 15 May to send thirty members of the Australian Army Training Team Vietnam (AATTV) – specialists in guerrilla warfare drawn from the jungle training school at Canungra – to Vietnam. Australia's was the largest commitment of any other Western country.

After Rusk's visit, Barwick noted with satisfaction that the secretary of state had mentioned that the future of the two countries was 'inextricably intertwined'.[78] Inextricable intertwinement was precisely the policy goal of the Australian government.

Intertwinement was also happening at a broader level. In May 1962 Australia and the United States had entered into an agreement for Washington to establish a naval communications station at North West Cape in Western Australia. The role of the facility was to provide low-frequency radio communications to America's Polaris nuclear submarines, which were patrolling the Indian Ocean with their intercontinental ballistic missiles. It therefore embedded ANZUS more directly in the structure of global deterrence and established a likely nuclear target in the event of war with the Soviet Union.

The agreement came to parliament in May 1963. It required the US to provide no more than minimal consultation with Australia over the operations of the facility and, as an exchange of letters made clear, consultation did not 'carry with it any degree of control over the station or its use'.[79]

The issue split the Labor Party. After intense internal debate, the ALP finally agreed to support 'this grim and awful necessity', as Whitlam, the deputy leader, expressed it, while promising to secure greater participation in its control.[80] Nevertheless, the divisions the debate revealed (and the newspaper photograph of Opposition leader Calwell and Whitlam, waiting in the streets for the final decision on the matter to come from the 'fifty-six faceless men' who comprised the Special Party Conference) helped to ensure Labor's comprehensive defeat in the following election.[81]

By the middle of 1963 Vietnam had begun to dominate US foreign policy debate. Opposition to Diem's repressive regime was growing. The self-immolation of a Buddhist monk in June horrified Western television viewers. In November the United States finally acquiesced in an army coup that overthrew Diem. But what followed was further instability in the south and a succession of military governments.

Paul Hasluck

In April 1964 Paul Hasluck replaced Barwick as Minister for External Affairs. Few parliamentarians would have seemed better fitted for the ministerial appointment. Hasluck was a former diplomat, a fine writer and historian, and after twelve years as Minister for Territories he had extensive administrative experience. He had reflected deeply on the world and Australia's place in it. Power was central to the way he thought about Australian foreign policy. 'The possession of power is the main determinant of what happens' in the world, he told parliament in his first speech as minister in 1965. 'We might like it otherwise but we cannot ignore the fact.'[82]

The international situation, as he saw it, was shaped by this struggle for power: a grim prospect, but one that had to be addressed realistically. He returned to the theme in parliament three years later: 'let us face the reality that we live in an ugly world – a world in which there are many shortcomings.

Nevertheless, it is the world in which we live. It is the world with which we have to deal. It is the world in which international relations must be conducted.'[83] In that world, Asia was important to Australia, but the region's problems could not be separated 'from the major problems of the power situation in the whole world'.[84] And Australian power was limited. It should not have aspirations that were too grand. As he told department secretary Arthur Tange in September 1964:

> Our responsibility as an Australian government is to ensure that, so far as the nature of world events and the world situation will allow, we make Australian decisions to meet Australian needs and interests and that, in those situations in which a lasting difference of opinion between the United States and Australia would be unendurable, we try to shape the United States decision so that it will come as far towards our way of thinking as is possible before the compromise is accepted ... [W]e have very little power to force any compromise and we have to seek to gain acceptance for a point of view mainly by intelligent persuasion.[85]

Yet, whatever his strengths as a thinker, and however psychologically penetrating he could be about his colleagues' motivations, Hasluck was an unsuccessful minister. Overly influenced, perhaps, by his distaste for Evatt's playing of favourites and administrative untidiness, he was a distant minister. He preferred written communications to engaging in debate. He had only infrequent personal contact with Tange, with whom he had a mutually unsatisfying relationship. His approach to ministerial responsibility was so rigid that he would not tell his own department what his advice had been to cabinet.[86] He attended fastidiously to grammatical errors.

As a result, he was unable to harness the resources of his department as Barwick had done. Many who worked with him told similar stories: 'In contrast to Barwick, Hasluck could be suspicious, querulous, resentful when queried about a decision, frequently remote, and intrusive in matters of departmental administration with which a Minister would not normally be engaged,' a future departmental secretary, Philip Flood, would later record.[87]

Hasluck's biographer, Geoffrey Bolton, noted that Arthur Calwell may have put his finger on a reason for Hasluck's problems with his department when he observed that Hasluck's 'great fondness for his world power struggle theory ... I suspect derives from his desire, as an historian – and a very distinguished one – to provide a consistent and self-contained philosophical basis for his activities and attitudes, in a Department which works in an atmosphere that is full of inconsistencies and contradictions'.[88]

At a time when Australian foreign policy was encountering a world increasingly full of just such inconsistencies and contradictions, in which the policies of its closest allies were changing, Hasluck was not the man for the job.

Unlike Barwick, who had focused his ministerial attention on Indonesia, Hasluck saw China and its southward expansion as the greatest threat to Australia. From his first visit to Vietnam in 1964, his objective was to encourage the United States to involve itself more deeply in the country.[89] Soon after he took over, the size of the training team in Vietnam was doubled. Australia's purpose, he instructed the Australian ambassador in Washington in 1965, was to 'remove any hesitation on the part of the Americans and, within our limited resources, to go with them but not to rush out in front'.[90]

Claims by the US administration – later revealed to be incorrect – that North Vietnamese torpedo boats had launched unprovoked attacks against American naval vessels in international waters in the Gulf of Tonkin on 2 and 4 August 1964 persuaded Congress to give President Johnson extensive new powers over the deployment and use of forces in Vietnam. Escalation had begun.

Responding to the new situation, the Menzies government increased the Australian defence budget and introduced national service for overseas service through a system of balloting. Menzies himself was the most powerful influence on Australian policy. He shared Hasluck's analysis: 'I see, moving down from the North – Peking to Hanoi, to the war-torn jungles of Laos and South Vietnam and Cambodia – Chinese communism with its undiluted Marx-Engels doctrines and practices ... I subscribe to the Domino Theory', he wrote in his memoirs in 1970, four years after he left office.[91]

In December 1964, in response to a request from President Johnson for a further 200 advisers, the Australian cabinet decided, in principle and subject to a formal request from South Vietnam, to provide a battalion instead. Debates about what an Australian battalion would do and where it might operate continued until its public announcement in April 1965.[92]

In February 1965 President Johnson had begun Operation Rolling Thunder, bombing strategic targets in the north, and on 7 April he announced that US ground troops were to be sent in. On the same day, the Foreign

Affairs and Defence Committee of Cabinet confirmed the commitment of the Australian battalion in support of the US forces. But the formal request it wanted from the Republic of Vietnam proved surprisingly difficult to arrange. It was not until 27 April that the Americans persuaded Saigon to make the request and the decision was made public.

'The vital thing for Australia was to have the United States remain in the area and everything else must be measured against this,' the Foreign Affairs and Defence Committee of Cabinet noted in January 1966.[93] Only the presence of American troops in the region could ensure that their support would be there if Australia needed it.

The Labor Opposition had mostly offered cautious support for the Vietnam deployments, but the amendment of the *Defence Act* in 1965 to permit conscripts in the new national service scheme to be sent overseas, with its echo of the great conscription debate of World War I, added emotional intensity to the national argument. Labor was now interpreting the conflict as 'a civil war aided and abetted by the North Vietnamese Government', as its leader, Arthur Calwell, told parliament, and therefore one that could not be solved by military means alone.

Calwell firmly opposed the new commitment of Australian troops. In a powerful speech in parliament in May 1965 he set out the basis for Labor's opposition:

> We do not think it is a wise decision. We do not think it is a timely decision. We do not think it will help the fight against Communism. On the contrary, we believe it will harm that fight in the long term. We do not believe it will promote the welfare of the people of Vietnam. On the contrary, we believe it will prolong and deepen the suffering of that unhappy people so that Australia's very name may become a term of reproach among them. We do not believe that it represents a wise or even intelligent response to the challenge of Chinese power. On the contrary, we believe it mistakes entirely the nature of that power, and that it materially assists China in her subversive aims. Indeed, we cannot conceive a decision by the Government more likely to promote the long term interest of China in Asia and the Pacific.[94]

The Australian battalion was sent to South Vietnam in May 1965, and would soon operate in the coastal province of Phuoc Tuy. It was expanded to a battalion group in August, and in March the following year the deployment was further built up to two battalions plus supporting units.

With Menzies' retirement in January 1966 Australia had, in his successor, Harold Holt, a prime minister less emotionally attached to Britain and more at ease with the United States. He fully shared the view that, 'In the long run, the threat to South Vietnam is a direct threat to Australia.'[95]

On his first visit to Washington in July 1966, riffing off Johnson's campaign slogan, Holt assured the American president that Australia would go 'all the way with LBJ'. The federal election in November that year, fought heavily on the issues of Vietnam and conscription, showed that, although the public was more cautious about sending national servicemen to fight in Vietnam than they were about the war itself, public opinion was strongly with the Coalition; it delivered them their largest-ever parliamentary majority.

Late that summer, as signs that the British were leaving Southeast Asia intensified, the Holt government began a gradual reappraisal of Australia's defence and foreign policy in Southeast Asia. What should Australia do about its own military presence in Malaysia and Singapore if Britain went? It had never before committed troops overseas without either the British or the Americans alongside. In this tenuous environment it would be more important than ever to send the right signals to Washington. If the British were going, it was surely more important that the Americans should stay.[96]

So, in September 1967, Holt committed, in principle, a third battalion group to Vietnam. But early in 1968 optimism about progress in Vietnam was shattered by the major countrywide offensive launched by the Viet Cong and North Vietnamese forces during the Tet religious holiday. Despite the huge casualties sustained by those forces, the offensive was a political triumph, persuading many in the United States that the strategy of attrition was not working.

In March Johnson announced a partial halt to the bombings and the opening of peace negotiations. Politically damaged, he said he would not contest the next election. In April his new defence secretary, Clark Clifford, announced that the president had no intention of further increasing US personnel numbers in Vietnam. The turning point had come.

Johnson's successor, Richard Nixon, felt that American prestige would not survive a unilateral withdrawal of forces from Vietnam, but he came to office with a program of 'Vietnamisation', meaning that the United States would gradually withdraw while building up the capacity of the South Vietnamese army. Peace talks between the United States and North Vietnam finally began in Paris in January 1969, and in June Nixon announced that the US would begin pulling its troops out.

Then in July Nixon codified his views of the relationship between the United States and its allies in what became known as the Nixon Doctrine, or alternatively, the Guam doctrine, after the Pacific island where he had first outlined it during a plane stopover. It was later elaborated in a 'New Strategy for Peace', which he put to Congress in February 1970.

Under the Nixon Doctrine, the United States reaffirmed its treaty commitments but made it clear that it expected its allies to carry a greater share of their own security burden. In future, the US would avoid Vietnam-type commitments in areas on its periphery and would look 'to the nation directly threatened to assume the primary responsibility of providing the manpower for its defence'. 'We will help', said Nixon, 'where it makes a real difference and is considered in our interest.'[97]

Australian ministers recognised that Australia faced a new situation. Where would the United States consider it was in its interest to intervene? Through 1968 and 1969, from the period of Johnson's decision to stop escalation of the conflict to the Nixon Doctrine, the Australian government consistently found itself defending US policy only to discover that, without consultation, the policy had changed. In September 1969 the Minister for External Affairs, Gordon Freeth, summarised the uncertainty: 'There is a widespread feeling that in Asia and the Pacific old patterns are breaking up and new ones emerging and that Australia's own relationship with the region may be entering a period of change and readjustment.'[98] But caught by their own convictions and established policies, and in a political environment in which their reliance on the preferences of the anti-communist Democratic Labor Party had increased, ministers were unable or unwilling to make the necessary adjustments.

Within Australia, public opinion, which had consistently supported the war, was beginning to fragment. This was less a reflection of developments on the ground in Vietnam than of uncertainty about the American position. In February 1967 Whitlam, an altogether more formidable politician than Calwell, had been elected as leader of the ALP. He had gone into the 1969 elections pledging withdrawal of Australian forces by mid-1970. Gorton's parliamentary majority was reduced from forty to seven. Throughout 1970 and 1971 anti-war demonstrations – the Vietnam moratorium movement – grew in scale. Crowds of more than 100,000 marched in the streets in May and August 1970. Even so, as late as January 1970 Gallup polling showed that

65 per cent of respondents – 75 per cent in the younger age group – still supported a gradual rather than immediate withdrawal of Australian forces.[99]

But with its hand forced by the Americans, the Gorton government announced the withdrawal of the first Australian battalion in April 1970. In August 1971 Gorton's successor, the hapless William McMahon, who had taken over in March, announced that most Australian combat forces would be brought home by Christmas.

The security environment Australia had tried to support was crumbling. Its oldest defence partner, Britain, had announced its withdrawal east of Suez, and all Australian efforts to keep the United States engaged looked to be failing.

It is impossible to separate the Vietnam War's entangled strands of meaning and consequences. Even for Australia, the war was many things: a military operation in which around 60,000 Australians served and 521 died; an explosive domestic political controversy; a vector of social and cultural change. But considered as foreign policy, what can be said about its consequences?

Certainly the government's clear objectives at the beginning were not met. The Menzies government went into the war with the aim of keeping the United States involved in the region, so that when Australia needed the shelter of the ANZUS umbrella, it would be ready at hand. But it ended up with the Nixon Doctrine, an American determination that there would be 'no more Vietnams' and a prolonged American reluctance to expend its power in Asia.

The strategic assumptions that lay behind Australia's engagement in the war and that Australian ministers believed, or convinced themselves they believed, were obviously flawed. The war was not a manifestation of an aggressive southward thrust by Chinese communism. Its roots lay much more deeply in Vietnam's own political and social divisions and nationalist convictions.

Vietnam became communist, but the rest of the region did not follow. As early as June 1964 the CIA was advising the Johnson administration that 'With the possible exception of Cambodia it is likely that no nation in the area would quickly succumb to Communism as a result of the fall of Laos and South Vietnam. Furthermore, a continuation of the spread of Communism in the area would not be inexorable and any spread which did occur would take time – time in which the total situation might change in any number of ways unfavourable to the Communist cause.'[100]

And the total situation did change. Claims by Asian leaders like Lee Kuan Yew that the Vietnam War gave the rest of the region time to inoculate itself against the communist threat are impossible to prove. But any attempt to measure the war's impact has to address the questions 'At what cost?' and 'What were the alternatives?'

On the other hand, as foreign policy, Australia's participation did no serious damage to its standing with its key ASEAN neighbours, all of which either directly supported (Thailand, the Philippines) or were not displeased with (Indonesia, Malaysia) the American position. And whatever the great and unnecessary cost of the war, it taught Australia some important lessons in alliance management. Its support had been politically vital to the US administration, and that experience would have a long-term impact on the way Australian policy-makers thought about their contribution to the alliance and on the way Americans thought about Australia.

Despite the divisions over Vietnam, throughout the war both the government and the Opposition regarded the American alliance as central to Australian security.

4

ORGANISING THE WORLD: THE 1940s TO THE 1960s

The third of the elements that would together create an Australian foreign policy was a commitment to an international order based on clear laws that Australia itself had helped to determine. Even before the United States entered World War II it was evident that a new sort of global system would have to replace the one that had ended.

The basic framework was agreed by Winston Churchill and Franklin D. Roosevelt when they set out 'certain common principles in the national policies of their respective countries on which they base their hopes for a better future for the world' in a statement issued in August 1941 after their secret meeting aboard the USS *Augusta* in Placentia Bay, Newfoundland. This became known as the Atlantic Charter. These principles included no territorial aggrandisement; the right to self-determination; free and open trade and secure access to raw materials; collaboration between all nations to secure improved labour standards, economic advancement and social security; a secure peace 'that all the men in all the lands may live out their lives in freedom from fear and want'; freedom of the seas and the disarmament of the aggressors in the war; and an easing of the crushing burden of armaments. The charter described a liberal internationalist order that would embrace collective security, economic openness and social progress. The objectives reflected the 'Four Freedoms' – of speech, of worship, from want, from fear – which Roosevelt had set out in his State of the Union address in February 1941.

In January 1942, just weeks after Pearl Harbor, Australia, along with twenty-five other Allied governments, signed up to these principles at a Washington meeting to coordinate Allied military strategy. This 'Declaration by United Nations' was the first contemporary use of that term. The Atlantic Charter provided Australia, H.V. Evatt said, with a 'sure and certain guide to future policy'.[1]

The institutions of the post-war world

Even at the beginning of the Pacific War, thought was being given to what the world would be like when it was over.

The organisations and approaches of the past had demonstrably failed to preserve security or sustain economic growth. Politicians and scholars were looking for something new. How could you combine the reality of power with moral force in ways that would avoid the ineffectiveness of the League of Nations? How could you prevent the boom and bust economic cycles that had led to the Depression? In his 1936 *General Theory of Employment, Interest and Money*, J.M. Keynes had suggested that these cycles could be moderated, even controlled, by more active government management of fiscal and monetary policy, so aggregate demand would be high enough to maintain full employment. For one of the most influential Australian economists of the post-war years, Herbert Cole 'Nugget' Coombs, the publication of this book, was 'for me and for many of my generation the most seminal intellectual event of our time'.[2]

Partly in response to the Atlantic Charter, a post-hostilities section was set up in the Department of External Affairs in April 1942, just two months after the fall of Singapore, at the suggestion of Paul Hasluck, who would lead it, to deal with the diplomacy of reconstruction and to protect Australia's political and economic interests as the arrangements for the future were settled.[3] The approach mirrored externally the domestic work of the Department of Post-War Reconstruction, created in late 1942 and headed by Coombs.

Ever alert to Australia's exclusion from decisions that might affect it, Evatt's irritation that the great powers had announced, without consultation, at their Cairo Conference in November 1943 decisions about the disposition of Japan's territories after the war provided a further catalyst for Australian and New Zealand thinking about post-war organisation. Australia became an active participant in a series of conferences on agriculture, labour, security and economic cooperation, which throughout 1943 and 1944 began to shape the new international institutions.

In October 1943 the American, British and Soviet foreign ministers announced plans for a United Nations Organisation that would maintain global peace and security. These were elaborated at a meeting held in August 1944 in a Georgetown mansion called Dumbarton Oaks. The 'Big Three' proposed a structure for the new organisation in which they, together with France and China, would be permanent members of a Security Council and able to veto any of its decisions. They would be joined on the Council by temporary members elected from a General Assembly of all member states. The Council would have sole responsibility for maintaining the peace and imposing economic and military sanctions. The Assembly's role would be restricted to the consideration of general principles.

Evatt and the Department of External Affairs began thinking about an Australian response to the Dumbarton Oaks draft and to the problems of collective security more generally. This was one of the main subjects discussed by Australia and New Zealand at an ANZAC conference in Wellington in November 1944.

Roosevelt's death in early April 1945 left the new president, Harry Truman, with the task of constructing the post-war order. Later that month, representatives of forty-six nations, with 850 delegates and 3500 support staff, met in San Francisco to draw up the United Nations Declaration. The challenge was enormous. Every section of the Charter of the new organisation had to be agreed by a two-thirds majority. A steering committee of the heads of delegations was created but even this was too large and the task of preparing draft proposals was delegated to a fourteen-member Executive Committee.

Curtin had sent the deputy prime minister, Frank Forde, an amiable old-style Labor man, as leader of the Australian delegation, presumably to keep Evatt under control. If so, it didn't work. Forde presented Australia's opening statement which set out substantial reservations about the Dumbarton Oaks draft. But it was Evatt's thinking that informed it. Observing him at close quarters, Hasluck, who was a member of the delegation, wrote, 'Day after day for ten weeks from early morning to late at night his concentration on the task and the intensity of his efforts had a ferocity that made me wonder what strange demon had possessed him.'[4]

Evatt recognised that any new organisation needed the support of the great powers and accepted that America's absence had been an important reason for the failure of the League of Nations to prevent Japan's aggression. But he insisted from the start that the great powers should not shape the post-war world alone, that the responsibility had to be shared with (and by) smaller nations. As he had told the Australian parliament: 'No sovereign state, however small, will wish to think that its destiny had been handed over to another power, however great. Nor does history at all support the view that wisdom is confined to the strongest nations or that knowledge is found only at the centre of power ... [A] successful world organization requires an enthusiastic contribution from smaller powers, both in counsel and in material support.'[5]

Evatt was appointed as one of the members of the Executive Committee. The chief changes Australia sought in the amendments it proposed to the draft Charter – thirty-eight in all – were to raise the status of the General Assembly; expand the functions of the Economic and Social Council (ECOSOC) so that greater attention was paid to social, economic and human problems; bring all dependent peoples into a mandate or trusteeship arrangement; and greatly limit the use of the great powers' veto over the business of the Security Council and amendments to the Charter.[6]

Evatt argued strongly for the strengthening of the UN's role in human rights. The Atlantic Charter – as well as the terrible revelations about the Holocaust now coming to light – provided the background to the emphasis on 'faith in fundamental human rights, in the dignity and worth of the human person, in the equal rights of men and women and of nations large and small' which was written into the preamble of the UN's Charter. A Commission on Human Rights was formed as one of the ECOSOC's subsidiary bodies, and Australia was elected to it. As president of the General Assembly in December 1948, Evatt presided over the adoption of the Genocide Convention and the Universal Declaration of Human Rights, the basis for subsequent major human rights instruments such as the International Covenant on Economic, Social and Cultural Rights and the International Covenant on Civil and Political Rights, both drafted in 1954. Throughout 1946 and 1947 Evatt also argued for the establishment of an International Human Rights Court, although he could not attract sufficient support.[7]

Only one woman, Jessie Street, was a member of the Australian delegation, but through her Australia was also prominent in issues relating to women, including the establishment of the Commission on the Status of Women, of which Australia was a founding member.

The idea that a trusteeship process should be introduced for all dependent territories, requiring colonial powers to account for the interests of the people they administered, with self-government the ultimate objective, was one Evatt held strongly. In this he was closer to the views of the US state department than was Curtin, who shared the caution of the British Colonial Office.[8] (It did not, however, prevent his arguing strongly against UN intervention in Australia's policies in Papua and New Guinea.)

The outcome of the San Francisco conference was a substantial achievement for the Australian delegation. They failed to limit the scope of the great powers' veto on Charter amendments, or to bring all non-self-governing territories under the purview of the trusteeship system. But they succeeded in expanding the UN's economic and social remit and in giving the General Assembly equal authority with the Security Council to deal with and make recommendations to the Council, on 'any matters within the scope' of the Charter – except those currently before the Council.

Evatt was the acknowledged leader of the smaller powers and established a reputation for Australia. It was a formidable feat of intellect, energy and willpower. An exhausted Hasluck wrote to his wife: 'The effort has been worth it ... Australia's name stands higher in world affairs and we have won a great deal of respect and many friends ... [Evatt] has made me proud to be an Australian and particularly to be one of the same team. He really has fought magnificently and with great judgement in difficult circumstances.' [9] Hasluck would have plenty of reasons to criticise his minister in future, but this was Evatt's great hour. Australia had successfully managed its introduction to an essentially new form of diplomacy – multilateral coalition-building. In 1965, at the end of Evatt's life, his body frail and his mind wandering, Hasluck visited him at his home in Sydney. Their last conversation was of San Francisco.[10]

Bretton Woods and the global economy

Security was not the only consideration in the remaking of the post-war order. The immediate economic aim was relief and rehabilitation: devastated economies had to be rebuilt, and displaced people fed and given shelter. But it was also generally agreed that significant change was needed in the way countries coordinated their economic policies.

The war had fundamentally altered the balance of economic power in the world. The flow of US military and economic support to Britain and the other Allies (including Australia after November 1941) through the Lend Lease program came with American conditions. Article VII of the Mutual Aid Agreement, which bound all the recipients, required them to agree to the 'elimination of all forms of discriminatory treatment in international commerce and ... the elimination of tariffs and other trade barriers'.

In Australia's case, this commitment, unavoidable in the circumstances of the time, represented a revolutionary change in the way it thought about its economic interaction with the world. Ever since Federation, the Australian economy had been based on imperial preferences in trade and strong tariff protection of industry.

Within the Labor government the suspicion of international finance and free trade ran very deep. But a brilliant group of economic advisers including Coombs, L.F. Giblin, Roland Wilson, John Crawford and Leslie Melville, influenced by Keynes, provided the government with a policy solution to its political problem. While acknowledging the importance of the Mutual Aid Agreement commitments to free and open trade, they placed them in the context of broader obligations to secure full employment, industrial development and rising living standards.[11]

Called the 'positive approach', this became the way for Chifley to reconcile international obligations, national ambitions and party political requirements. It became a recurrent theme in all Australian contributions to the development of the new institutions. It was why Evatt fought hard and successfully to have a commitment to higher standards of living and full employment included in the UN Charter.

During 1943 and 1944, conferences on food and agriculture at Hot Springs (partly a legacy of work Stanley Melbourne Bruce had done in the League of Nations) and international labour issues in Philadelphia helped provide building blocks for the United Nations system.

For Coombs, Australia's objective was 'clear and relatively simple: to ensure a United States economy which would, by its consumption pressure, power the demand for internationally traded goods, and which would open its markets to the products of other countries. Unless we could achieve such an outcome I saw little prospect of the Australian Government, Mutual Aid Agreements notwithstanding, dismantling existing protections'.[12]

Australia was one of the forty-four nations represented at the United Nations Monetary and Financial Conference (better known as Bretton Woods) in July 1944 in New Hampshire. The conference was designed to find ways of preventing a recurrence of the currency wars and market restrictions of the 1930s; its intellectual drive came from Keynes and the US treasury secretary, Harry Dexter White. Their objective was to establish an open economic system in which trade could flow and capital move.

The conference created the International Bank for Reconstruction and Development (IBRD), which would evolve into the World Bank, and the International Monetary Fund (IMF). The purpose of the IBRD was to speed post-war recovery by helping to finance reconstruction projects, especially in Europe. The IMF's job was to oversee the stability of the international monetary system through an adjustable system which would tie currencies to the US dollar, which was linked in turn to gold. All members were to subscribe to the IMF's capital and the Fund would provide short-term financial assistance to countries experiencing balance of payments difficulties. Governments could revise exchange rates by up to 10 per cent and regulate the flow of capital.

A companion proposal for an International Trade Organization with rules and regulations governing overseas trade was eventually killed off by the United States senate but an interim step – a General Agreement on Tariffs and Trade (GATT) – provided the foundation for an open, non-discriminatory trading system in which every concession extended to one trading partner would automatically flow to all parties to the agreement.

The ratification of the legislation bringing Australia into these new institutions provided a very tough test for Curtin and Chifley. Powerful opponents within the party argued that the new bodies would threaten imperial preferences and protection, create a 'world money monopoly' and tie the Australian economy too closely to America's. They fought tenaciously against ratification through the parliamentary caucus and party forums. The left-wing government minister Eddie Ward spoke against his own side in the debate over ratification in March 1947. But Chifley prevailed. As he told parliament: 'Just as political isolation in the world would be an impracticable policy for Australia so do I think that economic isolationism would be disastrous.'[13] His success was one of the most important international achievements of the Labor government.

The GATT was ratified in 1948, this time with the Opposition, which had supported the Bretton Woods bills, opposing. Menzies said, 'unless we can continue to make discriminatory bargains we shall come off very badly in our search for world trade'.[14] 'Let us make no mistake about what

this agreement means,' added the future trade minister John McEwen, ' ...
It represents the cutting up of the British Commonwealth.'[15] Nevertheless,
the Liberal–Country Party Coalition, which was elected in December
1949, decided that it would not withdraw from the GATT and delivered a
large measure of continuity in international economic policy.

Aid and the Colombo Plan

The most immediate economic problem facing the victors at the end of
the war, however, was how to relieve the devastation and dislocation of
the conflict. Australia's experiences here provided the foundation for
what would become an important instrument of Australian foreign policy: the aid program. The organisation charged with food, shelter and
other relief was the United Nations Relief and Rehabilitation
Administration (UNRRA), set up in November 1943. Australia became
an active participant in its work, and by the time its functions were transferred to other UN agencies in 1947 Australia was the fourth-largest
contributor. An Australian official, Robert (later Sir Robert) Jackson, who
would go on to make a distinguished contribution to international development issues through the United Nations, was a driving force of the
organisation as deputy director.

So when the Australian government changed in 1949, the idea that it
should provide aid for others was an established part of Australia's international policy. The Coalition came to power planning to continue such
assistance, but with less focus than Labor on the United Nations and Europe,
and more on helping non-communist Asia, especially the members of the
Commonwealth.

Many elements of what would become the Colombo Plan were already
under consideration in the Department of External Affairs under Evatt, but
when Percy Spender became minister, he seized upon the idea and became
its most prominent advocate. The war had ravaged Asia as much as Europe.
Food was scarce, birth rates high and health problems growing. 'The whole
area dwells on the edge of famine,' Arthur Tange, who was one of the
Australian officials most responsible for the Colombo Plan's development
and early implementation, noted in a secret memorandum.[16] In 1950 Asia's
main rice-exporting areas, Burma, Thailand and Indochina, were shipping
only half as much as they had in 1938. For Spender and other ministers,
this was a political as well a humanitarian issue. In the growing global

ideological competition with communism, it was imperative that non-communist Asian states should keep their people fed.

Just two weeks after he took office, Spender had to travel to Colombo to attend the first-ever meeting of Commonwealth foreign ministers. With the help of two of his senior officials, including Tange, he spent the journey working up a proposal to put to the conference. Ceylon's finance minister had suggested a larger Marshall Plan–like development scheme for Asia, but with the economic pressures facing Britain, that was never likely to eventuate. The more modest Australian proposal, which called, essentially, for the coordination of aid programs individually set by each country – both donors and recipients – was adopted. As Spender acknowledged, it was not really a plan at all. The details were to be worked out by a Consultative Committee, which Australia offered to chair. 'In that way Australia could keep its hand upon the tiller,' Spender noted shrewdly.[17]

The Consultative Committee met at Admiralty House overlooking Sydney Harbour in May 1950, and agreed on a program that would encompass the training of students and the provision of technical experts as well as food aid and longer-term finance for public investment.

In developing the Colombo Plan, Australia had several aims. It wanted to help Asia's immediate humanitarian needs and build the confidence and capacity of the new postcolonial states to deal with economic development. It wanted to shore up the countries of the region against communism. It wanted to develop its own ties with its neighbours through the sort of people-to-people contact that training and technical assistance would deliver. And for both strategic and practical reasons it wanted to involve the United States as a donor, and non-Commonwealth countries like Indonesia as recipients.

The Colombo Plan began operation in July 1951. The United States joined before the end of that year, greatly increasing the available resources. By 1954 the seven founding members of Australia, Canada, Ceylon, India, New Zealand, Pakistan and the United Kingdom had been joined by Burma, Cambodia, Indonesia, Laos, the Philippines, Thailand, the United States and Vietnam. Not without reservations on Australia's part, Japan joined in 1954.

Australia learnt how to deliver aid. An Economic and Technical Assistance section was set up in the Department of External Affairs in 1952, the forerunner of subsequent aid administrations. By the end of 1959, 2650 Asian students had arrived in Australia under the Colombo Plan and Australia was the leading provider of places for education and training.[18]

The impact of the Colombo Plan shouldn't be overstated. The volume of Australian aid was still relatively small. Spender's successor, Casey, had difficulty keeping his ministerial colleagues up to the mark. He complained in his diary that many were 'hostile to the UN, hostile to the Colombo Plan, and unsympathetic to Asia ... That we are not pulling our weight internationally doesn't cut any ice.' He noted that Australia's Colombo Plan contributions per head in 1953–54 were lower than those of New Zealand or Canada, and less than half those of the United States for South and Southeast Asia alone. He would not be the last Australian foreign minister to complain that after trying to help the Treasury keep costs down, his prudence was now working to his disadvantage.[19]

That situation did not change much during the 1960s. By the end of the decade more than $115 million of Australia's total external aid of $166 million was still allocated to Papua New Guinea.[20] And not all the people-to-people experiences were happy: some of the arriving students got a closer look at the operation of the White Australia policy.

But the Colombo Plan was important. It was the first multilateral Asian aid scheme engaging the Asian countries themselves. It represented a well-planned and coordinated Australian initiative to shape the region. It established development assistance as a central part of Australia's relations with Asia and it made its mark on Australians themselves. No dimension of the Australian aid program afterwards had such widespread public recognition. That was why sixty-three years after it first began, one of Spender's successors, Julie Bishop, branded her government's program to send Australian students to study in Asia as a New Colombo Plan.

The Commonwealth

It seemed to all the Australian policy-makers of the immediate post-war period, whatever their political affiliation, that although much had changed in Australia's world, the British Commonwealth of Nations, the legacy of the Empire, would provide a continuing anchor for Australian foreign policy and an important parallel to the United Nations. From 1944 John Curtin was urging the establishment of a new Commonwealth secretariat to formalise these arrangements, although he was unable to attract much support for the idea.[21] No statement on foreign policy by either side of politics in the 1950s and early '60s was complete without an acknowledgement of the Commonwealth's continuing importance.

Chapter 3 examined the shift in Australia's attitudes towards Britain, but the Commonwealth had a different role. It was seen as a bridge that could carry Australian foreign policy from the old, intimate, imperial world, linked by loyalty to the Crown and a common sense of Britishness, to a modern, multiracial future. It offered a prospect of reassuring continuity in a period of great change, and a way for Australia to project its own interests in the world through a broader group of countries.

Although Churchill had famously declared that he had 'not become the King's First Minister to preside over the liquidation of the British Empire', that process had begun as soon as the war was over. The new states of Asia – India, Pakistan, Ceylon and Burma – were first.

In October 1948 the Commonwealth Prime Ministers' Conference took a fundamental step when India, a republic, became a member on its independence. This broke the bond between the British monarch and membership of what now became known simply as the Commonwealth of Nations. Two other new states – Burma, and later Eire – decided not to join at all.

Each side of Australian politics put the weight of its support for the Commonwealth in different places. For the Coalition, and particularly for Menzies, it was the ties to the past that mattered – the link to the Crown and the continuation into the contemporary world of British history and values. Menzies' hopes for the institutions were high: 'there is no meeting of any group in the world that is quite so intimate, so significant and so informed as is a meeting of prime ministers who can speak for so many different races in so many parts of the world,' he told parliament in March 1951 [22], sounding a little like a man trying to persuade himself. But he saw dangers ahead: 'We must not, at our peril, allow this precious family association ... [to] become no more than a loose association of nations which are in temporary alliance but which spiritually have no common roots in the ground.' [23]

Labor gave less weight to the past than to the link the Commonwealth provided to the new world of emerging Afro-Asian powers. For Gough Whitlam, speaking a decade later, 'the fate of the Commonwealth is of very great sentimental as well as practical significance to Australia. The Commonwealth is the best bridge – in many ways it is the only bridge – between the European-type countries on the one hand and the countries of Asia and Africa on the other hand.' [24]

The expansion of the Afro-Asian membership of the Commonwealth came faster than almost anyone expected. Ghana was the first of Britain's African territories to become independent, in 1957. The West Indies followed in 1958, and just eight years after Harold Macmillan declared in February 1960 in Cape Town that 'the wind of change is blowing through this continent', almost all remaining British territories were independent. This deeply changed the nature and focus of the Commonwealth. By the mid-1950s Menzies was referring to a two-tier 'old' and 'new' Commonwealth.

Race was one of the issues that preoccupied the new Commonwealth. India was increasingly drawing attention to the treatment of Indians in South Africa, a fellow member of the Commonwealth, as it had been doing in the United Nations since 1952.

Throughout the 1950s Australia voted with very small and declining minorities against resolutions in the United Nations opposing apartheid. What lay behind these votes was not, the government insisted, support for the policies of the South African government but the principle, dating right back to Billy Hughes, that there should be no international interference with Australia's restricted immigration policy or its treatment of its Indigenous population.

The brutal shooting in March 1960 of sixty-nine black demonstrators in the African township of Sharpeville protesting against the apartheid requirement that they carry passbooks decisively tilted world opinion. In the Australian parliamentary debate that followed, Whitlam castigated Menzies' insistence on the principle of domestic jurisdiction: 'That is the great question in his mind, not the policy, not the morality, not the principle, but the legalism.'[25]

Two sets of global rules were at odds here. The rules the government preferred were those of Article 2(7) of the UN Charter providing that 'Nothing contained in the present Charter shall authorize the United Nations to intervene in matters which are essentially within the domestic jurisdiction of any state'. Whitlam put the emphasis on Article 55, which required member states to promote 'universal respect for, and observance of, human rights and fundamental freedoms for all without distinction as to race, sex, language or religion'.

White South Africans had voted to become a republic in October 1960 and in March 1961 the South African prime minister, Hendrik Frensch Verwoerd, attended the Commonwealth Prime Ministers' Conference in London, seeking continuing membership of the Commonwealth as a republic. He met heavy opposition, especially from India's Jawaharlal Nehru and Ghana's Kwame Nkrumah. Verwoerd decided that resignation was better than expulsion and South Africa left the Commonwealth formally in May.

Menzies greatly regretted this and tried to prevent it. This was not, he said, because he condoned apartheid, but because sovereignty within the Commonwealth – the ability to choose one's own form of government – was 'vital to the Commonwealth structure and spirit'.[26] The southern Africa issues transformed the Commonwealth for Menzies. He was irritated when Macmillan asked Nehru to chair the London meeting in his absence, rather than turning to Menzies as the senior Commonwealth leader. The prime minister was 'much put out by Mr Macmillan's apparent preference for a brown face', the Australian high commissioner complained to the British minister responsible.[27]

When Garfield Barwick succeeded Menzies as external affairs minister in 1961, he began arguing for a tougher anti-apartheid stance at the United Nations. He also differed from Menzies and the majority of his cabinet colleagues on the future of Southern Rhodesia. The decolonisation of the British territories in central Africa had taken many different turns during the 1950s, but London now had to decide whether Southern Rhodesia should be allowed to move towards independence before the implementation of majority rule, under a government dominated by white settlers. 'Australia, with its migration policy, Papua New Guinea and our past – and for that matter present – treatment of our aborigines (cannot afford to be) in support of a white minority government in Africa maintained by repressive legislation and perhaps by force of arms', he advised Menzies in 1963.[28]

By 1964 the question was dividing the Commonwealth. The white government of Ian Smith threatened to resolve the impasse by making a unilateral declaration of independence (UDI). Other Commonwealth countries demanded that Britain resist such action with force if necessary. While accepting that a UDI would be illegal, Menzies rejected the resort to force as 'repugnant to the people of Australia' and held 'very great reservations' about an arms embargo and economic sanctions'.[29]

When negotiations (including a British proposal, rejected by the Rhodesians, to have Menzies try to broker a settlement) failed, Smith announced a UDI in November 1965. Australia implemented some Commonwealth sanctions banning arms sales and imports of tobacco, but declined to attend a special meeting to discuss the matter on the grounds, as Menzies put it, that if the Commonwealth 'begins to claim the right to intervene in and give orders in relation to matters which are the proper concern of some individual members of the Commonwealth good relations cannot long continue, nor can the present Commonwealth structure long endure'.[30]

By the time of the next Commonwealth Prime Ministers' Meeting in September 1966, Menzies had been replaced by Holt, whose views on these questions were not very different. Within the Liberal Party some senior politicians were strongly supporting Smith. The tone of the September meeting was acrimonious, and the differences within the Commonwealth on full display. It was agreed that if Britain could not force a reversal on the Rhodesian regime it would seek sanctions from the United Nations. Harold Wilson did this in May 1968 when, for the first time in its history, the United Nations Security Council applied comprehensive and mandatory economic sanctions on a state.[31]

Australia had been unenthusiastic about the referral to the United Nations and, although it applied the mandatory sanctions, the attorney-general, Nigel Bowen, said publicly that 'many ministers found sanctions distasteful'.[32]

By the late 1960s the Commonwealth had diminished as a central feature of the way Australia thought about itself in the world. It had become clear that it could not offer either side of politics the sort of foreign policy advantage they sought from it: the ties with the past were too tenuous and the links to the new Afro-Asian world too amorphous.

Britain itself mattered less in Australia's foreign policy. Australia's independent relationships with Asia were becoming deeper and more complex. They existed independently of the Commonwealth relationship (although common membership did enhance them). And it was not only African issues that divided the Commonwealth. The dispute over the contested territory of Kashmir led to war between India and Pakistan in September 1965.

The Commonwealth would linger on. Heads of Government Meetings would be held and declarations made. Both Fraser and Hawke would use it effectively to address issues of race and representation in southern Africa. But the Commonwealth would never again be seen by Australia in quite the same way as an instrument for its engagement with the world.

Arms control and the nuclear threat

No fact more clearly divided the world after 1945 from that which had gone before than the existence of nuclear weapons and their capacity to end history. Resolution 1(1) of the United Nations at its opening session on 24 January 1946 dealt with 'problems arising from the discovery of atomic energy and related matters'. It declared that atomic energy should be used 'only for peaceful purposes', called for the elimination of atomic weapons from national arsenals and established a new UN Atomic Energy Commission (AEC).

Evatt chaired the first meeting of the AEC, supporting an American plan for comprehensive international control over nuclear technology and sanctions against states that misused it. But in a sign of the tensions that were already consolidating into the Cold War, the Soviet Union was dragging its feet on the issue, to Evatt's increasing irritation. Finally, the Soviet Union joined the nuclear ranks with its own nuclear explosions in August 1949.

The Menzies government's scepticism about UN arms control initiatives grew after the revolution in China and the Korean War. It accepted the theoretical desirability of disarmament, but did not think this was yet the time for it. Menzies expressed concern that the Soviet Union would use arms control to trick and outflank the West.[32] So Australia stood on the sidelines of the arms control debates throughout the 1950s as the Cold War intensified.

An important reason for this was the government's continuing uncertainty about whether Australia itself should pursue nuclear energy and develop nuclear weapons. That was also a factor behind Menzies' offer of support to the British when the United States became reluctant to continue its nuclear cooperation after the war. British nuclear tests were conducted at the Monte Bello Islands off the Pilbara coast from 1952 and subsequently in South Australia throughout the 1950s, with minor trials continuing at the Maralinga site until 1963.

Menzies was ambivalent about whether Australia should procure nuclear weapons, but he believed in keeping the path open if circumstances demanded it. In 1961 cabinet was seeking 'recognition now of the United Kingdom's obligation to provide Australia, if ever necessary, with a nuclear capability'.[34]

As France became the fourth nuclear weapons state in 1960 and the Soviet Union resumed nuclear tests in the atmosphere in December 1961, the focus of the international arms control debate shifted from the question of what the United States and the Soviet Union should do about their own nuclear arsenals to how to prevent the weapons spreading further. In 1961 an Irish motion in the United Nations called on nuclear states to prevent the transfer of nuclear technology to others, and on non-nuclear states to refrain from acquiring them. Australia's support for the resolution was decidedly muted, shaped by the fear that China would go nuclear and the possibility that it might need to do so itself.[35] But the near-catastrophe of the Cuban missile crisis in October 1962, when the world came so close to nuclear war, tipped the debate's momentum in the direction of nonproliferation.

In the face of growing public concern about radioactive fallout, the nuclear powers negotiated the Partial Test Ban Treaty in 1963 prohibiting testing in the atmosphere, in outer space or under water. And, in another development that Australia found unsettling, there was a growing move towards the declaration of nuclear-weapons-free zones (NWFZs).

Through Casey, Australia had already been an important player in establishing the first nuclear-free zone. In 1933 Australia had taken over British territorial claims (based in part on Douglas Mawson's exploration) to more than 40 per cent of Antarctica. The Antarctic Division was set up within the external affairs department in 1947, and Casey, with his interest in science, was an active supporter of Australia's work there. After the war, Antarctica still seemed a possible site for military bases and a source of minerals.

However, Australia's sovereignty was never accepted by the non-claimant states, including the United States and the Soviet Union, and faced with that reality, Casey became an influential participant in the 1959 Washington conference where the Antarctic Treaty, which would come into force in 1961, was signed. The treaty froze all territorial claims and established a regime for exploration and scientific research. It declared Antarctica a nuclear-free zone. The treaty was an important signal that, despite the Cold War, international cooperation was still possible.

China joined the nuclear club in 1964 and exploded its first hydrogen bomb in 1967. And with proposals for a NWFZ in Latin America gathering force, Australia wanted to avoid a precedent for the Pacific that would preclude its own possible nuclear ambitions. But the nuclear states increasingly recognised a common interest in limiting the access of others to the technology they possessed, so in 1967 a Treaty on the Non-Proliferation of Nuclear Weapons (NPT) was negotiated. The nuclear states agreed not to transfer nuclear weapons technology and non-nuclear states agreed not to acquire it; the nuclear states also agreed to share the benefits of peaceful nuclear technology and to pursue negotiations leading to nuclear disarmament. A system of 'safeguards' monitored by the International Atomic Energy Agency (IAEA) was set up to ensure that nuclear materials provided for peaceful use were not diverted for weapons purposes. Australia's uranium exports would be affected

When the treaty was opened for signature in July 1968 the Australian government was divided. Hasluck, and increasingly the defence department, felt that pressure from allies and the likely reaction of neighbours like Indonesia gave Australia no alternative but to sign.[36] The prime minister,

John Gorton, with more nationalist instincts on defence policy, was opposed, however, and was supported by scientists and officials from the Australian Atomic Energy Commission. The US secretary of state, Dean Rusk, reported to Washington that he had run into a 'full battery of reservations about non-proliferation' from Gorton during their discussions in Canberra in April 1968. 'He sounded almost like de Gaulle in saying that Australia could not rely upon the US for nuclear weapons under ANZUS in the event of nuclear blackmail or attack on Australia.'[37]

In February 1969 Gorton proposed the construction of Australia's first nuclear power reactor, at Jervis Bay, including an enrichment plant. The reason given was to provide Australia with an alternative energy source, but the scarcely hidden objective was to give the nation the technical capacity to go nuclear if the need arose.[38]

During the 1969 election campaign Gorton said he would not sign the NPT if he was returned to government, but as important states like Japan and West Germany signed up the pressures on Australia grew. When, in early 1970, Australia finally became the second-last country to sign before the treaty came into effect, Gorton noted that it would still not apply until it was formally ratified.[39]

The Jervis Bay project was shelved by Gorton's successor, William McMahon, in 1971, but it was not until Whitlam became prime minister, pledging 'strong and unequivocal support for efforts to check the spread of nuclear weapons', that Australia ratified the treaty.[40]

Differences between the parties were also emerging over the role in global nuclear strategy of United States–operated defence facilities in Australia. The establishment of the North West Cape Communications Centre in 1963 had been followed by announcements of a 'joint defence space research facility' at Pine Gap in 1966 and a 'joint defence space communications centre' at Nurrungar, near Woomera, in 1969. Both facilities, which were linked to the top-secret United States satellite early-warning and intelligence-gathering systems, were swathed in much greater secrecy than North West Cape. Defending the agreements, the government had cited the requirements of Article 11 of the ANZUS Treaty for both parties to 'develop their individual and collective capacity to resist armed attack'. 'There is a price to pay for the alliance,' said the defence minister, Allen Fairhall, 'and the price we pay takes the form of the facilities provided at Woomera, Pine Gap and North West Cape.'[41] The debate within the ALP about that price would continue.

Trade, the GATT and the Australia–Japan Commerce Agreement

Coming out of the war, the Australian economy was characterised by preferential trade with Britain, which took around half the country's exports, import quotas, high tariffs, and a currency tied to the British pound and managed by the government. Subsidies and guaranteed prices protected smaller primary industries; tariffs and import quotas protected manufacturers. Wool dominated Australian exports. As every Australian schoolchild learnt, the Australian economy rode on the sheep's back. There was no clear demand for this comfortable position to change.

But whether or not Australia wanted it, the commitments under Article VII of the Mutual Aid Agreement with the United States to the 'elimination of all forms of discriminatory treatment in international commerce' had set Australia on a new policy path. John Crawford, between 1950 and 1960 the influential Secretary of the Departments of Commerce and Agriculture, and then Trade, later wrote: 'all major developments in Australian post-war trade policy, at least up until the late 1950s, can be traced back to the commitment in Article VII.'[42] By the early 1950s the GATT had emerged as the vehicle through which that commitment would be implemented.

By establishing a framework within which first Japan, then Korea and later China could enter – then become central to – the global economy, these rules provided the foundation for Australia's remarkable late-twentieth-century economic growth.

For the first twenty-five years of the GATT's operations, however, Australia remained a largely passive member. The agreement was seen as a threat to the heavily protected Australian manufacturing industry and a hindrance to the restoration of some earlier imperial preferences, rather than an opportunity to expand exports. Australia identified itself with developing country agricultural exporters and unsuccessfully sought changes to help agriculture, where the barriers to exports were quantitative restrictions rather than tariffs. The battle against agricultural protectionism would be a recurring theme in Australia's efforts to influence the global rules.

Throughout the 1950s and '60s, Australian industrial tariffs remained as high as they had been in the 1920s. In 1970 they were higher than those of every other wealthy country except New Zealand.[43]

Still, it was clear that, given Britain's post-war economic weakness, Australia had to find new markets for its exports. Both Crawford and

Coombs advised Chifley, and then the Coalition, that Australia needed to shift the focus of its trade towards Asia and the United States.

Anti-Japanese sentiment in the Australian community after the war led the government to impose restrictions on Japanese imports while Australian exports, especially of wool, wheat and barley, were becoming significant. In 1952–53 the trade imbalance in Australia's favour was nearly 18 to 1.[44] By November 1953 Japan was warning that, without 'expeditious' steps, it 'might find itself unable to continue imports from Australia on the pace and scale as in past periods'.[45] When Tokyo reduced the value of Australian wool imports by nearly 30 per cent the following year, it became clear to Menzies and the government that something had to be done to protect Australia's market.

In August 1954 ministers considered Australia's fundamental policy towards Japan. 'Generally,' the cabinet minute noted, 'the view was reluctantly adopted that, overall, Australia should adopt a more liberal policy towards Japan because of (i) the very real danger over the next few years of Japan becoming aligned with Communist China; and (ii) the need for Australia to join with other nations particularly the United Kingdom and the United States in taking measures to avoid that result. Trade is an essential factor in achieving political results'.[46] Although it was true that Japanese officials had expressed interest in renewing trade with China, Australian trade, rather than politics, seems likely to have been the deeper motivating force behind this decision.[47]

Even so, Australia proceeded more slowly than comparable countries. Britain and America had extended 'most favoured nation' (MFN) treatment to Japan (guaranteeing it the same treatment as other GATT partners on like products), and Canada and New Zealand had already negotiated agreements. But the domestic politics were difficult for the government. The public was resistant, the Labor Party was threatening political heat and the public service was badly divided between McEwen's commerce and agriculture department, which favoured a new framework for trade with Japan, and the protectionist trade and customs department.

Debate within the government dragged on. In September 1955 Japan became a full member of the GATT. Article 35 of the agreement still gave Australia the ability to opt out of extending MFN commitments to Japan but it was becoming harder to hold the line with a partner whose importance to Australia was growing.

Informal (and unpublicised) talks with Japan finally began in October 1955, and a large bureaucratic impediment to progress was removed in

January 1956 when all aspects of overseas trade were brought under the control of McEwen and Crawford in a new Department of Trade.

Japan asked Australia to negotiate a comprehensive Treaty of Friendship, Commerce and Navigation that could govern all the aspects of commercial relations, but Australia was reluctant, sheltering behind the flimsy excuse that this would be difficult in a federal system. The agreement was to be limited to trade questions alone.

Preliminary negotiations began at the end of August 1956 and the final deal was submitted to cabinet for decision on 16 May 1957. Menzies was more cautious about the Japanese trading relationship than either McEwen or Casey and was absent from the critical meeting, leading to speculation that he wanted to be able to disassociate himself from the agreement if things went wrong.[48]

The agreement was signed in July 1957. Australia gave Japan MFN tariff treatment and promised not to discriminate against it in import licensing. Australia retained the right, after consultation, to raise tariffs against any Japanese goods that endangered Australian industries (under Article 35 of the GATT). Japan agreed to 'voluntary restraints': in effect, it would manage Japanese exports to limit the damage to Australian manufacturers.

By the time the treaty came to parliament for ratification in August 1957, the wartime bitterness had begun to drain from the public debate (although some Labor politicians refused to meet Nobusuke Kishi when he made the first visit by a Japanese prime minister in December), and the reaction to the agreement was largely positive.

In the ratification debate, Labor criticised the safeguards for Australian industry. Evatt – mirroring the tenor of McEwen's complaints during the debate over the ratification of the GATT – accused the government of sacrificing British commercial interests for the sake of trade with Japan. 'Never before has the United Kingdom textile industry ... been faced with the possibility or probability of complete elimination from the Australian market. I do not think the Australian people would approve of that,' he said.[49] But contrary to the fears that Australian manufacturers would be devastated, Japan managed its voluntary restraints skilfully, especially in areas like textiles. No disaster followed for Australian industry. The result instead was a huge expansion of bilateral trade, including in Japanese exports to Australia. By 1958 Japanese cars were becoming more familiar on Australian roads. When the agreement was extended in 1963, it was clear that the residual right to impose special tariffs was unnecessary, and Australia agreed to give it up.

The Commerce Agreement with Japan had been a long time coming, but it represented a revolutionary turn in Australia's economic relationships, and, more deeply, in its foreign policy. McEwen drove it, and he and the trade department continued to dominate the management of the whole relationship with Japan until his retirement in 1971.

In 1966 Japan surpassed Britain as Australia's largest export market. By 1970 it was Australia's biggest trading partner overall.[50] Just before the Commerce Agreement was signed, 16 per cent of Australia's total trade was with Japan. In 1970/71 it was 41 per cent.[51]

The structure of the trade changed too. Australia's embargo on iron ore exports, imposed in 1938, was relaxed at the end of 1960, leading to a massive growth in exports of iron ore and coal. By 1970 resource exports surpassed agricultural exports in value.[52]

A network of new institutions such as the Australia Japan Business Co-operation Committee, which was established in 1963, was emerging to deepen the people-to-people links between the two countries. Difficulties remained, of course: not least, Australia's discriminatory policies on the provision of long-term visas for Japanese businesspeople. And, from the other side, complaints began to be heard later in the 1960s that Australia was becoming a 'Japanese quarry'.

But policy-makers were talking with new ambition about the potential for the relationship. Since 1963, when Hayato Ikeda made a second prime ministerial visit to Australia, the possibilities were being floated for political as well as economic cooperation. As early as January 1966 Hasluck had spoken of an 'Asian tripod' – Australia, Japan and India – 'the three powers best fitted by their resources to make a massive contribution to the region itself, to the rebuilding of Asia'.[53] Japan's successful drive to establish the Asian Development Bank (ADB) in 1966, with Australia as an active contributor, was a further manifestation of its growing weight and economic impact in the region.

As Britain moved to join the EEC in May 1970, McEwen sought cabinet approval for 'the development of a new dynamic relationship with Japan'.[54] He argued that in a world where worries about trading blocs were growing, 'Japan and the surrounding countries offer the best possible prospects for increasing Australian exports in the world, and are the only area where, in developing closer relations, we can hope that the doors are open to us.'[55] What McEwen had in mind was the increasing frustrations Australia was encountering elsewhere in the global trading system. Britain's entry to

Europe was the most important of these, but difficulties also emerged regularly with Australia's second-largest trading partner, the United States, over import restrictions and competition with wheat and other commodities in foreign markets. The Kennedy Round of world trade negotiations under the GATT, which concluded in 1967, had brought little relief for Australia's agricultural exporters. In January 1966 Australia had signed a free trade agreement – NAFTA – with New Zealand, its fourth-largest market and biggest market for manufactures. It was an important building block for the future, but it was limited in its coverage and generated persistent squabbles over agricultural products.

Australia's broader international economic policy was also shifting. In 1971 a long-building crisis in the international monetary system came to a head. The Bretton Woods system of fixing currencies to a US dollar pegged to gold at $35 an ounce had served the post-war international economy well. But it was doing so no longer. A steady decline in the US balance of payments, fuelled in part by the costs of overseas military engagement and economic aid, was exacerbated by the expense of the Vietnam War. From 1970 even the US balance of trade was in the red. In 1971 the German government held more gold than Fort Knox. A major adjustment was needed to the exchange rate between the US dollar and the currencies of the major surplus countries, especially Japan and Germany.

In August 1971 Richard Nixon took matters into his own hands by effectively suspending the dollar's convertibility into gold and imposing a 10 per cent surcharge on import duties. A global response to the 'Nixon Shock' came in December 1971 when industrialised countries agreed in Washington to realign their currencies: the US devalued the dollar relative to gold and revoked the import surcharge in return for a revaluation of the yen and European currencies.

With the system of pegged exchange rates crumbling, Australia had to decide how to respond. For two hundred years, sterling had been the basis for Australia's currency, but the changing patterns of its trade and global economic interests no longer made this an obvious choice. A three-day meeting of cabinet later in December decided, in a complex decision, to fix the Australian dollar primarily in terms of the US dollar.[56]

In the same year Australia became a full member of the industrialised countries group, the Organisation for Economic Co-operation and Development (OECD). This reflected the country's growing acceptance (helped by McEwen's departure from politics)[57] that it was now a fully developed economy rather than an occupant of a vague 'middle zone' between the developed and developing countries. Membership of the OECD opened the economic debate in unexpected ways. Outside public reviews of its economy were conducted regularly and Australia became more involved in the coordination of international economic issues. Around the same time, the Tariff Board, which had been founded in 1921 to advise the government on tariff levels, was beginning to interpret the costs of tariffs to the community more broadly, and in 1971 began a systematic review of the Australian tariff. It was the beginning of a long transition in official economic thinking from protection to productivity.

For twenty-five years after the end of the war the Australian economy had experienced a golden age of economic growth, with unemployment at around 2 per cent and inflation around 3 per cent. But there were clear signs now of a more uncertain economic future, including as a result of the huge foreign exchange inflow that followed the realignment of the Australian dollar.

It was becoming obvious, however, that Australia's fibre, food and minerals were a natural complement to the economies of Northeast Asia. From the late 1960s onwards, discussion in academic and business circles was turning to the need for some sort of regional economic organisation to provide a framework for such cooperation. By 1968 two private organisations in which Australians were active participants – the Pacific Trade and Development Forum (PAFTAD), a group of policy-oriented economists, and the business-led Pacific Basin Economic Council (PBEC) – had been formed, largely at Japanese initiative.

The Australian government was cautious about any more formal arrangements, but Australia was seeing the first stirrings of the debate about regional architecture that would engage its foreign policy in different ways through the rest of the century.

Cul de sac

By 1972, thirty years after Australia had ratified the Statute of Westminster, the country itself and its idea of its place in the world were very different. Its population in 1942 of 7.1 million had nearly doubled, to 13 million. Australian society had been transformed by the arrival of three million immigrants, drawn from an increasingly diverse range of European countries, especially the Netherlands, Italy, Greece and Yugoslavia.

The machinery by which Australia engaged with the world had expanded massively. A handful of overseas missions had become a network of sixty-seven embassies and high commissions. The Department of Foreign Affairs (its name changed from External Affairs in 1971) had become an important part of the machinery of the Australian government. Australia was represented at all the major forums of the United Nations and other multilateral organisations. It had made contributions to UN peacekeeping operations in the Middle East, India, Pakistan and Cyprus.

An economy heavily based on agriculture and trade with Britain had diversified into one in which resource exports played a greater role and the main prospects for growth lay in Asia.

The international environment to which Australia was responding was also very different. The world had been divided into two rigid blocs, as Washington and Moscow competed for influence in a global arena. By 1972 the most dangerous period of the Cold War – the years from the Berlin airlift to the Cuban missile crisis – had passed. The two sides had worked out new ways of managing the still-real dangers of nuclear conflict. But their competition remained intense, and a new fluidness had entered international politics as China emerged from the disruption of the Cultural Revolution.

In the space between the two superpowers and their allies, the collapse of European colonialism had created a new Afro-Asian and non-aligned world, which included Indonesia and many of Australia's other close neighbours. The modest hopes at the end of World War II that new forms of cooperation would be found between the wartime allies had been quickly dashed by the Cold War. By the end of the 1950s the great expectations for the United Nations had been disappointed. As a means of collective security it hadn't worked, and voting had become bloc-based. As the UN got bigger in the 1950s and '60s, and the focus on racism and colonialism intensified, Australia was increasingly on the defensive.

The broad consensus that had marked Australian foreign policy in the late 1940s and early '50s had broken down towards the end of the decade, as the Labor Party split over the issue of communism. Even so, both sides of politics continued to support in their policy statements the same trio of issues – regional engagement in Asia, support for a close alliance with powerful friends, and a commitment to a rules-based order – that had been present from the beginning.

Labor tended to put forward an idealised version of the United Nations that had hardly existed even at the beginning of the period. The Coalition prided itself on a hard-nosed, power-based view of the world. It saw global motivations behind regional developments. And it was more cautious about adhering to UN conventions like the International Covenant on Civil and Political Rights because of domestic political concerns that this might enable Canberra to override areas of state jurisdiction.

Nevertheless, both sides of politics continued to acknowledge the importance of the United Nations. Even Hasluck , the most power-oriented of the Liberal foreign ministers, believed that 'Power is not enough. In a world of power, peace is only maintained on a precarious balance and it is plain that recourse to power as a means of security is in essence a readiness to have recourse to war. There will never be full security for anyone unless and until the exercise of power is made subject to agreed principles of international conduct and, in a world of national states, that means the possessors of power restrict by their own pledges their own use of power.'[58]

The most important change in the way Australians looked at the world had been in the way most of them thought about the relationship with Britain, and in their own sense of identification with Britishness. This shift had been driven more by the actions of Britain than the desires of Australia. In retrospect, it was clear that Australia's efforts to engage Britain in the security of Southeast Asia, to preserve imperial trade preferences, and to develop united Commonwealth positions on international issues could never have succeeded in the circumstances in which Britain found itself after the war.

But Australia was slow to give up the idea that it did not have to choose between Britain and the United States. The ANZUS relationship developed cautiously on both sides. Major players in each country had reservations. Nevertheless, the dominance of America in the post-war world was clear from the beginning and, in Korea and then Vietnam, Australia became engaged in the first of a series of what might be called the 'Wars of American Engagement'. Conflicts, that is, whose rationale was less the places and circumstances in which they were fought, or their strategic purpose, than the desire to demonstrate allied support and solidarity: to pay the insurance premium.

By 1972 the Liberal–Country Party Coalition had been in office for twenty-three years. The foreign policy achievements of those years had been substantial: the creation of an effective diplomatic service and foreign policy machinery, the development of close relations with the countries of Asia, the successful management of the relationship with Indonesia through the stormy passages of Confrontation, the building of a substantial economic relationship with Japan, and an alliance with the United States achieved against the odds.

In universities and non-government organisations like the Australian Institute of International Affairs, an 'engaged public' had emerged to debate foreign policy. Ordinary Australians, exposed to the world through personal travel and television, were more literate about international issues than their parents had been before the war.

But, as the 1972 election drew closer, the pile of unfinished business was growing. The political dominance of Sir Robert Menzies, with his nostalgic resistance to unnecessary change in Australia's historic links with Britain – and with 'little inclination for Eastern cultures', as the former Secretary of External Affairs put it[59] – had given Australian foreign policy a conservative tone and a reactive posture. This had been reinforced by the political importance of Democratic Labor Party preference votes.

After Menzies retired in 1966, his successors, Holt, Gorton and McMahon, had neither the capacity nor (Gorton aside, perhaps) the desire to change much. The post-Hasluck Coalition foreign ministers – Gordon Freeth, William McMahon, Les Bury and Nigel Bowen, cycling through the job in little more than three years between them – had little chance to influence the direction of policy.

Time and again in those years, Australian foreign policy was caught short by developments. The depth and impact of the divisions between Moscow and Beijing, the declaration of the Nixon Doctrine, America's opening to China and the emerging international consensus on nuclear non-proliferation all surprised the policy-makers in Canberra. Events were moving faster than Australian policy was responding.

Australian ministers knew that change was necessary on the recognition of China, on the formal termination of the discriminatory immigration policy, on complete military withdrawal from Vietnam. But they fiddled. They could not summon the resolve, or build the political momentum, to do what they knew needed to be done. Old mantras were no longer working and, like many long-term governments before them, they found themselves trapped in a policy cul-de-sac from which the only way of escape was to abandon the very arguments that had put them there.

It was time for change.

5

TRANSITIONS: THE 1970s

T he election of Gough Whitlam's Labor Party government on 2 December 1972 released a torrent of change in Australian foreign policy. Diplomatic relations were established with China, disengagement from the Vietnam War was completed, Australian votes in the United Nations on issues of race and decolonisation were reversed, and all remnants of the racially based immigration policy erased. The major elements of the foreign policies of previous governments for twenty years had clearly run their course. But as Whitlam himself acknowledged in 1973, 'even if there had been no change of government, there would have been a change of policy; and I am not so churlish as to suggest that it would not have changed for the better.'[1] When the Coalition returned to power under Malcolm Fraser less than three years later, the principal elements of Whitlam's reordering continued.

These changes were more than the outcome of a long domestic policy debate in Australia. They were also necessary responses to the global environment in which Australia found itself in the 1970s. Both Whitlam and Fraser faced a world in which Australia had more options, but which was more difficult to manage. The United States was looking inwards after the traumas of the Vietnam War and Watergate. With the Helsinki Accords of 1975, which recognised the post-war settlements in Eastern Europe, and in the negotiation of strategic arms control agreements, the gravest tensions between the superpowers were being moderated. But to some, including some in Moscow, it seemed that this détente was facilitating a shift in the balance of military power away from the West. Britain, which joined the European Economic Community (EEC) in 1973, was more remote from Australian interests. China was developing a more normal pattern of diplomatic engagement with the rest of the world and, by the end of the decade, entering its period of economic reform. Australia's relations in its own region were complicated by the aftermath of the Vietnam War, by the development of ASEAN's regionalism and by Indonesia's takeover of Portuguese Timor.

As the global economy deteriorated after the 1973 oil shock, and with the United States struggling to absorb the costs of the Vietnam War, the international focus, and Australia's too, shifted from security to the economy. The chambers of the United Nations and other multilateral organisations filled with newly independent states and a North–South debate emerged between developed and developing states, complicating the established East–West strategic divisions.

This chapter traces the transitions in Australian foreign policy over the eight years between the election of the Whitlam government and the Soviet Union's invasion of Afghanistan in December 1979, which brought détente to an end and threw the global settlement into question again.

The two prime ministers of the period, Whitlam and Fraser, dominated Australian foreign policy-making more completely than any of their post-war predecessors. For all their liberal internationalist sentiments, both Whitlam and Fraser thought of themselves as foreign policy realists, looking in a clear-eyed way at Australian interests and at the world as it was, but each of them saw that reality differently. Whitlam was a pragmatist. He supported the US alliance, but believed that a failure to accept the inevitability of change – whether this was communist control of China or the nationalist sentiments driving the Vietnamese resistance – brought trouble with it. 'The real test of a successful foreign policy is the extent to which a balance is struck between a nation's commitment and a nation's power,' he said.[2] He was confident in his own judgements – over-confident in some cases, as became clear – and generally disinclined to consult much with his cabinet (an unwieldy twenty-seven members) or caucus colleagues on foreign policy.

It was partly as a result of his demands for a realistic, illusion-free foreign policy that in mid-1974, as acting foreign minister, Whitlam accepted departmental advice that Australia recognise de jure – that is, as a legal fact – Soviet sovereignty over the Baltic states of Latvia, Lithuania and

Estonia, which had been forcibly incorporated into the USSR at the start of World War II. The foreign affairs department argued that such recognition would remove an anomaly and make it easier to provide consular assistance to Australians of Baltic origin by making it possible for embassy staff to travel there. The decision revealed some of the risks involved in Whitlam's approach to foreign policy. Baltic community groups and the Opposition reacted to the decision with outrage. How did this square with the government's insistence on the right to self-determination in places like Africa? The response was an example of the price Whitlam paid for his reluctance to take his cabinet colleagues into his confidence on foreign policy. They would surely have warned him of the likely domestic political effects of the decision. The Fraser government revoked the recognition at the end of 1975.

Fraser, too, saw himself as a realist: 'The guiding principle for Australia's role in the world ought to be an active and enlightened realism,' he told parliament. Under Whitlam, he declared, 'unrealistic notions that an age of peace and stability had arrived encouraged a neglect of power realities – a neglect that did not serve our interests'.[3] For Fraser, that realism lay in understanding the fragile nature of détente, the advantages which he saw the Soviet Union accruing from it and the dangers that lay in challenges to the credibility of US foreign policy. Some of these, in the post-Watergate period, stemmed from America's own internal problems. Ideology was not irrelevant to him, but it could not be a guiding principle. 'Whatever the basis of a regime,' he said, 'whatever the organisation of its domestic government, the chief determinant of our relations will be that country's approach to foreign relations, how it meshes with ours and, of necessity, the extent of the interests we share.'[4]

Gough Whitlam

When Edward Gough Whitlam was finally elected as prime minister in December 1972, bringing about the first change in the party of government in Australia since 1949, he knew what he wanted to do. He had been shadow foreign minister, had travelled and thought about Australia's place in the world and had worked hard within the ALP to changes its policies. 'It is time to clear away the rubble. We need a fresh start,' he had told parliament after President Nixon's Guam doctrine.[7] He wanted Australians to end 'the old stultifying fears and animosities which have encumbered the national spirit for generations'.[6]

Born in Kew, Melbourne, in July 1916, Whitlam had come to Canberra with his father, the Deputy Crown Solicitor, in 1928. He attended school in Canberra, then the University of Sydney. After wartime service in the RAAF, he completed his law degree in 1946 and was called to the bar. Tempted into politics, he won, at a second attempt, a by-election for the outer suburban Sydney seat of Werriwa in February 1953. With his intelligence, energy and eloquence there was never, as his biographer Graham Freudenberg wrote, 'any time when it would have been inherently improbable to say, "this fellow will be prime minister".[7] He was elected to the caucus executive (shadow ministry) in 1959, became deputy leader in 1960 when Evatt stepped down, and eventually replaced Arthur Calwell as leader in 1967. He brought Labor close to victory in the 1969 election and finally led it there in 1972.

On 5 December he and his deputy leader, Lance Barnard, were sworn in to all ministerial positions until the full ministry could be elected on 18 December. Whitlam took on the foreign affairs portfolio. Within the first exhilarating days of the rule of 'the duumvirate', the things that could be done quickly were done: new instructions were given to negotiators with China on diplomatic relations, conscription for military service was ended, the final military advisers were withdrawn from Vietnam, and military aid to Vietnam and Cambodia ceased.

In his first press conference as prime minister, Whitlam set out his objectives for Australian foreign policy in words drafted for him by Richard Woolcott, then the media spokesman in the Department of Foreign Affairs: 'The general direction of my thinking is towards a more independent stance in international affairs, an Australia which will be less militarily oriented and not open to suggestions of racism, an Australia which will enjoy a growing standing as a distinctive, tolerant, cooperative and well-regarded neighbour not only in the Asian and Pacific region, but in the world at large'.[8]

Whitlam remained as his own foreign minister for almost a year, before handing the portfolio to Senator Don Willesee. Willesee was a diligent and capable minister who shared most of Whitlam's outlook but brought independent views on a number of issues, including East Timor. Nevertheless, Whitlam remained the dominant foreign policy figure throughout Labor's term in office. He wanted to make a mark on the world, and his overseas travel was frequent and indulgent. The political price he paid for this would be noted by all his prime ministerial successors.

Race and immigration

Determined to avoid charges of racism, Whitlam took the final steps towards abandoning the remnants of the White Australia policy. Labor's carefully cobbled together policy platform had reaffirmed the importance of avoiding 'the difficult social and economic problems that may follow from an influx of peoples having different standards of living, traditions and cultures', but committed the party to 'the avoidance of discrimination on any grounds of race, or colour of skin or nationality'.[9] During 1973 and 1974 uniform selection criteria were introduced and the preference for British immigrants eliminated.

On 8 December 1972, Human Rights Day, Whitlam announced plans to expedite Australian ratification of the UN's International Convention on the Elimination of All Forms of Racial Discrimination. This finally happened in 1975 after the passage of the *Racial Discrimination Act*. The requirement imposed on Australia to report on these issues to the United Nations marked a fundamental change from the decades during which Australian governments had argued that matters of immigration and race were purely domestic issues. Three states challenged the Act, but it was finally upheld by the High Court in 1982 under the external affairs power of the constitution.

Whitlam recognised that Australia's reputation on race did not depend simply on Australia's international behaviour. 'More than any foreign aid program, more than any international obligation which we meet or forfeit, more than any part we may play in any treaty or agreement or alliance,' he told Australians in his policy speech on 13 November 1972, 'Australia's treatment of her aboriginal people' was the thing upon which the rest of the world would judge it.[10]

Indochina

Australia's involvement in the Vietnam War had dominated the country's foreign policy debate since 1965. The Paris peace agreement of 27 January 1973 finally brought about a formal ceasefire in Vietnam after five years of negotiations and nine years of direct American military engagement. The United States began to withdraw its troops and it was agreed that elections would be held in the south, ostensibly paving the way for reunification.

The agreement gave Australia the opportunity to establish parallel diplomatic relations with Hanoi, as well as Saigon. Although Whitlam resisted the urgings of the left of his party to recognise the communist Provisional

Revolutionary Government in the south and to cut aid to the Saigon government, he believed that reunification on the north's terms was inevitable and the only way of finally resolving the conflict.[11]

Any fragile optimism about the ceasefire in Vietnam soon disappeared as it became clear that neither side was committed to the outcome. Fighting resumed throughout the south. On 30 April 1975 Saigon finally fell to the communist forces. Whitlam told the House of Representatives on 8 April: 'who rules in Saigon is not, and never has been, an ingredient in Australian security. Our strength, our security, rest on factors and relationships that are unchanged by these events.'[12] By July 1976 formal reunification was complete.

The US-backed Cambodian government also fell in April 1975, to Khmer Rouge forces that had been gradually consolidating their control of the countryside. The Australian embassy had been evacuated the previous month. Australia recognised the new regime, known as Democratic Kampuchea, but as the extreme policies of the new rulers became apparent, with reports of the execution of officials of the former government and the brutal expulsion of city dwellers to the countryside, Australian diplomats did not return to Phnom Penh.

As in many other areas, the incoming Fraser government did not greatly shift Australian policy towards Indochina when it took over at the end of that year. In contrast to the United States, it maintained diplomatic, aid and trade relations with Hanoi and supported the admission of the Indochinese states to the United Nations. 'Nothing will be gained by either Australia or the region ostracising, ignoring or setting out to alienate these governments', the foreign minister, Andrew Peacock, told parliament on 15 March 1977.[13]

The end of the Vietnam War remade the strategic situation in Southeast Asia. Vietnam's triumph left it with a larger and vastly more experienced army than all the ASEAN countries combined. The nervousness of the non-communist Southeast Asian states stemmed in part from the threats Malaysia, Thailand and the Philippines still faced from small, internal, communist-supported guerrilla groups of their own. Vietnam, always concerned about Chinese domination – something which was by then apparent to all observers – pursued closer relations with the Soviet Union. The Chinese, in turn, saw this as an effort by Moscow to encircle it on its southern border and prepared to respond. The Sino-Soviet dispute had arrived in Southeast Asia.

The regional upheaval had humanitarian as well as geopolitical repercussions. In the four years after October 1975, more than one million people fled the three Indochinese states. Australian governments had a first taste of one of the most difficult policy issues they would face over the following decades: the movement of refugees from and through the region. The Whitlam and Fraser governments, like those of Howard, Rudd and Gillard later, found themselves trying to balance humanitarian imperatives, international legal obligations under the Refugee Convention, domestic political anxieties and the competing demands and pressures of regional states, both friends and adversaries.

The Vietnamese refugee exodus began before Saigon fell, as tens of thousands of civilians tried to escape the increased fighting in the south and the United States began evacuating some 140,000 Vietnamese who had served the American and South Vietnamese governments. Australia faced similar pressures to give sanctuary to Vietnamese who had served it during the war. Although Whitlam was prepared to fund and support international responses to the problem, he stood in the way of any large-scale Australian response. He was reluctant to give weight to fears of a bloodbath if Hanoi took over and was concerned that a liberal entry policy would simply encourage a rush of further departures. After the recent uproar caused by Baltic community groups when he recognised legal Soviet control of Estonia, Latvia and Lithuania, he was also worried that he would be facilitating the creation in Australia of a new conservative émigré group of 'Vietnamese Balts'. He tightened entry criteria and moved more slowly than Willesee wanted. As a result, only 342 of the nearly 4000 Vietnamese who applied to enter Australia before the end of the war were deemed to have met the conditions.[14]

As the fall of Saigon approached, and facing a heavy media campaign, the government approved special flights to bring out Vietnamese orphans who had the approval of the South Vietnamese authorities and potential Australian adoptive parents. Of the 1132 refugees who had been accepted in Australia by the time Labor left office, nearly 300 were orphans.[15]

Although the first wave of around 12,000 refugees making their way by boat to neighbouring countries[16] seemed to have subsided, the numbers in camps in Southeast Asia were still a serious burden. Soon after it took office, the Fraser government announced that Australia would accept more refugees, mostly from Thailand.

The number of people fleeing from Vietnam increased again after 1976 as the government began moving city dwellers – mainly ethnic Chinese – to 'new economic zones' in rural areas. More than one million people were sent to re-education camps and, from early 1978, the expropriation of private businesses was underway. By the end of 1978, nearly 62,000 'boat people' had made their way to camps in Southeast Asia. Hong Kong and China itself became new destinations. Large-scale people-smuggling operations involving sizable vessels began. In the first half of 1979 it became evident that the Vietnamese government was actively involved in arranging some of the departures. Facing domestic hostility to the camp dwellers, Malaysia, Thailand and Singapore began to push new arrivals back to sea and announced they would accept no more.

For the Australian government, the politics of refugees changed dramatically in April 1976 when a 25-year-old Vietnamese, Lam Binh, steered his small boat into Darwin Harbour after a two-month voyage from Vietnam using a page torn from a school atlas to navigate.[17] Lam and his four young passengers were the first of 2000 boat people to arrive on Australian shores in the following years.

The Fraser government's response was to try to channel more arrivals through the official refugee program, which rose to 9000 per year from 1978, while threatening to deny permanent residency and send back to Southeast Asia those who arrived in Australia by boat.[18] It also began to work with the ASEAN countries – a foretaste of future searches for regional solutions to the problem – and to encourage greater international burden-sharing. Its efforts to internationalise the problem helped bring about a major United Nations conference on Indochinese refugees in July 1979 in Geneva. The result was a three-way deal under which worldwide resettlement pledges were doubled to 260,000, and Vietnam agreed to curtail illegal departures and support orderly family reunions from its own territory. Regional processing centres were set up. Australia increased its resettlement pledge to 14,000.

Between April 1975 and October 1980 Australia accepted nearly 42,000 Indochinese refugees, the highest number per capita of any country of asylum except Hong Kong.[19] Public opinion was consistently reluctant, and in respect of boat arrivals, fanned by Labor criticism of government policy. An *Age* opinion poll in June 1979 found that 30 per cent of respondents thought Australia should take fewer refugees, and 37 per cent no more at all. Just 7 per cent thought the program should be more generous.[20]

One of the new drivers of refugee outflows was increasing border tension between Chinese-supported Cambodia and Vietnam after 1977. This tension also caused the Australian government to look again at the arguments for restoring diplomatic relations with the Khmer Rouge regime, despite the growing concerns about human rights abuses. In December 1978 Peacock announced that the government would begin negotiations with Phnom Penh over the resumption of diplomatic representation. But in the same month, fortified by a formal Treaty of Friendship it had signed with Moscow in November, Vietnam invaded Cambodia. By 11 January 1979 it had driven the Khmer Rouge out, preparing the way for the installation of a pro-Vietnamese government under Heng Samrin. More than 300,000 more refugees fled to camps along the Thai–Cambodian border.

Australia joined ASEAN and the United States in condemning Vietnam's actions. It cut off its aid, generating a debate that would continue in different forms in the following decades about whether the principal role of the aid program was to support national policy aims or to alleviate poverty. Coordinating its policy closely with ASEAN, Canberra withheld diplomatic recognition from the newly installed government in Phnom Penh and continued to recognise the Khmer Rouge government in exile, although it also continued, for humanitarian reasons, to provide aid to Cambodia.

China's response was more robust. It mounted its own short but costly military incursion by ground forces across the border into northern Vietnam in February. The embarrassing tactical shortcomings this revealed would lead to Deng Xiaoping's subsequent reform of the People's Liberation Army. Nevertheless, China's 'lesson' was a signal to the ASEAN countries of Chinese determination to resist Vietnamese expansion.

The consequences of the fall of Saigon shaped Australian foreign policy in important ways. Australia had to learn to work cooperatively with a group of Southeast Asian countries, understanding their different interests and their internal tensions, and balancing these against its own interests. The lessons learnt would be important in the larger policy efforts that would come a few years later regarding Cambodia and regional institution-building.

The events, and particularly the tragedy of the Cambodian genocide, also raised for Australia the enduring contest between values and interests in foreign policy. As Cambodia went dark, the details of the crimes being committed emerged slowly and were hard for some to believe. The Khmer Rouge forced perhaps two million city dwellers into the countryside and began a millenarian fundamentalist program in which markets, money, religion, education and property were abolished. The best estimates are that 1.7 million Cambodians (one in five of its people) lost their lives under the regime. It was among the worst genocides of the twentieth century and the only one conducted by the perpetrators against their own people.

The Fraser government had to balance its geopolitical interests in resisting Vietnamese and Soviet expansion in Asia, and maintaining solidarity with the ASEAN countries against the growing evidence of crimes against humanity by Pol Pot and his henchmen. Responding to the Vietnamese invasion, the Australian Permanent Representative in New York told the United Nations that 'we cannot accept that the internal policies of any government, no matter how reprehensible, can justify military attack upon it by another government.'[21] Later in the century, other slaughters in Rwanda and the Balkans would lead some in the international community to different conclusions when weighing the claims of state sovereignty against the responsibility to protect against mass atrocity crimes.

ASEAN and Asian regionalism

One of the liveliest issues of Australian foreign policy in the 1950s and '60s, the commitment of Australian forces to the defence of Malaysia and Singapore, drained away over 1972 and 1973. Some typically clumsy references by William McMahon in 1972, before the election, seeming to throw into question the importance of the Five Power Defence Arrangements (FPDA), which had come into operation in November 1971, as well as growing discussion about Southeast Asian neutrality by leaders such as the Malaysian prime minister, Tun Razak, made the Labor Party's commitment to the withdrawal of Australian forces from Singapore seem less controversial.

Over the year from February 1973, the Whitlam government pulled its infantry battalion and artillery battery out of the ANZUK force in Singapore, although it kept 150 support troops in Singapore and two squadrons of Mirage aircraft at the Malaysian air base at Butterworth, with an infantry company rotating from Australia every three months as part of the FPDA. The British also pulled out their forces. 'We no longer look on the countries of South East Asia as buffer states or as some northern military line where a possible future enemy should be held,' Whitlam told parliament. 'Rather, we look upon them as countries having a common interest with Australia and New Zealand in consolidating the security and stability of the region as a whole.'[22]

For Whitlam, the best way of avoiding any future return of Australian forces to the region was to help its neighbours become self-reliant through training, exercises and aid. Indonesia, Malaysia and Singapore continued to be large recipients of Australian military assistance.

As the Vietnam War drew to an end, the attitudes of Southeast Asian countries were changing. In September 1973, at Australia's suggestion, the Council of the South East Asia Treaty Organization (SEATO) ceased all military planning, and in September 1975 Australian and Thai proposals to phase out the organisation entirely were accepted. SEATO was finally dissolved in 1977.

While the ASEAN states remained formally open to future cooperation with Indochina, they worried about the security implications of a reunited Vietnam. But as the American forces withdrew and US military bases in Thailand closed, they addressed this concern by insisting that the great powers respect Southeast Asia as a Zone of Peace, Freedom and Neutrality (ZOPFAN). One by one they overcame their concerns about China and established relations with Beijing.

A summit meeting in Bali in February 1976 underlined a new sense of solidarity in ASEAN. Orchestrated by President Suharto, members signed a Treaty of Amity and Cooperation, which gave form to the ideas of neutrality and adopted a more formal structure and a broader agenda for the group.

In April 1974 Australia had become the first non-member state to establish formal relations with ASEAN, providing aid to the group as a whole. This process of engagement continued under Fraser with the establishment in 1977 of an annual ASEAN-Australia Forum. Australia's experience formed the template for ASEAN's relations with other countries and helped provide the building blocks for a broader relationship between it and the outside world.

But Australia also found itself being tested by ASEAN's growing solidarity, as the member states began to understand the power of collective action. Australia's handling of refugees from Indochina and its efforts to protect its textiles, clothing and footwear industry from foreign competition fuelled coordinated ASEAN criticism. Civil aviation policy was a particular problem. With the introduction of the Boeing 747 aircraft in the early 1970s, the era of mass air travel was beginning. Singapore Airlines had only been founded in 1972 but by 1978 had captured about 30 per cent of the growing market for air travel between Australia and Europe. In the highly regulated environment of the time, Australia and Qantas responded to the threat by trying to limit the participation of overseas carriers in the market and imposing steep charges on stopovers in countries like Singapore. Although this was essentially a problem for Singapore, it used ASEAN solidarity very effectively to frame Australia's actions in North–South terms, as a developed country selfishly protecting itself against a developing-country competitor. Australia basically capitulated in 1979.

These trade and civil aviation problems reminded Australian policy-makers of the important lesson that Australian policy towards Asia could no longer be managed in separate diplomatic and economic boxes. It required much closer coordination among departments in Canberra.

It was not just trade and economic differences that raised ASEAN suspicions of Australia. Soon after coming to office, Whitlam floated a proposal for the establishment of a new regional grouping that would potentially encompass all the Asian countries from India to China. He wanted to seize the opportunities of the 'new realities' in the regional environment to establish an 'organisation genuinely representative of our region, without ideological overtones, conceived as an initiative to help free the region of great power rivalries that have bedevilled its progress for decades and designed to insulate the region against ideological interference from the great powers'.[23]

The concept was vague and the membership non-specific. Whitlam promised to consult Australia's neighbours about these questions. But the neighbours were not impressed. The proposal looked to the ASEAN countries like a competitive threat. 'The time is not ripe, some countries in the area have not really worked out their economic relations with Japan and some have no political or economic relations with China,' the Indonesian foreign minister, Adam Malik, announced.[24]

By mid-1973 Whitlam was downplaying the concept as 'a slow and delicate growth'.[25] He soon had more important political priorities and nothing came of the idea although it was an ideational forerunner of later Australian proposals like Keating's APEC Leaders' meetings and Rudd's East Asian Community.

A more immediately promising path towards regional institution-building was emerging with a specific trade and development focus. Ideas for a Pacific Free Trade Area had been advanced by the Japanese foreign minister, Takeo Miki, back in 1967 and developed by the business members of the Pacific Basin Economic Council (PBEC) and economists like Dr Peter Drysdale at the Australian National University. In 1976 a report by Sir John Crawford and the Japanese economist Saburo Okita, commissioned by the Australian and Japanese governments, recommended that the two governments formally endorse the idea of an Organisation for Pacific Trade and Development (OPTAD) that would help drive trade, investment and resource development among the market economies of the Pacific region. By January 1980 Fraser and his Japanese counterpart, Masayoshi Ohira, had agreed that this Pacific community 'represented a significant longer term objective' and had put it to further study. The seeds of what would become APEC had been sown.

Indonesia and East Timor

Indonesia was central to Whitlam's Asia policy. The goal of achieving 'closer relations with our nearest and largest neighbour' was one of the main international commitments in his 1972 policy speech. He visited Jakarta in 1973 and 1974 and hosted Suharto in Australia in 1975. Despite criticisms from the left, the Whitlam government continued the large bilateral defence assistance program to Indonesia that McMahon had announced in June 1972, including the transfer of sixteen RAAF Sabre fighter aircraft to the Indonesian air force. A seabed boundary agreement between Indonesia and Australia was ratified and the PNG–West Irian border delineated in February 1973. Whitlam pressed on Port Moresby the case for good relations with Indonesia and accelerated joint mapping of the Indonesia–PNG border.

The task of developing the relationship was not simple. The political turmoil of 1965 and 1966 had left many thousands of political prisoners in the jails of the New Order government, and human rights were part of the difficult diplomatic agenda for visiting Australian ministers and officials. Wild riots, arrests and a media crackdown in Jakarta in 1974 during a visit by the Japanese prime minister reinforced a public impression of instability and repression. But it was political turmoil on the other side of the world that would have the greatest impact on the Australia–Indonesia relationship for decades to come.

Embedded within Indonesian territory, and just 400 kilometres from Darwin, was the small enclave of Portuguese Timor, first settled by the Portuguese in the sixteenth century and formally colonised in 1702. Australian governments had thought about the future of the territory before. Australian troops were sent there in 1941 and fought a guerrilla campaign against the Japanese with the assistance of Timorese fighters. In 1943 Curtin and Evatt discussed possible post-war negotiations with Portugal about 'the inclusion of Portuguese Timor into an Australian defence zone' and the development of closer economic relations.[26] The Portuguese were reluctant to follow up, but Indonesian behaviour at the time of Confrontation revived their interest in closer defence cooperation. However, the Menzies cabinet had concluded in February 1963 that there was 'no practicable alternative' to Timor's incorporation into Indonesia.[27]

On 25 April 1974 young Portuguese army officers, driven by opposition to the human and financial costs of Portugal's wars against liberation movements in its African territories, staged a coup that brought down the forty-year-old conservative authoritarian regime in Lisbon. The new leaders of the Armed Forces Movement (ARM) announced they would pull the army out of Angola and Mozambique and support self-determination in Portugal's overseas colonies. The ARM drifted quite quickly to the left, with the Portuguese Communist Party exerting increasing influence.

The impact of the coup on the sleepy, undeveloped outpost of Portuguese Timor was rapid. Within weeks, three political associations had formed among the population of 650,000, representing different strands of thought about the future. The Timorese Democratic Union, or União Democrática Timorense (UDT), favoured continued association in some form with Portugal. The Association of Timorese Social Democrats, which became Fretilin, wanted independence. The Timorese Popular Democratic Association (APODETI) supported integration with Indonesia.

Policy-makers in Canberra and Jakarta were responding to developments against the backdrop of a very uncertain international environment. Cold War tensions were high. Washington was disengaged, preoccupied by events in the Middle East and distracted by the unravelling of the Watergate affair. Saigon fell to the forces of the North and the Viet Cong in April 1975. The idea that a left-leaning Timor might become a Cuba-style outpost in the middle of Indonesia did not seem so far-fetched.

Whitlam's response to developments in Timor was complex. In all his thinking about foreign policy he emphasised the need to face up to the realities of the world. He believed Timor would be unviable as a small independent state and that its incorporation into Indonesia was the best option for all the parties, including Australia. He had already argued strongly within the Labor Party for the return of West New Guinea to Indonesian control. China was determined to negotiate the integration of Macau, the other Portuguese colonial remnant in Asia. The earlier Indian takeover of Portuguese Goa by force in 1961 had passed without lasting international repercussions.

Whitlam was concerned about the 'way in which the Australian people, in the face of the rumours of an invasion of Portuguese Timor, had been shown to be overly nervous and fearful of Indonesia'.[28] He did not want Indonesia to replace China as the locus of an Asian threat for Australia. Nor did he want to position Australia on the side of a European colonial power against its close neighbour. And he was determined that Australia should stay out of further Vietnam-style fights in Asia. On the other hand, the principle of self-determination was central to his government's views about the remaining colonial regimes in southern Africa and its approach to Papua New Guinea.

By the time Whitlam visited Jakarta for a second time in September 1974, Canberra was already aware that Indonesia was planning covert operations to encourage Timorese support for integration. The prime minister told Suharto that Australian policy was not yet settled, but his view was that 'Portuguese Timor should become part of Indonesia', albeit 'in accordance with the properly expressed wishes of the people of Portuguese Timor'.[29]

His further remarks that 'Portuguese Timor was too small to be independent' and that 'independence would be unwelcome to Indonesia, to Australia and to other countries of the region' because it would inevitably become the focus of others outside the region,[30] were hardly calculated to restrain Indonesia, however.

There was a serious gap in the information coming to the government from inside Portuguese Timor. The Australian consulate in Dili, which had been opened in 1941, was closed to save money in 1970. 'We see no likelihood that internal developments in Timor will become significant from Australia's point of view,' the secretary of the department advised his minister.[31]

Without its own sources on the ground, the government had to depend on intermittent visits from officers of the embassy in Jakarta to gather information. And while the Jakarta embassy had excellent insights from well-placed informants into Indonesia's planning for intervention in Timor, the government was stymied in its use of that information by the need to avoid compromising its sources. Whitlam opposed reopening the consulate in case it embroiled Australia further in a dispute he wanted to stay out of.[32]

Differences of view emerged between Whitlam, the foreign minister, Don Willesee, and the defence minister, Lance Barnard, and their advisers, about what Australia's interests in Timor were, how assertive its policy should be, whether it should try to persuade Indonesia to live with an independent Timor and how the forums of the United Nations should be used. In February 1975 Barnard wrote to a sympathetic Willesee, copying his letter to Whitlam, saying he was 'deeply disturbed by the present indications that the Indonesian government is considering military action to seize

Portuguese Timor'. If this happened, 'years of effort to induce a sober and responsible approach to the development of a constructive relationship with Indonesia could be undone'.[33] Australia must 'make a determined effort to deflect them from any immoderate action', he wrote.[34]

But Whitlam's was the dominant voice. As a result, Australia's policy was permeated with the unresolved tension between what the prime minister wanted to happen and how that objective could ever be attained. Whitlam expressed his dilemma to foreign affairs officials: 'I am in favour of incorporation but obeisance has to be made to self-determination. I want it incorporated but I do not want this done in a way which will create argument in Australia which would make people more critical of Indonesia.'[35]

Shortly after Barnard's intervention, on 28 February 1975, the incoming ambassador, Richard Woolcott, presented Suharto with a letter from Whitlam. While sympathetically couched, it reiterated Australia's support for self-determination and noted the sensitivity of parliamentary and public opinion to any unilateral action by Indonesia. It went on to say that 'no Australian government could allow it to be thought, whether beforehand or afterwards, that it supported such action'.[36] Woolcott added, however, that Whitlam had told him that the 'long-term importance of the Australian/ Indonesian relationship was (the) overriding issue and any possible complications in our relationship should be seen in that context'.[37] Suharto asked Woolcott to tell Whitlam that Indonesia had 'no intention' of attempting to integrate Portuguese Timor by military force.[38]

Australia's allusive, ambivalent message was reaffirmed in April 1975, when Whitlam met Suharto again in Townsville. He told the president that he desired closer relations with Indonesia and would ensure that Australia's actions with regard to Portuguese Timor 'would always be guided by the principle that good relations with Indonesia were of paramount importance to Australia'.[39]

In the second half of 1975 tensions inside Portuguese Timor deepened. Relations between UDT and Fretilin soured. Behind the scenes, Indonesia manoeuvred to influence the UDT leadership. On 10 August the UDT, with Indonesian encouragement, staged a pre-emptive show of force against Fretilin. In response, Fretilin captured an arsenal of Portuguese weapons recently shipped from Mozambique. On 27 August the governor fled from Dili to the small offshore island of Ataúro, 25 kilometres away, effectively abandoning Portuguese administration of the territory and leaving behind him 15,000 rifles, which Fretilin seized. Forty thousand refugees fled into West Timor. The civil war had begun.

The Indonesians were determined to prevent a Fretilin victory. By 17 August Woolcott was reporting that Australia was now dealing with a 'settled Indonesian policy to incorporate Timor'.[41] The situation was complicated by the continuing absence of any clear policy direction from Lisbon, where the ARM was paralysed by a power struggle between pro-communist and moderate members. Developments in Africa, particularly in Angola, were much more important to Portugal than anything going on in Asia. 'It is difficult to avoid the conclusion that the Portuguese have decided to write off the Timor problem', the ambassador in Lisbon reported on 21 August.[41]

Over the following three months Fretilin leaders visited Australia, seeking support and warning of imminent Indonesian invasion. The memory of the assistance Timorese people provided Australian soldiers during the war, concerns about the future of the Roman Catholic Church in Timor, and darker worries about what the developments suggested about Indonesian ambitions in PNG all contributed to a heightened public concern in Australia. Accusations were circulating in the media that an 'Indonesia lobby' was driving policy in Canberra. At the same time, and more urgently, the government was dealing with the political and budgetary crisis that would soon lead to its dismissal from office.

Australian policy was becoming tortuously complicated. The prime minister directed the foreign affairs department that Australia should 'not be in a position where we could be held to be approving in advance Indonesian intervention without a Portuguese request or in effect giving a signal to undertake it. On the other hand, we should equally not wish to be made responsible for blocking Indonesian intervention if the Indonesians for their own reasons have decided they must undertake it.' He told his officials that Australia needed to avoid being used by Suharto's advisers to further their own views. At the same time, they should not indicate to the press how closely Australia was in touch with the Indonesians and be careful of references to Jakarta 'giving us warning of intervention or seeking Australian understanding of it'.[42]

Whitlam rejected proposals for Australian initiatives to mediate the conflict, to involve the United Nations or to become involved in some future joint administration. The Australian government did not 'regard itself as a party principal in Portuguese Timor', he told parliament on 26 August: 'We continue to hold that the future of the territory is a matter for resolution by Portugal and the Timorese people themselves with Indonesia also occupying an important place because of its predominant interest.'[43]

By the end of September, Fretilin controlled most of the territory and had begun to establish a government. Indonesia shifted its response from covert operations to infiltrating commandos. Australia knew from mid-October that Indonesia intended to intervene militarily by November. Popular support for the Fretilin cause in Australia, and disappointment in Jakarta that Australia was not showing sufficient support for Indonesia's dilemma, raised new tensions in the relationship.

Then, on 17 October, came the first reports that five Australia-based journalists had been killed during an Indonesian attack near Balibo in Timor. Australia had known in advance about a proposed Indonesian operation in the area but, as a 2002 review of the intelligence information showed, the embassy did not know of the presence of the journalists and the government held no information that could have alerted it in advance to the possibility of harm to the journalists.[44] Nevertheless, Woolcott wrote later, 'I sensed even then that, in Australia, attitudes towards Indonesia would be poisoned for years to come.'[45]

The government's response to the shootings was severely complicated by its reluctance to compromise its sources or damage its interests in Indonesia further by acknowledging publicly that it knew Indonesian troops were operating inside East Timor, despite Indonesia's denials.

The killing of the journalists came the day after the Opposition voted in the Senate to delay supply. In the days that followed, political survival in Canberra rather than events overseas preoccupied the government. On 11 November Whitlam was dismissed by the governor-general and Malcolm Fraser sworn in as caretaker prime minister until elections could be held.

The Opposition had been critical of Whitlam's handling of the crisis, but Fraser asked Woolcott to deliver a message to Suharto on 20 November in which he acknowledged 'the need for Indonesia to have an appropriate solution to the problem of East Timor' (making no mention of the need for self-determination) and foreshadowed an early visit by the foreign minister if the Coalition won the election on 13 December.[46]

On 28 November Fretilin issued a unilateral declaration of independence. Under Indonesian pressure, UDT and APODETI announced their support for integration with Indonesia. This triggered the open Indonesian military intervention, which began on 7 December with an air and sea attack on Dili, ostensibly in support of anti-Fretilin forces. Fretilin troops were driven into the hills and a pro-Indonesian government was installed, calling for incorporation with Indonesia.

The caretaker Liberal government issued a rather cautious statement regretting the use of force by Indonesia.[47] It intended to move amendments to a UN General Assembly resolution calling on Indonesia to withdraw but, caught in a confusing and rapidly moving series of events in New York, was unable to do so.[48] On 12 December it voted in favour of the resolution. Indonesia responded resentfully, especially as Malaysia, the Philippines, Thailand and Japan had opposed the vote and the United States and Singapore had abstained. Demonstrations were held outside the Australian embassy in Jakarta.

In the Australian elections on 13 December, Fraser led the Coalition to a landslide win. On 22 December the UN Security Council unanimously called on Indonesia to withdraw its forces and enable the people of East Timor to exercise freely their rights of self-determination.

Andrew Peacock, foreign minister in the new government, visited Jakarta the following month. The Fraser government's response to the situation involved criticising Indonesia's use of force, calling for self-determination and declaring its willingness to consider a contribution to an international presence. At the same time, it was trying to protect the broader relationship.[49] In April, Peacock told the Indonesians in Jakarta that Australia would not ignore public criticism but would not break relations with Indonesia. He said that 'the overwhelming majority of Timorese' had to have a say in their future while accepting that how this should be done was not for Australia to say.[50]

By late 1976 the question for Australia had turned to how to recognise the Indonesian incorporation, which was formally declared in July. Australia had stayed away from the meeting in Dili on 31 May which Indonesia organised to legitimise its control. The government did not finally decide on the issue of accepting Indonesian control of East Timor until January 1978, when it recognised the incorporation de facto to help it deal with issues of family reunion and aid, as Peacock explained. In the words of its legal advisers, it then 'slipped' into de jure recognition, during negotiations over the delineation of the seabed in early 1979.[51]

In the second half of the 1970s, despite efforts on both sides to keep relations on an even keel, the Australia–Indonesia relationship was battered by the long legacy of the Timor crisis and the Balibo killings, media criticisms and the expulsion of journalists. The high hopes Whitlam had expressed earlier in the decade were lost.

All the major external players – Portugal, Indonesia and Australia – as well as the internal Timorese factions, misjudged and mismanaged the events around Portugal's decolonisation, with tragic results. In Australia's case, the hard work of officials in Canberra, Jakarta, Lisbon and New York could not compensate for the absence of clarity on the part of the policy-makers about what they wanted and how to get it, nor for the muffled and mixed delivery of messages. The failures of Australian foreign policy during the Timor crisis were those of imagination, ambition and understanding. Policy-makers – mostly Whitlam – were too limited in their conception of what might be done, and too constrained in their willingness to utilise Australian influence. They were hobbled by an abundance of information from Jakarta that they could not effectively use and too little understanding of what was going on inside Timor. The result was wishful thinking disguised as foreign policy.

China

As the chaos of the Cultural Revolution began to subside after 1968, and relations with the Soviet Union deteriorated dangerously with border clashes in March 1969, Mao Zedong began exploring greater contacts with the United States. In Washington he found interested interlocutors in Richard Nixon, who was elected president in November 1969, and his national security adviser, Henry Kissinger. Both were looking for ways of expanding US strategic options and bringing the Vietnam War to an end.

In this new environment, Canada, a major competitor for Australian wheat sales, had established diplomatic relations with China in October 1970, and Beijing had promised 'to consider Canada first as a source of wheat as import needs arise'.[52] This was becoming politically sensitive in Australia.

The Coalition government knew that changes were coming in China's international position, and from late 1970 it was again considering the question of recognition. But the government was conscious of the domestic political issues at stake; its objective was to secure improved relations and to protect the wheat market while maintaining continued recognition of Taiwan in some form. 'Remember please that we have a DLP – and that its reactions must be considered!' foreign minister McMahon wrote, annotating a note covering a departmental policy planning paper on China in November.[53]

Cabinet decided in February 1971 that, with efforts to prevent Beijing taking the 'China seat' in the United Nations looking increasingly vulnerable, it needed to review Australian policy. Nevertheless, it continued to stipulate that 'the interests of the people of Taiwan be upheld and [that]

Taiwan should be preserved as a separate entity and as a member of the United Nations if it so desires'. Ministers noted that the government would 'wish at all times to maintain close concert with the United States in particular'.[54]

In May 1971 the Australian ambassador in Paris, Alan Renouf, was instructed to open a dialogue with Beijing through the Chinese ambassador. The contacts were to be kept secret. In his discussions he was to 'avoid explicit references to recognition or diplomatic relations'.[55] It was hardly surprising that with such instructions the discussions moved slowly and without great enthusiasm on the Chinese side.

The ALP had been committed to the recognition of the People's Republic of China (PRC) since the time of the Chifley government. In April 1971 the ALP party secretary, Mick Young, who had visited China before the Cultural Revolution, suggested to Whitlam that he should seek an invitation for the party's rural affairs spokesman, Rex Patterson, or an ALP delegation, to visit China. Whitlam sent a cable to Premier Zhou Enlai and the message was followed up through intermediaries. Silence followed. It was a high-stakes gamble by Whitlam.

But on 11 May the Chinese People's Institute of Foreign Affairs, a Party organisation, provided an invitation. A delegation, led by Whitlam and accompanied by journalists and a television crew, entered China on 2 July. In Beijing Whitlam met Zhou three days later for a conversation unexpectedly conducted in the presence of the journalists. Although Whitlam was critical of the Vietnam War and SEATO, he defended the ANZUS Treaty and Australia's participation in it. Back in Australia, William McMahon, now the prime minister, condemned the visit. 'The Whitlam policy would isolate Australia from our friends and allies in Southeast Asia and other parts of the western world as well,' he declared on 12 July.[56] 'It is time to expose the shams and absurdities of his excursion into instant coffee diplomacy … Mr Chou had Mr Whitlam on a hook and he played him as a fisherman plays a trout.' For good measure he added: 'What an impertinence to the leader of the United States, and it is not likely to be forgotten by the American Administration.'[57]

On 15 July, alas, McMahon received an emergency cablegram from the Australian ambassador in Washington, James Plimsoll, advising him that Secretary of State William Rogers had just telephoned with the news that Kissinger had been secretly in Beijing during Whitlam's visit to begin talks about normalisation. The president was about to announce that he would visit China the following year.[58] Although bravely asserting in public that there was no difference between Australian and American policy positions, McMahon wrote a plaintive letter to the president three days later, noting that 'it is apparent to the Australian press that there was no consultation between our two Governments. This has naturally led to the conclusion that our relations are not as close as they should be, which is surely something that neither of us want.'[59]

On 2 August 1971 Rogers announced that the United States would support action to transfer the China seat in the United Nations to the PRC, while seeking to preserve representation for Taiwan. In October, the General Assembly adopted by 76 votes to 35 (including Australia), with 17 abstentions, a resolution to 'restore all its rights' to the PRC and recognise its representatives as the only legitimate representatives of China in the United Nations.

Australia abstained in subsequent voting on China's admission to other international organisations such as the International Civil Aviation Organization (ICAO) and the International Atomic Energy Agency (IAEA). On 10 December 1971 the McMahon government acknowledged publicly that talks 'had been held in certain European capitals on the matter of the normalisation of relations between Australia and the PRC'. In February 1972 Nixon's historic visit to China finally took place.

When the Labor government took office in December 1972 it found that the foreign affairs department had prepared extensive briefings on the steps towards recognition.[60] Negotiations resumed under new instructions in Paris. They took fewer than twenty days to complete and revolved around the wording of Australia's acceptance that there was only 'One China' and the timing of the removal of the Taiwanese mission from Canberra. In a fine diplomatic distinction, Australia 'acknowledged' China's position that Taiwan was one of its provinces, rather than 'noting' it as Canada had done. The communiqué establishing diplomatic relations was signed on 21 December.

Whitlam appointed the 35-year-old former foreign affairs officer and ANU China scholar Stephen FitzGerald, who had accompanied him to Beijing as interpreter and adviser, as Australia's first ambassador. Whitlam visited China as prime minister in October 1973.

After the election of the Fraser government, the basis was set for an essentially bipartisan approach to China. Peacock, the new foreign minister, announced 'there should be no change in Australian policy towards Taiwan' and that 'the general approach should be to manage contacts with Taiwan as they had been managed for the last three years'.[61]

But an unexpected difference soon emerged between Fraser's policy and Whitlam's, reflecting their responses to the deterioration in Sino-Soviet relations. Where Whitlam sought to balance Australian foreign policy between Beijing and Moscow, Fraser saw an opportunity to secure China's leverage against the more powerful, and in his view more dangerous, of the communist states. He told parliament: 'A realistic view requires us to recognise that despite ideological differences there are important areas where our interests overlap'.[62] He saw these especially in China's support for an effective American presence in the Pacific and Indian oceans.

Fraser's first overseas visit as prime minister was to Tokyo and Beijing, signalling his break with earlier Liberal Party attitudes. The Chinese welcomed Fraser's robust anti-Soviet posture. Their approval was signalled by the thousands of cheering workers and children who greeted Fraser on his arrival in Beijing on 20 June 1976. The *People's Daily* praised his wisdom. On the other side of the divide, representatives of the Soviet Union and the Soviet bloc boycotted the formal ceremonies.

An ailing Mao Zedong was too sick to see him, but Fraser held eight hours of talks with Hua Guofeng, a Mao loyalist who had become premier after the death of Zhou Enlai in January. The Australian record of the first session of talks, in which Fraser argued for the development of a balance of forces in the Indian Ocean while criticising Indian policy and noting the impact of differences between the administration and Congress on US policy-making, was accidentally leaked to the press.[63] It seemed to suggest the idea of a coalition of interests between the United States, China, Japan and Australia against the Soviet Union.

On Southeast Asia, Hua told Fraser that, in the future, party-to-party relations should not affect state-to-state relations – foreshadowing the end of Chinese support for local communist insurgencies in Southeast Asia. The rest of Fraser's visit was heavily oriented to defence arrangements. He was flown to the sensitive area of Urumqi, near the Soviet border, and shown the routes along which his Chinese hosts expected a Soviet invading force to advance.[69] In Washington at the end of July, Fraser admonished his hosts for not engaging China more carefully. Kissinger responded tartly that the Chinese were trying to play the Americans through their allies.[65]

After Mao's death in 1976, Deng Xiaoping's influence grew slowly, and the elements of the reform program that would transform China, and with it the Australia–China relationship, were put in place. For the rest of the decade the bilateral relationship developed steadily, accumulating all the usual paraphernalia of two-way visits, exchanges and agreements.

Japan

Japan was already central to Australian trade, but the nature and scale of that trade changed in the 1970s as Australia became integrated into Japan's energy structure, a foretaste of a larger pattern to come in North Asia. The transformation was driven fundamentally by Japan's demand for minerals and energy – steaming coal, iron ore and uranium, then liquefied natural gas – and Australia's capacity to supply it. But beyond the economic, the decade also saw the development on both sides of broader understanding of the range of political and strategic interests they shared.

In October 1973, in response to Washington's support for Israel during the Yom Kippur War, Arab oil producers reduced production, embargoed supplies to the United States and, within a couple of months, nearly quadrupled prices. The 'oil shokku' heightened Japan's anxiety about the supply and cost of its vital commodity imports. Both Whitlam and Fraser wanted to address that concern and were personally central to the Australian response. In each case they stared down opponents within their own parties at important moments. From slightly different angles, each of them saw Japan as an important regional partner rather than simply a marketplace.

Reporting on his visit to Japan in 1973, Whitlam told the National Press Club that 'it was above all my design to reassure Japan ... about the stability, the security, the steadiness of supply of the raw materials she needs from Australia'.[66] The Fraser government delivered the same message. For Whitlam, the mark of his commitment to reassuring Japan was the decision to negotiate a Basic Treaty of Friendship and Co-operation. This agreement, also known as the Nara Treaty, set out a broad framework for closer relations between the two states and finally addressed the persistent Japanese suspicions, dating back to the behaviour of Billy Hughes at Versailles, that Australia was not prepared to deal with Japan on a genuinely equal basis.

In 1957 Australia had rejected the idea of a broad Treaty of Friendship, Commerce and Navigation of the sort Japan had with many other countries, citing the lack of precedent and problems of negotiating with the states in a federal system. It opted instead for the simpler Commerce

Agreement. When the Japanese raised the proposal again in 1970 and 1971, Australian officials dutifully re-examined their reservations but quickly reaffirmed the view that a treaty dealing with issues such as immigration, investment policy and shipping 'would cause very considerable difficulty for Australia'.[67] The McMahon government conveyed the decision to Japan.

But when Whitlam asked again about the idea, he declared the same advice from officials 'appalling'.[68] Persuaded by the doyen of Australian trade policy, Sir John Crawford, then at the Australian National University, that Australian interests would, in fact, be well served by establishing a 'framework of principles' for the relationship, he demanded a reassessment. Returning from a visit to Japan in October 1973, he announced that the old 'begrudging, negative, timid and unimaginative' Australian attitude to Japan's request for a treaty was at an end.[69]

Officials in the Department of Foreign Affairs then began the complex job of coordinating an Australian position on a wide-ranging treaty – enshrined in law – that would deal with trade, investment, arbitration, and entry and stay arrangements for businesspeople, while being flexible enough to adjust to changing circumstances.

Talks on the Basic Treaty ground on through 1974 and 1975 as officials debated the meaning of phrases such as 'fair and equitable' terms of trade.[70] Their task was complicated by the resource nationalism which was a strong feature of the 1970s global environment. Japanese investment in Australia was tiny compared with that of the Americans and British, but from 1971 onwards, as its foreign exchange reserves accumulated, Tokyo was actively encouraging Japanese equity investments in overseas resources. From its perspective, any new Australian restrictions on foreign investment seemed aimed disproportionately at Japan.

Whitlam had come to office on a platform of increasing Australian ownership and control over the nation's resources, and his Minister for Minerals and Energy, Rex Connor, known as 'the Strangler', was a pugnacious nationalist. Concern that Japanese steel mills were playing Australian producers off against each other in driving down prices was widespread in Australia. Connor declared that 'the Japanese are world-ranking exponents of playing off one company against each other to achieve the best deal and pursue a policy of divide and conquer with great effect'.[71] The Fraser government shared these suspicions and in 1978 it, too, briefly played with a policy of export price control to secure 'fair and reasonable' prices.[72]

As would be the case for the following forty years, agricultural exports, subject to the entrenched political power of the Japanese rural lobby, were a constant irritant. To protect its own beef producers, Japan embargoed Australian imports in 1974, causing severe problems for the Australian industry. Even when this was resolved, the need to haggle over beef quotas every six months, as well as problems with fisheries and sugar, continually tested the capacity of Australian trade diplomacy.[73] On the other side of the equation, Japan raised its frustration with Australian restrictions on motor vehicle imports and other manufactured imports as a formal complaint under the General Agreement on Tariffs and Trade (GATT) in 1974.[74]

Negotiations on the Basic Treaty were incomplete when Malcolm Fraser took office in November 1975, but aware of Japan's wish for a quick resolution, Fraser instructed his officials to conclude it on the basis of the current draft, overruling several of his ministers in order to maintain the momentum.[75]

By the time Fraser and his Japanese counterpart, Takeo Miki, met in Tokyo in June 1976 they were able to sign the treaty, the first of its kind Australia had ever concluded. It set broad guidelines for the future development of the relationship and satisfied Japan's longstanding concern that its businesses operate under the same principles as those applying to all other nationalities.[76]

But none of the ongoing friction deflected the trend lines. By 1979/80 Japan was still Australia's largest trading partner, with annual total trade of $A7.6 billion and, with 21 per cent of the total, the third-largest source of foreign investment after Britain and the United States.[77]

Beyond the economic relationship, the range of people-to-people contacts between the two countries was also expanding. A cultural agreement was signed in 1974. Two years later, one of the first pieces of legislation passed by the Fraser government established an Australia-Japan Foundation, an initiative begun under Whitlam to expand non-governmental contact and exchanges. A working holiday scheme, unique for both countries, was introduced in 1980.

Both the Whitlam and Fraser governments saw Japan as an important international partner for Australia. For Whitlam it had the potential to become 'the first great industrial power to break the nexus between economic strength and military strength' and a potential partner in a regional forum. Fraser pointed to the common alliance with the United States and a shared interest in regional stability as a basis for cooperation. In April 1978 he and Prime Minister Fukuda met specifically to discuss not bilateral problems but international issues such as the multilateral trade negotiations, the North–South dialogue and common fund proposals.[78]

A symbolically important moment came in 1979 when Japan sought to have Australia included in the Tokyo summit meeting of the Group of 7 (G7), which had been established in 1975, by the seven large industrialised countries to informally coordinate global economic matters. Washington blocked Japan's move, but it was a clear sign of how aligned the regional and global interests of Australia and Japan were becoming. Discussions between Australia and Japan begun during this period would eventually have a deep impact on the development of regionalism in Asia and the Pacific.

Papua New Guinea and the Southwest Pacific

In January 1972 the Coalition's slow approach to change in Australia's nearest neighbour, the trust territory of Papua and New Guinea, was given a new sense of urgency when the Minister for External Territories, the uninspiring Country Party stalwart Charles 'Ceb' Barnes, retired and was replaced by the ambitious young Liberal Andrew Peacock. Peacock visited Papua New Guinea seventeen times during his short tenure and brought the government's policies into something like bipartisan agreement with those of Labor.

There was certainly no universal desire for independence in Papua New Guinea (PNG), as the territory was formally renamed in 1972. Bougainvilleans wanted independence, Papuans did not want to be lumped in with New Guineans, and, many people in the remote New Guinea Highlands, the most populous part of the country, wanted Australia to remain in charge until they had caught up economically with the rest of the country.

But Australia's task of decolonisation was made easier when Michael Somare, a former schoolteacher and journalist from the Sepik region, successfully manoeuvred himself into the position of Chief Minister after the April 1972 House of Assembly elections. Somare was a canny and gregarious politician with moderate views, and his Pangu (Papua and New Guinea Union) Party, which campaigned under the slogan 'One Name One Country', was the only political party with truly national aspirations.

It had been clear since Whitlam's visits to PNG as Opposition leader in 1970 and 1971 that he was determined to deliver self-government within a year of coming to office and full independence within his first term. Self-government was proclaimed in December 1973, and independence finally came in a flurry on 16 September 1975. Frustrated by the slow progress of the House of Assembly's constitutional planning processes, Whitlam had simply transferred the defence and foreign affairs powers to PNG in advance of independence in March 1975. Although the process was completed faster than almost anyone in PNG or Australia had anticipated a few years earlier, PNG's first governor-general, Sir John Guise, was able to note during the independence celebrations that Papua New Guineans were lowering the flag of their colonisers, not tearing it down.[79]

The Fraser government, with Peacock now as foreign minister, maintained the same approach to PNG. Unlike almost any other administering power, Australia did not have the option of walking away from the problems of its former colony, even if it had wished to do so. The country was too close and the continuing links too deep. By 1980 almost half Australia's aid program was still directed to PNG, mostly in the form of direct support to the PNG budget.[80]

The issues of support to the military and Australia's residual defence commitments to PNG were delicate matters for both sides. Neither Canberra nor Port Moresby sought a formal defence treaty. Defence cooperation and assistance continued, however, and in 1977 the Fraser government signed a formal status of forces agreement and settled the question of how the remaining Australian personnel would be used in politically sensitive situations.

PNG's independence was the most important of the developments that transformed the Southwest Pacific. The number of independent states continued to grow as the Solomon Islands and Tuvalu (1978) and Kiribati (1979) became independent. Despite French resistance, even the condominium of New Hebrides, jointly ruled by France and the UK since 1906, was moving to independence by 1980. In February that year, however, just before the new constitution entered into force, a group of rebels on the island of Espiritu Santo, with support from French settlers, announced their own unilateral independence. France refused to allow the mobile police force to suppress the rebellion, but when PNG troops arrived to help celebrate Vanuatu's independence in July 1980, the new government dispatched them, together with backup from Port Moresby, to regain control. This PNG intervention in Vanuatu represented a significant departure from past approaches to security in the region. Australia had quietly encouraged the move.[81]

This growing number of independent states had a new agenda to discuss, but the existing regional organisation, the South Pacific Commission, included the remaining colonial powers, Britain, France and the United States, and non-self-governing territories. It was not a forum in which political discussions could take place. In 1971, at the instigation of the independent island leaders, a new body, the South Pacific Forum, was established to represent the independent states. Australia supported the change and hosted the second meeting.

The Forum's agenda grew during the decade. The proclamation of the new 200-nautical-mile exclusive economic zones established under the Law of the Sea Convention gave tiny island states rights to some of the world's largest fisheries resources and a major new source of income. This led to disagreements with the United States, in particular, over the control of valuable, highly migratory species of fish such as tuna, which American fleets were fishing. A Forum Fisheries Agency was established in 1979 with Australian support, to provide the island members with expertise and technical assistance to help manage the resources. Regional concerns about French nuclear testing also continued.

The balance of trade with regional countries was heavily in Australia's favour, and it found itself under regular pressure from Forum members over greater access for their products. In 1980 a South Pacific Regional Trade and Economic Co-operation Agreement (SPARTECA) was signed.[82] But Australia's largest impact on the economies of the regional states was through aid.

After a long period during which Australia's relations with New Zealand had been taken for granted, Whitlam deliberately chose Wellington for his first overseas visit to emphasise the importance of the Pacific and to restate the principles of the 1944 Canberra Pact, the first treaty both countries had signed. Even under Whitlam, there were differences over the proposal by the New Zealand prime minister, Norman Kirk, for a nuclear-free zone in the South Pacific, and over immigration issues. Although Fraser's election coincided with a similar political change in New Zealand, where his fellow conservative Robert Muldoon took power, the trans-Tasman relationship became abrasive. The two leaders had very different personalities and took different philosophical approaches to issues like sporting links with South Africa. Policy rivalry in the Pacific, where Muldoon resented Australia's new aid and diplomatic efforts in Polynesia, also played a part. The symbolic nadir of trans-Tasman relations would come later, with the underarm bowling incident during a one-day international cricket match in Melbourne in 1981.

Despite this niggling policy friction, progress was made on the economic relationship with the assistance of Muldoon's deputy, the well-liked New Zealand foreign minister Brian Talboys. Following a tour of all Australian states in March 1978, and after discussions with Fraser at his rural property in Victoria, both sides agreed that the existing New Zealand–Australia free trade agreement was no longer effective and that something more was needed to promote deeper economic integration. In March 1980 Fraser and Muldoon agreed on the goal of a Closer Economic Relations (CER) agreement, with the objective of 'a gradual and progressive liberalisation of trade across the Tasman for both industrial and agricultural goods produced in each country'.

In April 1976 the South Pacific unexpectedly emerged as part of the Cold War geopolitical struggle. During a visit to Tonga to present his diplomatic credentials, the Soviet ambassador to New Zealand raised the prospect of Russian aid for the expansion of an airport in return for rights to an onshore fishing base. The ambassador's offer coincided with a growing consciousness in Canberra of the extent of Australian responsibility for the security of the region. The colonial powers were packing up and the Americans had made it clear that the ANZUS Treaty did apply to the independent regional states: this was a part of the world in which Washington expected its allies to do some real burden-sharing.

Fraser responded dramatically to the Russian move. He announced the opening of new Australian diplomatic posts in Western Samoa and Tonga and quadrupled development assistance. By the end of 1980 Australia had risen from third place to first among the aid donors to the Pacific.[83] For Fraser, this was a dangerous example of exactly the sort of Soviet expansionism he had long been warning about.

It turned out, in the end, that the Russians were not coming. Moscow established diplomatic relations with Fiji, Tonga and Western Samoa, but its diplomacy was clumsy and its interests limited. No bases appeared. But the incident was a sign of the extent to which the Cold War was now becoming a global contest.

The US alliance

For all Australian governments of the 1970s a degree of uncertainty hung over the United States alliance, especially over the question of how America's allies were to interpret the 1969 Nixon Doctrine, in which the United States made it clear that it expected them to take a larger measure of responsibility for their own defence. Buffeted by the defeat in Vietnam and the energy crisis, self-absorbed and introspective, America was re-examining its role in the world and had reached no clear answer to the questions it was asking itself.

Despite the policy mistakes he thought the United States and Australia had made in Vietnam, Whitlam was a supporter of the alliance. The problem, as he put it later, was: 'How to oppose American intervention without opposing America: how to denounce the war without denouncing the United States.'[84] As the American withdrawal from Vietnam began, he saw new opportunities to remake the relationship. But this meant moving away from 'the narrow view that the ANZUS treaty is the only significant factor in our relations with the United States and the equally narrow view that our relations with the United States are the only significant factor in Australia's foreign relations.'[85] 'I believe this alliance is old enough and strong enough to stand a little frankness on both sides,' Whitlam said in July 1973.[86] By that time, the assumption was being well tested.

On Christmas Day 1972, just weeks after the new Australian government was elected, President Nixon ordered a resumption of American bombing of North Vietnam. In massive raids over twelve days, B-52 bombers dropped 20,000 tonnes of explosives on targets in Hanoi and Haiphong. Nixon's objective was to pressure Hanoi into resuming the Paris peace talks. Three of the new Labor ministers, fresh from the anti-Vietnam campaign and speaking outside their portfolio responsibilities, were damningly critical. The trade minister, Jim Cairns, called the bombing 'the most brutal indiscriminate slaughter of women and children in living memory'.[87] Labour minister Clyde Cameron described the administration as 'maniacs'. To another ministerial colleague, Tom Uren, they were mass murderers. Maritime unions placed bans on US shipping.

Whitlam wrote privately to Nixon expressing his concern in more measured tones, although he foreshadowed an intention to seek support from other East Asian leaders for a public appeal to Washington and Hanoi to return to serious negotiations.[88] The reaction from the White House was indignant. Nixon did not reply to the letter and his national security adviser, Kissinger, rang the Australian embassy to complain. The Australian government was placed in a diplomatic freeze and Australia's relations with the United States were as severely strained as at any point in the ANZUS relationship.[89] According to the US ambassador in Canberra, Marshall Green, a senior career diplomat, only Sweden outranked Australia among Nixon's most-disliked Western nations.[90]

For the next half-year, a diplomatic tussle took place over whether Whitlam would be invited officially to the White House. Whitlam wanted to go but did not want to beg. For his part, Nixon could be relied on to hold a grudge. In the end a visit was brokered through Kissinger with the assistance of Green and Whitlam's chief of staff, Peter Wilenski.

Suspicion eased a little after that visit in late July, but it would take Nixon's resignation after the Watergate scandal in August 1974 and the accession of Gerald Ford to the presidency to improve things substantially.

For both Canberra and Washington, one of the central issues in the relationship was the presence in Australia of the US defence facilities at North West Cape, Pine Gap and Nurrungar. The development of satellite systems to collect signals intelligence and provide early warning of ballistic missile launches had become central to the United States intelligence program in the course of the 1970s. This increased the importance of the facilities in Australia.[91] As Whitlam later wrote, slightly portentously, 'The United States is important to Australia as it is the most powerful and vital nation on earth. Australia is important to the US as it occupies a crucial position on the earth's surface and in relation to the heavens above and the waters beneath.'[92]

The issue was very divisive within a Labor Party energised by the anti-Vietnam movement. The left wing of the party saw the facilities as violations of sovereignty, entangling Australia in American strategies and risking nuclear attack in the event of war. Briefings on the role of Pine Gap and Nurrungar in early 1973 persuaded Whitlam that the installations were not weapons systems but part of an early warning system that helped ensure that 'the great powers do not have the ignorance and suspicion of each other that leads to war'.[93] This recognition of the role of the facilities in nuclear deterrence was to reframe the debate within Labor. The platform on which Labor had come to power opposed foreign bases on Australian soil but Whitlam worked hard to moderate its implementation.

Even so, irritations continued. Whitlam was angered when he was not given advance warning when US armed forces, including those in the Australian facilities, were placed on high alert during the Yom Kippur War of October 1973. His rebuke exasperated Washington.

Still, in January 1974, the defence minister, Lance Barnard, and his American counterpart, James Schlesinger, were able to conclude an agreement for joint operation of North West Cape, which would install an Australian as deputy commander. Significantly, they tied the agreement to the alliance, noting that 'the status of the station is a bilateral arrangement in the framework of the ANZUS Treaty'.[94]

Anti-base protests grew. A practical and unthreatening proposal for Australian participation in an Omega navigational system, available to all ships and aircraft, became a focus of suspicion. A senior minister, Jim Cairns (who as deputy prime minister did not ask for, and was not given, briefings on the role of the facilities),[95] accepted appointment as president of the Congress for International Co-operation and Disarmament, an organisation which supported the removal of foreign defence facilities from Australia.

Whitlam continued to face down critics within his own party and more broadly. The lease arrangements for Pine Gap were due to expire in 1976 and a non-renewal notice could be given by the end of 1975; Whitlam had alarmed the Americans in 1974 by seeming to suggest that it might be given.[96] In February 1975, however, he told the delegates to the federal conference that 'I would give no such notice'.[97] Nevertheless, the febrile atmosphere at the time of Whitlam's dismissal, which coincided with American anger at media reports that Pine Gap was under the control of the CIA, contributed to a flowering of conspiracy theories.

Relations with Washington were smoother with the election of Malcolm Fraser. He came to office committed to ensuring that the ANZUS alliance did not 'fall in to disrepair and dispute'. America, he told parliament, was the only power that could balance the might of the Soviet Union: 'If America does not undertake the task it will not be done. If it is not done, the whole basis of peace and security is unsupported.'[98] On his first visit to Washington in July 1976 he took offers to President Ford of access for US naval ships to Australian ports and further discussions on defence installations.[99]

Even so, Fraser distinguished between cooperation and subordination. As he told the House of Representatives, 'The interests of the United States and the interests of Australia are not necessarily identical. In our relations with the United States, as in our relations with other great powers, the first responsibility is independently to assess our own interests. The United States will unquestionably do the same.' He also made his views clear on Washington's post-Watergate political problems: 'Mutual recriminations about the causes and effects of foreign events, differences between President and Congress on the conduct of American foreign policy, are producing some concerns about America's capacity to act with full effect around the world.'[100]

Malcolm Fraser

Malcolm Fraser came from a family of graziers. He had entered parliament for the Victorian rural seat of Wannon in 1955 at the age of twenty-five, fresh from Oxford. He spent ten years on the backbench before being appointed Minister for the Army in 1966. Later, under John Gorton, he served as Minister for Education and Science and Minister for Defence, although his disagreements with Gorton eventually precipitated the latter's resignation as prime minister. He took over as leader of the Opposition from the ineffectual Billy Snedden in March 1975 and thereafter rode the gathering chaos of the Whitlam government relentlessly to become caretaker prime minister in November 1975. He was then elected in his own right with a record majority.

The dour realism of Fraser's approach to foreign policy was, in fact, washed by an unexpected and almost romantic attachment to great causes. His view of the world with which Australia should engage was larger than that of his Liberal Party predecessors. He believed in the cause of the Western alliance but wanted Australia to make its own independent contribution to it, especially in Australia's environment of Southeast Asia and the surrounding Pacific and Indian oceans. 'If that environment is going to change,' he had told the House of Representatives as defence minister in 1970, 'we want to be able to play a meaningful part in the changes.'[101]

Administratively, he was as much a centralist as Whitlam. The prime minister's department became the centre of Canberra's foreign policymaking. He was demanding – sometimes unreasonably so – with public servants and those around him. 'The prime minister has all the flexibility of a steel girder,' one of his staff commented tiredly to this writer during an overseas visit in 1976.

Despite political rivalries and different temperaments, Fraser and his foreign minister from 1975 to 1980, Peacock, had similar approaches to global developments and Australian interests, and worked effectively together.

Détente and its discontents

Fraser came to office at a time when détente with the Soviet Union was coming under new stress. Both liberal and conservative elements in the United States were resisting the balance of power realpolitik by which Nixon and Kissinger had shaped US strategy. Anger about Soviet policies towards the emigration of Jews and the treatment of dissidents led Congress to impose trade sanctions on the USSR under the Jackson–Vanik amendment to the *Trade Act* in early 1975. Then came the conclusion of the Conference on Security and Co-operation in Europe (CSCE) in Helsinki in June 1975. This looked to some, including in Moscow, like a Western acknowledgement of the permanent political division of Europe. But the commitments it included to the UN Charter and the Universal Declaration of Human Rights would turn out to have entirely unexpected long-term consequences for the Soviet Union and its satellites.

For the time being, however, the global correlation of forces, as the communists put it, seemed to be changing in Moscow's favour. In the former Portuguese territories of Angola and Mozambique, Soviet and Cuban forces were supporting leftist leaders in a proxy struggle with the West. Moscow's support for a Marxist regime in South Yemen and, after 1978, for the Ethiopian revolutionaries in their war against Somalia provided it with direct influence in the Indian Ocean and the Red Sea through the base at Berbera and brought Soviet forces close to the Persian Gulf with its oil wealth. A Marxist coup in Afghanistan in April 1978 brought another Soviet-supported regime to power. For Fraser, the Third World was the forum in which the struggle against Soviet threats would have to be fought and Australia's western approach, the Indian Ocean, was central to the outcome.

The Indian Ocean

Before the 1970s Australia's major maritime connection with Europe had been comfortably dominated by Britain through its bases in Aden and Singapore. But the situation was changing. Britain's military withdrawal east of Suez, an increasing – if modest – presence by the Soviet navy in the region, and the growing economic importance of Western Australia all served to increase Australian attention on the region. Its sensitivity was illustrated by the political furore caused in 1969 when the Coalition foreign minister Gordon Freeth commented that Australia 'need not panic whenever a Russian appears'. Freeth lost his West Australian seat in the following election, possibly for unrelated local reasons, but the lesson was not lost.

The Coalition was anxious to encourage the United States to stay in the Indian Ocean, not least because of nagging doubts about whether the ANZUS Treaty applied to that ocean as well as the Pacific. Despite private reservations about the wisdom of Washington's dispatch of a carrier battle group led by the USS *Enterprise* into the Bay of Bengal during the Indo-Pakistani war of December 1971, the McMahon government welcomed the American naval presence. It encouraged the development of an American base on the tiny British-owned atoll of Diego Garcia in the central Indian

Ocean and offered the Americans the use of the new naval facilities then being developed at Cockburn Sound in Western Australia (the current HMAS Stirling).

Labor was less worried about the Soviet naval presence in the Indian Ocean, which Whitlam saw as 'a completely natural and expected development'.[102] Still, after its early problems with the Nixon administration, Labor responded in carefully moderate tones to the upgrading of the American facilities in Diego Garcia in 1974 and permitted the US to stage flights there through Australia's Cocos Islands. Fraser set a different and more urgent tone from the beginning. 'The Soviet leaders now have ... a capacity to influence and even to intervene ... well beyond the periphery of the established zones of Soviet security interest,' he told the House of Representatives in his first major foreign policy speech as prime minister. 'Reasonable people can ... reasonably assume that the Soviet Union still seeks to expand its influence throughout the world in order to achieve Soviet primacy.'[103]

His concerns about the Russians were not shared fully in Washington, which was still trying to balance its interests between China and the Soviet Union, nor in Australia. Labor thought Fraser was over-egging the pudding and there were sceptical voices within his own party. A parliamentary report chaired by a Liberal Party senator produced a much more cautious assessment of Soviet capabilities.[104]

Australia's relations with India, the largest of the Indian Ocean states, had never been close despite common membership of the Commonwealth. The personal relationship between Menzies and India's first prime minister, Jawaharlal Nehru, had been strained. Australian policy had tried to maintain a balance between India and Pakistan and avoid taking sides in their conflicts. India's friendliness with the Soviet Union, despite its commitment to non-alignment, placed natural limits on strategic relations with Australia. A breakthrough of sorts occurred during the war between India and Pakistan in December 1971, when India intervened to support secessionists in East Pakistan fighting to form the new state of Bangladesh. Although Australia had voted with Pakistan, China and the United States in United Nations votes calling for a ceasefire, it had been more sympathetic to India's position than most Western governments and became one of the earliest countries to recognise Bangladesh.

Whitlam made efforts to revitalise ties with New Delhi, and his visit in June 1973 was the first by an Australian prime minister since 1959. His government reacted in measured terms to the first Indian nuclear test in May 1974. But in the absence of any driving economic, strategic or political interests, the relationship under both Whitlam and Fraser remained limited.[105]

Southern Africa

Developments in Southern Africa were having a greater impact on Australian foreign policy. By the time Whitlam took over, Australian voting in the United Nations on apartheid had already changed. The McMahon government had supported most of the anti-apartheid resolutions put to the 1971 General Assembly, although it had abstained on calls for an arms embargo against South Africa and the end of sporting ties. It was not government bans but increasing protests in Australia that brought about the cancellation of the 1971 cricket tour by South Africa.

Whitlam's election platform in 1972 included a pledge that Labor would not permit the travel to, or passage through, Australia of racially selected sporting teams. The government pressured the Australian Cricket Board not to send a cricket team to South Africa.

Australia began co-sponsoring, rather than simply supporting, anti-apartheid resolutions in the United Nations, and in 1974 voted for the first time in favour of South Africa's expulsion from the UN. Defence links were reduced when the South Africans were not permitted to replace the defence attaché in Canberra.[106]

Trading ties, however, which were heavily in Australia's favour and especially important for manufactures, were not cut. Even the trade minister, Jim Cairns, an emblematic left-winger, agreed that Australia could not stop trade because it disapproved of a country's policies: 'If we did that, we would stop trading with just about every country except Sweden and Switzerland.'[107]

Namibia, administered by South Africa, was also attracting attention. In 1971 the International Court of Justice reversed its 1966 decision, taken on the casting vote of Percy Spender as president, and declared South Africa's continuing presence in Namibia illegal. With the revolution in Portugal in April 1974, and the promise of independence for Portugal's African colonies, anti-colonial pressure intensified on South Africa and Rhodesia.

Malcolm Fraser was, as his biographer noted, 'the most scathing critic of apartheid of any Liberal parliamentarian in the early 1960s'.[108]

His views became clear to his international counterparts at the June 1977 Commonwealth Heads of Government Meeting when he launched an attack on racism as 'an offence to human decency and a scourge to the dignity of man'.[109] At that meeting he was an important figure in negotiating the Gleneagles agreement, which averted a looming boycott of the Commonwealth Games by committing all member countries to withhold support for competition with any country where sport was organised on the basis of race.[110]

In 1978 continuing international sanctions against Rhodesia and military pressure from the rebel Zimbabwe African National Union Patriotic Front (ZANU-PF) of Robert Mugabe and Joshua Nkomo, led Ian Smith's white minority government in Rhodesia (which Fraser was now calling Zimbabwe) to pursue an internal settlement. After elections, which were boycotted by the Patriotic Front, it transferred nominal power to a black government under Bishop Abel Muzorewa. White control over the army, police, judiciary and civil service continued, however.

The settlement was not recognised internationally, but as the 1979 elections in the United Kingdom approached, comments by the Conservative Party leader, Margaret Thatcher, raised fears that she would recognise the Muzorewa government and end sanctions when she came to power. Fraser took on the task of trying to moderate the new prime minister's views.[111] He lobbied key African and other Commonwealth leaders, like the Jamaican prime minister, Michael Manley, with whom he was close, to avoid pushing Thatcher into a corner. At the Commonwealth Heads of Government Meeting in Lusaka in August, he helped shift her away from recognition of the Muzorewa administration to acceptance of a communiqué that was broadly acceptable to the African Commonwealth members.[112]

Britain then hosted a constitutional conference at Lancaster House in September which led to a Commonwealth-monitored ceasefire and fresh elections under British auspices. Australia provided a 154-person contingent to the ceasefire monitoring force. The election was won by the ZANU-PF party of Robert Mugabe (who managed to remain in office thereafter). Australia was the first country to announce the appointment of a high commissioner to Zimbabwe and delivered a sizeable aid program. Fraser attended the independence celebrations in Harare in April 1980. He was able to speak persuasively to all sides in a way no other leader could, and at cost to his relationship with Thatcher; his role in the settlement had been substantively and tactically significant.

He and Peacock carried their Africa policy against significant internal party dissent. Before Fraser left for Lusaka, he had faced public calls from

the National Council of the Liberal Party and his own Victorian state executive for recognition of the Muzorewa government. As so often happens in
Australia, success in international affairs did not help the government politically. After Lusaka, Fraser's approval rating as prime minister reached an
all-time low of less than 30 per cent.[113]

The Commonwealth

Australia's membership of the Commonwealth was an important instrument for Fraser's foreign policy-making. For his conservative predecessors
the Commonwealth's importance lay principally in the historic and emotional connections it provided back to Britain. Fraser used it instead as a
means of connecting with the Third World, and extending the global reach
of his policies.

In the hope of strengthening the body, he proposed the establishment of
regional meetings of Commonwealth heads of government. He hosted the
first of these, with twelve leaders from Asia and the Pacific, in Sydney in
February 1978. It was marred by tragedy when a bomb exploded in the early
morning outside the hotel at which the leaders were staying, killing three
people. The army was called out to provide security. The initiative did not
survive Fraser's leadership, but it was another version of Australia's search
for effective regional architecture.

The Middle East

From 1947, when Evatt played a significant role in Israel's establishment,
first as chair of the UN Special Committee on Palestine, then as President of
the General Assembly, Australian policy on the Arab–Israeli dispute had
been largely bipartisan and low profile.

'Neutrality' and 'even-handedness' were the words used by both sides
of politics to describe their approach, which was based on the principles
outlined in UN Security Council Resolution 242, passed after the Six-Day
War in 1967. This called for Israel's withdrawal from territories it had
occupied and asserted the right of every country in the area 'to live in
peace within secure and recognised boundaries free from threats or acts
of force'.[114]

In practical terms, this usually meant, as the Liberal foreign minister
Nigel Bowen told parliament in May 1972, that the government 'supported

United Nations resolutions which were concerned with the welfare of those who have suffered from the dispute, but … abstained on those which tended politically to favour one side or the other.[114]

From the time of the Yom Kippur War in October 1973, when Israel was attacked by the combined forces of Syria and Egypt, the Middle East began to attract greater political attention in Australia. The Arab oil supply boycotts and price increases that followed the war established a link between the Arab–Israel issue and Australia's economic interests in the region. The Arab world provided 30 per cent of Australia's crude oil, a valuable market for its agricultural products and, it soon became apparent, a potential stock of investment funds.

Under Whitlam, Australian votes on Arab–Israel resolutions shifted. Although it continued to reject efforts to expel Israel from the UN, support the use of force to resolve the dispute or equate Zionism with racism, 'even-handedness' was now interpreted as meaning that Australia would vote in favour of resolutions that offered balanced criticism of both sides. So in July 1973 Australia voted for a resolution, vetoed by the United States, which 'deplored Israel's continuing occupation of territories occupied as a result of the 1967 conflict'.[115]

After the Palestine Liberation Organisation (PLO) leader Yasser Arafat addressed the UN General Assembly in November 1974, the Assembly passed resolutions reaffirming 'the inalienable rights of the Palestinian people to self-determination, national independence and sovereignty and return to their homes and property' and granting the PLO observer status at the UN. Australia abstained on both issues on the grounds that 'the existence of the state of Israel has to be accepted', although it voted in favour of PLO representation in some of the UN's specialised agencies.[116] The Australian representative at the United Nations told the General Assembly that 'when a new state alongside Israel in the former Palestine emerges from a negotiated agreement among those parties, Australia will be prepared to accept it and deal with it on the basis of equality'.[117]

Australian policy had moved from one in which the Palestinian issue was seen as essentially a refugee problem to one which acknowledged the right of the Palestinians to their own state. The government's new attitude to visits to Australia by PLO officials and efforts to establish a PLO information office in Australia generated criticism from the Australian Jewish community (which had traditionally been close to Labor), the Opposition and, most starkly of all, from within the ALP itself. The PLO at this time was tainted by acts of terrorism such as the attack by the splinter Black September group on Israeli athletes at the Munich Olympic Games in 1973. It refused to accept Israel's right to exist. The two sides of the dispute within the ALP were led by the party president – and head of the Australian Council of Trade Unions – Bob Hawke, who criticised the attitude to the PLO as 'abhorrent', and the Victorian leftist – and member of the federal executive – W.H. (Bill) Hartley, who led the pro-Palestinian faction. In early 1975 Hartley tried to organise a visit to Australia by a PLO group. In what one close academic observer described as 'the first genuinely "collectivist" foreign policy decision since Labor's election in 1972', cabinet decided by a narrow margin to ban the visit despite the wishes of Whitlam and Willesee.[118]

In other parts of the Middle East, Australia was seeking trading opportunities and a share of the growing pool of 'petro-dollars', US dollars flowing into the coffers of the increasingly rich Arab producers as a result of the oil price rises. The involvement of Whitlam's ministers, minerals and energy minister Rex Connor, and Treasurer Jim Cairns, in efforts to raise huge petro-dollar loans from dubious sources helped precipitate the crisis that led to the government's dismissal.

The Fraser government reverted to a more traditional interpretation of even-handedness, when it came to office. 'In the Middle East the only future lies in negotiation – in a proper and broad recognition of the rights of all groups within that troubled area; in an absolute recognition of the right of Israel to survive as a nation; and an equal recognition of the problems of the Palestinian refugees', Fraser told parliament.[119] The Coalition criticised the PLO's refusal to acknowledge Israel's right to exist but it, too, moved to acknowledge 'recognition of the legitimate rights of the Palestinian people to a homeland alongside Israel'.[120]

The regional dynamics changed with the September 1978 negotiation of the Camp David Peace Accords, brokered by President Jimmy Carter, followed by a peace treaty and diplomatic recognition between Israel and Egypt. The agreement offered, Fraser noted optimistically, 'new and exhilarating prospects of real and lasting peace'.[121]

An even greater change to the regional order came in early 1979, however, when the Shah of Iran, America's close ally, was driven into exile and Shi'a revolutionaries installed a theocratic Islamic Republic headed by Ayatollah Khomeini, who returned triumphantly from exile. None of this was a function of the East–West struggle. Instead it foreshadowed a much larger change to come with the emergence of radical Islamism as a political force. Peacock recognised this. 'The indications are that the resurgence of Islam could cause significant far-reaching changes in the world. It is a revived force of great dynamism which is being generated in the context of social and cultural changes,' he told the House of Representatives in February.[122]

But the Iranian Revolution further weakened American confidence in the country's international role. The seizure of hostages from the American embassy in November 1979, and the failure of President Carter's attempt to release them, added to the sense of drift. Australian policy on Iran was firm in condemning the breach of international law involved in the hostage-taking but less resolute on the question of a practical response. Cabinet split on the question of a total trade boycott because of the value of Australian wheat and other agricultural exports.[123] One consequence of the Iranian Revolution was that the decade ended with another oil price shock, further extending the global economic malaise.

Australia and the international economy

When the Whitlam government came to office, the Australian economy was booming. Iron ore and coal, manufactures and agriculture were all in high demand internationally. Only inflation looked like a problem. It was partly to address inflation that Whitlam dramatically cut all Australian import tariffs by 25 per cent in July 1973. He also took steps to sever the link between the interests of Australia's domestic manufacturers and its trade-focused export industries by breaking up John McEwan's formidable bureaucratic citadel, the Department of Trade and Industry, into separate departments of Overseas Trade and Secondary Industry. And he renamed the Tariff Board as the Industries Assistance Commission, giving it a broader remit to address productivity.

But in 1973 the oil exporters' organisation, OPEC, imposed supply boycotts and quadrupled prices as a response to the Yom Kippur War (and also to help restore value to their long-term supply contracts). As the terms of trade of oil-importing countries collapsed, inflationary pressures grew and real incomes fell. What followed globally was a period that required the invention of a new name to describe it: stagflation, a debilitating combination of lower growth, rising inflation and growing unemployment. Demand for Australian resources and manufactured exports slumped and in 1974 the country entered a stagflationary period that would last until the end of the decade.

Whitlam's tariff cuts had been broadly welcomed, but as inflation rose and unemployment grew the Australian public quickly rediscovered its protectionist instincts. In September 1974 the government reimposed import quotas on a range of consumer goods, including motor vehicles, clothing and footwear. Together with a devaluation of the Australian dollar, this increased Australia's effective rate of protection by 50 per cent.[124] The quotas did not do much to relieve unemployment or reduce inflation but they particularly hurt Australia's Southeast Asian neighbours just entering new areas of manufacturing, especially clothing and textiles. Their angry response to Australia's actions reflected the growing sense among the developing countries that the international order was stacked against their interests, particularly those of the food and commodities producers. They used their growing numbers in international organisations to push for change.

In 1974 the United Nations General Assembly adopted a Declaration on the Establishment of a New International Economic Order 'based on equity, sovereign equality, interdependence, common interests and cooperation among all states'. This was to be accomplished through a 'North–South dialogue' between developed and developing countries which would, in turn, facilitate measures such as the development of an international code of conduct for transnational corporations.[125] For the remainder of the 1970s and early '80s this debate was a centrepiece of global discussion in the United Nations and its forums, especially the United Nations Conference on Trade and Development (UNCTAD).

One of the major proposals under discussion was the creation of an international fund to finance the purchase of buffer stocks of commodities produced by developing countries. Together with measures such as controls on production and exports in order to manage the supply side, this was seen as a way of stabilising prices. A second arm of this Common Fund would provide producers with development assistance and promotional help.

As in earlier international economic debates, Australia had dual interests. It thought of itself as both a developed country and a primary commodity producer. It was also more alert to the concerns of its developing-country neighbours than were many other members of 'the North'. The success of the OPEC oil cartel had strengthened interest in the idea of cooperation between commodity producers. As one of the world's top five producers of bauxite, iron ore, tin, nickel, silver, lead, zinc, manganese and uranium, Australia toyed with producers' associations but only joined the International Bauxite Association, set up in 1974.[126]

The question of who owned the nation's resources returned to the public debate as fears that Australia was becoming a quarry for the Japanese aligned with demands to 'buy back the farm'. In 1973, 44 per cent of Australians surveyed thought the government was not doing enough to control foreign ownership. The Whitlam and Fraser governments both wrestled with efforts to find the most effective way of managing foreign investment, and policies shifted during the period.

Labor's views were divided between the nationalist instincts of Connor – for whom the major issue facing Australia in the 1974 election was 'Who owns Australia? How do we stem the tide? How do we turn it back?'[127] – and the greater pragmatism of Whitlam, Crean and, especially, Whitlam's final treasurer, Bill Hayden.

Whitlam extended laws introduced by McMahon to regulate foreign takeovers and ensure maximum Australian equity in new investments. The Fraser government's response differed only in tone and scale. It modified some of Labor's rules but largely continued policies with regard to non-bank financial institutions and insurance companies, new large mining and natural resources projects, and some real estate.[128]

A farmer himself, and close to his rural Coalition partners, Fraser brought to the debate a strong identification with the complaints of the agricultural exporters. Like Whitlam, he saw advantages for Australia in resources diplomacy: 'Australia is a resource-rich country in a resource-tight world,' he noted.[128] He appointed John Howard as Minister for Special Trade Negotiations in 1977 to deal with the EEC, whose Common Agricultural Policy continued to distort world markets by limiting Australian agricultural exports to Europe while subsidising its own exports to other countries.

A good deal of Fraser's foreign policy energy, particularly in 1978, was directed towards arguing directly to the Europeans and North Americans the case for the developed countries to take greater account of the developing world. He supported compulsory direct funding by governments of the Common Fund, which he saw as something like the Australian wool price stabilisation scheme. For Fraser, this was a strategic as well as a humanitarian argument. As he told an audience at the University of South Carolina in 1981, his position was not typical. He had taken, from the beginning, a tough line on East–West relations but an accommodating position on North–South issues: 'I believe ... that the two sets of issues are closely interlinked, that what happens or equally importantly what does not happen, with respect to one will have crucial implication in what happens to the other.'[130]

A measure of his interest in the Third World was the appointment in April 1978 of a high-level Committee on Australia's Relations with the Third World, chaired by Owen Harries, a distinguished international relations academic who had become an influential adviser to Peacock and Fraser. The purpose of the review was to identify Australia's policy options with this group of states. Its recommendations were sensible and comprehensive but it was a mark of the times that it was done at all. An element of the report's conclusions that was reflected in the foreign policy of the Fraser government generally was its insistence, like Whitlam's, on an Australian international identity separate from that of the West in general. 'We must be as ready to disaggregate "the West" as we are to disaggregate the Third World,' the report advised. 'Sometimes what is called Western policy reflects no more than the particular interests of one or two Western countries, from which Australian interests may differ markedly.'[131]

But for all the effort the Fraser government devoted to the issue, the results were limited. The New International Economic Order was a regulation-based, not market-driven, response to the problems of economic development. Globalisation would soon enough change the nature of the debate profoundly.

The rules-based order

Whitlam, a lawyer, regarded the framework provided by a rules-based international order as central to Australia's interests. He and Labor also saw it as a means by which the Commonwealth's responsibility for 'external affairs' under section 51 of the constitution might be used to bring about changes in domestic policy that were otherwise state responsibilities.

On 18 December 1972 he personally signed the two 1966 international covenants – on Economic, Social and Cultural Rights and Civil and Political Rights – that had flowed from the adoption of the Universal Declaration of Human Rights. To implement their provisions, he introduced a human rights bill, although this lapsed with the double dissolution in 1974 and because of fears of a successful High Court challenge by the states was not revived.[132] He ratified as well a number of important International Labour Organization, UNESCO and other conventions.

While less full-throated, the Fraser government's approach to the UN was also generally supportive. 'A number of the attacks on the United Nations have largely sprung from an unrealistic view of what the United Nations could hope to achieve … The problems faced by the United Nations in no way diminishes the need for all nations to support the organisation and make it a more effective instrument for peace,' Fraser told parliament in 1976.[133] With the inauguration of Carter as US president in 1977, human rights became the cornerstone of American foreign policy. 'Because we are free, we can never be indifferent to freedom elsewhere,' he declared in his inaugural address, expressing sentiments that would be closely echoed in the following century by neo-conservative policy-makers. The international focus on human rights intensified and, under Fraser, Australia became an active member of the United Nations Human Rights Commission in 1978 and supported proposals for the establishment of a United Nations High Commissioner for Refugees.[134] It joined the new United Nations Committee on Disarmament.

Law of the sea and Antarctica

Of all the international rules the international community was seeking to strengthen, none were more important to Australia than those governing the law of the sea. Questions of the extent to which a country could claim sovereignty over the seas around it mattered deeply to the island continent, which depended on maritime trade for its prosperity and controlled potentially rich offshore resources, including around its Antarctic and other territories.

Earlier international conferences to codify the law of the sea in Geneva in 1958 and 1960 had agreed that coastal states possessed sovereign right to explore and exploit the natural resources of the sea and seabed but had been unable to resolve how far that sovereignty stretched. The question began to matter more as global interest in the resources of the seabed grew from the 1960s onwards, and especially after the oil shock of the early 1970s.

In 1967 Malta proposed that seabed resources beyond the continental shelf should be declared the 'common heritage of mankind' and developed in the interests of all states. This was a novel legal concept and appealed strongly to the developing countries. In 1970 the UN General Assembly convened a third Conference on the Law of the Sea to establish an international regime for the seabed and ocean floor.

After extensive preparatory meetings, the conference met in 1973 with representatives of 160 nations.[135] One of the main tasks for negotiators was to decide how far from its shores a littoral state could assert full sovereignty over the sea. International practice differed. Like many states, Australia claimed a three-mile territorial sea. Most claimed six or twelve miles, some two hundred. Some archipelagic states, like Indonesia and the Philippines, which comprised thousands of islands, claimed sovereignty over all the seas lying within straight lines drawn between their outermost islands, and wanted to measure their territorial seas outwards from these lines. Such claims by Australia's neighbours potentially harmed its interest in securing maximum freedom of passage for its maritime trade.[136]

It was evident that the states which claimed extensive territorial seas would not be prepared to cede those claims unless they were compensated in some way. This generated proposals for an exclusive economic zone (EEZ) extending for 200 nautical miles beyond the territorial seas. Within this zone, coastal states would have the rights to explore and exploit resources as well as to control scientific research and preserve the marine environment. But all other states would enjoy freedom of navigation and overflight within the EEZ and the right to lay submarine cables and pipelines.

When it was finally ready for signature in October 1982 the draft Convention on the Law of the Sea, to which Australia had been an active contributor, was one of the twentieth century's most important achievements in international law. It determined the extent of the 12-nautical-mile territorial sea and the 200-nautical-mile EEZ; it established rights of navigation through archipelagic waters and narrow straits; it dealt with the conservation and management of living marine resources and established a marine research regime. It established a Tribunal for the Law of the Sea to settle disputes over the law and declared the seabed beyond the national jurisdiction as the common heritage of mankind, with an International Seabed Authority to control activities there.[137]

Sixty countries had to ratify the convention before it could come into effect. This finally happened in 1994. Because of Congressional opposition, the United States was the most important state to remain outside the convention, although it accepted its provisions as a codification of customary international law.

Australia's 200-nautical-mile EEZ gave it control over the world's third-largest maritime jurisdiction. As with any international treaty, these provisions all had to be translated into Australian legislation, and this meant dealing with the states. To resolve continuing differences with the states over the Commonwealth's earlier legislation to assert its sovereignty over the territorial seas and the continental shelf – the *Seas and Submerged Lands Act 1973* – in 1980 the Fraser government negotiated an Offshore Constitutional Settlement. This package of different pieces of state and

Commonwealth legislation gave the states responsibility for the regulation of offshore exploration and exploitation to the three-nautical-mile limit of what were now termed 'coastal waters'. Beyond that, Commonwealth legislation was responsible.

The 1970s also delivered progress on the rules governing the management of the resources of Antarctica, which, like those of the deep seabed, had begun to attract greater interest. Australia's claims to 42 per cent of the continent had, like those of all other claimants, been placed in abeyance by the Antarctic Treaty of 1958, but not abandoned.

Beginning with a meeting in Canberra in 1978, a new agreement was negotiated in May 1980 to conserve the krill, fisheries and other living resources of Antarctica. The Convention on the Conservation of Antarctic Marine Living Resources (CCAMLR) was the first international agreement to take an approach based on the ecosystem as a whole. The headquarters of CCAMLR were established in Hobart.[138] A temporary moratorium was agreed in the mid-1970s on the exploration and exploitation of Antarctica's potentially rich mineral and energy resources. The issue would return a decade later.

Nuclear issues

On coming to office the Labor government quickly signed the Nuclear Non-Proliferation Treaty and committed itself to the nuclear inspections regime administered by the International Atomic Energy Agency (IAEA). Although it accepted that nuclear weapons had a place in maintaining deterrence between the superpowers, it supported the expansion of nuclear-weapons-free zones and other measures like the 1971 ASEAN proposal for a Zone of Peace, Freedom and Neutrality in Southeast Asia. Concerned about the implications for port visits by the US Navy, it paid little more than lip service, however, to a New Zealand proposal for a South Pacific Nuclear Free Zone, launched just before it left office, foreshadowing further disagreements to come on nuclear issues between the two countries.[139]

Australia criticised above-ground nuclear tests conducted by China and by India, which tested its first device in 1974, but it was French atmospheric testing at Mururoa, an atoll in the Pacific, that concerned it most. Under the Coalition government Australia had already made its opposition to French testing clear, but Labor took a tougher position. In May 1973 it asked the International Court of Justice (ICJ) for a restraining order against French tests, on the grounds, among others, that radioactive fallout from the tests was potentially dangerous to Australia and therefore a breach of its sovereign rights over its territory. France, which had claimed an exemption for national defence matters when it accepted the jurisdiction of the ICJ in 1966, took no part in proceedings.[140]

The ICJ issued an interim decision in June 1973 that France 'should avoid nuclear tests causing the deposit of radioactive fallout in Australian territory' while a final decision was being made. France ignored the decision and detonated five nuclear devices in July and August 1973.[141] Public protests and trade union black bans on French transport followed. Australia sent a naval ship to join a New Zealand protest to the testing area and protested internationally. When France announced in 1974 that it intended to cease testing in the atmosphere, the ICJ decided that a dispute no longer existed and that it did not, therefore, have to rule on the case.[142]

The most complex policy questions Australian governments had to face in the nuclear area, however, were the consequences of the country's own desire to develop and export uranium. At the beginning of the 1970s, and especially after the oil price shocks of 1973, it seemed to many people that uranium offered Australia an important strategic resource whose value would grow as global demand rose. This belief was reinforced by the discovery in 1974 of the world's largest high-grade deposits of uranium oxide in the Alligator Rivers area of the Northern Territory, which was under the control of the federal government.

The circumstances under which Australia would develop and export uranium, and the role of foreign investment in it, were matters of continuing review and change under Labor. The minerals and energy minister, Connor, wanted to maximise the profitability of the uranium resource by undertaking processing in Australia. He banned new uranium sales contracts in the expectation that prices would rise. The Australian Atomic Energy Commission was given responsibility for developing the Northern Territory deposits in partnership with the government-owned Australian Industry Development Corporation (AIDC).

Before leaving office in 1975 the Whitlam government set up an inquiry, headed by Justice Russell Fox, into the overall question of whether Australia should mine uranium and the circumstances under which it should export it. The commission reported to the Fraser government in October 1976, with a final report in May 1977. Fraser accepted its principal recommendations, and announced that Australia would only export uranium to countries with which it had negotiated bilateral agreements that ensured its use was monitored by the IAEA.

To implement this policy, Australian foreign affairs, trade and nuclear officials began an intensive round of negotiations. By September 1981 bilateral safeguards agreements had been signed with sixteen countries.[143] But public disquiet over uranium mining was growing and feeding into broader concerns about nuclear weapons. The ALP shifted its policy to oppose all uranium exports.

The end of the 1970s

The 1970s were, in many ways, a sour and anxious time for Australian foreign policy. Nevertheless, by the end of the period the elements of a foreign policy that would be recognisably Australian for the following forty years had emerged. The Whitlam government had made changes that were urgently needed and Fraser maintained most of them, although the bitterness of the domestic political debate after the dismissal obscured the degree of continuity at the time.

Speaking at the end of the decade Andrew Peacock reflected that during his time as minister, since 1975 'international affairs have been largely dominated by economic issues, international recession, inflation, the drift towards protectionism, concerted pressure for economic change by the developing countries and the ensuing dialogue between north and south'.[144]

Australia's economic and political relationship with Japan had been deepened and the long and fruitful link between Asia's economic growth and Australia's energy resources had been forged. Australia had finally recognised China, and Fraser cemented the deal with the establishment of a subtler political relationship. By the end of the decade Deng Xiaoping had begun the most important economic reforms in Asia since the Meiji Restoration in Japan.

In Southeast Asia the Vietnam War had ended and Australia had begun to learn how to deal with its neighbours as a group. The Southwest Pacific had also changed, and new institutions like the South Pacific Forum were emerging. Papua New Guinea had been brought successfully to independence.

The ending of the White Australia policy and Fraser's openness to Vietnamese refugees, as well as the strong Australian position under both Labor and the Coalition on decolonisation and racism in Southern Africa, had shaped a new image of Australia in the world.

Whitlam and Fraser had each found themselves at odds in some ways with their major ally. With the United States and Britain withdrawing from Southeast Asia, the strategy of 'forward defence' had outlived its usefulness for Australia. It was formally buried by defence minister Barnard in 1973. What replaced it in Australia's doctrine was a greater emphasis on self-reliance and the defence of the continent and its approaches, but neither Labor nor the Coalition effectively defined what this new strategy might be. Under neither Whitlam nor Fraser were any Australian service personnel engaged in combat, and, notwithstanding Fraser's warnings about international dangers, defence spending did not move much. Between 1976 and 1980 it represented between 2.6 per cent and 2.8 per cent of GDP, roughly where it had been under Labor.[145]

The period also saw fundamental reform of the Australian intelligence agencies. A royal commission conducted by Justice Robert Hope was appointed by Whitlam in 1974 but made its final report to Fraser. Hope found the Australian intelligence agencies to be fragmented and poorly coordinated. They 'lacked proper guidance, direction and control'.[146] Fraser accepted Hope's recommendation for the establishment of a new and independent statutory agency – the Office of National Assessments (ONA) – which would report to the prime minister and provide the government with independent analysis and assessment of global political, economic and strategic developments. That turned out to be a mixed blessing when the new Office delivered an assessment of the Soviet invasion of Afghanistan out of tune with his own judgements.[147]

On Christmas Day 1979, 10,000 Soviet troops crossed the border into Afghanistan to try to impose order on the fratricidally divided Marxist regime which had been in power since April 1978 and which was already facing a growing Islamist resistance. KGB special units attacked the Presidential Palace, killing the president and many of those around him. A new man was installed.[148] The frail Soviet leader, Leonid Brezhnev, expected it all to be over 'in three or four weeks'.[149]

President Carter's national security adviser, Zbigniew Brzezinski, had spoken a year earlier of an 'an arc of crisis' stretching along the shores of the Indian Ocean, but it was the Soviet invasion of Afghanistan that fundamentally altered perceptions that the balance of power in the world was changing in Moscow's favour. For Fraser, the Soviet actions vindicated all he had been saying for a decade about the dangers of détente and the threat posed by the Russians. They posed 'dangers to world peace greater than any in the last

35 years'. The invasion gave Moscow the potential to 'gain control of, or influence over, Middle East oil production, that would enable it to destroy the economies of the advanced world'.[150]

Neither he nor the Americans nor the Russians themselves foresaw the role this catastrophic error would have on bringing an end to the Cold War and to the Soviet Union itself. That required a different cast of characters and a different decade.

6

OPENING UP: THE 1980s

T he prime minister heard the news that thousands of Soviet troops had invaded Afghanistan on 27 December 1979, when the head of his department telephoned him at his rural property, Nareen, in western Victoria. For Malcolm Fraser, the action was incontrovertible evidence of the dangerous Soviet expansionism about which he had been warning for so long. 'In the first weeks of 1980,' he told parliament, 'the world is facing probably its most dangerous international crisis since World War II.'[1] From Afghanistan, he asserted, Soviet forces would be in a position to control the Strait of Hormuz leading into the Persian Gulf and the sea lanes of the Indian Ocean, especially given the uncertainty in Iran, where radical student followers of the Islamic revolutionary government of the Ayatollah Khomeini had recently seized US diplomats as hostages. These developments, Fraser was convinced, changed 'substantially for the worse the strategic order underpinning Australia's security'.[2]

The ripples of the Soviet invasion would shape the world. Impossible as it seemed in 1979, in just ten years the Cold War would be over. But the process of getting there was to be hard and, at times, dangerous. For most of the decade a Labor government in Canberra had the difficult task of managing its relationship with a conservative administration in Washington while holding true to reforming foreign policy objectives. The result would be a reframing of the basis of the ANZUS alliance. New issues like the environment appeared on the international agenda and required the development of new rules and approaches. Underpinning all Australia's foreign policy through the period, however, was the pressing need to restructure a domestic economy that could no longer deliver the growth and innovation the country required. The great economic reforms of the period were mirrored and supported by a foreign policy designed to open Australia to the region around it.

But that was still to come. To help shore up a common response to the Soviet move Fraser quickly arranged to visit Washington and Western Europe. What was needed, he said on his return, was a clear demonstration of international resolve to meet the new challenge. This was particularly important in the case of the United States, he added pointedly, 'not only because of its indispensable leadership role but because – and to say this is only to state the obvious – the twin traumas of Vietnam and Watergate have undermined the credibility of American resolve in recent years'.[3] In fact, President Jimmy Carter had already sharpened the American response by declaring on 23 January that an attempt by any outside force to gain control of the Persian Gulf region would be regarded as an assault on the vital interests of the United States and would be repelled by any means.

The Australian government responded with a series of sanctions on the Soviet Union, including a ban on Soviet naval visits and the withdrawal of fisheries approvals. Trade, as so often, was trickier. Australia agreed not to fill any gap in wheat exports caused by a US ban that Carter had instituted, but Fraser emphasised that 'the essential criterion must be the effectiveness of the measures taken in terms of their impact on the Soviet Union'.[4] With time, the dilemma over Canberra's response to the American grain embargo became easier to manage, as Carter's political opponent in the coming elections, Reagan, declared he would lift it.

The Opposition was more cautious in its reading of the invasion of Afghanistan than Fraser. Its leader, Bill Hayden, emphasised Labor's opposition to the Soviet move and its concern about its implications, but he interpreted Moscow's actions as a sign of its paranoid concerns about its own border security and a mark of its weakness rather than an attempt to seize oil supplies or 'a confident step in an expansionist drive' to a warm water port.

But in sport-obsessed Australia, it was Fraser's proposed boycott of the Olympic Games in Moscow in July 1980 that attracted most public interest and overshadowed the issue of Afghanistan. The government decided it would not itself prohibit athletes attending but passed the decision-making to the Australian Olympic Committee, which voted narrowly against a boycott, leaving individual sporting bodies to decide for themselves. The sporting community and the

Australian public were deeply divided. In the end, 120 Australian competitors competed in Moscow under the Olympic, not the Australian, flag.

More important for Fraser were measures to help strengthen the Western alliance and the military balance against the Soviet Union. He declared that Australia would increase defence spending by 7 per cent in real terms over five years and deepen military engagement with the United States. An ANZUS Council meeting, brought forward by several months to February, agreed to intensify operational cooperation. The Australian government offered home porting facilities for the US Navy in Western Australia and, later, staging facilities in Darwin for B-52 bombers operating surveillance flights in the Indian Ocean.

'Whatever can be salvaged of the concept itself,' Fraser had told the House of Representatives, 'the age of detente is now over'.[5] The clearest possible sign of that was the sweeping victory at the end of the year of an optimistic, confident, new American president, Ronald Reagan. Fraser, who had himself been returned for a third time in October, welcomed the change. He told Reagan at their first meeting in June 1981 that 'in recent years our societies have simultaneously suffered from comforting illusions about their enemies, and from doubt and uncertainty about themselves. The feeding of these illusions and doubts has become a major intellectual growth industry'.[6] In 1982 Russia was seen by 26 per cent of respondents to a Morgan Gallup poll as the greatest security threat facing Australia, easily surpassing Indonesia, which was next in line.[7]

Doubt was not a weakness from which either Reagan or the British prime minister, Margaret Thatcher, suffered. Thatcher came to office in 1979 and was re-elected in a landslide in 1983 after sending British forces to retake the remote Falklands Islands from Argentina. Australian policy over the next decade would have to respond to a tense global atmosphere, as these two leaders sharpened competition with the Soviet Union, but in a regional environment which was largely marginal to the great powers.

Southeast Asia

After the high dramas of the 1960s and '70s, Australia's relations with Southeast Asia settled into a steadier pattern. The ASEAN economies were becoming more industrialised and diversified. New notes of assertiveness were appearing. In Malaysia, for example, Dr Mahathir Mohamad, the prime minister after 1981, worked to shift Malaysia's interests towards Asia, particularly Japan, and away from the West. Australia had its own periods of tension with Mahathir when Hawke criticised as 'barbaric' the execution of two Australian heroin traffickers. More problems were to come.

For both the Fraser and Hawke governments a central problem in relations with the region was how to respond to the pressure from its closest partners in Southeast Asia to continue to support the ASEAN-backed opposition forces in Cambodia, which included elements of the Khmer Rouge. At the core of the Cambodian dispute was a struggle for influence in Indochina, principally between the ASEAN countries and Vietnam, but with Chinese, Soviet and American interests all engaged. A key objective of ASEAN diplomacy was to deny international recognition to the Vietnam-backed Heng Samrin government – the People's Republic of Kampuchea (PRK) – by ensuring that the former Democratic Kampuchea (DK) regime held onto the Cambodia seat in the United Nations. The ASEAN countries also wanted support for regular United Nations resolutions calling for the withdrawal of Vietnamese troops.

Australia had opposed the invasion, and was concerned by Vietnam's increasing economic and security ties with the Soviet Union, but the genocidal legacy of the Khmer Rouge remained a disturbing reality in the public mind. Fraser's foreign minister, Andrew Peacock, used the government's support for the seating of the DK in the United Nations as a token in his political rivalry with Fraser. Just before the election in October 1980, he threatened to resign, protesting that cabinet had not been asked to consider Australia's continued recognition of the Khmer Rouge. He agreed to stay only on condition that Australia withdrew its diplomatic recognition of Pol Pot's government (although it would continue to support its seating in the United Nations). This change was announced in February 1981. By that time Peacock had been transferred from foreign affairs and replaced as foreign minister by Tony Street. He finally resigned from cabinet in April 1981, at which point the story of his earlier threatened resignation was leaked to the press.

In 1982 ASEAN tried to address the public relations problem by brokering the formation of an uneasy new Coalition Government of Democratic Kampuchea (CGDK), bringing the Khmer Rouge under the same umbrella as the two non-communist republican and royalist resistance groups.

Bob Hawke

In contrast to Whitlam's victory ten years earlier, foreign policy was not an issue in the election that swept the ALP and its leader, Bob Hawke, into power in March 1983.

Hawke's name was well known to most Australians long before he became prime minister. The son of a Congregationalist minister, he was born in 1929 in South Australia and grew up in the West. Rising through the trade union movement, he became president of the ACTU in 1969 and a key figure within the ALP. By the mid-1970s the story of the bright student from Perth Modern School, Rhodes scholar, legendary beer drinker, good bloke and the nation's negotiator-in-chief, had become folklore. He was drafted into parliament in 1980, and then into the leadership of the ALP just weeks ahead of the 1983 election.

His rapport with the public – his 'love affair with the Australian people' – ran deep. The man he replaced as leader, Bill Hayden, recounted in his memoirs experiencing 'an instance of that extraordinary, indefinable personal quality of his ... the same quality he was able to transmit to the public in a great variety of ways. "Love me, trust me, you know you can depend on me ... and most of all you know I can't live without your love," seems to be its message.'[8]

Hawke came to the job with wide experience of international issues through his work with the International Labor Organization. His election policy speech pointed to a high degree of 'continuity, consistency and con-sensus' in Australian foreign policy.[9] The Labor government would pursue 'an independent and self-respecting foreign policy based on a cool and objec-tive assessment – hard-headed if you like – of Australia's genuine national interests', Hawke told the Washington Press Club a couple of months later.[10]

Any colleague or public servant who was around him for long enough would eventually hear the prime minister recount the adage that in the race of life one should always back the horse called 'self-interest'. At least you knew it was always trying.

The incoming government had learnt the lessons of the indiscipline of the Whitlam period, and Hawke's own qualities as an inclusive chair of cab-inet and a diligent administrator were a key to his government's success. He was not a centralising leader like Whitlam or Fraser. Ego, an essential quality in any successful political leader, may have been more marked in Hawke than most, but it gave him the self-confidence to work with the other strong personalities around him.

Differences of approach and emphasis were evident between the prime minister from the right of the party and his two foreign ministers, Hayden from the Centre Left faction, and Gareth Evans, with his deep liberal inter-nationalist instincts, but they complemented each other and worked well together. Hawke allowed his ministers space to act.

In any case, by choosing successively as his chiefs of staff some of Australia's most able diplomats – Graham Evans, Chris Conybeare, Sandy Hollway, Dennis Richardson – and with the backing of his longstanding international adviser John Bowan, and later Hugh White, Hawke helped to ensure that even when policy differences emerged with his ministers, these were massaged and managed through effective processes of the public service.

Australia has never had a prime minister more convinced of the power of human agency. Personal relationships were central to Hawke's understanding of international relations. He had high faith in his own ability to reconcile and bring together contending parties on the basis of enlightened self-interest. He saw opportunities everywhere – in the Middle East, in South Africa, in China. He wanted, Hayden wrote, 'to fine tune the major trouble spots of the world'.[11]

The three recurrent themes of Australian foreign policy – engagement with the region ('enmeshment' in Hawke's words), the centrality of the US alliance and support for a rules-based order, especially one in which trade arrangements were fair and open – were central to his government's policies.[12]

Indochina was a particular problem, however. The Labor Party platform committed the new government to resume aid to Vietnam, a policy that was certain to be opposed by the ASEAN countries, China and the United States. With memories of the foreign policy dramas of the Whitlam period still fresh in the ALP's collective mind, Hawke was looking for a way of avoiding an immediate confrontation on this matter.[13] He proposed to the new foreign minister, Hayden, that he should explore opportunities to resolve the stalemate in Indochina, an issue that was certainly central to the future security of Southeast Asia.

Bill Hayden

Hayden had become foreign minister in personally difficult circumstances. A former Queensland police officer, he had represented the Queensland seat of Oxley since 1961. After serving as a reforming social security minister and treasurer in the Whitlam government, and then as Labor leader from 1978, he had done a great deal to restore the party's economic and social policy credibility. With excessive self-deprecation he described himself in his memoirs as a 'grey personality'.[14] More accurately, he wrote of his 'natural diffidence of character some described as an inferiority complex, caution about others, a tendency to personal remoteness'.[15]

Just before the 1983 election which, Hayden memorably asserted, could have been won for Labor by a drover's dog, he was replaced as leader by Hawke, a man who 'had glitter and offered excitement'.[16] Given a choice, he decided to take on the portfolio of foreign affairs. Hayden had a restrained sense of Australia's national capacity: 'a small country ... [but] not without influence'.[17] But he strongly believed that the nation's interests embraced not only political, economic and strategic concerns but issues of 'moral duty' such as human rights, world poverty, arms control and the resolution of conflict.[18]

He unsettled his officials. He had, one of them recorded, an 'acute capacity to discern pretence, falsity and pomposity a mile off'.[19] For his cabinet colleague and successor, Evans, he was 'an extraordinary bundle of contradictions'[20] and 'quite irrepressible in wreaking his vengeance'.[21]

In temperament and outlook Hayden and Hawke were poles apart, but they complemented one another's strengths. 'There were not many important differences on matters of principle between us,' Hayden acknowledged.[22] As a leading member of the Centre Left faction, Hayden had the reputation for independence that was critical in shifting the party towards Hawke's more moderate positions on the US alliance, East Timor and Irian Jaya.[23]

So, despite his reservations about 'strolling into this particular pastry shop and upsetting the wares so carefully if unsteadily arranged',[24] Hayden took on the Indochina issue in a round of visits and discussions. Australia, he told parliament, should 'stake some of our national imagination on the development of broad perspectives regarding the future of Southeast Asia'.[25] The elements of an eventual deal on Cambodia were clear enough. Any solution would have to incorporate Vietnam's withdrawal from Cambodia, some sort of guarantee against the return of the Khmer Rouge, an act of self-determination by the Cambodian people and the return of refugees. The restoration of normal relations between Vietnam, China, ASEAN and the West would follow.

There were lively confrontations at ASEAN meetings, including admonitions from the US secretary of state, George Shultz. Australia stopped co-sponsoring the annual ASEAN resolution on Cambodia in the United Nations in 1983 on the grounds that it was unbalanced in its treatment of Vietnam and the Khmer Rouge.[26] In 1986 Hayden proposed the idea of 'some sort of tribunal to determine once and for all the culpability of the Pol Pot leadership'.[27] The idea of such a tribunal attracted international interest but strong opposition from ASEAN. A series of seminars at Griffith University brought together all parties to the conflict except the Khmer

Rouge. By 1989 Australia was delivering the largest bilateral aid program in Cambodia, channelled through an unofficial office of Australian aid groups.[28]

In the end, Hayden's efforts got nowhere. As his chief adviser (and future secretary of the department), Michael Costello, commented later: 'Regional balance of power considerations and American passion and emotion meant that it just wasn't possible to shift anybody. It just wasn't.'[29]

Still, the efforts were far from fruitless. Australian actions – including the Fraser government's de-recognition of the Vietnam-supported government in Phnom Penh – gave it standing in the discussions of the future of Cambodia. Hayden's work kept the international focus on Cambodia and pointed to ways forward. The Australian foreign policy bureaucracy and academics developed a solid understanding of the issues involved. The foundations were laid for the active Australian diplomacy that would follow within a few years when a changing alignment of international interests made different outcomes possible.

Indonesia

Relations with Australia's closest Southeast Asian neighbour, Indonesia, remained the most difficult for Australia to manage. Concerns about East Timor and the killings of journalists at Balibo ran deeply in the media and within the Labor Party. The 1984 ALP conference came close to calling on the government to withdraw Australian recognition of Indonesia's incorporation of East Timor. Hayden had to grapple with what he later called 'a cluster of impractical or imprudent foreign policies written into our party platform in slacker times', including a retributive policy towards Indonesia for its occupation of East Timor, while trying to maintain a solid way forward in the relationship with Jakarta.[30]

From the early 1980s until 1988 Indonesia banned resident Australian media representatives. Tension deepened in April 1986 with the publication by the *Sydney Morning Herald* of an examination of the wealth of the Suharto family, comparing the president with his rapacious Filipino counterpart, Ferdinand Marcos, who had been forced from office by 'people power' demonstrations in February.[31] Indonesia responded by cancelling a ministerial visit, suspending visa-free entry for Australians and banning all press visas for Australian journalists. Recurrent concerns erupted about developments along the border between Papua New Guinea (PNG) and Irian Jaya, which Australia worried might bring it into conflict with Indonesia.

The situation became easier in 1988 when Gareth Evans and Ali Alatas each became foreign minister at around the same time. They formed a strong personal and professional relationship. 'Let's just stop taking the temperature of this relationship like a neurotic set of doctors,' Evans recalled telling Alatas. 'Let's just get on with issue by issue, one step at a time, rebuilding it and trying to find ways in which we can work together.'[32]

Annual talks were instituted between senior officials, and frequent ministerial discussions were held. The Australia-Indonesia Institute was established in 1989 to promote people-to-people links and understanding. But the most substantial achievement came with the agreement between the two countries to a treaty delineating the sea boundary between Indonesia and Australia at the resource-rich area known as the Timor Gap. Differences over where the line should be drawn had dragged out over nearly ten years of negotiations. They were now set aside and a new joint development zone created in the disputed area. Evans and Alatas signed the treaty in December 1989 in an aircraft circling above the Timor Sea.

South Pacific

In Australia's other main regional theatre, the Southwest Pacific, relations became more complex as the internal dynamics of the region changed. By 1981 most of the island states apart from the French colonies of New Caledonia and Polynesia were independent, but they were small and vulnerable. The threats Australia saw came from outside, and its policy objective was to keep potentially hostile external powers out of the area. But by the time the decade ended, it was the fragile politics of the island states themselves that were causing the greatest problems for Australian foreign policy.

As Cold War tensions grew, Fraser worried about Soviet encroachment. He saw dangers in the emergence of a more non-aligned foreign policy in Vanuatu under Prime Minister Walter Lini and the establishment of diplomatic relations between Cuba and Vanuatu. Labor, too, when it came to power feared that Soviet fishing activities might provide a cover for intelligence gathering.[33] Driving these concerns was the sense among Canberra policy-makers that the South Pacific was Australia's backyard, the place where it was expected to fulfil its broader responsibilities as a Western ally.

In late 1986 and early 1987, contacts between political figures in Vanuatu and the New Caledonia independence movement and agents of the radical Libyan government of Muammar Gaddafi, which was aiding terrorist groups in the Middle East and Europe, became an unexpected source of Australian anxiety.

Fearing that a Libyan People's Bureau would be established in Port Vila, Australia expelled its own Libyan diplomats. Hayden made a dramatic dash across the Tasman in May 1987 to try to persuade a sceptical David Lange, the New Zealand prime minister, to join Australia in regional action.[34] Australian diplomats were dispatched into the region to spread the message.

Although the Libyan panic subsided, French colonialism remained a source of tension, especially after the appointment of the uncompromising Gaullist Jacques Chirac as prime minister of France in 1986. Chirac took a harder line against demands for Kanak independence in New Caledonia, and the Hawke government responded by supporting regional efforts to reinscribe New Caledonia on the United Nations list of non-self-governing territories. Relations between Canberra and Paris, already complicated by differences over nuclear testing and agricultural subsidies, were strained. The French banned ministerial exchanges and expelled the Australian consul-general from Noumea. Things improved again after 1988 when Chirac's successor, the socialist Michel Rocard, negotiated an agreement between loyalists and separatists providing for a ten-year delay until a vote on self-government in New Caledonia.

But it was regional rather than external players who caused the greatest difficulties for Australia and foreshadowed problems to come. In May 1987 Sitiveni Rabuka, a lieutenant-colonel in the Fiji military force, burst into the Fiji parliament with a group of masked and armed gunmen to unseat the newly elected government of Timoci Bavadra, which was dominated by Fijians of Indian descent.

The coup came as a surprise to Australia, challenging its assumptions about a peaceful and democratic region. With 4000 Australian tourists in Fiji, the defence minister, Kim Beazley, and the government contemplated using Australian military assets to evacuate Australians, to rescue the deposed prime minister or even to intervene militarily. Naval ships were sent to the area and troops placed on stand-by.[35] But no-one could be sure that military intervention would achieve any of Australia's policy aims. In any case, the Australian Defence Force's amphibious capability was revealed to be limited, an issue that would be addressed in the defence white paper to come.

When Rabuka's first coup failed to deliver the wholesale changes to the constitution he wanted, he had another go in September, declaring a republic and taking Fiji out of the Commonwealth. The dilemma Australian

policy-makers faced in Fiji (and which their successors would also confront) was how to respond to a challenge to democracy in their own
neighbourhood. The coup makers seemed to have the support of indigenous Fijians, most of whom saw them as defending their rights. Other
regional governments were mostly relaxed, arguing that the Fijians should
be left alone to sort out their own problems. So although political and economic sanctions by Australia would send a strong message of support for
democracy, they might marginalise other Australian interests. What, finally,
did 'democracy' mean in the context of South Pacific societies?

A minute prepared for cabinet in September outlined the dilemma. If
Australia were to cut its longstanding defence relations with Fiji, 'Rabuka
would clearly look to alternative sources of military assistance, some of
which could be damaging to our strategic interests'. Furthermore, regional
countries saw this as an assertion of indigenous rights: 'If we take a hard line
towards Fiji, this is very likely to provide opportunities to others, particularly France, to usurp our influence and possibly some of our commercial
opportunities.'[36]

So, after early attempts to marshal opposition through the South Pacific
Forum and the Commonwealth, the Australian government eventually rejected
calls for harsher responses, including economic sanctions. By August 1990
Hawke was again meeting formally with Ratu Mara, the former leader who had
been returned to power as acting prime minister by the coup plotters.

Fiji was not the only problem. In April 1988 riots in Vanuatu's capital of
Port Vila led the prime minister, Walter Lini, to request Australian assistance. Riot control equipment was quickly dispatched.

The greatest difficulties emerged with Australia's closest neighbour,
PNG. It was accepted that the relationship, to which proximity, aid dependence and colonial history each added their own complex notes, needed to
be placed on a more formal footing. Several efforts were made to do this.

In 1984 Sir Gordon Jackson, a distinguished businessman, had conducted the first extensive review of the Australian aid program, central to
the relationship with the South Pacific as a whole. The Jackson Report's
recommendations, largely accepted by the government, included a clearer
statement of the objectives of the aid program, a greater regional focus,
more professionalism in its management and an aspirational goal of providing 0.7 per cent of national income as development assistance. For
PNG, Australia's largest aid recipient (it received assistance worth $8 bil-
lion in 1990 prices between 1975 and 1992),[37] the report recommended a

transition from direct budget support – in effect, a cheque to the central government – to support for individual aid projects.

In December 1987 Hawke and the PNG prime minister, Paias Wingti, signed a Joint Declaration of Principles on the conduct of the bilateral relationship. Using language similar to that in the Five Power Defence Arrangements with Singapore and Malaysia, it included a stronger commitment by Australia to the defence of PNG. The two governments agreed that in the event of external attack they would consult for the purposes of 'deciding what measures should be taken, jointly or separately, in relation to that attack'.[38]

In contrast to Hayden, whose interest in the South Pacific was limited, Evans gave it a high priority, setting off on a visit to all regional countries soon after he took office and articulating in September 1988 a policy framework he branded as 'constructive commitment'. This meant respect for the sovereignty of regional states, partnership and mutual respect.[39] Evans and Beazley worked well together, but there were discernible differences between them on the possible use of Australian military assets in Fiji and on the PNG island of Bougainville.

From around 1988 tensions over the distribution of benefits from the giant Bougainville Copper mine had been growing between landowners and the mine owners. A resistance force calling itself the Bougainville Revolutionary Army and demanding secession from PNG had begun acts of sabotage against the mine. Violent clashes broke out between the rebels and the PNG police. In March 1989 the mine (which provided 17 per cent of PNG's national revenue)[40] was closed. The Papua New Guinea Defence Force (PNGDF) was sent in to maintain order, but instead caused further problems.

The conflict raised serious issues for Australia. The mine was a subsidiary of an Australian company, Rio Tinto, and Australia had a consular interest in the fate of around 850 Australians working on the island. These individuals were eventually evacuated in civilian aircraft, although planning was in train for an Australian military operation to get them out. Australia faced a deeper strategic question: how much did it matter to its national interests that PNG remained as a single unified state? The answer at the time was that the balance of those interests weighed heavily in favour of the central government in Port Moresby.

In January 1990 Australia announced new defence support for PNG, including $12 million to finance an expansion of the defence force by 450 soldiers and the supply of four Iroquois helicopters to be used for transport and reconnaissance purposes.[41] Evans noted that the fragmentation of the country was an outcome 'we would like to see avoided at all costs'.[42]

But those costs, political as well as financial, were rising. The next month, news emerged that the helicopters had been used to strafe villages and then to transport and dump at sea the bodies of armed Bougainvilleans who had been tortured and executed by PNGDF members. The problems on Bougainville were rising.

Internationalising the economy

It was the economy, not foreign policy, that had driven Fraser from office in 1983. By the early 1980s Australia was in recession. This, it was true, reflected a broader global downturn, but the longstanding rigidities in the closed, centralised and heavily protected Australian economy impeded an effective response. It was clear what needed to be done. In 1981 an inquiry into the financial system by the businessman Sir Keith Campbell had recommended substantial economic reforms of the sort that would follow later in the decade, but Fraser shied away from implementing them.

When Hawke became prime minister in 1983, the level of unemployment had reached 10 per cent, wages were skyrocketing and Australia's exports as a share of GDP had reached historic lows. It was clear to the new government that large structural reforms were needed.

From early 1985 the Australian dollar fell sharply as the world prices of Australia's export commodities collapsed, leading to sharp fall in the terms of trade (the price Australia received for its exports compared with the price it paid for its imports). The country was being squeezed out of global markets for high-value-added manufactures, intellectual property and services. Its share of global trade declined from 2.5 per cent to about 1 per cent, and it dropped out of the top twenty-five trading nations.[43] Net overseas debt was rising. In May 1986 the treasurer, Paul Keating, warned that Australia was in danger of becoming a banana republic.

The story of the reforms of the Hawke and Keating governments – the floating of the dollar, the removal of exchange controls, financial deregulation – is not the subject of this book. But their fundamental objective was to force structural change on the Australian economy by exposing it to international competition. The internationalisation of Australia that resulted had a deep impact on foreign policy. Foreign policy and economic policy became more aligned than at any period since the Chifley government and post-war reconstruction. The scale of Australia's international engagement expanded greatly during the two decades that followed.

The most visible bureaucratic sign of these changes was the decision in July 1987 to bring together into a single department the separate departments of Foreign Affairs and Trade, ending their decades-long rivalry for influence with the government and changing the cultures of both.

Australia appeared increasingly isolated in a world in which the West seemed to be coalescing into different economic blocs centred on North America, the European Community and Japan. The post-war trading system, with its focus on multilateral negotiations and non-discrimination, looked fragile. By 1987 Canada and the United States had negotiated their own free trade agreement. Across the Pacific, tensions were building rapidly between the United States and Japan over the persistent US trade deficit and the value of the yen.

In 1985 the European Community had agreed to move towards a single European market by 1992. Goods, services, capital and people were to be allowed to move as freely between the member states as within them. François Mitterrand, the president of France, and Jacques Delors, president of the European Commission, were pushing the political goal of the European Union.

Australia's basic trade problem with Europe was with the Common Agricultural Policy (CAP), a program that subsidised European farmers to maintain price levels above world prices and then compounded the affront by supporting them again for export, undercutting Australian producers. Australia wasn't looking for agricultural markets in Europe but it wanted to avoid losing them elsewhere. The new uncertainty was whether a single market in Europe would open up economic opportunities for Australia or just create a more tightly integrated protectionist bloc.

The American response to the Europeans simply piled on additional problems for Australia. Congress was already directing $50 billion in taxpayers' funds to American farmers, but in 1985 a new Export Enhancement Program was introduced to directly subsidise US grain exports to meet European competition.[44] The situation, Hawke noted later, was 'insanity: the costs of distortions of grain, livestock and sugar markets amounted to US$36 billion a year (in 1980 prices)'.[45] It wasn't only export subsidies to which Australia objected, but the whole range of barriers to agricultural trade. But Australia was small and of declining importance in global trading terms.

In the middle of the global recession in 1982, the eighty-eight member countries of the General Agreement on Tariffs and Trade (GATT) had met in Geneva hoping to launch a new round of global trade negotiations to lower barriers. But with the Europeans and the Japanese resisting American efforts to include agriculture, the meeting failed. It was a debacle, declared the Australian trade minister, Doug Anthony.[46]

A few years later, however, wanting to expand US markets and contain growing protectionist pressures brought on by an overvalued dollar and the huge trade deficit, the new American president, Ronald Reagan, sent his trade negotiators back to the table.

Under American pressure, GATT members agreed at a meeting in Punta del Este in Uruguay in September 1986, to begin negotiations on an ambitious and comprehensive agenda to lower trade barriers. Reflecting the changing nature of global production and trade, it included for the first time in such negotiations a range of new issues, such as intellectual property rights, investment measures and trade in services. The sensitive issues of agriculture and textiles and clothing were also included, as was a review of the functioning of the GATT system itself.[47]

A month before the Punte del Este meeting, the Australian trade minister, John Dawkins, who had been in the job since 1984, invited fourteen agricultural exporting countries, drawn from developed and developing economies on five continents, to a meeting in Cairns. The Cairns Group of agricultural fair traders, as it became known, accounted for 25 per cent of world trade in agriculture. Its formation helped ensure that the Uruguay Round included a broad mandate for agricultural negotiations.[48] In the arduous negotiating slog over the next eight years, Australia chaired the group and represented it in three-way negotiations over agricultural subsidies with the United States and the European Union. The newly integrated Department of Foreign Affairs and Trade (DFAT) provided much of the intellectual drive and research backing for the case for agricultural fair trade.[49] The Cairns Group was an important example of a successful Australian initiative in coalition-building and shaping the rules-based order.

The government's domestic reform program, particularly the round of unilateral tariff cuts announced in the May 1988 economic statement and further reductions in 1991 strengthened Australia's negotiating credibility in the Uruguay Round. Its international competitiveness was improved by micro-economic reforms of government utilities and the labour market. Services exports were increasingly important. From 1985 the government permitted overseas students to be enrolled without numerical limits in

Australian educational institutions. The results were immediate. In 1987, 9654 overseas students were studying in Australia; by 1996 there were 53,000. More than 90 per cent of them were from Asia.[50] In addition to its economic impact, the export of education would contribute mightily to deepening Australia's ties with key Asian countries and to the composition of its immigration program.

The conditions had been set for a period of sustained economic growth and more diversified trade. Asia, where growth was averaging 8 per cent a year from 1982, was central to that process. In speeches and papers like the 1989 report from Hawke's former economic adviser Ross Garnaut, 'Australia and the Northeast Asian Ascendancy', the case for 'enmeshment', as Hawke called it, was being made to the Australian people.

China

It was the decade in which opportunity replaced threat in the Australian view of China, though it was to end in a setback.

The economic reforms which Deng Xiaoping, the great survivor of the Maoist upheavals in China, had initiated in December 1978 were spreading out from the countryside and into the cities. In October 1984 new reforms gave greater decision-making power to managers of individual factories and began to loosen the allocation of workers by the state. The phenomenon of 'Factory China' was born. To the wheat and wool that had dominated Australian trade with China, the resources needed for China's industrialisation were being added.

Hawke seized upon the China relationship with enthusiasm as the centrepiece of his hopes of enmeshing Australia with Asia. Soon after Hawke took office, the Chinese premier, Zhao Ziyang, visited Australia and Hawke returned the visit in 1984. An important element in Fraser's interest in China had been the potential he saw for it to help the West contain the Soviet Union. Hawke made it clear that, for him, 'our relations with China are of great importance in their own right. They do not come about because of the interests we may have elsewhere.'[51]

He began to see the economic and political liberalisation underway in China as the most important thing that was happening in the world.[52] 'A substantial relationship ... acknowledging China's important role in the region and the world, should be central to Australian foreign policy,' he declared in 1984.[53]

He saw a special role for Australia and himself 'in augmenting international understanding about China' and helping to broker its economic and political entry onto the world stage.[54] Australia and China could provide a model for the sort of relationships that could be established by countries with different political and economic systems.

Hawke took pride in the close relations he established with the Chinese leaders, both Zhao, who accompanied him for several days as he travelled to the outer provinces during his second visit in 1986, and the party secretary, Hu Yaobang ('like a chirpy little sparrow ... a complete extrovert').[55] A stream of other senior Chinese leaders also visited Australia. 'It was acknowledged in diplomatic circles that no other leader had spent so many hours in direct, intimate discussion with the Chinese leadership,' Hawke declared.[56] Real power in China continued to reside, however, in the diminutive frame of Deng Xiaoping.

With his economic adviser, Ross Garnaut, appointed as ambassador to China in 1985, Hawke pursued the economic relationship and especially the potential for the integration of Australian resources and the Chinese steel industry. Wheat still dominated, but sales of manufacturing inputs such as mineral ores were growing. By 1986 China was Australia's fourth-largest export market after Japan, the United States and New Zealand. Australia was China's fifth-largest trading partner.[57] (Even so, and without any official help, Australia's two-way trade with Taiwan was as large as that with the mainland right through to 1993.) In 1986 a Joint Ministerial Economic Commission was set up to coordinate the plethora of committees and working groups which by then were scattered over the bilateral economic landscape.

In 1981 Australia became the first Western country to provide development assistance to China, which by 1988 was receiving more Australian aid than any other area outside the South Pacific and Southeast Asia.[58] Australia was also an important supporter of Chinese participation in regional and global multilateral institutions such as the Asian Development Bank (ADB), the Pacific Economic Cooperation Council (PECC) and the GATT. Australia became a testbed for China's overseas investment. By 1987 China had invested close to $100 million in Australia, mainly through a joint venture in the development of the Mount Channar iron ore mine in Western Australia and a 10 per cent stake in the Portland aluminium smelter in Victoria.

But in 1989 the romance was punctured. Hu Yaobang had been forced from office in 1987, blamed for responding too softly to an outbreak of student demonstrations. The news of his death from a heart attack in April

1989 was met by an outpouring of public grief. Students began to gather in Tiananmen, the central square in Beijing, to mourn and protest.

In May, finance ministers from across the region were due to arrive in Beijing for a meeting of the ADB with a visit by Mikhail Gorbachev, the reformist Soviet leader, to follow. Zhao Ziyang, who had replaced Hu as party secretary, pleaded with the students not to damage the Sino-Soviet summit. He was ignored and the students began a hunger strike. On 19 May, with Gorbachev safely out of the country, Deng Xiaoping, seeking to preserve both Communist Party control and the economic reform program, ordered the mobilisation of troops from the People's Liberation Army and the declaration of martial law. The 100,000 students in the square refused to disperse and on the evening and early morning of 3–4 June the troops moved in to clear them out. The number of students killed is unknown but the best estimates range from 300 to 2600.[59]

Shocked by these events, Hawke presided over an emotional rally in the Great Hall of Parliament House on 9 June. Reading from what turned out to be an incorrect intelligence report that students had been run down by tanks, he wept for those who had been killed.[60] Australia's relations with China were frozen. Ministerial visits including Hawke's own planned visit for October were cancelled, and aid and defence cooperation activities suspended. Without seeking cabinet approval, Hawke extended the visas of all Chinese students then in Australia. The prime minister's tears at the memorial ceremony, wrote his speechwriter, Stephen Mills, 'were also shed for the death of his dreams of a powerfully beneficial relationship with China'.[61]

It would take some time to restore equilibrium to the relationship, although the ban on ministerial visits was lifted in January 1990, following similar decisions by the United States and Japan.

Japan and Korea

After the successful negotiation of the Basic Treaty of Friendship and Cooperation in 1976, Australia's economic relationship with Japan continued to flourish. But structural changes in both Japan and Australia, along with American economic and political pressure, gave it a different tone in the 1980s and caused an old anxiety to be revisited.

As the United States worried about growing trade deficits with Japan (over $40 billion annually from the mid-1980s) and the undervalued yen, it put the squeeze on Tokyo to improve access for American exporters to

Japanese markets. Australia became collateral damage. On Hawke's first visit to Tokyo in February 1984, he was delighted to find in the new Japanese prime minister, Yasuhiro Nakasone, an outward-looking Japanese leader, well disposed to Australia and with whom he could establish his favoured sort of personal 'Bob' and 'Yasu' relationship.[62] Soon after the prime minister returned to Australia, however, Japan announced a reduction in the Australian share of the Japanese beef market to accommodate more American imports. Hawke protested: if Japan did not live up to Nakasone's promises that the US trade problem would not be solved at Australia's expense, he said, 'it would seriously jeopardise confidence in the relationship'.[63]

Australian mineral exports were also under pressure. The Japanese steel industry had not recovered from the global downturn of the early 1980s and was undergoing a major restructuring. As a result, prices and volumes of Australian iron ore and coal were already declining, but US pressure was now giving American producers an edge in the market. In some cases they were securing higher prices for long-term contracts than their Australian competitors.[64]

The problem for Australian trade with Japan was one the government had already identified more broadly for the Australian economy – its over-reliance on commodity exports. So Japan also became a test case for Australia's efforts to modernise its manufacturing as Hawke argued the case for increasing Japanese investment in export-oriented manufacturing industry. In 1986 and 1987 large business missions toured each country exploring investment opportunities.[65] Despite competing pressure from the United States and Europe, Japanese investment in Australia did increase between 1987 and 1990, helped by a rising yen which made the Australian dollar more competitive. But apart from the motor manufacturers Nissan, Toyota and Mitsubishi, most of this went into tourism, agricultural land, the cattle feedlot industry and Queensland real estate.[66]

The Japanese investment triggered one of the periodic waves of fear in Australia that the country was selling off the farm to foreigners. All the ambivalence about Japanese investment seemed to coalesce in a 1987 Japanese proposal that Japanese companies and research institutes should invest in building a futuristic new Australian city of between 100,000 and 250,000 people as a hub for high-tech manufacturing research, leisure and tourism. The idea was put to study but it failed to get traction. Its name – the Multifunction Polis (MFP) – was hardly designed to stir the imagination of the Australian people. It was to become a minor issue in the 1993 election campaign as the Opposition took up popular suspicions that the MFP would become an enclave for Japanese retirees in Australia. Nevertheless, the Hawke government largely resisted public pressures to restrict foreign investment.

The complications in the Australia–Japan relationship went beyond the economic. They also reflected global political changes. As Cold War competition between Washington and Moscow intensified after the election of Reagan, the United States looked to an increasingly prosperous Japan to carry a greater share of the defence burden in the Western Pacific. In particular Washington wanted Japan to increase its defence spending and take on responsibility for the security of sea lanes out to 1000 nautical miles from the home islands. In Nakasone, Reagan found a more enthusiastic and nationalist Japanese partner. These proposals were received cautiously in Australia, however. Was a more militarily assertive Japan a good thing, even as a Western asset in the Cold War? The Australian government was keen to encourage more active Japanese diplomacy in the region and to work with it, but calls for greater Japanese long-range operational capacity kindled in some Australians an old anxiety. Japanese government polling in Australia showed almost 60 per cent of respondents feared that a re-armed Japan might emerge as a direct military threat to Australia.[67]

As the government's strategic planning document, the *Strategic Basis of Australian Defence Policy*, put it in September 1983: 'there remain significant differences … between the strategic perceptions of Japan and the United States … Australia should not encourage the extension of Japanese defence activity into our region. There is a risk of displacement rather than supplementing of the United States presence there.'[68] Visiting Tokyo in July 1983, Hayden said, 'Australia would be concerned if – either as a result of the external pressure or internal decision – there were a shift in Japan's basic defence posture or a dramatic acceleration of defence spending.'[69]

Future prime minister John Howard, now the Opposition leader, took a different view, arguing in 1988 that Japan should review its constitutional constraints on rearmament, including the defence budget, and participate more actively in regional military affairs. 'I believe there is scope for a wider range of defence cooperation between Australia and Japan beyond what has currently been contemplated,' he said.[70] Changing views in Washington with the end of the Cold War and a reversion to more cautious Japanese leadership under Nakasone's successors took some of the urgency out of the defence debate. But despite the problems, trust and intimacy, as well as trade, continued to grow. After the 1989 ministerial committee meeting, Evans recounted one of his Japanese colleagues saying, 'Japan doesn't have many friends and Australia is one of them.'[71]

Japan's neighbour, South Korea, was also emerging during these years as a more important partner for Australia as it moved through a process of democratisation and away from the authoritarian leadership of the past. In 1987 a former general, Roh Tae-woo, was elected president in the country's first popular direct elections. The economic relationship continued to expand as Australia became South Korea's most important supplier of iron ore, coking coal and steaming coal. By the mid-1980s South Korea was Australia's fourth-largest export market.[72] Roh's political reforms opened up new opportunities for greater diplomatic cooperation with Australia. The clearest sign of this was Hawke's decision to launch a proposal for a new Asia-Pacific economic organisation in Seoul.

APEC

With the Asian 'tiger' economies growing, Japan's economic dependence on regional production chains deepening and new global trade negotiations underway, discussions about broader regional economic cooperation in Asia and the Pacific entered a new phase. New ideas, many of them from Australia, were being canvassed about what further steps the region should take. Region-wide non-governmental organisations like the Pacific Basin Economic Council (PBEC) were operating and, since 1980, regional officials had been participating in a regular informal dialogue with academics and businesspeople in the Pacific Economic Cooperation Council (PECC). Ideas for a 'Pacific OECD' or a 'Pacific Basin Forum' were coming from leaders in Japan and the United States.[73] In 1983 Hawke himself had called on regional countries to develop a coordinated response to global trade liberalisation.

But by 1989 no broad institution yet existed in which the governments of the Pacific Rim could directly discuss global trade negotiations and regional barriers to trade. On a visit to Seoul in January 1989, Hawke raised this gap in his discussions with President Roh and found an interested partner. As a result, a major speech Hawke was due to deliver to a Korean business forum the following day was rewritten by the 'concerted efforts of eight senior Hawke staffers and public servants sitting around a hotel between the hours of midnight and 4 am on the morning of the 31 January,' as Hawke's speech-writer, Stephen Mills, recalled.[74]

In his speech Hawke argued that the time had come 'to assess what the region's attitudes are towards the possibility of creating a more formal inter-governmental vehicle of regional cooperation'. A meeting of ministers to investigate this would be useful. He made it clear that he wasn't talking about an Asian trading bloc. The basis for economic cooperation in Asia would be 'open regionalism', in which any trade liberalisation would be extended to others on a non-discriminatory, most-favoured-nation basis, rather than the closed regionalism being developed in Europe and North America.

Hawke left questions such as membership and broad functions open for discussion.[75] The very name APEC – Asia-Pacific Economic Cooperation – (which did not appear in Hawke's speech) was a sign of fluid purpose: 'four adjectives in search of a noun', in Evans' memorable phrase.[76] The speech generated immediate interest and, after garnering polite support from his Thai hosts on the next leg of his visit, Hawke wrote to the heads of government of Japan, South Korea, the ASEAN countries and New Zealand, explaining his views and seeking their support for further talks.

Hawke dispatched the secretary of DFAT, Richard Woolcott, on a mission to consult all the potential members of the new organisation, including China and the United States, about its membership and purposes. A number of questions had to be resolved. Should China be in it? Although it was on a strong economic growth path, China was not nearly as central to the regional economy as it would later become. The associated 'Chinese economies' of Taiwan and Hong Kong were almost as significant. But would China permit them to be involved in an organisation of sovereign governments?

The ASEAN countries, especially Malaysia's difficult prime minister, Mahathir Mohamad, were worried that any new body might dislodge ASEAN from the central position it claimed in regional institutions. In Japan, responses were complicated by the different approaches of the rival bureaucratic fortresses of the foreign ministry and the Ministry of International Trade and Industry (MITI).

Perhaps most significant, however, was the question of American membership. The absence of any reference to the United States in Hawke's original speech had caused irritation in Washington. Hawke claimed later that he had never wanted to leave the United States out of APEC, but had thought it better tactically to leave membership open in order to prevent nervous ASEAN countries immediately spiking the idea.[77] This does not seem to have been clear to the Australian public service, however. A departmental briefing to Evans soon afterwards noted: 'we understand that Mr Hawke does not regard it as automatic that the US and Canada would be members of the proposed regional arrangement … although this question is to be the subject of further ministerial consideration.'[78] The result was that when Evans arrived in Washington on a visit in mid-March, he was met by a diplomatic bollocking from the secretary of state, James Baker, who 'laid the real mark of Zorro on me, slash, slash, slash.'[79]

These were the issues which Woolcott, one of Australia's most experienced diplomats and Asia hands, was tasked to resolve. He found broad general support for such a meeting, although caution about any institutionalisation or bureaucratisation.[80] There was a general disposition to include the United States and to find a place for Taiwan and Hong Kong. Arriving in Beijing just as the student demonstrations in Tiananmen Square were gathering steam, Woolcott found officials willing to go along with the fine legal distinction that because the new body was intended to be a meeting of economies rather than governments, Taiwan and Hong Kong – defined as parts of the Chinese economy – should not be ruled out.

In a remarkably short period as these things go, the first APEC meeting was held in Canberra in November 1989. The six ASEAN countries, Japan, South Korea, the United States, Canada and New Zealand took part, with an agenda centred on global and regional trade liberalisation and regional economic cooperation. It was agreed that further ministerial-level talks would be held in Singapore in 1990 and Korea in 1991. It was only at the third meeting in Seoul that China became a participant, under a deal by which Taiwan would be represented by its trade minister, not its foreign minister.

The successful effort to bring APEC, the first trans-Pacific governmental organisation, into existence was not the result of a precise blueprint or detailed pre-planning but fortuitous timing and effective, determined diplomacy. As Evans later said, 'Right from the outset there was a compelling logic for the creation of APEC. If it hadn't been inaugurated by Australia in Canberra in 1989, it was only a matter of time before some other country took the initiative.'[81] Still, Australia was there and ready to lead: big enough to marshal effective diplomatic resources, but not so large as to frighten others. This was the beginning of a productive new period of Asian regionalism in which Australian policy played a significant part.

The ANZUS alliance and defence

For Fraser, more than any of his predecessors, the ANZUS alliance formed part of a global coalition against a real Soviet threat. The United States alone could lead that response. So he welcomed Reagan's more robust approach and wanted Australia to play a part, but he had little of Hawke's capacity to identify emotionally with Americans and was cautious about the scope of Australia's engagement. He decided against committing Australian forces to work with the US rapid deployment force in the Middle East in March 1980 or to participate in British and US naval exercises in the Persian Gulf during the Iran–Iraq War.[82]

Hawke liked Americans and felt at home in Washington. (He was 'nothing if not consistent in his passionate support for all things American', noted Evans in 1985.)[83] But he came to power juggling two pressures on the alliance – painful political memories of the difficulties the Whitlam government had experienced over the American relationship, especially with a more assertive Republican administration in the White House, and a party and an electorate which by the early 1980s were more worried by global nuclear dangers than any security threat from Australia's immediate region.

It was one of the major achievements of Hawke's government to balance these various pressures so effectively and to craft by the late 1980s a new and robust model of the alliance. It would require the close engagement of ministers with rather different ideas about Australian security and foreign policy – Hawke, Hayden, Beazley and Evans – to manage this.

Hawke's early signals to Washington were designed to show that his was a different sort of government from its Labor Party predecessor. He left the Australian ambassador, Sir Robert Cotton, a former Liberal Party cabinet minister, in place in Washington, and on his first, early visit to Washington stressed the continuity between his government's approach to the American relationship and the Coalition's.[84]

But the platform on which his party came to power had insisted strongly on a more independent Australian approach to the alliance and to the joint facilities. It had emphasised the importance of disarmament and arms control. And there was a real domestic political imperative here. As the hopes of détente faded and the Reagan administration made clear its willingness to contest Soviet actions such as the deployment of new missiles in Europe, public anxiety about the dangers of nuclear conflict grew. Just three days after the Australian election in 1983, Reagan publicly described the Soviet Union as an 'evil empire'. The incoming government faced what Hayden described as 'an efflorescence of support' for disarmament and anti-nuclear issues.[85] Traditional Palm Sunday peace marches across the country attracted huge numbers of people – an estimated 250,000 in 1984 – and votes for a new

Nuclear Disarmament Party cut into Labor support at the 1984 election, when the party won a Senate seat in Western Australia. The putative role of the joint facilities in any nuclear exchange came under renewed criticism.

Hawke's response to this was to call for a review of the ANZUS Treaty to address the concerns of the left of his party while reassuring the Americans that the objective of that review was to strengthen the alliance. 'The years 1983–88,' Hayden wrote, 'saw an extraordinary, sustained effort to preserve the integrity of the ANZUS treaty as a fractious New Zealand set about unravelling it.'[86]

Hawke made five visits to the United States as prime minister. He established strong relations with the key figures in the Reagan administration, particularly the secretary of state, George Shultz, whom he had met earlier when Shultz was head of the giant American construction company Bechtel. With Reagan himself, the relationship was easy. While the president did not 'have a black belt for detail or for intellectual prowess', Hawke wrote later, 'he was rock solid on the elementary verities that would shape the world to be passed on to future generations'.[87]

On his first visit, Hawke told Reagan that he wanted to review ANZUS and open up a discussion about the role of the joint facilities. The government's aim was to describe more fully the role of the facilities and to place them in a broader context: as a central element in the stabilising framework of deterrence between the superpowers through their capacity to monitor and verify arms control agreements. As Hayden, whose influence with the left of the party was important, expressed it: 'I came to believe that in the interests of deterring nuclear conflict between the superpowers, we were obliged to support America. That commitment was morally driven: it would be immoral to claim neutrality and non-alignment on such an issue when most life on the globe could have been extinguished by a major nuclear conflict. In those circumstances one has to choose and I chose, but with the important rider that our support for deterrence was committed on the expected basis we would vigorously push ahead with our arms control objectives'.[88]

That approach underlay the statement about the joint facilities Hawke made to parliament on 6 June 1984: 'The government takes the view that the joint facilities directly contribute to the security that we enjoy every day and that this tangible benefit outweighs the possibility that risks might arise at some future time from our hosting the facilities ... . Australians cannot claim the full protection of ... deterrence without being willing to make some contribution to its effectiveness'.[89]

The MX missile crisis

One of the ways in which the United States was addressing strategic competition with the Soviet Union was by introducing into its arsenal a new long-range land-based intercontinental ballistic missile carrying multiple warheads: the MX missile. Fraser had agreed in 1981 that test missiles could land in Australian waters off southeast Tasmania and US air and naval vessels could stage through Sydney to monitor the tests, although no public announcement of this was made. The incoming Labor defence minister, Gordon Scholes, had endorsed the tests, although the landing zone was moved to international waters. Hawke confirmed the deal to Shultz and the defence secretary, Caspar Weinberger, on his first visit to Washington.[90]

But the weapons system, which the Reagan administration had challengingly rebranded the 'Peacemaker', was seen by its opponents as a destabilising new element in an already dangerous nuclear stand-off. In February 1985, on the eve of Hawke's second visit to Washington, the *National Times* reported on the Australian's role in the tests. The reports caused uproar in the Labor Party. Hawke at first refused to back down in the face of 'a bout of residual anti-Americanism and pacifist naiveté within the party',[91] but travelling in Brussels on his way to Washington he was persuaded in telephone conversations with right-wing factional leaders that pressure was building for a special conference of the ALP aimed at overturning the decision. He feared it would damage ANZUS. It was also likely to damage him. He agreed that Australia needed to back away.

It was an embarrassing backflip, but his friend Shultz came gracefully to his aid, telling a joint press conference when Hawke arrived in Washington that the tests could be monitored in a number of different ways and that the United States had decided to proceed without Australian support. The incident underlined the differences that still existed within the ALP over the alliance and the unexpected pressures that were being applied by its fraternal party across the Tasman.

New Zealand

In 1984 the New Zealand Labour government of David Lange came to power with a policy of banning nuclear-powered and nuclear-weapons-capable naval vessels from entering its ports. Longstanding United States policy was to refuse either to confirm or deny the presence of nuclear weapons on board its ships. The objective was to maximise their deterrent

value by keeping potential adversaries uncertain. The New Zealand decision amounted, therefore, to an effective ban on US naval vessels entering
the ports of one of its allies. Washington was worried that Wellington's
anti-nuclear policies would leach through to other, more strategically
important, partners.

Amusing, intelligent, undisciplined and unpredictable, Lange frustrated
his Australian and American interlocutors. His enthusiasm for the policy
was hard to read and early in 1985 he seemed to point a way out of the
impasse. He announced that if his officials could tell him that a visiting vessel was not nuclear armed he would welcome it. The United States then
proposed sending the USS *Buchanan*, a conventionally powered guided-
missile destroyer, which was as near to a non-nuclear sure thing as the US
Navy could offer, to New Zealand. Washington thought the visit would be
approved (and 'after carefully reading the relevant cable traffic, especially
that out of Wellington, I understood why', wrote Hayden).[92] But in the face
of a public and internal party outcry when the news got out, the visit was
declined. Hawke and Lange, temperamentally poles apart, got on no better
than Fraser and Robert Muldoon had done. 'I had in the end nothing but
contempt for Lange and his vision on this,' Hawke said later.[93]

After the *Buchanan* incident, the Americans declared that their alliance
obligations to New Zealand were suspended: New Zealand was a friend but
no longer an ally. The ANZUS Council meeting was replaced with bilateral
Australia–United States Ministerial Consultations, known as AUSMIN. The
shift required Australia to work out new ways of continuing to engage with
Wellington on issues such as intelligence sharing so that the breach with
Washington did not damage trans-Tasman defence links.

The ANZUS Treaty (now given 'a firm and unequivocal reaffirmation'
after the government's review)[94] was not, however, an objective in its own
right but an element in Australia's broader defence strategy. So any review of
the relationship with the United States also required some fundamental
rethinking about the balance Australia had to strike in its defence policy
between alliance and self-reliance.

Kim Beazley and the 1987 defence white paper

Immediately after Labor's second electoral victory, in 1984, Hawke had
replaced Scholes as defence minister with the 35-year-old West Australian
Kim Beazley. It was a job for which Beazley's training, psychological

disposition and interests fitted him completely. Son of a long-serving Labor Party parliamentarian, Beazley had been a Rhodes scholar at Oxford, then a lecturer in politics, before being elected as member for the seat of Swan in 1980. He embraced all the dimensions of the portfolio 'from the most abstruse strategic concept to all the hardware of war',[95] as Hawke put it, with knowledge, energy and something approaching delight.

Soon after taking office, Beazley sought an external review of Australia's defence capabilities from the Australian National University academic and former defence department official Paul Dibb. Designed to provide a basis and rationale for the structure of the Australian Defence Force (ADF) over the following decade, it was released in 1986.[96]

The report foresaw a benign security environment for Australia and expected that the nation would have at least ten years' warning of any substantial change. The strategy Dibb proposed to balance Australia's strategic vulnerability against the resources available for it to defend itself was one of denial. Australia needed the military capability to deny any enemy the potential to cross 'the sea and air gap' protecting the approaches to Australia. This meant concentrating on Australia's area of 'direct military interest', an area stretching from the Cocos Islands to New Zealand and the Southwest Pacific islands, and from 'the archipelago and island chain in the north' (that is, Indonesia) to the Southern Ocean, within which Australia should be able to exercise independent military power. The report recommended a further move of defence assets to the north and northwest of the country.[97]

The report attracted critics for its 'concentric circles' approach to Australia's defence, which was a far cry from the expeditionary aims of forward defence. Officials in Washington voiced suspicions. The white paper (that is, the official statement of government policy) that followed – *The Defence of Australia 1987* – presented a more conventional strategy of 'defence in depth', rather than denial, and a more regionally engaged focus in both Southeast Asia and the South Pacific.

'Self-reliance within the alliance' remained the theme, however. As Beazley explained to a Washington audience in June 1988, Australia's contribution to the ANZUS alliance gave it the 'technological edge we need to enable less than 1 per cent of the earth's population to guard 12 per cent of its surface. Without this help, Australia cannot sustain a self-reliant defence posture in this fundamental way, our alliance is literally essential to our self-reliance'.[98] Like many of its predecessors and successors, the white paper's defence spending estimates proved optimistic. Instead of the real growth of 3.1 per cent which the white paper anticipated over the years 1989 to 1991, actual growth was closer to zero.[99]

Elements of difference remained between Australia and the United States – over the Reagan administration's policies in Central America, over the South Pacific Nuclear-Free Zone proposal and over Indochina. Australia declined to participate in Reagan's March 1983 Strategic Defense Initiative – the so-called Star Wars program to develop land- and space-based missile defences against intercontinental ballistic missiles – an approach that its opponents feared would undermine the basis of mutual deterrence by opening up the hope that nuclear war could be won.

And the warm rhetoric of the alliance was less evident in the area of trade, where strong disagreements persisted. Non-tariff barriers affected somewhere between 20 and 30 per cent of Australian exports to the United States, including dairy, meat, sugar, steel and some minerals, and Australia was seriously disadvantaged by the export subsidies American farmers received. Some Australians, including Hayden, asked why the joint facilities should not be used as a bargaining chip in the negotiations on agricultural subsidies, but Hawke would have none of it.[100] Even so, two-way investment continued to grow and by 1988 the United States was Australia's second-largest trading partner after Japan, although the balance was heavily in America's favour.

When the AUSMIN meeting was held in Sydney, just three weeks before the 1987 election and during the campaign period (that timing itself a startling reflection of Washington's comfort with the Hawke government's policies), defence secretary Weinberger told Australians that 'I think the military relationship is very strong, as strong indeed as it has ever been, and we want to keep it that way.'[101] Between them, Hawke, Hayden, Beazley and Evans effectively restored a bipartisan consensus to the alliance in Australian politics.

Disarmament and arms control

The other dimension of the Hawke government's remaking of defence policy was its plunge into an active diplomatic commitment to arms control and disarmament. It appointed an Ambassador for Disarmament, established a Peace Research Institute, supported the negotiation of a Comprehensive Nuclear-Test-Ban Treaty, worked on a treaty outlawing all forms of chemical and biological warfare, and drove the establishment of a South Pacific Nuclear-Free Zone (SPNFZ).

The initiative for a SPNFZ, part of Labor's election platform, was announced when Australia hosted the South Pacific Forum in Canberra in August 1983. Two years later, in August 1985, and helped by the election of the Lange government in New Zealand, the Treaty of Rarotonga was signed. The treaty banned the presence of nuclear weapons, their manufacture and testing, and the dumping of nuclear wastes anywhere in the territory of the South Pacific states, including Australia and New Zealand. To protect the ANZUS alliance, a specific exception was made for nuclear weapons aboard ships visiting ports, or navigating the territorial seas or aboard aircraft visiting or transiting. Even so, the Opposition pronounced it a nail in the coffin of ANZUS.[102]

The foundations were also laid for progress in replacing one of the oldest international arms control agreements, the now outdated 1925 Geneva Protocol on gas warfare. Efforts to do this had begun in the 1960s and had been given additional urgency by Saddam Hussein's use of chemical weapons during the Iran–Iraq War but negotiations had stalled. The Hawke government decided in November 1983 to support the goal. It took a series of steps including the convening in 1985 of the 'Australia Group' of like-minded Western governments seeking to improve controls over the export of substances used to make chemical weapons. A regional chemical weapons initiative followed in 1988, and in 1989 Australia convened a large conference of government and industry representatives from sixty-six countries to encourage the manufacturers and exporters of chemical equipment to commit to the elimination of chemical weapons and to cooperate in closing off avenues for their development. Hayden saw all this as 'a comprehensive program which allowed us to streak ahead and stay there'.[103]

The environment and the global rules

Environmental issues emerged as a new dimension of both foreign policy and domestic politics in the 1980s. Between 1972, when the United Nations convened the first intergovernmental conference on the environment – the Conference on the Human Environment in Stockholm – and 1992, when the Earth Summit was held in Rio de Janeiro, concepts like sustainable development, ecosystems and global warming all made the transition from the discourse of science to the world of international relations. Around the middle of the 1980s, dramatic demonstrations of environmental dangers like the explosion of the ageing Soviet nuclear power plant at Chernobyl and the discovery of a hole in the protective ozone layer over Antarctica brought the issue home to the general public all over the Western world. The green vote was beginning to have a political impact.

Efforts by the Tasmanian government to build a new dam that would have flooded the remote Franklin River valley, recently listed under the World Heritage Convention, became an issue in the 1983 election. Hawke promised to prevent the dam's construction. Following his victory, the Labor government introduced Commonwealth legislation to implement its international obligations by banning clearing and excavation work in the World Heritage area. The legislation was promptly challenged by the Tasmanian government, but in July 1983 the High Court decided broadly in favour of the Commonwealth. It found that the constitution's external affairs power (section 51 (xxix)) enabled the federal government to enact legislation to fulfil Australia's international legal obligations under certain conditions. The decision strengthened federal powers over the states in a number of areas that the Hawke and Keating governments would subsequently use, including World Heritage listing for the North Queensland rainforests.[104]

The Australian government became active internationally in most of the new global discussions on the environment. From a foreign policy perspective, Australia's particular relationship with the small countries of the South Pacific, so vulnerable to environmental change, gave it an additional interest. In 1989 Australia appointed its first Ambassador for the Environment, the former governor-general Sir Ninian Stephen.

Perhaps the most significant Australian contribution to the international environmental debate during this period came over Antarctica. In May 1989 Evans brought to cabinet a submission recommending that Australia sign the 1988 Convention on the Regulation of Antarctic Mineral Resource Activity (CRAMRA). Long in the negotiation, elegant in its legal approach, the convention was an effort to impose rigorous controls on any future minerals exploration or mining in Antarctica. Hawke, with the support of his advisers, took the view that any contemplation of mining in Antarctica's pristine environment should be opposed. He announced, to the surprise and irritation of the ministers most closely involved, that Australia would not be supporting the convention, but would instead press to preserve Antarctica as a wilderness reserve.[105] The decision was taken in a political atmosphere that was becoming increasingly competitive on environmental issues. The Opposition was already arguing against signing the minerals convention, and both major parties were competing with promises to cut greenhouse gas emissions.[106]

The decision to ditch the carefully stitched together minerals convention was not without risks. If the bid for a wilderness reserve failed, Antarctica might be left with no protection at all against mining. Australian ministers and officials set off to persuade and lobby. Given the recent history of antagonism between Australia and France, Paris seemed an unlikely environmental partner, but the French explorer and conservationist Jacques Cousteau had already expressed his opposition to the minerals convention and the treasurer, Paul Keating, had discussed the matter with the new socialist prime minister, Michel Rocard, in September 1988.[107]

Hawke spoke to both Rocard and Cousteau during a visit to Paris in June 1989 and received their support. President Mitterrand was a harder sell ('There was no "François" and "Bob" with this austere gentleman'),[108] but the French finally agreed.

The British and the Americans were opposed but Hawke received support from the future vice president and environmental advocate Senator Al Gore, who helped shape American attitudes. After a series of negotiations between the Antarctic Treaty partners, the Protocol on Environmental Protection (the Madrid Protocol) was finally signed in 1991. It designated Antarctica as a 'natural reserve, dedicated to peace and science', banned mining and made all activities on the continent subject to prior assessment of their environmental impacts. The ban was indefinite. After fifty years any party could seek a revision, but this could then be blocked by just one quarter of the current consultative parties. It may have been the most important of the series of contributions Australia had made to the preservation of Antarctica.

The Middle East

Of all Hawke's international interests, perhaps the one that engaged him most personally was Israel, a country he first visited in 1971. He had admired the leaders he met, like the Labor Party prime minister Golda Meir, and the work of its trade union movement. Hawke had been a key figure in the debate within the ALP during the Whitlam years over the party's approach to the PLO.

Out of Hawke's regard for the country and its people had come a broader interest in issues such as the efforts of Jews in the Soviet Union – the 'refuseniks' – to emigrate to Israel. In 1979 he had been embarrassed during a visit to Moscow by the 'vicious duplicity' of the Soviet authorities when they had reneged on a promise he had already announced to release a group of Soviet Jews.[109]

As a result of these experiences, and buoyed by his faith in his own strengths as a negotiator and conciliator, he was convinced that he was one of the few world leaders who could resolve the Arab–Israeli conflict.[110] On the day he was sworn in as prime minister, he told an interviewer he believed he might 'have a part to play' in the Middle East by making an official visit there.[111]

He was dissuaded by his staff from an immediate visit, but his interest did not abate. It was January 1987 before he got there, the first Australian prime minister to visit Israel and Jordan, and the first to go to Egypt since Menzies. He encountered a different Israel from the one he had first known, however. The Likud prime minister Yitzhak Shamir was a much less flexible leader than the secular Zionists of the Israeli Labor party, and relations between Palestinians and Jews were becoming tenser. By December that year they would erupt into the Palestinian uprising known as the Intifada.

The changes worried Hawke and reinforced his view that a settlement needed to be negotiated urgently. In discussions in Jordan, Israel and Egypt he talked privately and at length to his various interlocutors, some more responsive than others, about the need for an international conference that would bring in Israel and the moderate Arabs and a settlement based on Palestinian confederation with Jordan. The ground was not yet fertile, and his ideas did not find traction.[112]

Australia also became an important participant in the campaign to overturn United Nations Resolution 3379, which had equated Zionism with racism. This finally succeeded in December 1991. Hawke's long interest in the plight of Soviet Jewry was rewarded when, on his visit to Moscow in December 1987, and after intense diplomatic preparation, he raised the subject of the refuseniks with the Soviet leader, Gorbachev, and presented him with a list of names. The following day he was able to speak to a group of them at the Australian embassy and, just before departure, was handed a list of five whose release Gorbachev had approved.

This was the beginning of a much larger exodus of Soviet Jews, and in May 1988 the Australian Jewish community held an emotional reception in Melbourne for a group who had come to Australia. Hawke was the guest of honour.[113] To the shock of his audience, however, he chose this occasion to express his concerns about the future of Israel and the aspirations of the

Palestinians. 'The friends of Israel around the world are fearful that ... we may be witnessing again, after thousands of years, a giant, eyeless in Gaza. Is there not emerging the danger of Israel being blinded to the threat to its very soul and the vision of its founders?'[114]

Elsewhere in the Middle East, other forces were at work. In September 1980, war had broken out between Iran and Iraq, a resurgence of the deep divisions between Shi'a and Sunni that would plague the region in the following decades. Australia had economic interests at stake. Iran and Iraq were large markets for Australian agricultural exports and Australia continued to pursue wheat sales to Iran, restoring relations at ambassadorial level in 1985.

In a small but useful way Australia also contributed to peacekeeping operations in the region. After the 1979 Israel–Egypt peace treaty, Australia sent troops to the Multinational Force and Observers (MFO) in the Sinai (a non-UN force because of a threatened Soviet veto) and contributed personnel to the United Nations Iran–Iraq Military Observer Group supervising the 1988 armistice when that war ended.

Southern Africa

Hawke continued Fraser's engagement with southern African issues, but the diplomatic focus moved from Zimbabwe to the more difficult task of ending apartheid in South Africa, where the regime was tightening repression internally and acting aggressively towards neighbouring states. For Hawke, like Fraser, the Commonwealth was the vehicle for Australian involvement. At Commonwealth Heads of Government Meetings through the mid- to late-1980s, in Nassau, Vancouver and Kuala Lumpur, he worked closely with other leaders such as the Canadian prime minister Brian Mulroney and India's Rajiv Gandhi, with whom he became particularly close, to establish and apply a regime of Commonwealth sanctions in the face of formidable opposition from Britain and Margaret Thatcher.

At the 1985 meeting in Nassau, Hawke proposed the establishment of an Eminent Persons Group to explore prospects for a negotiated deal between the South African government and the African National Congress to end apartheid. Should such a deal prove impossible, a slate of new trade sanctions would be introduced. Hawke nominated his old political opponent Malcolm Fraser as co-chair of the group. By the time the group reported six months later, it was apparent that the South African government would not move, so further sanctions were imposed.

It was soon clear, however, that trade and sports sanctions would not be sufficient to end apartheid. At the 1987 Heads of Government Meeting in Vancouver, Hawke discussed with Australian officials the idea that financial sanctions could be a more powerful lever against the regime. Major loans to South Africa from American and European banks were about to be rolled over, and the South African economy would be crippled if it could not get access to international finance. At Hawke's request, the Australian-born, New York-based banker Jim Wolfensohn flew to Vancouver for a private meeting to discuss the possibilities with Gandhi, African 'front-line' leaders and the Commonwealth Secretary-General Shridath Ramphal.[115]

What followed was an extensive research and lobbying effort in which a senior Australian Treasury official, Tony Cole, was sent off to explore the possibilities of persuading banks and the US government to lend their support. Cole's work and the resulting book, *Apartheid and International Finance*, which was published in 1989 with Australian government support, were influential in building international financial pressure, which slowly began to grind down on Pretoria. Despite Britain's opposition, sanctions were ratcheted up further at the Kuala Lumpur Commonwealth meeting in 1989.

Full of enthusiasm for the Commonwealth, Hawke was less successful with another Australian initiative, to run Malcolm Fraser for the position of Commonwealth Secretary-General. 'I never had a harder task in my life because he had no small talk whatsoever – no capacity to communicate at any ordinary level with any human being,' despaired Evans, who was asked to coordinate the campaign.[116]

In February 1989 a new South African leader, F.W. de Klerk, had taken over from P.W. Botha as South African prime minister. In September he was elected in his own right with a mandate for reform. Finally, in February 1990 he announced that his country was 'irrevocably on the road of drastic change'. Nelson Mandela was freed from prison after twenty-seven years and the African National Congress recognised as a legitimate political party. The South African government was ready to negotiate the end of apartheid.

On a visit to Lusaka a few days later, Evans became one of the first Western ministers to meet Mandela after his release from prison. 'Of all meetings with all the leaders and other international figures I have had during all the years of my public life,' he recorded later, this was 'the one which gave me most joy.'[117] Apartheid was brought down by many factors, internal and external, but Australia under Fraser and Hawke played a consistent and serious role in maintaining international pressure. De Klerk and other South African officials noted the importance of financial sanctions in this.[118] In October 1990, in a visit that would have been difficult to imagine five years earlier, Mandela came to Canberra to express his thanks.

Europe and the end of the Cold War

A Conservative government was in power in the United Kingdom for the whole decade. Hawke and Labor had a relationship with Margaret Thatcher (who, in Hawke's description, was 'applied, committed, dogged, dogmatic, determined and certainly courageous'[119]) that was often tense but was in some ways easier than the one Fraser had had with her. Perhaps that was because expectations were lower.

Australia's slow drift away from Britain continued, though not without regrets in some quarters. In 1986 London and Canberra passed virtually identical legislation – the *Australia Act* – terminating remaining legislative and legal links between the two countries by ending the possibility of appeals from Australian courts to the UK's Privy Council and cutting residual connections between the United Kingdom and state governments.[120]

In 1983/84 immigration to Australia from Asia exceeded for the first time immigration from Europe, largely because of the refugee intake.[121] Remarks by the historian Geoffrey Blainey in 1984 calling for a slower pace of Asian immigration precipitated an intense public debate that showed how far the country had moved since the days of the White Australia policy.[122] By the end of the decade, despite public discomfort with some aspects of the speed and composition of the migration program under Labor, and internal debate on the conservative side of politics, most notably involving the future prime minister John Howard, the principle of a non-discriminatory policy was reaffirmed by all the major political parties.

Hawke had become prime minister just as the ageing and infirm Soviet leader, Leonid Brezhnev, died. Signs of a fraying Soviet system were already apparent as the world took note of the blundering actions and subsequent cover-ups around events like the September 1983 shooting down of a Korean civilian airliner, KAL007, with the loss of 269 lives, and the Chernobyl nuclear explosion in 1986.

Brezhnev's successors, Yuri Andropov, who died from kidney disease, and the enfeebled Konstantin Chernenko could not change anything. When Chernenko died in March 1985, the Politburo leaders finally turned to a younger man. The 54-year-old Mikhail Gorbachev came to office recognising that the Soviet system could not go on as it had. He brought a fresh face and new thinking to Soviet foreign policy, downplaying ideological competition and emphasising the need for economic, political, social and cultural reform.

Australian policy and intelligence officials, like their counterparts elsewhere in the West, were unsure whether Gorbachev and his policies of openness and restructuring represented genuine change in the Soviet system or were simply an attempt to modernise the state and strengthen the Communist Party's control. In fact, it turned out, Gorbachev was trying to do both, but could not.

In a major speech in Vladivostok, Russia's city on the Pacific, Gorbachev called in July 1986 for a build-up of the Soviet Far East and greater Russian integration into Asia and the Pacific. Talks on the Sino-Soviet border, which had been suspended for nine years, resumed in February 1987. The Soviet Union signed and ratified the South Pacific Nuclear-Free Zone Treaty and became a dialogue partner of ASEAN.

Hawke visited Moscow in November 1987. He was thrilled by his meeting with Gorbachev, which lasted more than three hours. 'The timing and extent of our discussions, the rapid fire way in which we were able to exchange opinions and information, the parity of views we held on so many important issues, made for a totally exhilarating experience,' he recalled.[123] Convinced that Gorbachev represented a sea change, he shared his impressions in a five-page letter to Reagan.[124] The Soviet prime minister, Nikolai Ryzhkov, followed up with a visit to Australia in February 1990.

Unfortunately, in the middle of all this reform, the first visit to Australia by an East European head of state turned out to be that of the brutal Romanian leader Nicolae Ceauşescu, who arrived on an official visit to Canberra with his wife in April 1988 as part of a complicated plan concocted by the mining magnate Lang Hancock and the West Australian Labor leader Brian Burke to sell iron ore into Eastern Europe. The visit may have represented the nadir of the Hawke government's foreign policy. On Christmas Day the following year, a decade after Malcolm Fraser had learnt with apprehension that the Soviet Union had sent troops into Afghanistan, the Ceauşescus were executed by firing squad by their own people.

1989

Reagan, who had fought the Cold War to the end but knew when to accept victory, stepped down in January 1989 to be replaced by George H.W. Bush.

Hawke told Reagan at their last meeting in Washington in June 1988 that the world could live more constructively at peace 'in very large measure ... due to his ideas, to his persistence, to his strength, to his determination to shape the agenda'.[125] Unanticipated by politicians, unpredicted by intelligence analysts, 1989 would turn out to be a transformative year.

On 15 February Moscow announced that all Soviet troops had left Afghanistan, driven out by domestic pressure at home and relentless resistance from the Muslim warriors of the mujahedin – 'those who wage jihad' – armed with American shoulder-fired anti-aircraft missiles and supported by foreign fighters drawn to the conflict from around the Muslim world. Across Eastern Europe – in Hungary, Poland, Czechoslovakia and East Germany – communist parties were swept from power. The Iron Curtain drawn by the victories of the Red Army in 1945 simply rusted away. The crossing points in the greatest of all the Cold War symbols, the Berlin Wall, were thrown open on 9 November and Germans from both sides of the city danced on top of it.

In one of the largest strategic calls of the twentieth century, the West German chancellor, Helmut Kohl, made it clear that, despite British and American apprehension, he would accept no outcome short of German unification. For a European Union whose focus had been on deepening economic and political integration, the question now became one of broadening its membership.

Other parts of the world seemed bright with new possibilities, too. On the right as well as the left, autocrats were toppling. Free elections in Chile in December replaced the dictator Augusto Pinochet. In South Africa, de Klerk, elected in September, began dismantling the apartheid system. In the same month, the last Vietnamese forces left Cambodia. When Gorbachev became the first Soviet leader to visit Beijing for thirty years, in May, relations were declared normalised; the Sino-Soviet dispute was over. In an influential journal article in the summer of 1989, the deputy director of the US state department's policy planning staff, Francis Fukuyama, detected the end of history.

The Cold War, which had dominated Australia's world and shaped its domestic politics since the end of World War II, was moving fast towards its end.

7

A 'POST-' WORLD: THE 1990s

We were living in what seemed, in so many ways, to be a 'post-' world – Post-Cold War, post-modern, post-industrial ... Our language reflected our uncertainty about what was coming next.

PAUL KEATING, *ENGAGEMENT*

As the Berlin Wall fell and the Soviet Union disintegrated, Australian policy-makers faced a hopeful but uncertain new world. The two years since he had become foreign minister, Gareth Evans told the *Age* in October 1990, had been 'quite simply the most exciting ... in international affairs in this century and possibly the last two centuries since the French Revolution'.[1] The possibilities were great, and Australian foreign policy-makers – Evans and Paul Keating especially – foraged, poked, prodded and pursued opportunities, from building new structures for economic and security cooperation in Asia and global arms control to state-building in Cambodia. But the uncertainties were also great. Australia faced a 'more complex, fluid and less certain' world, the government's 1993 strategic review declared.[2]

In private, Australian leaders wondered what role the United States would now play. The great struggle with the Soviet Union had been the challenge that kept America engaged in the world at the end of World War II. Now the Cold War was over, how would Washington respond? Would it, Keating wondered, 'simply drift further and further towards its own shores, until its forces ended up in San Diego'?[3] That concern was bipartisan. 'Over time,' declared the Coalition defence policy in 1992, 'it is clear that the US military presence in the region will decline.'[4] It would not be wise, Evans told the Senate, 'to assume the United States will continue to maintain its present level of security activity in this part of the world'.[5]

The Cold War had been a perilous time, certainly, but its protagonists had finally, tenuously, learnt how to manage it. The fear that regional disputes might escalate to nuclear exchanges had helped hold conflicts in places like Angola and Afghanistan in check. What would happen now these restraining bonds had dissolved? How would China, Japan and the fast-growing countries of Asia manage their own relationships if the United States was not there as a broker and balancer?

It wasn't just the geopolitics that were changing. 'At the very core of the international system,' Keating wrote, 'subterranean rumblings foreshadowed a more profound change ... Like termites, the twin forces of globalisation and the information revolution were gnawing away at the struts and joists that had forever separated our national house from the world around it.'[6] You could see the evidence of globalisation in the expansion of global investment and trade. Direct investment abroad had risen from around US$50 billion in 1983 to US$250 billion in 1992, and the share of trade in the global economy had risen three times as fast between 1985 and 1994 as in the ten years before.[7]

Australia's response to this 'post-' world engaged three Australian prime ministers: Bob Hawke, Paul Keating and John Howard. It would end with a disastrous financial crisis that doused expectations of continued easy growth in Asia and precipitated the fall of Suharto's New Order government in Indonesia. The decade began with a flourish of hope, however, as the American president, George H.W. Bush, spoke of the possibility of a new world order 'where diverse nations are drawn together in common cause to achieve the universal aspirations of mankind – peace and security, freedom, and the rule of law'.[8] The first test of that order would be the world's response to an invasion of his neighbour by that perennial disturber of the regional peace, the Iraqi dictator Saddam Hussein.

The Gulf War and the new world order

On 2 August 1990 Saddam, pursuing an old claim, sent 100,000 Iraqi troops into Kuwait, bringing his forces right to the border of Saudi Arabia, storehouse of the industrialised world's oil supplies. In a promising sign that the United Nations might finally fulfil the hopes of its founders, the Security Council unanimously demanded Iraq's immediate and unconditional withdrawal. It imposed an embargo on all trade with Iraq and authorised the establishment of a multinational naval task force to enforce it.

Hawke, who had led the Labor Party to a fourth electoral victory in March but was now being stalked politically by his treasurer, Keating, was energised – and politically protected – by the war. The issues were large and the stakes were high. 'As the Cold War fades,' Hawke told parliament, 'the United Nations has moved back to the position its founders intended for it.'[9]

The government faced two interlinked questions: what help should it provide the United Nations, and what were the expectations of its ally, the United States? On 10 August Hawke advised Bush that three Australian ships would take part in the naval taskforce. They were being dispatched, he told parliament, not to serve the United States alliance but 'to protect the international rule of law which will be vital to our security however our alliances may develop in the future'.[10]

Saddam was unmoved by the UN's demands, and on 11 September Bush announced that the United States would use force if necessary to remove his troops from Kuwait. In response, Saddam seized all foreigners, including Australians, in Baghdad as hostages, threatening to use them as 'human shields' if he was attacked. Hawke saw opportunities to mediate and persuade. He was personally engaged in the developing crisis from the beginning, At Bush's request he telephoned the Canadian prime minister to keep him up to the mark on wheat sanctions[11] and toyed with the idea of personal intervention to try to negotiate a settlement with Saddam.[12]

By mid-November 1990 it was clear that war was inevitable; Hawke believed Australia had to take part.[13] In response to Iraq's intransigence, the Security Council passed a resolution authorising the use of 'all necessary means' against Iraq if Saddam did not withdraw by 15 January 1991. On 3 December Hawke told parliament that the role of the Australian ships in the Gulf had now changed from enforcing trade sanctions to supporting the huge allied ground force now being assembled in Saudi Arabia for Operation Desert Storm. The Australian naval vessels came under United States operational control.

In Australia, anti-war sentiment on the left was strong. The dispatch of Australian troops to conflict in the Middle East, which would become a familiar business after the turn of the century, divided the country. When the air operations against Iraq began on 17 January, parliament was recalled and in long debates on 21 and 22 January more than 100 members spoke. For all this reflection, the Australian contribution was, in fact, modest. A couple of medical teams and a team of naval mine clearance divers were also dispatched but no ground or air forces.

The air war over Kuwait concluded quickly and land attacks began on 24 February. By 28 February it was all over. Saddam withdrew his forces, having ordered them to set fire to the oil wells of Kuwait as they departed. President Bush, adhering to the terms of the UN resolution that had authorised involvement, halted his forces at the Iraqi border rather than pushing on to Baghdad.[14] There were no Australian casualties.

The new world order that had shimmered so alluringly did not follow, and global politics soon reverted to older and more familiar patterns of power. The experience did, however, persuade some American policy-makers that military force could be used to good effect and with limited cost to the United States. The ease with which American goals were achieved in Operation Desert Storm would not be repeated in the Middle East conflicts to follow. And, yet again, an Australian political leader found that public approval for his handling of foreign policy did not translate into lasting advantage. Before the year was over, the Labor Party had abandoned Hawke for Keating.

Paul Keating

After years as the hard man on the domestic economy, and with his mastery of economic arcana, Keating was widely assumed to have little interest in foreign policy when he came to office, defeating Hawke in his second caucus challenge by 56 votes to 51. Keating had been a member of parliament since winning the western Sydney seat of Blaxland in 1969 at the age of twenty-five. In nine grinding years as treasurer, he had, with Hawke, helped construct a new economic model for a middle-sized developed economy.

Neither the foreign minister, Evans, nor the defence minister, Senator Robert Ray, a tough, taciturn, right-wing Victorian who succeeded Beazley in 1990, had supported Keating in the struggle for power, but they kept their positions. The general direction of Australian foreign policy did not change.

But Keating saw the world in a different way from Hawke. Foreign policy, for him, was essentially just one more instrument to achieve a single, larger aim: to refurbish Australia as a modern independent state. APEC, education, enterprise bargaining, the push for Australia to become a republic, relations with Indonesia, compulsory superannuation and Indigenous land rights were simply part of that project. The issue of 'who we are' was an important part of his broader effort to open up Australia economically and socially. If (to put it crudely on both sides) Hawke saw international relations through a prism of human agency – personal connections were an important driver of how the world worked – Keating's default position was structural. Foreign policy was an exercise in international landscape design. And Asia was in the foreground. A disclosure is necessary here: the writer was Keating's senior international adviser from 1993 to 1996.

Despite Hawke's later claims to the contrary, Keating had long had an interest in Asia. 'We are a European enclave in the south end of the Asian region and our future, both politically and economically, is tied up with that region . . . Australia should have the complexion of an Asian country and not a European country,' he told parliament in 1977.[15] He knew a number of key Japanese businesspeople well from his time as shadow resources minister and neglect of Indonesia was one of the charges he levelled at Hawke in the challenge that brought him to power. It was not that Keating's views on Asia were greatly different from Hawke's (his 'engagement' was simply a broadening of Hawke's 'enmeshment'), but the single-minded focus on Asia was new, and the broadening was important because it encompassed a strong dimension of identity. If Australia was to succeed in Asia, it needed to tell a new story about itself to the region – about its national character as well as its economic strength. Australia would 'go to Asia as we are. Not with the ghost of Empire about us. Not as a vicar of Europe or as a US deputy. But unambivalently. Sure of who we are and what we stand for.'[16]

Keating's conviction that 'our head of state should be one of us' and that Australia should become a republic was part of that. Inevitably, the issue of the republic became caught up in the historical complexities of Australia's relationship with Britain. In February 1992, soon after becoming prime minister, Keating launched a swingeing attack on the Opposition for 'cultural cringe to a country which decided not to defend the Malaysian peninsula, not to worry about Singapore, and not to give us our troops back to keep ourselves free from Japanese domination.'[17] It was an early battle in the History Wars.

During the 1993 election campaign, Keating promised that if re-elected he would establish a Republic Advisory Committee to develop options for a republic. In September that year he went to see the Queen 'on the unpleasant errand to tell her, in all conscientiousness, that we didn't need her any more'. She received him in the tartan-carpeted Drawing Room at Balmoral Castle. Its furniture, he recalled in a personal note, 'had the colour of a woody lemon reminiscent of amboyna or Karelian birchwood.'[18] The committee, chaired by a future Liberal Party prime minister, Malcolm Turnbull, recommended that an Australian head of state should be elected by two-thirds majority vote in a joint sitting of both houses of the Commonwealth parliament on the nomination of the prime minister and the cabinet. When the Coalition put a similar proposal to the electorate in November 1999, divisions within the republican movement over the form of election, and the firm opposition of the prime minister, ensured its defeat.

Keating was a nationalist (although he preferred the term 'patriot'), but he was not a sentimental nationalist. He thought Australia had to make its own way in the world. He had high ambitions for the country and believed its experiences offered useful lessons, but he did not see it particularly as a light to others. The debate at the time about whether Australia should think of itself as Asian was irrelevant to him: 'Australia is not, and never can be, an "Asian nation" any more than we can – or want to be – European or North American or African. We can only be Australian and can only relate to our friends and neighbours as Australian.'[19]

His view of the world was one international relations theorists would recognise as realist – economic weight mattered and power moved the international order. He had a strong sense of Australia's strategic advantages: 'A continent to ourselves,' he would note meaningfully to foreign visitors: 'They're not making those anymore.' But the realism was not deterministic. He saw always, as in his approach to nuclear disarmament, the prospect that the world could be made better.

His foreign policy priorities were clear and limited: 'the building of appropriate multilateral institutional structures in the Asia-Pacific, encouraging an open international trading system and the development of Australia's relations with our immediate neighbours.'[20] He was happy to leave much of the rest of the agenda to Evans, whose energy he admired and judgement he trusted.

As prime minister he had little interest in the raw intelligence that can titillate some politicians. What mattered was the big picture. What could be built? Just as important as the design was the execution. He admired craftsmanship in all its forms, from late-eighteenth-century French cabinets to elegant econometrics. His description of the 1989 national accounts as a 'beautiful set of numbers' was an aesthetic as well as a political statement.

He was a seductive advocate, in part because he believed so fully in the cause he was pleading, even if the arguments varied with the interlocutor. The talking points prepared by his officials or staff were usually inadequate to the task. His language and imagery were fresher than theirs. His mind, intuitive rather than analytical, gave him an unusual capacity to trace connections between seemingly disparate elements. The urgency of his need to teach and persuade was often evident in the litter of diagrams, freshly inked by his Mont Blanc fountain pen, which he used to demonstrate to his interlocutors the absolute urgency of the point he was making.

Just as the Australian economy had to be restructured to prepare the country for the new world, so too, Keating believed, did the institutions by which it engaged with its neighbours. And if they did not exist, they would have to be created.

APEC leaders' meetings

Since Evans chaired the first meeting of Asia-Pacific economies in Canberra in November 1989, APEC had consolidated itself. Its objectives and methods of operation were settled at a meeting in Seoul in 1992, and a small secretariat was established in Singapore. It was now agreed that regional trade liberalisation should be one of APEC's aims.

For the new prime minister, the most urgent of his foreign policy tasks was to host a long-planned visit to Australia by the US president, George H.W. Bush. Keating was looking for something to say to the president that would be fresh and would reflect his international priorities. At their first informal meeting in Kirribilli House, overlooking Sydney Harbour on New Year's Day 1992, Keating set out for the first time his belief that what the Asia-Pacific region needed, and which almost alone of the world's regions it lacked, was a regular forum at which its heads of government could meet to talk directly about its problems. Without such high-level leadership, he told Bush, it would be difficult to drive forward an ambitious APEC agenda.

Bush's response was positive but cautious. But it was sufficient for Keating to follow up with formal letters to Bush and the other regional leaders who would matter most, President Suharto in Indonesia and Prime Minister Miyazawa in Japan. He then floated the idea publicly in his first foreign policy speech in April, proposing a process of periodic Asia-Pacific heads-of-governments meeting, 'say every two or three years'.

Keating wrote more letters, receiving mostly favourable, if careful, responses. He believed that meetings of heads of government needed to be anchored in the structure of an existing body such as APEC, rather than standing alone. But the membership of China and the other two 'Chinese economies', Taiwan and Hong Kong, a problem already encountered when

APEC was established, was revived with greater sensitivity because heads of government were involved. The diplomatic solution was again found in declaring the meeting one of economies, not governments, with Taiwan and Hong Kong represented by more junior economic ministers.

Keating had been hoping for a first meeting during Indonesia's chairing year in 1994. But Bill Clinton's unexpected defeat of Bush at the end of 1992 offered a chance to speed things up. The United States was to host APEC the following year and Keating wrote an unusually substantive letter of congratulations to the new president, raising the idea of leaders' meetings 'as a way of filling a conspicuous gap in institutional links in the Asia-Pacific region, and of affirming a renewed US leadership role in Pacific affairs.'[21]

Clinton was searching for ways of reinforcing his own economic priorities, which included the burgeoning aerospace and information technology industries of the US West Coast. His advisers took up Keating's idea and by June the president had issued an invitation to APEC leaders to join him in Seattle for a meeting in November. Only the Malaysian prime minister, Dr Mahathir Mohamad, refused.

The APEC model of Asia-Pacific cooperation, which envisaged a single trans-Pacific economy based on 'open regionalism', under which any trade reforms would be open to all, was facing competition. The Seattle meeting was held against the background of the successful approval by Congress of the North American Free Trade Agreement (NAFTA), linking Canada, Mexico and the United States in a formal, restrictive trade pact. On the other side of the Pacific, Mahathir had proposed the establishment of an East Asian Economic Group, which would join the ASEAN countries with Japan, China and South Korea in an Asia-only institution. Mahathir's ASEAN partners had forced this into a more limited form as a Caucus (EAEC) operating under the APEC umbrella. Even so, faced with the question of whether Australia might try to join such a grouping, Keating was opposed: 'Leaving the United States institutionally disconnected from the Western Pacific with an important ally joining the EAEC to its exclusion, is not a policy we should embrace without a great deal of forethought,' he told Evans.[22]

Clinton's invitation to Seattle was an important start, but that meeting was planned as a one-off gathering and Australia needed more. So Keating started work on Suharto to persuade him to offer to host the leaders again in Indonesia the following year. Over nearly two hours of discussion in Jakarta in October 1993, the two of them stitched up a deal whereby Suharto would agree to do this if someone else asked him. Keating worked with two of his allies, Goh

Chok Tong of Singapore and Kim Young-sam of South Korea to arrange that.

The Seattle meeting in November 1993 went well. Clinton's glistening political skills were all on show. The leaders announced their goal of establishing 'a community of Asia Pacific economies' in which 'the spirit of openness and partnership deepens, enabling us to find cooperative solutions to the challenges of our rapidly changing regional and global economy'.[23] They agreed to meet again in Indonesia.

But if the APEC leaders' meetings were to be institutionalised, they would need a continuing agenda large enough to engage the annual attention of heads of government. Keating believed that had to revolve around lowering formal barriers and making it easier for businesses to operate around the region ('trade facilitation'). Drawing on an agenda suggested by an Eminent Persons Group, Keating, Evans, trade minister (from January 1994) Bob McMullan and their officials worked closely with Indonesia to prepare for the next meeting.

In the nine months leading up to the second leaders' meeting, Keating's diary recorded around thirty-six meetings and phone calls on the subject, mostly with other APEC leaders.[24] He visited Jakarta again in June. 'I collect APEC arguments like some others here collect postage stamps,' he told Suharto in their last conversation on the eve of the meeting.[25] He deployed a wide and occasionally contradictory array of them in his long campaign of advocacy and persuasion directed at the interests of each of the economies involved.

The meeting was held in the town of Bogor, 60 kilometres from Jakarta. A 'Declaration of Common Resolve', which Suharto pressed through against opposition from Mahathir, committed member economies to free trade by 2010 for industrialised countries and by 2020 for less-developed economies. The debate about whether APEC's approach should be preferential (available only to members) or open to all was resolved by declaring it would be 'GATT consistent', a fudge which could cover either option. Suharto had placed one of the world's largest developing countries behind a free-trade agenda, he had used his prestige to bring his ASEAN partners along with him, and he had done all this in close cooperation with the prime minister of Australia. Keating described the result as 'one of the most satisfying days of my political life'.[26]

The Bogor goals were not legally binding, so the challenge over the next few years was to decide how to measure progress. At Osaka in 1995 it was agreed that each APEC economy would develop an action plan detailing its progress towards the Bogor goals. But the difficulty of getting governments to act in the absence of formal legal requirements soon became clear. The

Bogor commitments were not met, but their impact was real. By suggesting that the Asia-Pacific countries had other economic options available, they helped bring the Europeans to the point of a deal in the global Uruguay Round of trade negotiations. And they helped cement the idea that Asia's prosperity depended on free trade. So, as Keating noted, 'when the Asian economic crisis came in 1997, with its pressures for governments to close up and look inwards, the significant thing was that APEC's free-trade goals and aspirations remained in place. The plot-line of the region's story did not take a sudden turn.'[27] The broader work of cooperation and trade facilitation continued in the years that followed, as the annual photograph of regional leaders in colourful shirts became a newspaper staple.

The establishment of the APEC leaders' meetings also had an important structural effect back home. Until Seattle, the Australian prime minister's international travel had revolved around the increasingly marginal Commonwealth Heads of Government Meetings and the South Pacific Forum. In APEC, then later in the East Asia Summit and the G20, the prime minister's role at the centre of Australian foreign policy grew.

Southeast Asia

By the early 1990s the prospects for Southeast Asia, the focus of so much of Australia's foreign and defence policy attention over the previous forty years, were looking more promising. Political divisions were breaking down. The great powers – the United States, the Soviet Union and China – had no further interest in playing out their conflicts through local proxies. Moscow cut its economic support for Vietnam and in 1989 began withdrawing its air and naval assets. The United States pulled out of its huge air and naval bases at Clark Field and Subic Bay when the Philippines senate signalled in 1992 that it would not renew the leases. The split between the ASEAN countries and Indochina eased as Vietnam signed the ASEAN Treaty of Amity and Cooperation in 1992 and became a full member of ASEAN in 1995. The countries of Southeast Asia slowly normalised their relations with China. In trade terms the ASEAN countries and Vietnam were Australia's fastest-growing markets.[28]

Cambodia

The most immediate effect of these changes came in Cambodia, the tragic object of so much of the earlier competition. Vietnam's decision in 1989 to withdraw its troops from Cambodia eased the concerns of Thailand, the frontline ASEAN state, but left open the awful prospect that in the ensuing gap the genocidal Khmer Rouge might return to power.

The political divisions that had impeded Bill Hayden's earlier efforts to resolve the conflict were disappearing. In July 1989 France, the former colonial power, and Indonesia convened a conference in Paris between the four Cambodian factions (the government of Hun Sen and the three externally backed opposition groups) and the main regional and external players, including the five permanent members of the UN Security Council and Australia. The Paris meeting came tantalisingly close to securing agreement on the establishment of a transitional administration in which all four factions would participate and which would lead to free elections. The stumbling block was that one of those groups was the Khmer Rouge.

The idea of placing Cambodia under some form of UN trusteeship had been raised in the past by Prince Sihanouk. Evans heard about it again in a meeting in October 1989 with the New York congressman Stephen Solarz, and became intrigued that this might be one way out of the impasse. In November he outlined to the Senate the idea of 'building a transitional administration directly around the authority of the United Nations'.[29]

This idea was developed into a plan, as a result of an extraordinary round of shuttle diplomacy in December 1989 and January 1990 by the deputy secretary (and later secretary) of DFAT, Michael Costello, involving more than thirty meetings in thirteen countries, including Cambodia, over twenty days.[30] Costello's diplomacy fed into a continual refining of Australia's proposal by Evans and his department. It was clear that so long as China supported the Khmer Rouge, the group could not be wished out of the equation: if it was not dealt into a settlement, the civil war would continue. United Nations engagement in a transitional administration seemed the only solution.

In February 1990 the Indonesian foreign minister, Ali Alatas, co-chair of the Paris conference, convened an informal meeting of the ASEAN countries, Cambodia, Laos and the four Cambodian parties in Jakarta. Australia was invited to participate as a 'resource delegation'. In preparation, Evans dispatched a team of Australian officials and experts to Cambodia, Thailand and the border region.[31] In a marathon eight-day drafting session, with Evans' participation throughout, a Cambodia task force in DFAT prepared a 155-page series of working papers, known as the 'Red Book'.[32] This report proposed the establishment of a symbolic 'National Council' that would embody Cambodian sovereignty during the transitional period, and set out details of how a comprehensive settlement under United Nations administration would work. The overall cost, it estimated, would be $US1.3 billion.[33]

The Australian proposals were central to the Jakarta discussions. The conference broke down over the question of whether the agreed record should refer to the past genocide of the Khmer Rouge, but in further meetings over the course of the following year progress continued. In August the UN Security Council permanent members agreed on the elements of a comprehensive political settlement, based on an enhanced United Nations role. On September 1990 the Cambodian parties accepted this as the basis for settling the conflict, and the whole framework was endorsed by both the Security Council and the General Assembly.

Negotiations dragged on, but finally, in June 1991, Prince Sihanouk, with the implicit support of China, reinserted himself in the process, calling a meeting in Thailand of the Supreme National Council, comprising the four Cambodian parties. This led to agreement on an unconditional ceasefire and the cessation of external military support. The Paris peace agreements on Cambodia were formally signed on 23 October 1991. Evans was present. The detail was very close to the plan developed by Australia two years earlier.

The UN Transitional Authority in Cambodia (UNTAC) was an enormous enterprise. Sixteen thousand troops, 3600 police and 1020 administrators from thirty countries were involved. Australia contributed 500 military personnel and an Australian, Lieutenant General John Sanderson, commanded the peacekeeping force.[34] The path was not easy. The Khmer Rouge generated continuing problems. Nevertheless, 365,000 refugees had returned from border camps by April 1993 and voters were registered. In May 1993 elections were successfully held, with a voter turnout of almost 90 per cent. No party attained a majority of seats, and a shaky coalition government was formed with Sihanouk's son, Prince Norodom Ranariddh, and Hun Sen as co–prime ministers. With the inauguration of the new constitution in September 1993 the Kingdom of Cambodia was re-established, under Prince Sihanouk as constitutional monarch.

The hopes of the early 1990s soon encountered the realities of a society traumatised by violence and beset by corruption and human rights abuses. In 1997 Hun Sen consolidated sole power in Phnom Penh amid concerns about a return to civil war. Nevertheless, Cambodia ceased to be a source of regional tension and its people were given a chance to recover. Slowly the Khmer Rouge faded away.

Australia's role in the Cambodian settlement, dating back to Hawke's first commission to Hayden, was important to the final resolution. Evans' determination, his close relationship with Alatas, the skilful work of Australian diplomats and the willingness of the government to contribute human and financial resources to the solution were all important. It was Australia's most significant contribution to resolving a regional problem since its involvement in the Indonesian independence struggle, forty years earlier. Its role, Evans reflected, had been that of 'map maker and persuader. It was much more an intellectual than a political or military role.'[35]

Indonesia

Australia needed to establish 'beyond doubt', Keating said in his first foreign policy speech in April 1992, 'that Asia is where our future substantially lies; that we can and must go there; and that this course we are on is irreversible.'[36]

Indonesia was at the symbolic heart of that objective. It was the country to which he had pointed when asked how his own policies would differ from Hawke's. 'I was not after a "special relationship" with Indonesia', he wrote later, 'a phrase I never used, and a category of international relationships in which ... I did not believe. But I did want a relationship appropriate to two neighbouring countries of our size and with our potential for development. And we did not have it.'[37]

Gareth Evans and the Indonesian foreign minister, Ali Alatas, had already embarked on the same project. Evans wanted to add what he called 'ballast' to a relationship blown too easily off course. To that end, they had instituted annual officials' talks, finalised the border by negotiating the Timor Gap Treaty and established the Australia-Indonesia Institute to deepen people-to-people relations.

Just as Keating took over, another of the always-threatening storms blew in. On 12 December 1991 more than 100 East Timorese demonstrators were shot dead by Indonesian troops near the Santa Cruz cemetery in Dili. The massacre was a reminder of how difficult the brutality and ineptitude that marked Indonesian rule had made the goal of integrating East Timor into the Indonesian Republic. Evans described the killings as 'savage, brutal and unconscionable.'[38] He was in Jakarta to express Australia's concern and press for a credible response on 19 December when Keating defeated Hawke. Suharto ordered an inquiry into the shootings.

Despite the developments in East Timor, Keating made Indonesia the destination for his first overseas visit as prime minister in April 1992. 'I was not prepared to make the whole of our complex relationship with 210 million people subject to this one issue,' he wrote.[39] He was the first Australian prime minister to visit Jakarta for nine years.

Keating knew that his hopes of shifting the relationship to a new level would depend on President Suharto, who had now been in office since 1965. Drawing his power from the military, Suharto was unchallenged in his political dominance. His government had delivered unprecedented economic growth to Indonesia, that growth was spread widely, and the regime's formal philosophy of Pancasila (Five Principles) emphasised religious tolerance against more Islamist pressures. Keating frequently noted that the coming to power of the New Order government had been the single most beneficial strategic development for Australia in the previous thirty years. An impoverished, divided or hostile Indonesia would have soaked up much higher levels of Australia defence expenditure.[40] On the other hand, the signs were already clear that Suharto was unwilling to confront the increasingly pressing question of political succession.

In their first meeting, Keating told Suharto that his visit was intended to 'make clear to Australians the priority he meant to attach to relations with Indonesia'. The meeting lasted more than two hours and the two men discovered in each other a strong strategic sense and a conviction that the relationship between Australia and Indonesia could bring mutual benefits, and help stabilise an increasingly uncertain Asia-Pacific region. Suharto agreed to Keating's suggestion that the two countries establish a Ministerial Forum, which would meet regularly with economic as well as foreign ministers, and which Keating hoped would become something like the Australia–Japan Ministerial Committee.

Keating visited Indonesia five more times over the next four years, pursuing an agenda that mixed the development of APEC (on which it would have been impossible for Keating to achieve his aims without Suharto's support), bilateral economic relations and the security relationship. He told Australians that 'no country is more important to Australia than Indonesia', placing it with the United States and Japan at the apex of Australia's foreign relationships.[41]

The problems in the relationship, including on questions of human rights, did not disappear. But the new tone was clear when another of the periodic crises broke out. In June 1995 reports emerged that Indonesia had

nominated as its ambassador General Herman Mantiri, a senior army officer. Mantiri was well regarded by the Australian military for his role in
improving discipline in the Indonesian armed forces but he was on record
defending and justifying the actions of the Indonesian military during the
Dili massacre. There was a public outcry in Australia. The difference now
was that, although the Australian government did not formally request it,
Suharto decided to withdraw the appointment in July. When they met in
Bali in September, Suharto told Keating, 'If we had allowed the appointment
to go ahead ... it would have provided bait for those who wanted to harm the
relationship. We had to prevent ourselves falling into this trap.'[42]

In February 1994 the government had considered a Defence Strategic
Review which concluded that 'more than any other regional nation, a sound
strategic relationship with Indonesia would do most for Australia's security.
We should seek new opportunities to deepen the relationship in areas that
serve both countries' interests.'[43] Keating agreed with the proposition but
thought the suggested policy response inadequate. He began pushing for the
idea of a bilateral security agreement with Indonesia that would complete
the circle of defence arrangements Australia already had with its other close
neighbours – New Zealand, Papua New Guinea, Singapore and Malaysia.
Officials – not opposed, but mostly sceptical that Indonesia, with its strong
tradition of non-alignment, would be willing to sign up – began exploring
language. Keating raised the idea with Suharto when they met again in
Jakarta in June 1994. When Suharto brought up the subject of defence
cooperation, Keating responded that 'from Australia's point of view, we
now saw strategic trust between Indonesia and Australia. We were willing
to put our cards on the table, face up, and to make a declaration that such
trust existed.' Suharto agreed – cautiously – that the two countries could
'study the matter further with the eventual aim of declaring what sort of
cooperation we were embarking on for the future.' They agreed that they
would themselves be the channel for future discussion and that their emis-
saries would carry the work forward.[44]

Keating appointed General Peter Gration, the former chief of the defence
force, who had worked hard to develop links between Australia and
Indonesia. Suharto's nominee was his close political counsellor, the state secretary, Moerdiono.

Gration visited Jakarta in September 1994 and a 'non-paper' setting out
Australian views on what an agreement might encompass was given to
Moerdiono in October. But the issue then abruptly fell into a black hole.

Gration turned up in Jakarta in November 1994 to find that scheduled meetings had been cancelled. Keating decided that the matter should rest there,
and nothing more was heard until Suharto himself unexpectedly told
Keating when they met in Bali in September the following year that Indonesia
was now in a position to look at a draft text.

The ageing Javanese general and the working-class warrior from Sydney
were unlikely partners. Yet they made an immediate connection and real
warmth developed. Keating was so unlike most of the interlocutors who passed
through the doors of the Presidential Palace that an observer in the room could
see the pleasure Suharto derived from his company. Uncharacteristically for an
Australian politician, Keating could comfortably wait out the pauses and
silences in Javanese conversations. Suharto became relaxed enough to conduct
part of their conversations in English. His 'friendship with the prime minister
would be there always', Suharto told Keating at their meeting in Bali.[45]

Gration flew to Jakarta on 15 November 1995 to negotiate the text of the
treaty with a wider Indonesian group. Because the Indonesians wanted to
avoid suggestions that this was a military pact, the document was restyled as
an Agreement on Maintaining Security (AMS), and the phrase 'external
threat' was changed to read 'adverse challenges'. The document committed
the two governments to consult at ministerial level about their common
security; develop security cooperation; consult each other in the case of
'adverse challenges to either party or to their common security interests and,
if appropriate, consider measures which might be taken either individually
or jointly and in accordance with the processes of each party'.[46]

In its focus on all external security challenges rather than military threat
alone, the agreement foreshadowed the more expansive idea of national
security to come in the following decade. On 13 December Keating announced it to a startled media conference in Canberra, much of the surprise
coming from the fact that the agreement had not been leaked. General
Gration and senior officials then spread out to brief regional leaders.

On 18 December 1995 Keating flew to Jakarta to sign the agreement,
taking with him the most senior Australian delegation ever to visit another
country: deputy prime minister Kim Beazley, the foreign and defence ministers and the chief of the defence force.

The Opposition responded positively. 'I thought in principle it was an
excellent initiative … It will give us a framework to develop the security
dialogue', said Alexander Downer, Evans' successor as foreign minister,
soon after the Howard government took office.[47] And over the following

couple of years the AMS became the core of a deepening security and military-to-military relationship.[48] But it did not survive the intensity of the East Timor crisis. In September 1999 Suharto's successor, B.J. Habibie, announced that he was abrogating it in response to Australia's decision to review security cooperation over developments in East Timor.

Malaysia

Australia's policy objective of closer integration with Asia faced an unexpected impediment in the form of the Malaysian prime minister, Dr Mahathir Mohamad, a prickly nationalist whose vision of Asia's future did not include Australia. Australia's historical links, people-to-people relations and defence commitments were closer with Malaysia than with any other regional country except Singapore, but under Mahathir crises in the relationship kept erupting over claimed insults in media reports, films and television shows. When the Malaysian government took offence at an ABC television series, *Embassy*, set in a fictional country that it took to be Malaysia, the Australian high commissioner in Kuala Lumpur was banned from official government functions for a time. To smooth matters over, Hawke ended up making an impossible promise to Mahathir in October 1991 that the Australian government would disassociate itself from 'insulting and inaccurate' media reporting about Malaysia.

These incidents were all proxies for a deeper difference between the two countries: whether Australia was a natural part of the region and had the right to participate in Asian institutions. Australia did not fit into Mahathir's view of Asia's future. Mahathir had boycotted the Seattle APEC meeting in November 1993 as he pursued his own East Asia economic grouping. So when Keating told journalists that 'APEC is bigger than all of us – Australia, the United States, Malaysia, Dr Mahathir, and any recalcitrant',[49] and Malaysia responded with outrage at his 'extreme comments', a pattern was being repeated. As Keating noted, reasonably enough, 'it was not ... one of the more searing insults of international diplomacy, or even of my own political career.'[50]

In the days that followed, a series of threats to Australian interests in Malaysia were canvassed. Persuaded to write to Mahathir, Keating handdrafted a letter which, although carefully couched, was not an apology but set out the differences between the two men.[51] This generated further outrage in Malaysia. Keating decided that 'Australia's relationship with Malaysia had to break out of the cycle of overreaction, and that it had to be made clear to the Malaysian government that we had a two-way relationship which needed commitment from both sides.'[52] Australian officials were instructed to prepare options for an Australian response to any Malaysian action.

By chance, two senior ministers, the trade minister, Peter Cook, and the defence minister, Robert Ray, had already planned visits to Malaysian in early December 1993. They made it clear to their Malaysian counterparts that it should not be assumed that Australia would let any Malaysian actions against its interests pass without response, and that defence and capital controls would not necessarily be off limits.[53] Coupled with a television interview in which Keating said he had not intended to offend Mahathir and was sorry if he had taken offence, the message was delivered and relations calmed down. Keating and Mahathir met again at the APEC meeting in Jakarta, and Keating visited Malaysia in January 1996.

'What was at stake,' Keating wrote, 'was a fundamentally different view of Australia's legitimate role in the region. This was a matter about which – certainly from Australia's side – we could not compromise, because compromise would mean accepting a permanent outsider status in the region that meant most to us.'[54] The differences persisted under the Howard government when Mahathir vetoed Australian inclusion in the Asia-Europe Meetings (ASEM).

Vietnam

After decades of warfare and tension, opportunities were now opening up for Australia in Vietnam. With the settlement in Cambodia, Vietnam normalised relations with China in November 1991. And despite the loss of Soviet aid (which had amounted to 11 per cent of GDP) an economic reform program introduced by the Communist Party in 1986 was beginning to show results. Vietnam remained a very poor country but in 1992 it was growing at 8 per cent annually.

Australia had been the first Western country to resume aid after the Cambodia settlement, promising $100 million over the four years to 1994/95. And by the early 1990s Australia was the third-largest investor in Vietnam after Taiwan and Hong Kong. Companies like BHP and Telstra saw opportunities there before the rest of the world caught up.

In May 1993, the Vietnamese prime minister, Vo Van Kiet, visited Australia, his first visit to a Western country. Keating, in turn, became the first Australian prime minister to visit Hanoi and a unified Vietnam in April the following year. He announced a doubling of Australian aid. At late notice, a meeting with the powerful 78-year-old general secretary of the Communist Party, Do Muoi, was added to his program. Do Muoi was clearly intrigued by Keating, who gave him a lengthy exposition on regional strategic developments and ended up discussing the electricity grid. Keating invited him to visit Australia, promising that they would travel together. That visit, only Do Muoi's second outside Vietnam, took place in July and August 1995. In addition to a visit to the Gladstone alumina refinery and port, Keating ended up giving the old guerrilla fighter advice about the development of Vietnam's tourism industry while driving him in a golf cart around the Mirage resort in Port Douglas, 'Christopher Skase's glittering temple to 1980s capitalism.'[55]

Australia's Vietnamese community, about 140,000 strong, remained suspicious of the growth of the relationship. Those political considerations lay behind Howard's refusal as Leader of the Opposition to meet Do Muoi during his visit. But although there were problems in the early period of the Howard government over aid matters, dialogue soon resumed, with a visit by the foreign minister in March 1997 and the prime minister in April 1999. The Vietnamese, Keating noted, 'have lived through much and they are the hardest of hard thinkers.'[56]

Regional security

The search was underway for structures that would help maintain the regional security order at a time when every Australian strategic assessment proclaimed that the world was becoming increasingly fluid and complex.[57] (In fact, it's hard to find an Australian strategic assessment over seventy years that hasn't made the same claim.)[58]

Evans' response to the changing environment was to deliver in November 1989 a statement in which he advocated a 'multi-dimensional' approach to regional security. This meant, he said, thinking about national security policy as something in which 'all the components of Australia's network of relations in the region – military and politico-military capability; diplomacy; economic links; assistance with development and so-called non-military threats; and the exchange of people and ideas – work together to help shape a security environment which is favourable to Australia's interests.'[59] As well as being a policy response to a new strategic environment, this was also a bureaucratic move to insert Evans' department into the hard space of national security.

Just as APEC was seen as a means of redressing the absence of any region-wide economic architecture in Asia, so Evans saw a need for a new forum in which all the regional states could discuss the new challenges to their security. In Europe, the Conference on Security and Co-operation in Europe (CSCE) had from the mid-1970s drawn European countries into discussions about their common security interests and helped set the conditions for the end of the Cold War. Was something like that needed or possible in Asia? Evans asked his department to begin work on ways in which a regional security dialogue could be facilitated. At a meeting of ASEAN foreign ministers and their dialogue partners in July 1990, he floated the idea of a Conference on Security and Cooperation in Asia (CSCA). The response was cool. The ASEAN countries were again concerned about any new institutions that might detract from ASEAN's centrality and worried about what they might be asked to sign up to. The Americans did not want to see any multilateral constraints on their naval capabilities in East Asia and preferred to keep the focus on their bilateral alliances.

Evans accepted that the only way forward was to give ASEAN the central role. Backing away from talk about a CSCA, he reassured his Southeast Asian colleagues that ASEAN was the most appropriate framework for developing a dialogue on security issues.

In January 1992 ASEAN agreed to 'intensify its external dialogue in political and security matters' in regular meetings with its dialogue partners'.[60] American policy also began to loosen up, especially after the Clinton administration took office in early 1993. But something more was needed to engage the other key countries with an interest in Asian security – Russia, China, Vietnam – but which were not officially dialogue partners of ASEAN.

An important breakthrough occurred at a senior officials' meeting in Singapore in May 1993. Singapore had become the easiest of Australia's ASEAN partners. Goh Chok Tong, who replaced Lee Kuan Yew as prime minister in 1990, had been helpful to Keating in developing APEC and managing Mahathir. Lacking its own strategic space, the small island had leased space at Pearce airforce base in Western Australia in 1990 to train the Singapore air force.

By agreement with the Singapore chair, Australia proposed that ASEAN foreign ministers, who were meeting in Singapore the following month, should invite those other states, as well as their formal dialogue partners, to participate in an ASEAN Regional Forum (ARF), the reassuringly bland name Australia had suggested for the new security meeting.[61] The ministers agreed, and the first formal meeting of the new body was held in Bangkok in July 1994.

The ARF's role was circumscribed by the caution of its ASEAN core. By 1995 members had agreed that the forum would adopt 'a consensual approach to security issues', which meant no voting, and movement 'at a pace comfortable to all participants'.[62] Major breakthroughs were unlikely and, for the most part, the forum members paddled around in the easy shallows of security discourse – confidence-building measures and dialogue – rather than risking the deeper waters of preventive diplomacy to address problems like the emerging differences between China and others in the South China Sea. It was probably too much to expect any more ambitious outcome, given the diversity, and occasional incoherence, of security views among member states. But the ARF did create for the first time a forum in which all countries of the region and their main external partners could discuss prospects for regional security. The ARF was not the result of Australian initiative alone, but as with other regional institution-building in those 'post-' years – APEC, the Cambodia settlement – it benefited from Australia's ideas-broking and its diplomatic energy.

The new post–Cold War defence environment and its consequences for Australia were explored in the government's 1993 strategic review and the white paper, *Defending Australia*, which followed in November 1994. Both these documents continued the focus on Australia's responsibility for its own defence, which had marked the 1987 white paper. The difference now was recognition that the development of new military capabilities within the region would provide Australia with shorter warning time for conflict but also offered opportunities. 'Our defence relationships with South-East Asia will be characterised by the concept of partnership,' the strategic review reported.[63] For the defence minister, Robert Ray, 'The clear message of this review is that Australia's security – like its economic future – lies in and with our region. This means we must be a participant, not an onlooker, in regional security and other areas'.[64]

India and the Indian Ocean

From the late 1980s, the economic and political transformation in Asia and the Pacific shifted Australia's foreign policy interest firmly eastwards. Any remaining strategic anxiety about hostile navies in the Indian Ocean eased with the end of the Cold War and the Soviet withdrawal from Afghanistan, while the end of apartheid deflected Australia's policy attention away from the issues of southern Africa. The region about which the

Australian government was thinking and speaking was the Asia-Pacific or, as Evans tried to reframe it in 1995, an 'East Asian hemisphere', of which Australia was an intrinsic part. Neither India nor the Indian Ocean featured on these maps. Australia had obvious strategic interests in the Indian Ocean, Evans acknowledged, but they were 'not pressing and ... not easily given regional cohesion'.[65]

The friendship between Hawke and the Indian prime minister, Rajiv Gandhi, forged in their cooperation over southern African issues in the Commonwealth, led to reciprocal prime ministerial visits, but warm speeches could not bring Australia's strategic interests into closer alignment with India's, nor substitute for the deep economic complementarity which underpinned Australia's links with Northeast Asia.

Trade was growing, especially after the deregulatory economic reforms initiated by Gandhi's successor, Narasimha Rao, in the early 1990s, but it remained modest in scale and limited in composition. And policy irritations continued to niggle away. New Delhi resented Keating's opposition to Indian membership of APEC, which Keating justified on the grounds that the new organisation needed to consolidate before it expanded,[66] although India's demonstrated reluctance to embrace the trade liberalisation agenda was a factor in his thinking. The two countries also had continuing differences over India's (and Pakistan's) nuclear ambitions and its refusal to accede to the Nuclear Non-Proliferation Treaty. These would come to a head in 1998 with the series of nuclear tests in South Asia.

The idea of creating a new institution that would lead to greater cooperation around the Indian Ocean rim appealed to both countries. The Australian government was conscious of the lopsided nature of its regional policies and politically alert to the different global outlook from Western Australia. It announced its own 'Look West' policy in August 1994 and supported Mauritian efforts to convene an Indian Ocean regional dialogue in February 1995. It underwrote a broad academic and business 'second track' dialogue in Perth later that year. But it differed from India over which countries should be involved and how broad its aims should be. India was determined to exclude Pakistan and to keep security matters out of the mandate of any new body. These various efforts coalesced with the formation in 1997 of a new regional organisation, the Indian Ocean Rim Association for Regional Co-operation, saddled with the forgettable acronym of IOR-ARC. Even the members of the new group held out hopes for it that were modest at best.

Gareth Evans

Gareth Evans was the personal generator of much of the energy in Australian foreign policy during these years. Born in 1944, he joined the Labor Party after a stellar record of legal achievement at the University of Melbourne and Oxford, then as a barrister. Taking his seat in the Senate in 1977, a member of the moderate Labor Unity faction, he became a reforming attorney-general when Labor was elected in 1983. His ambitions were bruised when political problems and policy differences led Hawke to move him after the 1984 election to Resources and Energy, then Transport and Communications. But the job he most wanted, foreign minister, finally became his in September 1988 when Hayden was appointed governor-general, and he held it until Labor lost office in 1996. Between 1993 and 1996 he had the additional heavy responsibilities of Leader of the Government in the Senate, overseeing the passage through parliament of the *Native Title Act 1993*, which implemented the High Court's Mabo decision.

Evans' interest in international affairs had been shaped during his student days by his participation in the anti-apartheid movement. What sustained him in public life, he wrote, was 'a fairly unquenchable sense of optimism: a belief that even the most horrible and intractable problems are soluble; that rational solutions for which there are good, principled arguments do eventually prevail; and that good people, good governments and good governance will eventually prevail over bad'.[67]

He was a foreign minister of rare energy and intellectual force and firmly in the tradition of Evatt in his belief in the value of global institutions and a liberal international order. He believed that the recognition of universal human rights, an expanding body of international law, and effective global multilateral institutions were necessary to underpin progress to international peace and justice. Australia's citizenship was global. In this world, Australia had its own range of national interests, of course, which had to be protected, but those interests would also be served by the broader objectives of a just international order. If policy-makers were to do their work effectively, rather than simply respond to passing events, it was essential, he believed, that they were informed by detailed thinking and conceptual clarity. That meant taxonomy, and the naming of parts – 'constructive commitment', 'comprehensive engagement', 'multidimensional security', 'good international citizenship'. Evans was too clever and subtle a player to believe that logic and good argument alone would change the world. But he was too convinced by it himself to imagine that it wasn't part of it.

His energy was prodigious. At the end of his term as foreign minister, he had made 280 visits to 101 countries and spent 766 days outside Australia.[68] 'This is a driven man,' said the High Court judge Michael Kirby, 'not content to force himself to the brink of exhaustion and achievement but determined to inflict the same motivation upon everybody who comes into his circle.'[69] His capacity to process information was enormous and few briefings with him were relaxed. His departmental officials complained to each other but, for the most part, forgave the demands and the explosions of anger as a price worth paying for the exhilaration of the ride and the knowledge that their work would be put to good use.

The times and the man were perfectly suited. The achievements of Australian foreign policy during Evans' long tenure were greatly assisted by the unique qualities of the post–Cold War world. As the fundamental building blocks of the international system shifted, objectives which had been unobtainable – a peace settlement in Cambodia or a Chemical Weapons Convention – suddenly became possible, and Evans had the imagination, energy and determination to seize the opportunities and drive them home. Had he become foreign minister ten years earlier or ten years later, things would still have been done, but the options would have been fewer and the impact more limited.

His relationships with his two prime ministers were neither competitive nor antagonistic but complementary. Both Hawke and Keating had a more practical sense of the world that could be brought into play when necessary to temper Evans' conceptual purity with the broader political interests of the government or to settle down irritations in Washington.

Good international citizenship

An important conceptual weapon in the battle for structure and coherence which Evans fought against the unruly, fissiparous tendencies of Australian foreign policy was the idea of good international citizenship. It was the term he used to define the different reasons a country like Australia concerned itself with issues such as arms control, disarmament, the protection of the global environment, the defence of human rights and the struggle against apartheid and racism. 'Purposes beyond ourselves', as he often said, drawing on the words of the Australian scholar Hedley Bull. Good international citizenship was not 'the foreign policy equivalent of Boy Scout good deeds', but a recognition of the reality of global interdependence.[70]

The times made a policy response to these matters both possible and necessary. As the rigidity of the Cold War faded, new opportunities for cooperation were opening up. It seemed possible, especially at the beginning of the decade, that sterile debates between Washington and Moscow in the United Nations Security Council might yield to something more productive. In the Strategic Arms Reduction treaties (START) of 1991 and 1993, the United States and Russia agreed to reduce, not just limit, their nuclear arsenals. Yet notwithstanding this good news at the centre, intractable new regional and intrastate conflicts, violent in their intimacy, were breaking out in places like the Balkans, Somalia, Rwanda and Haiti.

Never one to let a problem go unprobed, Evans began teasing out, in a series of speeches and papers, the meaning of concepts like security in the post–Cold War world. At the United Nations General Assembly in September 1993 he launched a book called *Cooperating for Peace*, which he wrote with input from DFAT staff and academics, in order, he said, 'to bring some conceptual clarity ... into the definition of security problems' and explore ways in which structures and processes, especially in the United Nations system, could be improved.[71]

Evans was thinking beyond the idea of the sovereignty and security of the state to the broader concept of human security. Threats arose, he argued, not from military sources alone, but from economic and social deprivation, from ignorance of countries about each other, and from a failure to address problems that by their nature cross international boundaries. Any effective international security system had to operate at all these levels simultaneously.[72]

The brutality of intrastate conflict in places like Somalia and the former Yugoslavia was raising new challenges for the international community. It was likely, Evans told the General Assembly in September 1992, 'that the UN will be increasingly confronted by situations where the principle of non-intervention in internal affairs will be matched by a compelling sense of international conscience.'[73]

The Rwandan genocide of 1994 and the Srebrenica massacre in 1995 would strengthen the view that in extreme cases where states were unable or unwilling to protect their own citizens against mass atrocity crimes, the international community had a responsibility to intervene to protect them. This idea was a challenge to the doctrine of state sovereignty, which had been enshrined in the international order since the Peace of Westphalia ended Europe's Thirty Years' War in 1648. Evans' work at this time, and his notable contributions in his post-ministerial life as head of the International Crisis Group, would eventually help promote the emergence of a new international norm – the 'responsibility to protect'.[74]

Australia continued to contribute to the broad range of arms control and disarmament negotiations underway in the Conference on Disarmament, the UN's negotiating forum for arms control in Geneva. It played an important role in securing the indefinite extension of the Nuclear Non-Proliferation Treaty (NPT) in 1995 and was a lead co-sponsor of the Comprehensive Test Ban Treaty (CTBT) when formal negotiations began in January 1994. It helped to define the scope of the treaty, to develop the detailed model text and to support the international seismic monitoring network that would help monitor the ban.

The Chemical Weapons Convention

The single largest Australian contribution to global arms control in the 1990s began a month after the first Gulf War ended. Following the withdrawal of Iraqi forces from Kuwait, the United Nations Security Council authorised the creation of a United Nations Special Commission (UNSCOM) with the task of eliminating Saddam's weapons of mass destruction (WMD). Chemical weapons were part of his arsenal.

Australia was already a significant player in the international efforts to ban chemical weapons. Since 1984 it had chaired the informal 'Australia Group' of countries working to coordinate the control of exports that might help potential chemical weapons programs. The Australian regional chemical weapons initiative and its government–industry conference on export controls had followed in the late 1980s. But the most important goal was a formal treaty to ban the production and use of these weapons.

Negotiations for such a convention had been going on in the Conference on Disarmament since 1984. A 'rolling text', 220 pages long, had emerged, but final agreement seemed distant. Twenty per cent of the text remained in square brackets – the negotiators' term of art for the areas, always the most difficult, which were still unresolved. In May 1991 Evans told a United Nations conference on disarmament in Kyoto that he had written to the foreign ministers of the other member countries of the CD to suggest a meeting at ministerial level to look again at a treaty. 'The need is fresh in everybody's mind, the political environment is favourable, and much of the groundwork has been done. All that is now needed is that extra element of creativity and political will to produce the resolution of the final issues,' he said.[75]

Intense diplomatic discussions and a great deal of work by Australian diplomats followed. In March the following year, Australia tabled a fresh draft of the negotiating text. It drew on the work that had already been done but included explanatory text on the issues still in dispute and suggested compromise language in areas of disagreement. The Australian initiative was critical to breakthrough in negotiations. It was a fine example of the capacity of a middle power to contribute to the resolution of a thorny international problem: Australia had the human and financial resources and, with no direct national interest beyond the aim of achieving a lasting outcome, it had the trust of the other parties. In January 1993 the Chemical Weapons Convention, banning the development, production, acquisition and use of chemical weapons and imposing a stringent verification regime, was signed in Paris by 130 countries.

French nuclear tests

Nuclear issues moved from the remote world of diplomats and strategists to the centre of Australian politics in June 1995, when the French president, Jacques Chirac, announced that France would conduct a series of eight underground nuclear weapons tests at Mururoa Atoll, 6000 kilometres east of Australia, in French Polynesia. The tests were to begin in September. The announcement ended a moratorium on testing put in place by Chirac's predecessor, François Mitterrand. It was not unexpected: the Australian government had been lobbying Chirac against the decision, sending Evans and a delegation of ministers from the South Pacific Forum, which Australia was chairing, to Paris to argue against it. And the announcement came with the welcome promise that France would then close the Pacific test sites and sign the CTBT.

Travelling in Tokyo, Evans told journalists that the decision was 'deeply disappointing' and that Australia would respond. But he also answered 'Certainly' when asked if he agreed that the decision was 'not as bad ... as it could have been?'[76] This was undoubtedly true, but it played badly as domestic political outrage against the tests grew. Talkback radio and tabloid newspapers – the 1990s equivalent of social media – exploded with calls for boycotts of French products. There were demands for the dispatch of Australian warships to the test zone. An arsonist attacked the honorary French consulate in Perth. 'It felt at times,' Keating wrote, 'as if the dead and wounded of the Battle of Agincourt had only just been carried from the field.'[77] In Keating's words, 'What people wanted was a validation of their understandable emotional responses not just action. We did not provide it strongly enough or quickly enough.'[78]

As a result, the government was impelled into a series of responses. The Australian ambassador to France was recalled for consultations, defence contacts were curtailed and senior defence representatives pulled out of Paris. Gordon Bilney, the Minister for Development Cooperation and Pacific Island Affairs and a fluent French speaker, led a parliamentary delegation to Europe to put the case against testing. Australia called a special meeting of South Pacific Forum environmental ministers. France's dialogue status with the forum was suspended.

This was, Keating recalled, 'foreign policy-making at its most frustrating: reactive, essentially a matter of rhetoric and gesture and unlikely, we all agreed to, to succeed in deflecting the French government from its course'.[79] He decided that the outrage expressed against the French tests would be put to better use if the government began to address the deeper problem of nuclear weapons themselves. Their role in maintaining the Cold War balance of terror was now over and the Gulf War had shown that conventional weapons of unprecedented accuracy and power were able to fulfil some of their functions.

On 24 October Keating announced Australia's sponsorship of a high-level international commission whose task would be to develop 'concrete and realistic steps for achieving a nuclear-weapons free world'. This was the objective to which all the established nuclear states had formally committed themselves under the Nuclear Non-Proliferation Treaty. The members of the commission included scientists, disarmament experts, hard-headed military strategists, former generals, and political leaders such as Michel Rocard, the former French prime minister. The Canberra Commission completed its work in August 1996. Declaring that only the elimination of nuclear weapons could provide complete defence against their use, it provided a list of practical and realistic suggestions for progress towards this goal.[80]

The final report of the Commission was handed to the incoming Coalition government in 1996. By then, France had ended its testing series after only six tests, signed the CTBT and, in early 1996, the South Pacific Nuclear-Free Zone Treaty. The new government accepted the report and presented it to the United Nations, but did not advocate for its recommendations. Nevertheless, there was some broad policy continuity on arms

control. 'The care and maintenance of international arms control agreements', wrote the new foreign minister, Alexander Downer, was a cause to
which Australia would continue to devote 'a significant part of its national
foreign policy resources'.[81]

Downer certainly played a critical role in rescuing the CTBT from the
margins of the Conference on Disarmament in Geneva and placing it before
the General Assembly in New York in 1996. Australia, the minister claimed,
had 'snatched the CTBT from untimely death in the conference on disarmament by – if I do say so myself – a daring and imaginative feat of Australian
diplomacy'.[82] The General Assembly's endorsement of the treaty by a large
margin undoubtedly provided it with greater international legitimacy,[83]
although it has not yet entered into force because of the failure of some of
the nuclear and threshold states to ratify, or in some cases sign, it.

Human rights

For Evans, strong and consistent Australian support for the civil and political rights set out in the Universal Declaration of Human Rights was central
to good international citizenship. Australian diplomats were instructed to
raise and pursue allegations of human rights abuses including those
broached by organisations like Amnesty International. In 1993, Evans said,
Australia raised 534 individual and group cases with 90 countries, as well as
following up earlier cases.[84] Australia was also an active participant in the
broader multilateral work of the United Nations Human Rights Commission
in Geneva.

The tenor of the times was optimistic. Progress on human rights was
seen, to some degree, as a concomitant of economic progress. 'Many of the
problems with civil and political rights in developing Asian countries,' Evans
thought, 'are likely to be transient in nature: as economic liberalisation pro-
ceeds … it will drag political liberalisation along in its wake.'[85] But in the
meantime the problems in Australia's neighbourhood kept coming: in
China, to which Australia dispatched two human rights delegations in 1991
and 1992; in Indonesia, with the Dili massacre in 1991; shootings of democracy demonstrators in Thailand; and the military's arrest of the opposition
leader, Aung San Suu Kyi, in Myanmar and its refusal to abide by the result
of democratic elections. As Evans said, 'Any government's handling of
human rights issues constantly requires a fine balance between, and judgement about, when to act and how to act and how forcefully and publicly to

act.'[86] It is possible to detect tonal and practical differences in the way the Australian officials responded to human rights abuses during this period, but no Australia government before or since has sought, or achieved, so high a degree of consistency in its human rights diplomacy.

Greening the international order

The Earth Summit – the United Nations Conference on Environment and Development (UNCED) – held in Rio in 1992 was an important step in a process the former secretary of DFAT, Stuart Harris, called 'greening the international order'.[87] Adding to the growing international interest in biodiversity and climate change, environmental issues were beginning to have an impact on the trade and finance agenda in organisations such as the World Trade Organization (WTO), the Organisation for Economic Co-operation and Development (OECD) and the World Bank.[88]

At the global level, Australia was heavily involved in the negotiation of a range of new conventions and instruments designed to limit ozone-depleting gases (the Montreal Protocol), preserve world heritage (the World Heritage Convention), protect endangered species (CITES, the International Convention on the Regulation of Whaling), address desertification (the Convention to Combat Desertification) and manage the transportation of hazardous waste (the Basel Convention). And regionally in the South Pacific, Australia led on a range of environmental initiatives such as the handling of nuclear waste, bans on drift-net fishing and the management of fishing stocks and logging. In APEC and the South Pacific Forum, ministers for the environment (now a separate portfolio in most countries) began to meet regularly.

Climate change was emerging as the most important and the most divisive of the international environmental negotiations. The Intergovernmental Panel on Climate Change – formed to develop an agreed base of scientific data on climate – met for the first time in 1990. In 1992 Australia ratified the United Nations Framework Convention on Climate Change (UNFCCC), which had emerged from the Rio Summit as the basis for future international negotiations on climate change.

From the time of the Rio meeting, differences were sharpening over who should pay for the costs of avoiding future environmental problems and remediating current ones. Why, asked the developing countries, should they have to pay for problems that the developed world had caused and from which it had benefited so abundantly? How could the problem be solved, responded the developed countries, unless outputs from the developing countries, unquestionably the largest source of potential future emissions of carbon dioxide, were limited? A Global Environment Facility (GEF) was established as a financial mechanism to provide funding to developing countries.

The environment was one of several areas of Australia's national life in which the divisions between domestic and foreign policy were being eroded. Climate change was the ultimate globalised problem. As a result, Australia was now being held internationally accountable for its reliance on fossil fuels for the majority of its domestic energy needs and its heavy dependence on energy-intensive exports like coal, aluminium and other processed minerals. Australia responded, as it had done in similar economic circumstances in the past, by arguing the case for its own special position as a developed country with the profile of a developing country. In the UNFCC, it called for its own special situation to be taken into account as part of the 'common but differentiated' responsibilities of the various parties.

The election of the Coalition government in 1996 brought no great change in declaratory policy on international environmental issues, but the tone and approach were different. The new government was more sceptical about multilateral solutions of all sorts and favoured what it called a more 'hard-headed pursuit' of the national interest. The differences would emerge more clearly in Australia's participation in the 1997 Kyoto negotiations on climate change.

China

In terms of relative importance to Australian foreign policy, the greatest change during the 1990s was in the relationship with China. When Keating set out the rough hierarchy of Australia's international relationships in the early 1990s, China did not appear in the top group. Yet by the end of the decade no general speech about foreign policy by an Australian leader would have omitted it.

After the national trauma of Tiananmen Square, Deng Xiaoping gradually, and against solid internal opposition, managed to consolidate power around a pro-economic reform group in the governing Politburo. His ideologically inventive commitment to a 'socialist market economy' was entrenched in the constitution. By 1992 Deng's triumph was complete and China was set to become the world's fastest-growing economy.

Zhu Rongji was one of the reformers installed by Deng. In April 1992, as vice-premier, he was the first senior Chinese visitor to Australia after post-Tiananmen sanctions were eased. Keating had liked and admired Zhu since he greeted him in Shanghai in 1989 with the declaration that, as the city's mayor, he had the most difficult job in the world.[89] In June 1993 Keating became the first Australian prime minister to visit Beijing since 1986. Two-way trade was up by 29 per cent to nearly $4.2 billion in 1992. Australian investment was growing strongly and Australia was the largest overseas destination for Chinese foreign investment.[90]

But the relationship with China went well beyond the economy. The agenda for any high-level discussions included human rights, China's seizure in 1995 of islands in the South China Sea claimed by the Philippines, nuclear testing, and difficult consular cases. A particular problem was the arrival in Australia in late 1994 and early 1995 of 835 Sino-Vietnamese boat people from southern China claiming refugee status because of China's one-child policy. Australian officials negotiated a memorandum of understanding with Beijing in October 1995, enabling 465 of them to be repatriated to China, while 370 were given asylum.

Unlike Hawke, Keating was not romantic about China. 'We have nothing to fear from China,' he told the *Australian* newspaper, 'but do we want to be in the Chinese orbit? In other words, the pull of gravity of China? No, of course we don't.'[91] The answer to dealing with China, he thought, lay in 'encouraging China into the world community and acknowledging the legitimacy of its position in it, but also in ensuring that the world into which it is moving is self-confident and, in ASEAN's term-of-art, "resilient"'.[92] That meant embedding China in the development of APEC and supporting its participation in the wider system of global rules like the WTO.

Japan

Notwithstanding China's growth, in the mid-1990s Japan still represented 70 per cent of the entire East Asian economy. Even if Japan grew by just 1 per cent a year, Keating reminded Australians, that was the equivalent of the entire New Zealand economy.[93] Japan remained Australia's most important economic partner, the destination for one-quarter of the country's exports and the third-largest source of foreign investment, including into manufacturing industry like the Toyota car plant in Victoria. Around 750,000 Japanese honeymooners and other tourists visited Australia each year.

Japan was changing, however. The bursting of the bubble economy in 1990 heralded the beginning of what became known as the 'lost decades'. Long-term deflation became entrenched and average annual economic growth between 1992 and 2001 was just 0.8 per cent.[94] In 1995 a large earthquake in Kobe and a terrorist gas attack on the Tokyo subway system underscored the growing sense of political uncertainty. That was also the year Japan's working-age population peaked and its steep demographic decline began. In a search for relief from the burden of the high yen, Japanese industrial production was being shifted offshore: in the three years to 1995, about $US160 billion worth of Japan's production – roughly half the value of Australia's annual economic output – had followed this path, according to the Ministry of International Trade and Industry.

Partly reflecting these uncertainties, Japan's domestic politics were also in upheaval as the dominant Liberal Democratic Party (LDP) split into several factions. The turnover of prime ministers was unusually high. By far the most unlikely of these was the leader of the leftist Japan Socialist Party, Tomiichi Murayama, who held office from 1994 to 1996 in coalition with his party's historic opponents, the LDP.

Japan was also being challenged over its international role. From the United States came charges that it was free-riding on the system, evidenced by its failure to play a larger part in the Gulf War. For its neighbours, however, the fiftieth anniversary of World War II revived longstanding questions about Japan's response to its own past and its imperfect acknowledgement of responsibility for the disasters of the war. Murayama, a pacifist and socialist, responded to those concerns with dignity and compassion.

Driven by Australia's economic interests but buttressed by a relationship that was now familiar and comfortable, Hawke, Hayden, Evans, Keating, Downer and Howard all made the relationship with Japan a priority. Keating visited Japan four times as prime minister. On his visit in September 1994 he told Murayama that he saw Australia's two key partners in the region as Japan and Indonesia: 'We had consistently taken Japan's side and we should build on this partnership.'[95]

One recent example of that was Keating's decision to bring Australia firmly down on Japan's side in one of its frequent trade conflicts with the United States. As Washington pressed Tokyo for greater access to the Japanese car-parts market, and for a specified share of its market, Keating told a business lunch in Tokyo in September 1992 that Australia 'would see no overall gain from entering into any trading pact which discriminates against Japan or which in one way or another is directed against Japan'.[96] American officials were privately indignant. What Keating sought from Tokyo in return was a pledge – familiar by now as an Australian aspiration – to ensure that Japan did not settle its disputes with third countries at Australia's expense.

With the greater integration of Japanese industry in the broader region, Japan was becoming more important as a partner in regional institution-building. Much of Keating's focus was on how Australia could use Japan's weight to help drive regional reform, especially through APEC.

Since the 1980s Australian governments had supported a more active and constructive Japanese role in international affairs. 'The health of the international system as a whole requires the world's second-largest economy to play a more substantial role in the world,' Keating wrote.[97] In September 1992, following legislative changes, Japan sent Self-Defense Force personnel and civilian police to Cambodia in a support role. Reciprocal visits by Australian and Japanese defence ministers in 1990 and 1992 began a pattern of more regular defence contacts, exchanges and strategic discussions, including political-military and military-to-military talks, held for the first time in February 1996.[98] Australia had moved by this time to support Japan's permanent membership of the UN Security Council.

The Joint Declaration on the Australia–Japan Partnership that Keating signed in 1995 described a 'relationship of unprecedented quality', on which foundation both countries pledged to build 'an enduring and steadfast part-nership'. Japan affirmed that Australia was 'an indispensable partner in regional affairs'.[99]

Continuity in policy was evident in the visit by the new foreign minister, Alexander Downer, to Japan in June 1996. 'Australia values highly the con-tribution Japan makes to regional stability through supporting the strategic engagement of the United States in the Western Pacific,' Downer told his Japanese audience.[100]

The United States

The form of Washington's strategic engagement with Asia was tested in the 1990s. With the closure of its giant naval and air bases in the Philippines in 1992, its anxiety about economic competition from Japan, the move to NAFTA and the 1993 'Bottom-Up' defence review, which recommended substantial force reductions, the Americans seemed to be preparing for a future closer to home.

In both Australia and the United States, the bilateral agenda was very different from the past. 'The economy, stupid' was the slogan which had driven Clinton's successful campaign team in 1992 to defeat Bush, the victor of the Gulf War, after a single term in office. When Keating paid an early visit to the new president in September 1993, the list of the topics they discussed, Clinton told the media, had begun with the General Agreement on Tariffs and Trade (GATT), the Uruguay Round of trade talks and APEC. Keating told Australian journalists later that his talks with Clinton over lunch ranged across healthcare policy, corporate taxation and the work of the child support agency.[101] 'The lack of discussion here about the security angles of Australian-American relations reflects the state of the world,' remarked one of the journalists in the room.[102]

The language used about the alliance was also very different from the rhetoric of the past (or of the decade to come). Defence relations with the United States were 'important for our national strategic posture', the 1993 strategic review declared, but as the strategic outlooks and policies of the two countries changed, 'we will need to work harder to maintain the benefits of the defence relationship, and to ensure that the United States sustains its engagement in the region'.[103] The words used by Labor and Coalition politicians to speak about the relationship and the alliance were similar, and honed by long use. The old Australian objective of maintaining United States involvement across the Pacific drove both policies. Labor's trans-Pacific economic objectives were central to the security aim of avoiding a rift between Australia's major trading partner and its security ally (an objective that would return in a much more challenging way with China twenty years later). Still, there were fewer adjectives when Labor leaders spoke about ANZUS and more balancing clauses to the statements of commitment. The 'alliance does not mean – and does not demand – obeisance,' wrote Evans.[104] 'Australia would not be performing much of a service if we were no more than Washington's Antipodean cheer squad,' Keating argued.[105]

The relaxed claim by the defence minister, Robert Ray, after the Australia–United States Ministerial (AUSMIN) talks in Washington in 1995, that 'We have a shared strategic viewpoint and there are no outstanding bilateral issues to cause any friction between the two countries', was true.[100] But it was indicative of some sort of shift in the centrality of the alliance that Australia only thought it necessary to brief the United States about the negotiation of the Australia–Indonesia Agreement on Maintaining Security the day before it was announced.[106]

The United States remained an important economic partner for Australia: in 1993 its largest source of imports, second-largest export destination and principal source of overseas investment. The tensions over the impact of America's agricultural programs on Australia's farmers continued to rankle, but it was clear that only a global resolution of the Uruguay Round would resolve that issue.

The South Pacific

The Labor government's commitment to good international citizenship was less evident in the area of development assistance, which by 1995 had fallen to a level of just 0.33 per cent of GDP, well below the 0.5 per cent it had reached in the early 1980s and substantially less than average of the wealthy industrialised countries in the OECD.[107] It was to fall to a new historic low of 0.25 per cent in 1999/2000 under the Howard government.[108]

The South Pacific remained the primary destination of that aid. Although they were well out of the international limelight and mostly ignored by the Australian media, the countries of the South Pacific continued to occupy the foreign policy attention of Australian governments. Keating assessed that he spent more time dealing with 'the complex, psychologically sensitive bilateral relationship' with PNG than with any other relationship, apart from Indonesia.[109] But during the 1990s Canberra's past concerns about great power competition, external intervention and domestic political instability in the island states were replaced by worries about the stubborn 'economic, environmental, cultural and demographic pressures' they faced.[110]

In 1993, the World Bank estimated that the real GNP of the Pacific Island countries had increased by less than 1 per cent over the preceding ten years, although they received aid flows ten times higher than for comparable small countries.[111] High population growth, poor education, inadequate management of fisheries and forestry resources, environmental degradation and an underdeveloped private sector all played a part in this 'Pacific paradox', as the Bank called it.[112]

Although the United Nations Convention on the Law of the Sea had given them sovereignty over 20 million square kilometres of ocean, the island countries received a cut of just over $A70 million a year from this rich fishing resource, which had an estimated commercial value of around $1.5 billion. Corrupt Asian logging companies were stripping timber from forests in Solomon Islands at four times the sustainable limit.[113]

Keating was struck by these problems during his first experience of the South Pacific Forum in the Solomon Islands capital of Honiara in July 1992, and then a year later as he looked out on the moonscape of Nauru, just 21 square kilometres in size. 'I felt,' he wrote later, 'Australian policy needed to be more direct and honest. I also accepted that such an approach would require active engagement by Australia at the highest level.'[114] He followed that up, attending all meetings of the South Pacific Forum as prime minister and, after the 1993 election, appointing Bilney, a former diplomat to a new position as Minister for Pacific Island Affairs. With a gregarious personality, Bilney handled the region's leaders skilfully, but he also brought to the job a hard-headed economic realism. '[W]hatever policies we've been following in the South Pacific – and by 'we' I mean Island countries and donor countries alike – are demonstrably not working,' he told the Foreign Correspondents' Association in Sydney in June 1994.[115] The level of interest of foreign investors and donor countries would largely depend 'on the implementation of sound and sustainable policies by national governments'.[116]

By the time Australia hosted the South Pacific Forum in Brisbane in 1994, Keating and Bilney were determined that some meaningful progress towards economic reform had to be made. The Brisbane Forum took as its theme 'Managing Our Resources'. Forum members agreed to seek better returns for their tuna catch, to work towards a code of conduct on logging and to examine options to rationalise money-losing regional airlines. At Australia's suggestion, a meeting of finance ministers of the forum was established.

The Australian experience of economic reform in the 1980s and '90s was introducing a new note into the talking points for Australian ministers during this period – and not just in discussions with Pacific leaders. This was, in essence, that Australia had demonstrated that it had made the difficult economic reforms and now had the right, and perhaps responsibility, to share its experiences with others as some sort of model. As Bilney put it, 'Island countries may need to ask themselves, as Australians have had to do in recent years, whether some old social and economic habits and attitudes might need to be adapted, or even abandoned, if positive and beneficial changes are to be secured and longer-term social and economic aspirations met.'[117]

PNG's problems were mounting. It was still the recipient of one-third of Australia's aid, but its economic situation was increasingly unstable, reinforced by a political situation in constant flux. Low investment, low competitiveness and misdirected expenditure – one-third of the education budget, for example, was going to fund the 2 per cent of students in tertiary institutions – left the country badly prepared to manage its development challenges. Keating described the dilemma all Australian policy-makers faced in one way or another in dealing with their closest neighbour: 'Australia was too closely involved ... and our interests were too great to enable us to walk away. On the other hand, we had neither the resources, nor the right, to resume a more interventionist role. The difficult policy goal was to find the right balance.'[118] That would be a challenge for all Australian governments.

In 1994 and 1995 PNG faced several crises over short-term debt and support for new investment projects and sought Australia's help. The government agreed to provide a stand-by facility, but only if PNG negotiated adjustment programs with the World Bank and the IMF, whose help was conditional on tough managerial and administrative reforms.

The economic problems were exacerbated by a deteriorating law and order situation, as the capacities of the security forces declined. Foreign investment, especially in badly needed resource projects, was being deterred. Australian support for training, infrastructure and personnel exchanges made little difference. The situation on the island of Bougainville was a particular problem. The undisciplined PNG defence force had been unable to reclaim control of the central part of the island from the rebel group known as the Bougainville Revolutionary Army (BRA), despite the desire of many of the islanders for peace. Sir Julius Chan, first as PNG's foreign minister, then from August 1994 as prime minister, sought a negotiated settlement. Arrangements for a peace conference on Bougainville, for which Australia agreed to provide support for a Pacific Peacekeeping Force, broke down before it began. A Bougainville Transitional Government was eventually formed in April 1995 with more moderate participants, but the hardcore rebels remained intransigent and the process eventually collapsed. Chan's frustrations would finally lead to the search for external mercenary support that would bring down his government.

New Zealand remained Australia's closest partner, and Keating and the National Party prime minister, Jim Bolger, established a good relationship. Closer Economic Relations, one of the world's most comprehensive free trade agreements, had brought great benefits to both countries, and merchandise trade had become completely free in July 1990, five years ahead of schedule. But differences arose over social security, taxation and efforts to develop a single aviation market behind a common border. And Australia worried that much lower New Zealand defence spending would begin to impair interoperability between the two forces. Keating explained the inbuilt dynamic: 'Because the relative importance of the relationship is so much greater for New Zealand than for Australia, we had a constant, if vague, sense that we were being outsmarted by the New Zealanders while we weren't paying attention. They often felt affronted that we seemed to ignore them or take them for granted.'[119]

Trade and the Uruguay Round

As the principal, if inconsistent, champion of the global free trade system, the United States had already begun looking away from non-discriminatory arrangements and towards bilateral free (or, more properly, preferential) trade deals. The first sign had been its 1989 free trade agreement with Canada ('in its own way', thought Evans, 'almost as significant as the breach of the Berlin Wall').[120] This was followed by the negotiation of NAFTA in January 1994. On the other side of the Atlantic, the 1993 Maastricht Treaty was driving a larger and more comprehensive trading bloc in Europe.

But in the end, after several near-death experiences, mutual fears of a fragmented global future were sufficient to drive the negotiators to bring the Uruguay Round, the largest trade negotiations ever conducted, to a successful conclusion on 15 December 1993. The negotiations had lasted for seven years, three months and seven days, long enough to run through five different Australian trade ministers.[116] In addition to large cuts in manufacturing tariffs, the agreement brought new disciplines to trade in agriculture (although many fewer than Australia hoped) and introduced multilateral rules in the fast-growing new areas of global trade such as services and intellectual property. The WTO was established as the governing body for global trade. The agreement, Keating told a press conference that same day, was 'a tip-top outcome for Australia, well worth the wait, the largest world trade deal ever done, a great thing for the world economy, a bull point for markets around the world and giving Australia the trading environment it could only have dreamed of seven years ago'.[121]

Despite the trade-offs and the disappointments, the outcome was an achievement for which the exhausted Australian negotiators – ministers and officials alike – could take some credit. Australia's role in the creation of the Cairns Group and its active and independent engagement in the negotiations of the General Agreement on Trade in Services (GATS) helped shape the result.[122] But even as the Round was being negotiated, there were signs that the whole global multilateral system put in place at the end of World War II had reached a point of exhaustion. Trade issues were moving beyond simple deals about cuts to industrial tariffs into complex new areas such as the protection of intellectual property, labour rights, competition policy and the environment. The line between trade and domestic policy was being blurred, raising the political stakes for governments. At the same time, with the proliferation of new sovereign states claiming seats around the global table, largely the result of the break-up of the Eastern Bloc, it was becoming harder to find consensus.

The Coalition takes office

Foreign policy played virtually no role in the decision of voters when they swept the Coalition to power with a 45-seat majority in the election of March 1996. The substance of the foreign policy set out in the government's 1997 foreign affairs and trade white paper, *In the National Interest*, did not differ markedly from that of the past. Globalisation and the economic rise of East Asia were expected to be the major influences on Australian foreign and trade policy over the following fifteen years. The Asia-Pacific would be the region of highest foreign and trade policy priority for the government, and 'within the Asia Pacific, Australia's most substantial interests are with the region's three major powers and largest economies – the United States, Japan and China – and with our largest neighbour – Indonesia.'[123] In his first major speech, the new foreign minister, Downer, gave 'an unequivocal message to the region: closer engagement with Asia is the Australian government's highest foreign policy priority'. 'No side of Australian politics,' he said, '"owns" the Asia vision.'[124]

But there were clear differences of emphasis and tone between the old and new governments. Big pictures and comprehensive frameworks were out. In the words of the white paper, on the draft of which Howard worked personally: 'Preparing for the future is not a matter of grand constructs. It is about the hard-headed pursuit of the interests which lie at the core of foreign and trade policy.'[125] The Coalition preferred to rely on traditional bilateral relationships, rather than multilateral coalition-building – a sentiment reinforced in October 1996, when largely as a result of factors beyond its control, Australia was easily defeated in its campaign to be elected to one of the five non-permanent member vacancies on the UN Security Council.[126]

A particular point of difference between the two sides of politics was the broad issue of national identity: what Howard called Keating's 'cultural agenda'.[127] Closer engagement with Asia did not 'require reinventing Australia's identity or abandoning the values and traditions which defined Australian society', the white paper declared.[128]

All Australian governments since Whitlam's had adopted policies of engagement with Asia, non-discriminatory immigration and a multicultural rather than assimilationist approach to settlement. But over time, and in the face of continuous social and economic change, resentment and resistance had built up in parts of the community. The most visible symbol of these views came in the form of a small-business woman from Queensland, a single mother and former proprietor of a fish-and-chip shop. Pauline Hanson had been nominated as the Liberal Party candidate in the safe Labor seat of Oxley, formerly held by the leader of the ALP, Bill Hayden. Two weeks before the election she was stripped of party endorsement for comments criticising special treatment for Aboriginal people. Even so – or possibly with the help of this clear demonstration of her outsider's credentials – she won the election with the largest anti-Labor swing in the country.

Howard, a cultural traditionalist, had sympathy for some of her specific views on multiculturalism and 'political correctness', and even more for the underlying anxieties they revealed. Hanson represented, he felt, 'something of a metaphor for a group of Australians ... who believed that in different ways they had been passed over, left out or generally short-changed by the pace and the intensity of economic and social change which Australia had undergone over the previous 10 to 15 years.'[129]

On 10 September 1996 Hanson delivered her maiden speech in the House of Representatives. She challenged special programs for Indigenous Australians and complained that 'we are in danger of being swamped by Asians ... They have their own culture and religion, form ghettos and do not assimilate'.[130] Howard chose not to repudiate these views, but to signal sympathy for her general concerns, if not the specific comments. They were a sign, he told the Queensland Liberal Party State Council a couple of weeks later, that under his government 'the pall of censorship on certain issues has been lifted'[131] and that Australians could now 'talk about certain things without living in fear of being branded as bigoted or racist'.[132] The prime minister's failure to criticise Hanson's views directly became a major news story in Australia and Asia. Expressions of concern that Australia was reverting to the racist approaches of the White Australia policy appeared in regional newspaper editorials and political speeches, buttressed in this particular case by memories of Howard's own earlier criticisms (subsequently repudiated) of Asian migration in 1988.

For Howard, the decision not to engage with Hanson and her views was a matter of clear domestic policy judgement. 'Among other considerations,' he wrote, 'I wanted to retain the support of those former Coalition voters who were supportive of some of the things being said by Pauline Hanson.'[133] He saw the 'extensive and often lurid coverage in Asia' as the result, principally, of overheated reporting by Australian journalists, rather than as an autonomous reaction. Other ministers, including the treasurer, Peter Costello, the National Party leader and trade minister, Tim Fischer, and Downer were more openly critical of Hanson's views.

With Howard's support, the House of Representatives passed a bipartisan statement on racial tolerance on 30 October 1996, but this didn't stop the story. It was true that reactions from Asia were coming largely from the elites (and were sometimes self-serving) and that Asian news reports often drew upon the debate in Australia. But it was the elites and the media that were shaping attitudes and making decisions. By mid-1997 Downer was reporting that Australian ambassadors in Asia were 'uniformly concerned' that the Hanson debate had 'already done some damage to our national interests in the region and had the potential to do ... specific damage to our political and commercial interests'.[134] The number of Japanese tourists to the Gold Coast declined, and positive views among Asians of Australia as a business destination fell, although there was no discernible impact on longer-term commercial interests.

Howard's first comprehensive repudiation of Hanson's views came in a speech in Sydney in May 1997, following her decision to launch her own political party, One Nation. In the Queensland state election of June 1998, Hanson's party received 23 per cent of the primary vote and won eleven seats, eight of them on the preferences of the state Coalition government, which nonetheless lost office.[135] The political lesson that Hansonism was a greater danger to the conservative side of politics than to Labor was clear. The party received 8.4 per cent of first-preference votes in the subsequent federal election in October, more than the National Party,[136] but without Coalition preferences it was unable to translate these votes into seats.

Hanson was defeated in her own electorate and the party disintegrated. Nevertheless, the sentiments she represented did not disappear and could be heard in later echoes of another line from her maiden speech: 'If I can invite whom I want into my home then I should have the right to say who comes into my country.'[137]

The Coalition and China

The failure to repudiate clearly Hanson's anti-Asian comments also played into the most serious initial foreign policy challenge for the new government. Within its first few months a series of decisions – some deliberate, some coincidental – combined to drive Australia's relations with China to an unprecedented level of frostiness.

Just days after Howard's election, China began a series of military exercises and live missile firings into the seas north of Taiwan in an unsuccessful effort to deter Taiwanese voters from supporting pro-independence candidates in the island's first fully democratic elections. The Clinton administration responded by dispatching two carrier battle groups to the area. Downer, protested to the Chinese ambassador and publicly expressed support for the American actions.

Howard had promised to reinvigorate the ANZUS relationship, which, he said, was 'drifting due to the Labor government's neglect'.[138] The AUSMIN meeting in Sydney in 1996 provided the opportunity for the government to reinforce its commitment to the alliance. The two sides released a joint security declaration (the Sydney Statement) describing the alliance as 'a cornerstone of Asia-Pacific security into the 21st century',[139] and announced an upgrade of the joint defence facility at Pine Gap and an extension on the lease until at least 2008. To the Chinese, noting the recent reaffirmation of the United States–Japan security relationship, all this had a whiff of containment about it.

Other actions and incidents played into Beijing's suspicions: the government's cancellation of a concessional finance scheme for developing countries in which China had interests, a visit to Taiwan by the primary industries minister, the sharp Australian response to Chinese nuclear tests in June, Howard's meeting with the Dalai Lama and his failure to repudiate Pauline Hanson. By September the Chinese had banned Australian ministerial visits[140] and the Australian ambassador in Beijing was unable to secure access to Chinese officials for himself or visiting Australians.[141] Australia and Japan, the official People's Daily declared, were being manipulated by the United States like the 'claws of a crab'.[142]

The tension eased after November 1996 when Howard met the Chinese president, Jiang Zemin, at the APEC summit in Manila (an early example of the diplomatic opportunities those meetings offered). It was, Howard wrote, 'about as important a meeting [as] I held with any foreign leader in the time that I was prime minister.'[143] Howard was determined to get the relationship back on track. He told Jiang that participation by China in the region was a force for stability. He assured him that Australia's alliance with the United States was 'not in any way directed against China.'[144] He reiterated Australia's support for the One China policy and for China's membership of the WTO. As they left the meeting, Jiang said to Howard in English: 'Face-to-face is much better, isn't it?'[145] Howard later wrote that he found Jiang 'amongst the more astute and fascinating and genuinely interesting leaders that I met.'[146] Jiang invited Howard to visit China.

Those who accompanied the prime minister on that visit in March 1997 saw it as an eye-opening experience for Howard. 'How long has this been going on?' he asked as he stood looking at the view from the window of his hotel suite in Shanghai.[147] The deal Howard implicitly struck with the Chinese was practical and transactional: the relationship would be based on 'mutual interest and mutual respect', not sentiment. Those interests included the development of a highly complementary economic relationship. Australia would not abandon its alliance with the United States or its other values, but neither would it support efforts to contain China. It would respect China's interests, and would express any differences privately, behind the scenes. As part of that signalling, Australia later announced that it would no longer co-sponsor an annual resolution criticising China in the United Nations Commission on Human Rights in Geneva. Human rights differences with China would instead be discussed directly in an unprecedented formal annual dialogue of senior officials. Downer received an irritated call of complaint from the US secretary of state, Madeleine Albright.[148]

Ministers now began speaking of an 'economic strategic partnership' between Australia and China. Trade continued to grow – up by an average annual rate of 18 per cent between 1996 and 2006. But security links were also being developed, including defence-to-defence talks. 'I don't think we have to choose between the Americans and the Chinese. I don't think that at all,' Howard told the journalist Paul Kelly.[149] This mantra, comforting but untrue, would be used in some variant by the Australian governments to follow. In fact, such choices would have to be made almost every day. This was the beginning of the delicate balancing act between Australia's economic and strategic interests in which all future Australian policy-makers would have to engage.

In February 1997 Deng Xiaoping died, exercising his influence to the end from his sole formal position as honorary chairman of the China Bridge Association. In his successful struggle to unleash China's economic potential he was the foreign leader of the twentieth century who most influenced Australia's future. In July 1997, in a symbolically important end to the 'century of humiliation', the phrase the Chinese used to describe their country's treatment by Western colonial powers and Japan, the British government returned Hong Kong to Beijing's control. Downer attended the swearing in of the new legislature, a ceremony the United States boycotted.

The Asian financial crisis

As the British left Hong Kong, the outlook for Asia was about to change profoundly. The Australian government's foreign policy white paper of August 1997 predicted that 'economic growth in industrialising East Asia will continue at relatively high levels over the next fifteen years.'[148] It was a reasonable assumption: for the preceding ten years average rates of growth for those economies, part of the Asian 'economic miracle', were mostly between 7 and 10 per cent.[149] But within weeks of the white paper's publication, the slow-rolling disaster of the Asian economic crisis gathered pace. Before it ended, Asia would experience the worst slowdown in the developing world for thirty years. The economies of the five Asian countries most affected – Korea, Thailand, Indonesia, Malaysia and the Philippines – would shrink by 18 per cent, and 15 million people would be pushed below the poverty line.

Most of the so-called Asian tigers had established formal or de facto links between their currencies and the US dollar. This enabled them to borrow dollars at low rates of interest, assuming that the fixed tie to their own currencies would give them a natural hedge. The strategy served them well: it kept production costs cheap and facilitated the flow of foreign direct investment and new technology into the region. In the case of Thailand, capital inflow amounted to about 10 per cent of GDP per year between 1990 and 1996.[150] But between April 1995 and April 1997, the US dollar rose nearly 60 per cent against the Japanese yen, dragging the pegged Asian currencies up with it. Exports – now more expensive – began to fall and investors began to scrutinise the current accounts of regional economies. Thailand was the first economy to be hit. Speculation by currency traders, including some of the world's largest financial institutions, grew from May 1997. Unable to defend its currency, the Thai government was forced to float the baht in July. The currency fell by 13.5 per cent that day and ended the month 23 per cent lower.[151]

One by one, in slightly different ways, and facilitated by the growing interconnectedness of all the Asian economies, the currencies of Korea, Malaysia, Singapore, the Philippines and, finally, Indonesia succumbed to the infection. Short-term money was pulled out of regional banks and stock exchanges as foreign investors began nervously to question their commitment to Asia as a whole. The catastrophic result was a $100 billion reversal of capital inflows to Korea and the ASEAN countries in a single year from 1996 to 1997. By late 1998 the market capitalisation of the Thai stock exchange was less than 15 per cent of its dollar value three years earlier.

As the pressure increased, serious structural flaws were exposed in the economic systems of most of the affected countries. Their banks and other financial institutions were poorly regulated, lending was often politically directed and their legal systems were corruptible. The IMF and the World Bank offered financial assistance but insisted on ever more elaborate and intrusive reform and austerity measures, often in areas (such as the Indonesian government's monopoly on cloves) quite peripheral to the crisis. As Keating described it, 'When the emergency paramedics from the IMF and World Bank first arrived on the scene they nearly bludgeoned the Asian patients insensible.'[152] Actively driven by the United States Treasury,[153] the IMF used economic pressure to force broader political ends.

The interplay of American economic and political objectives had the deepest impact in Indonesia. As in Thailand, the government was unable to sustain the informal currency peg between the rupiah and the dollar and in August 1997, quite early in the crisis, the rupiah was floated. But it was not enough to stop the economic collapse. An extensive deregulation package in September, then an IMF loan delivered with strong structural reform commitments failed to restore market confidence. Instead, the closure of sixteen weak banks generated a run on the entire banking system. In January 1998 a further IMF package – the most intrusive yet – sought transformative change across the whole Indonesian economic and political system. A widely circulated photograph of the managing director of the IMF, Michel Camdessus, watching on with folded arms like a stern schoolmaster as Suharto signed the agreement, symbolised for many Asians all the reasons they could no longer rely on the economic institutions of the Washington consensus.

Increasingly ill and out of touch, Suharto did not stick to the deal, and through the first half of 1998 the economic and political chaos in Indonesia increased. The economy shrank by 20 per cent, unemployment more than doubled and inflation soared. The rupiah lost 85 per cent of its value.[154] The conditions had been created for the collapse of the New Order government.

The crisis was the first real discontinuity the Howard government had faced internationally. 'It is sometimes hard to believe that only 18 months ago the East Asian region seemed to set on an economic path that was onwards and ever upwards,' Downer reflected at the end of 1998.[155] Expectations were high, especially as the crisis spread to South Korea, that Australia would become a victim too.

Within the government, and among officials, views differed about how Australia should respond internationally to what Downer described as 'the most severe economic crisis since the end of the Second World War'.[156] The government's advisers in the Treasury, in line with the IMF's position, were cautious, arguing the case for assistance to regional governments only under conditions of rigorous structural reform. DFAT and, especially, the Reserve Bank of Australia (RBA), which had been working steadily through the 1990s to develop policy dialogues with Asian central banks, argued for a more generous Australian response. In the end, in an important shift in the management of Australian international economic policy, the treasurer, Peter Costello, went with the RBA's advice.[157] Australia's response, he decided should be 'to increase our engagement with the region'.[158]

With Howard's support, Australia contributed $US1 billion to each of the IMF financial stabilisation packages for Thailand, Indonesia and Korea – the only country apart from Japan to do so. Downer and Costello argued to the IMF and obdurate US Treasury officials the case for easing the IMF's tough conditions on Indonesia. Australia increased its aid to the countries most affected, targeting the new buzzwords of 'governance' and 'capacity-building', and upgraded trade insurance schemes. Australia was also part of broader efforts to examine the operations and stability of the international financial markets. It helped establish the Manila Framework Group to facilitate macro-economic coordination between countries in the region in 1997, and it joined the G22 – a gathering of finance ministers and central bank governors from 'systemically important' countries – when it met under US government auspices in April 1998. This was the precursor to the G20.

Imprudent lending, overvalued currencies, weak governance, political uncertainty and geopolitical shifts, particularly the declining importance of Southeast Asia to the United States after the Cold War, all played their part in the crisis. The IMF accepted subsequently that its prescriptions were seriously flawed. But it was too late for the Asian countries, whose trust in the Bretton Woods institutions evaporated, and which turned, instead, to the development of new institutions of their own. China burnished its reputation as a fully-fledged regional power by holding the value of its own currency, rather than joining in a competitive devaluation.

As it became clearer that Australia's flexible exchange rate, strong financial system and solid fiscal position would carry it through the crisis in good shape, Downer saw 'a new paradigm for the relationship' between Australia and Asia emerging.[159] Australia had 'ceased being the region's "demandeur", badgering its neighbours for attention and recognition, and became a genuinely close partner and regional friend, in good times and in bad.'[160] Rather than searching anxiously for similarities with Asia, Australians should understand, he thought, that 'one reason why Australia's advice and assistance has been sought out and valued during the crisis was for the very fact that we are different, and could offer a fresh perspective'.[161] It was the beginning of a shift towards a more self-confident – sometimes overconfident – sense of national regional leadership, which would be reinforced by the commitment to East Timor yet to come.

8

THE NATIONAL SECURITY
DECADE: 1998–2008

T he years between 1998 and 2008 revealed in dramatically different ways the effect on Australian foreign policy of the powerful forces of the digital and communications revolutions and the economic globalisation they made possible. Two financial crises, the first in Asia, the second global, bookended these years. Economic reforms accompanying its entry into the World Trade Organization (WTO) and the development of a global network of supply chains made possible China's startling economic growth and its emergence as Australia's major trading partner. But the same technologies facilitated a new challenge to governments from powerful non-state actors, including terrorists, people smugglers and cybercriminals.

Foreign policy was subsumed within a broader concept of national security. Ideas of what national security was, how it could be threatened and how it should be protected all changed.

Australia joined US operations in Afghanistan and Iraq, driving the highest tempo of Australian military activity since World War II and leading to deeper military integration with the United States. With the Australia–US free trade agreement, Australia sought a closer level of economic integration with its main security partner. Al-Qaeda's use of sanctuary in Afghanistan to plan its attacks on New York and Washington generated fears about what was going on in the global badlands of 'fragile states', leading Australia to think and act in different ways about its responsibilities in the South Pacific.

The United Nations and other institutions of the post-war multilateral order became harder to operate as the large number of new states which had emerged from the fragmentation of the former Soviet bloc joined them. In response, in areas from security to trade, countries began to partner in 'coalitions of the willing'.

East Timor

The most lasting impact of the Asian financial crisis was not economic but political. On 21 May 1998 the Indonesian president, Suharto, resigned from office after thirty-one years, just months after taking office for another term. Two years earlier, the news magazine *Asiaweek* had described him as the most powerful man in Asia, but the financial crisis brought to a head all Indonesia's growing problems of political stagnation and economic corruption.

There were few early warning signs. The nation's budget was balanced, its current account deficit modest. It had strong hard currency reserves. And the longer-term record was positive: poverty rates in Indonesia had declined from 60 per cent in 1965 to just 10 per cent in the early 1990s. But none of this helped with an immediate capital account crisis. From late July 1997, domestic and foreign capital began to flee the country. When the central bank was forced to float the currency in August, the rupiah's value collapsed from around 2500 to the US dollar to as low as 17,000 by January 1998. Indonesia's private foreign debt, it became clear, was larger by far than anyone, including the government, knew. Miscalculation of the policy responses at every turn by the IMF and the Indonesian government compounded the problems.

This was the catalyst for the end of Suharto's New Order regime, which, despite intermittent political stresses, including over East Timor, had served Australian interests well since 1965. It had provided a benign strategic environment after the chaos of Sukarno and had delivered cooperative leadership in the ASEAN region. The uncertainties for Canberra policy-makers were multiplying.

The man to whom Suharto handed the reins of government was his vice-president, B.J. Habibie, an eccentric aeronautical engineer without any independent power base in the army or politics. Habibie recognised the need for democratic reform in the country and committed himself to releasing political prisoners and opening up the political system.

In the face of the pressing economic and political crises, the continuing unrest in its distant province of East Timor was a marginal issue for Jakarta.

But on 9 June 1998 Habibie told a BBC journalist that he was ready to give East Timor a special status and release political prisoners 'under one condition, that East Timor is recognised as an integral part of the Republic of Indonesia.'[1] He was offering, the foreign minister, Ali Alatas, told UN Secretary-General Kofi Annan, autonomy in all areas of government except defence, foreign policy and monetary policy.

When the Australian ambassador, John McCarthy, visited East Timor a week after Habibie's proposal, he found deep uncertainty among the various Timorese factions about how to respond. It was becoming clear to the Australian government that it might finally be possible to resolve this long-running impediment to Australia–Indonesia relations – the 'pebble in the shoe,' as Alatas famously described Indonesia's Timor problem. But what outcome would best suit Australia's interests? And how should it act? A central objective, the prime minister's office and senior DFAT leaders believed, was to persuade the Indonesian government to treat East Timor as a domestic issue which needed to be resolved by engaging the people of East Timor, rather than as an international diplomatic problem to be debated in the conference rooms of the United Nations, where Indonesia, Portugal (the former colonial power) and the UN itself had been engaged in interminable discussions about Indonesian sovereignty since the original takeover.

'When I became prime minister,' John Howard wrote later, 'I had no intention of changing Australian Government policy towards East Timor. I had not thought about the matter much at all but, to the extent that I had, my view was that a continuation of good relations with Indonesia was an important foreign policy goal for Australia.'[2]

Alexander Downer visited Jakarta in early July to review the situation. He argued that Indonesia now had a chance to address the long-term damage the East Timor situation was doing to its international reputation by negotiating an acceptable outcome with the East Timorese. He offered Australia's help in testing a representative sample of East Timorese opinion. Rather unenthusiastically, Alatas agreed.

After consultations inside and outside Indonesia, DFAT concluded that there were clear divisions in the East Timorese community about how to proceed, but that Indonesia's demand for international recognition of integration as a precondition for further autonomy was unacceptable to almost all of them. To Canberra, it looked as if the best course would be for Jakarta and the Timorese to agree to a lengthy period of autonomy before making any final decision on self-determination. The independence leader, Xanana

Gusmão, still in jail in Jakarta, was a key figure, and the Australian govern-ment now called unequivocally for his release.

To help shift the policy focus in Jakarta away from the diplomats in the foreign ministry to the president and his office, Downer and Howard decided that the prime minister should write to Habibie setting out Australia's posi-tion.[3] The terms of the letter, known to only about ten people in Canberra, were settled in discussions between Howard and Downer. It was delivered to the president's office by Ambassador McCarthy on 21 December. In restrained and modest tones, Howard expressed concern at the lack of prog-ress in the UN talks and at the hardening of attitudes in East Timor. He urged Habibie to enter direct talks with the East Timorese, including Gusmão and Catholic Church leaders, rather than relying on the New York negotiations with Portugal. He noted that the 'decisive element' of East Timorese opinion insisted on an act of self-determination and suggested Habibie consider addressing this demand 'in a manner which avoids an early and final decision on the future status of the province'. One possibility, he suggested, 'would be to build into the autonomy package a review mech-anism along the lines of the Matignon accords in New Caledonia'. In 1988, this agreement had ended the conflict between indigenous Kanaks and French settlers in New Caledonia by instituting a ten-year period of limited self-government followed by a referendum to determine the future. 'Successful implementation of an autonomy package with a built-in review mechanism would allow time to convince the East Timorese of the benefits of autonomy within the Indonesian Republic,' Howard wrote.[4]

The letter did not represent a radical change in Australian policy. It restated Australia's support for Indonesian sovereignty over East Timor. As Downer reflected later, 'it was not a 180-degree change of course, it was a 30-degree change. But there had been no change for 25 years, so in that respect a 30-degree change was quite historic.'[5] The real shift was that, for the first time, Australia was no longer describing the integration of East Timor into Indonesia as 'irreversible'.

Howard's letter was leaked in stories by Jakarta-based Australian jour-nalists on 12 January 2009. In response, Downer held a press conference describing the letter as 'a historic policy shift'.[6] He affirmed the government's preference for a lengthy period of autonomy for East Timor followed by an act of self-determination.

Habibie called Ambassador McCarthy to see him on 22 January. He unequivocally rejected the comparison between Indonesia's rule in East

Timor and France's colonial role implied by the reference to the Matignon Agreements. None of the Australian drafters of the letter had given this much thought, but it was a diplomatic mistake. Habibie said that a plan for autonomy that incorporated a review mechanism would amount to his leaving a time bomb for his successor. Instead, he went further. He wanted the issue resolved quickly: early independence for East Timor would be preferable to letting the issue drag on. Why, he asked, should Indonesia continue to pay the high cost of supporting the province if the end result was to be secession? If autonomy in the form offered by the government was not acceptable to the people of East Timor, he was inclined simply to grant independence. Indonesia 'would not die without East Timor'.[7]

Habibie's response was personal. Other powerful forces in Indonesia, including elements of the military leadership and his main political opponents, Megawati Sukarnoputri and Abdurrahman Wahid, opposed his autonomy plans. Without Habibie's determination to push for a solution on East Timor before Indonesia selected its new president later in 1999, none of what followed would have happened. On 27 January the Indonesian cabinet agreed that an act of self-determination where East Timor could choose between autonomy within Indonesia and independence could be held within a year. Gusmão was released from prison.

How much Howard's letter had to do with this change is uncertain, but together with pressure from the US Congress and the European Union, and the parallel national preoccupation with the economic crisis, it was an important catalyst.

As the dynamics shifted, Australian policy-makers began to ask whether their preferred objective of East Timorese autonomy within Indonesia was realistic any longer. By mid-February, the government had decided to step up its engagement with East Timorese groups and to support diplomatic activity to build up a common international approach. Australia also increased aid to East Timor and asked to reopen its consulate in Dili, closed since 1971.[8]

When Downer visited Jakarta again in February, he told Habibie that the Australian government would still prefer to see the East Timorese choose to stay with Indonesia but sensed they were more likely to choose independence. Australia's major interest was that the process should be credible and fair. A United Nations civilian presence in the province would assist this, he said.

The Indonesian Armed Forces, the TNI, had about 18,000 troops on the ground in East Timor. They were supported by 20,000 local militia forces, long part of Indonesia's framework for order throughout the country. The pro-independence resistance forces, FALINTIL (National Armed Forces for the Liberation of East Timor), numbered around 2000.

From early 1999 violence and intimidation by pro-integrationist militia forces against independence supporters in East Timor grew. It was increasingly clear that the army was arming and encouraging the militia to help secure a referendum outcome in support of autonomy. Downer described this as the work of 'rogue elements' within the armed forces. He was reluctant to accuse Jakarta directly, concerned that 'it would have terminated our relationship with Indonesia'.[9] He continued to argue for the presence in East Timor of a UN mission and offered substantial Australian help for this. But although the need for peacekeeping forces was discussed, it was accepted that Indonesia would be totally opposed to any external military presence in the province while it retained sovereignty.

Following questioning in cabinet by Howard in February, the government announced in March that the army's Darwin-based ready deployment force, the equivalent of two brigades, would be raised to 28-day readiness by June.[10] This capability to deploy at short notice would later prove critical.

At the next round of tripartite talks in New York in March, Alatas agreed that an act of self-determination would take the form of a direct vote of all East Timorese. National elections were due in Indonesia in June, and Habibie wanted the consultations held in time for him to present the results to the opening session of the new parliament.

Violence increased in April, with more killings and attacks on independence supporters. It was clear that the Indonesian army could not, or would not, fulfil its function of maintaining order. Howard telephoned Habibie to express Australian concern about the military's behaviour and the two leaders agreed to meet for further discussions in Bali. At this meeting on 27 April, they talked alone for an hour and a half.[11] 'I came away from this meeting,' Howard wrote later, 'believing that Habibie himself had reached a realistic and pragmatic position about East Timor. He had to pay regard to sentiment within his own country, but he was plainly of the view that there was a limit to how much national effort from Indonesia should be invested in keeping East Timor.'[12] Howard made representations about TNI behaviour. Could he ask if Habibie would accept an international peacekeeping force? 'You can ask,' Habibie replied, 'but the answer is no.'[13] Australia was given approval to reopen its consulate in Dili.

On 5 May Indonesia, Portugal and the United Nations agreed that the autonomy proposal would be put to the East Timorese people in a direct, secret and universal ballot and that a UN mission would be established to organise the consultation process. If voters rejected the autonomy proposal, authority in East Timor would be transferred to the United Nations and the territory would begin its transition to independence. Until then, responsibility for maintaining security would remain with Indonesia. With Australia's active diplomatic engagement, the United Nations established the UN Mission in East Timor (UNAMET), a civilian political mission rather than a military one. By 11 June it had begun its operations to enrol East Timorese voters and conduct the ballot. Australia provided $10 million in cash and $10 million in in-kind support.

In late July, Downer made the first ever visit by an Australian minister to East Timor. The situation on the ground remained very uncertain and some UNAMET staff were being attacked. Canberra began developing contingency plans for evacuations. By late August UNAMET's 900 personnel had been joined by some 1300 election observers. As the likelihood of a vote for independence increased, militia forces went on a rampage through Dili on 26 August.

Polling day was 30 August, and in a moving display of commitment, 98.6 per cent of all registered voters turned out to polling stations. When the result was announced on 4 September, 78.5 per cent of them had rejected the autonomy offer. The transition to independence therefore began.

Violence erupted immediately. By late afternoon on 4 September, gunfire was heard in several areas of Dili and houses were burning. Thousands of people fled to the hills. The head of UNAMET asked Australia to evacuate 200 to 300 non-essential staff to Darwin. By the following day an extensive Indonesian government evacuation was underway and UNAMET staff were forced to pull out of five East Timorese towns. An Australian consulate vehicle carrying Ambassador McCarthy was fired upon. Several hundred East Timorese sought refuge in the UNAMET compound. On 6 August militia forces attacked and destroyed the home of the head of the Roman Catholic Church in East Timor and independence leader Bishop Carlos Belo and ransacked the neighbouring Red Cross office. Some of the 5000 people sheltering at Belo's residence were marched away by the militia. Indonesian military forces were clearly permitting and facilitating the violence.

On 6 September Australian evacuation flights from Dili began. Between then and 14 September the RAAF helped bring nearly 2600 people, almost 1900 of them East Timorese, to Darwin.[14]

Habibie declared a state of military emergency in the territory and assured UN Secretary-General Kofi Annan that if martial law failed to bring matters under control, he would be willing to ask for international help. Howard telephoned Habibie, urging him to consider an international force. Annan told a press conference that the United Nations would give Indonesia twenty-four to forty-eight hours to restore control. A Security Council mission was dispatched to Jakarta and Dili.

Discussion on the mobilisation of a security force was already underway in New York. It would take several weeks to deploy a UN force, however, and because of the urgency, any immediate peacekeeping assistance would have to be put together in a 'coalition of the willing', raised and funded directly by concerned nations.

Howard had already told Annan that Australia would be willing to contribute to a peacekeeping operation, although he made it clear that Australia expected to lead it.[15] It was agreed that such a force would need a UN Security Council mandate; would be of short duration, aimed at stabilising the situation in advance of the deployment of UN peacekeepers; should have strong regional representation; and that Indonesian consent would have to be obtained.[16]

On 6 September Annan formally asked Howard if Australia would be willing to lead an international force in East Timor. Howard agreed to provide 2000 troops ready for deployment within forty-eight to seventy-two hours' notice and to pursue contributions from other countries.[17] 'For the next week to 10 days,' Howard recalled later, 'I lived on the phone in pursuit of both diplomatic and potential military assistance.'[18] In addition, intensive diplomatic and defence efforts went into securing support from the United States, Indonesia, Portugal, Thailand, New Zealand and Singapore.

One of the most important of Howard's phone calls was to ask for direct US participation. Although Australia had been consulting the Americans closely during the crisis, the administration had made no clear decisions about any US role. Howard wanted the United States there, including for the deterrent signal it would send to Jakarta.[19] But when he spoke to Clinton on 6 September, the president's response was that although the United States would provide general support, it would not deliver any 'boots on the ground'. Howard was deeply disappointed. Downer complained publicly about the American position on CNN, and he and the secretary of state, Madeleine Albright, had a sharp telephone exchange. The administration took notice, however.

On 8 September the US government and the IMF sent warnings to Jakarta that financial aid could be suspended if the violence was not brought under control. The next day Clinton demanded that Indonesia admit

peacekeepers if it could not control the violence, threatened economic sanctions, and ordered the Pentagon to suspend formal contacts with the TNI.
On 11 September he announced the suspension of arms sales to Indonesia.[20]
On his way to a fortuitously timed APEC summit meeting in Auckland on
13 September, Clinton telephoned Howard to say that the United States
would provide extensive logistic and intelligence support, the necessary
transport 'lift' for any peacekeepers and greater diplomatic pressure on
Indonesia to accept a UN-sanctioned peacekeeping operation. Howard
noted: 'This last-mentioned commitment was most important and played a
significant role in finally shifting the Indonesians.'[21]

Meanwhile, the carnage in East Timor continued. By 14 September,
according to the report of the Security Council mission, only an estimated
200,000 of East Timor's 800,000 people were still living in their own homes.[22]
The violence, in which at least 1200 people were killed, was purposeful,
designed for retribution and to send a message to other potentially seces-
sionist areas of Indonesia.[23]

Although some violence had been expected, its extent surprised both the
Australians and the United Nations. A public debate began about whether it
could have been foreseen and whether anything could have been done to
secure a UN peacekeeping intervention in advance. This had a domestic
political dimension. Australian policy was no longer bipartisan. From 1997,
Laurie Brereton, the ALP foreign affairs spokesperson, had led a change in
Labor Party policy, and through 1999 was advocating for a heavy on-the-
ground presence of UN peacekeepers in East Timor. It would have been
impossible, however, to persuade the Indonesian government to agree to a
pre-emptive force of this sort.

Habibie was not present at the Auckland meeting, but it was made clear
to the Indonesian representative that Indonesia's access to international
finance would be imperilled if it failed to accept international help in restoring security to East Timor. Later, on 12 September, Habibie announced that
he had told Annan that he would invite peacekeeping forces of 'friendly
nations' to East Timor. He asked the Thai government to help organise an
ASEAN military contribution.

Early on 15 September the Security Council voted unanimously to establish a multinational force to restore peace and security to East Timor. The
tragic massacre of Bosnian Muslims while UN peacekeepers were forced to
stand by still weighed heavily on the conscience of the international community. For this reason, the new force, to be known as INTERFET

(International Force for East Timor), had a strong mandate to use 'all necessary measures' under the peace enforcement provisions of article VII of the UN Charter. American support was again vital.

Australia had firm commitments of military and financial support from New Zealand, the United States, Canada, Britain, Portugal, France and others, but a strong regional component was necessary to give it credibility in dealing with Jakarta. Habibie had asked for ASEAN participation, but it was not at all clear that Indonesia's neighbours would commit themselves, especially under Australian leadership.

With key support from Washington, Thailand agreed to provide 1600 troops, the largest contribution after Australia's 4500 (eventually 5500). The Philippines and Singapore also participated. South Korea made a substantial contribution. Japan provided financial support of $US100 million.[24]

Under the command of Major General Peter Cosgrove, the operation began with the deployment of Australian, New Zealand and Gurkha troops on 20 September. Within four days of the initial landing, a full battalion of troops, supported by armoured personnel vehicles, had arrived in Dili. The risks were very high: miscalculation or accident could easily have resulted in direct military confrontation between Australia and its largest neighbour. But Cosgrove worked delicately and effectively to manage the crucial relationship with the Indonesian general appointed to relieve and evacuate local commanders. He imposed clear and coherent rules of engagement and discipline and worked very effectively with the media. The Australian leadership of the operation reinforced the objective Cosgrove had set: 'I felt we could do our job in a way that would limit the damage [to Australia–Indonesia relations] and provide opportunities for returning to close relations in the future.'[25] INTERFET secured the main towns on the border with West Timor and began extending protection and humanitarian assistance, as well as restoring essential services. Suspected militia members were detained.

Anti-Australian feeling in Indonesia was running high. Stories of atrocities by Australian troops were spread and there were threats against the embassy. In response to dismissive comments by Howard about its relevance, the foreign ministry announced on 16 September that Indonesia had abrogated the 1995 Australia–Indonesia Agreement on Maintaining Security and was ending all military cooperation.[26]

INTERFET's role was always intended to be limited: to hold the line until a formal UN peacekeeping mission could be organised. On 25 October the Indonesian parliament formally relinquished Indonesia's claim to the territory, opening the way for the Security Council to establish the United Nations Transitional Administration in East Timor (UNTAET).

INTERFET's responsibilities were formally passed to the new body on 23 February 2000. Together with associated operations, it had cost Australia around $1 billion.[27] UNTAET would have the full executive, legal and administrative responsibility for East Timor until it became independent as Timor-Leste in 2002, the most comprehensive UN intervention since Cambodia. Australia provided continuing support, with an Australian serving as deputy to the Philippine and Thai force commanders.

The outcome in East Timor was not the one anticipated at the beginning of the crisis, and Australia's policy objectives changed at various stages along the way. But faced with the most fundamental change since 1965 in the politics of its largest neighbour, Australia's foreign and defence policy-makers responded effectively. Serious dangers littered the path, including possible military confrontation with Indonesia, but with good management and some luck they were avoided. For the first time since Borneo in 1945, Australia had developed and led a successful military campaign in the region.[28]

Within Australia, public support for the operation ran at around 90 per cent.[29] Domestic politics were not irrelevant: 'The success of the operation in East Timor was a real setback for many of my regular political critics,' Howard wrote.[30]

Reflecting on the lessons of East Timor, Howard pointed to the 'unique assets' Australia brought to its relationships with Asia as a Western nation next to Asia with strong links to the United States and Europe. Australia did not need to change, but to get on 'with the job of being ourselves in the region'.[31]

Reinforced by the government's successful navigation of the Asian financial crisis, the East Timor intervention gave Howard, those working closely with him agreed, a new confidence in his capacity to deal with the external world and a sense that he had found a foreign policy authentically his own.

The sense of confidence led to policy stumbles, however. In September 1999, by letting pass an interviewer's comment that he saw 'Australia acting in a sort of "deputy" peacekeeping capacity in our region to the global policeman role of the US', Howard opened himself to countless 'deputy sheriff' cartoons and tags.[32]

And confidence sometimes spilled over into arrogance. The triumphalism over the 'liberation of East Timor', the references to Australia's 'special burden of leadership',[33] the emphasis on the military ethos and the downplaying of the role of others, including Indonesia and the United Nations, rubbed against raw Indonesian nerves.

In the end, the success of the intervention depended on the government's effective use of each of the principal strands that we have seen running through Australian foreign policy – the alliance, engagement with the region, and the use of the rules-based international order.

Despite Howard's initial disappointment with Washington, the diplomatic and military support provided by the United States was critical. At the same time, Australia's longstanding investment in relations with its regional neighbours, including Indonesia, yielded dividends, despite the tense environment. The existence of so many formal and informal contacts – diplomatic and military – with Indonesia eased the management of a difficult process, as Cosgrove found. Australia could, and would, have done nothing in East Timor without Indonesia's acquiescence. Australia's support for Thailand during the financial crisis was reciprocated.

Finally, and despite the Howard government's general reservations about the United Nations, the legitimisation provided by the UN Security Council resolutions was essential, as Howard acknowledged. Without that, it would not have been possible to put INTERFET together.

The effective management of the crisis in Australia was important to the outcome and changed the way Australian foreign policy was made. The National Security Committee of Cabinet became the principal engine for policy development and crisis management, engaging ministers and their officials directly. At the height of the crisis it was meeting twice daily. This established a pattern followed by all subsequent governments.

The Australian Defence Force came to be seen in a new light, as a policy instrument that might be used in the regional environment in circumstances short of all-out war. The function of aid as a support for security policy aims also grew. It was clear that all government assets needed to be better aligned, and new coordinating models such as the cross-agency East Timor Policy Group under the Department of the Prime Minister and Cabinet were developed.[34]

John Howard

Howard had come to office thoroughly tested in and tempered by politics. He entered parliament in May 1974 after working as a solicitor in Sydney. He was appointed as Minister for Business and Consumer Affairs in Malcolm Fraser's

government in 1975 and spent a short few months as Minister for Special
Trade Negotiations (leaving him with lasting scepticism about the EU bureaucracy) before becoming treasurer in December 1977. He was Leader of the
Opposition from 1985 to 1989, ousted unhappily before being returned to the
leadership again in 1995 and leading the Coalition to a decisive victory the
following year. His policy experience had centred on the economy and industrial relations. No sober analyst would have predicted that his term in office
would be dominated by issues of national security.

In public administration, Howard was an innovator as well as a traditionalist. He wanted a high degree of ministerial involvement in policy-making
and established the National Security Committee of Cabinet (NSC), with a
wider membership (including the treasurer) and broader mandate than any of
its predecessors, to help achieve this. He wanted ministers to have authority
and to take responsibility for implementing policy in their areas. He established a close policy and political relationship with his foreign minister but
there was no doubt that his was the voice that made the ultimate decisions and
determined the political tactics. The prime minister's office and department
became more central to policy-making as the government grappled with the
cross-governmental dimensions of terrorism and people movement.

Howard came to power suspicious of officials who had worked under
Labor and, in an unprecedented purge of the public service, dismissed six
departmental secretaries, including the head of DFAT. He was mistrustful of
what he saw as a foreign policy establishment and its elitist views. However,
the international policy advisers he surrounded himself with in his office
and department were skilled professionals.

Howard's foreign policy grew from the foundation of conservative social
values that shaped his political philosophy. Australians had much to be
proud of and did not need to seek new identities or different destinations;
nation-states, not multilateral bodies like the United Nations, were the bedrock of the international system; Australia wanted the least possible external
interference in its national life; the county's security depended, in the end,
on old allies that shared its values and had been part of its history.

He was a practical man and suspicious of conceptual analysis. Indeed,
the words 'practical' and 'realistic' were favoured adjectives in his description of a good foreign policy. Howard's way of thinking about the world
always began from a domestic political core – a sense of what the Australian
people wanted – and worked its way outwards to policy conclusions. But
public views, he knew, were inconstant, and he kept his eye on the domestic

mood. When he sensed it changing (as with climate change) he was ready to change with it. So he expressed his views cautiously and incrementally, preferring talkback radio and off-the-cuff addresses to long set-piece speeches that offered hostages to fortune. His language was far from the soaring rhetoric of Bush or Blair. In foreign policy, Paul Kelly noted, he was 'at his best responding to events. He was an adroit opportunist.'[35]

The Coalition's articulation of its foreign policy began by emphasising the 'hard-headed pursuit' of the national interest as a reaction to Labor's language of 'good international citizenship'. Its two foreign policy white papers were called *In the National Interest* and *Advancing the National Interest*. From the time of the East Timor intervention, however, and especially after the terrorist attacks of 2001, Howard talked increasingly about values. But they were values he identified as those of the Australian community, not the universal values of the Declaration of Human Rights. He drew on elements of Australia's history, particularly its military experiences at Gallipoli and on the Western Front, to send symbolic messages linking the past to the present. In that sense, foreign policy became part of the broader culture wars his government was fighting against what it saw as the stultifying constraints of political correctness.

He frequently framed policy around the avoidance of choice. Australia did not have to choose, he insisted, between its geography and its history; between 'multilateral institutions and alternative strategies to pursue our national interests';[36] between its economic relationship with China and its alliance with the United States.

September 11, the United States alliance and the wars in Afghanistan and Iraq

Although Howard came to office promising to revitalise the relationship with the United States, his relationship with President Clinton was uncomfortable. The international agendas of the two governments, and the personalities of the two men, were very different. Clinton's focus was on human rights, democratisation and the environment. He offered strong public support for multiculturalism during his first visit to Australia in November 1996 at the height of the debate generated by Hanson. When Howard made his second visit to the United States in 1999, niggling trade problems dominated discussion. Clinton was late for their official meeting, which lasted just thirty minutes.[37]

Differences of approach between the two countries were evident in their response to the Asian financial crisis and East Timor. During the financial crisis, Downer alluded publicly to the Lewinsky scandal then roiling around Washington, noting that the United States was 'preoccupied with its own domestic political crisis, which risks limiting its capacity to show global and regional leadership'.[38]

The relationship was transformed by two events: the election of the Republican George W. Bush as president in November 2000, and the terrorist attacks in New York and Washington in September the following year. Howard had visited Bush in Austin, Texas, before the election. Bush's conservative political agenda and the Republican administration's more accommodating approach to trade problems had an immediate impact on the tone of the relationship.

Howard came to Washington in September 2011 to celebrate the fiftieth anniversary of the signing of the ANZUS Treaty. He met the president and made the familiar speeches about the relationship: 'there's no relationship more natural, more easy and one more deeply steeped in shared experience, in common aspirations for the kind of world that we want our children to grow up in.'[39]

On 11 September, the day after he delivered that speech, a plane hijacked by al-Qaeda terrorists was flown into the Pentagon in Washington, while Howard was holding a press conference at the Willard Hotel on the other side of the Potomac River. Rushed back to the Australian embassy by his security team and bundled into a sub-basement, Howard sent Bush a message offering 'Australia's resolute solidarity with the American people at this most tragic time'.[40] On the following day, he went with a small party down to the Congress, the only guests in the visitors' gallery of the House of Representatives. For this act of support, he received a standing ovation from legislators who had been in session all through the night.

The most important impact of the attacks on the twin towers of the World Trade Center in New York and the Pentagon was the change they wrought in American views of the world. Just as the Japanese attack on Pearl Harbor had done sixty years earlier, they punctured the country's confidence that its geography was its security. It was clear that an American military response was coming and there was never any doubt that Australia would be part of it. Howard saw the events as 'a paradigm shift of historic magnitude'.[41] He had experienced America's sense of vulnerability and was convinced that this was the moment for Australia to show itself as an ally.

'We haven't been requested to provide any military assistance but obviously if we were asked to help we would,' he told a press conference at the ambassador's residence on 12 September.[42]

Hearing of the decision by NATO countries to declare that treaty operational, Howard and Downer decided, as Howard flew on a US government aircraft across North American skies cleared of all except military planes, to do the same with ANZUS. This was above all a symbolic act; it was not a precondition for Australian action. The attack had been launched by a terrorist group rather than a powerful state, and New York was a long way from 'the Pacific area' referred to in the treaty. As Paul Kelly noted, 'Nothing could have been more remote from the 1950s vision of Percy Spender and John Foster Dulles.'[43] Back in Australia, the decision received strong bipartisan support.

Afghanistan commitment

On 28 September 2001 the UN Security Council passed a wide-ranging anti-terrorism resolution recognising the right of UN member states to combat the threat of terrorism 'by all means'. The United States stepped up preparations for an attack on al-Qaeda in Afghanistan and the puritanical Islamist Taliban government that sheltered it.

In Australia, the government announced on 2 October that special forces and aircraft would be sent to Afghanistan. Three days later, Howard called a federal election for 10 November. The campaign would be dominated by national security and asylum-seeker issues and the result was a clear victory for the Coalition against the political trends of the preceding few years.

The United States operation – 'Enduring Freedom' – began on 7 October. An early Australian deployment of special forces troops was expanded with naval, army and air force assets. Australians joined the first assaults on the Taliban by American and British forces. Public support for the operation in Australia was strong.

By 10 November 2001 the Taliban had been driven from power, although Osama bin Laden had escaped from his headquarters in the Tora Bora mountains along the border with Pakistan. Among the foreign fighters captured were two Australian citizens, David Hicks and Mamdouh Habib, whose subsequent treatment and detention at Guantanamo Bay would become a political cause in Australia.

The Australian government made it clear to the Americans in the case of Afghanistan and, later, Iraq that any Australian commitment would be given early and fully, but that Australia would not be present for the pacification and reconstruction that would follow. It pointed to its commitments in East Timor and the Solomon Islands. 'I was conscious,' Howard recalled later, 'that given the potential for difficulties in our part of the world, the right combination was to provide sharp-edged forces for a limited period of time during the hot part but not get bogged down in long drawn-out peacekeeping operations.'[44]

In late 2002 the Australian special forces were withdrawn from Afghanistan. Responsibility for Afghanistan's reconstruction was transferred to NATO in August 2003, the first time the treaty partners had been committed outside Europe's borders. Security was now in the hands of an International Security Assistance Force (ISAF) drawn initially from thirty countries.

Iraq preparation

Within hours of the attack on 11 September 2001 the Australian ambassador in Washington, Michael Thawley, one of Howard's closest advisers, told him 'that as a result of the attack, Iraq would be back on the agenda for the Americans.'[45] By the time Howard visited Washington again in June 2002 to address a joint session of Congress, Iraq was high on the list of matters discussed.

The First Gulf War of 1990 to 1991 had left many issues unsettled. Although his army was forced out of Kuwait, Saddam Hussein remained firmly in power in Baghdad. He had failed to comply with many of the obligations imposed on him by the ceasefire that ended the war, including the destruction of Iraq's chemical weapons and long-range missiles and its programs to build nuclear and biological weapons. Between 1992 and 2000 the Clinton administration pursued a containment policy against Iraq, with economic and military sanctions and no-fly zones enforced by American and British air patrols. The *Iraq Liberation Act* of 1998 made regime change the official policy of the United States government. At Clinton's request, Howard had agreed in 1998 to pre-position Australian Special Forces in the Middle East to back a proposed strike against Saddam, although this was abandoned when Iraq bowed to demands over UN weapons inspections.

By the end of the century, however, sanctions appeared to be causing more pain to Iraq's civilian population than damage to the regime. The international consensus on sanctions was weakening, and two of the permanent members of the UN Security Council, Russia and France, were calling for them to be lifted.

The September 11 terrorist attacks helped strengthen the conviction within the administration that the only way to keep America safe was to pre-empt future threats before they manifested themselves. Iraq and Saddam, rather than Afghanistan, were at the centre of this concern. Well before Bush came to office, an influential group of neo-conservative advisers had been pressing for American action to overthrow Saddam. The al-Qaeda attacks provided their opening.

In his January 2002 State of the Union address, Bush singled out Iraq, along with Iran and North Korea, as part of an 'axis of evil' that harboured ter-rorists and was developing WMD. Underpinning the US National Security Strategy released in September that year was the assertion that 'in an age where the enemies of civilisation openly and actively seek the world's most destructive technologies, the United States cannot remain idle while dangers gather'.[46] As the national security adviser, Condoleezza Rice, put it: 'we don't want the smoking gun to be a mushroom cloud.'[47]

It was clear from mid-2002 that Bush had decided to commit the United States to action against Saddam. 'From the very beginning,' Howard wrote later, 'we knew what was in the minds of the American military. We also knew how we might contribute in the most effective manner possible and in a way that safeguarded, as best one could, the position of any Australian troops which might ultimately be committed.'[48]

Preliminary 'operational planning' discussions between American and Australian officials took place in July, and by August Australian military planners were working with their US counterparts at Central Command in Tampa, Florida, in anticipation of a decision to join the military action.[49]

It was not until around September 2002 that the issue of Iraq fully entered the Australian public debate, however. In a statement to the House on 17 September, Downer argued that Saddam's 'ambition to develop and deploy chemical, biological and nuclear weapons' could not be ignored. Australia's national security interests were directly engaged by Iraq's defi-ance of the resolutions of the United Nations.[50]

In November, Howard said, 'the ultimate nightmare must surely be the possibility of weapons of mass destruction falling into the hands of terrorist groups. That is a powerful additional reason why a country such as Iraq, which has previously been willing to maliciously use weapons of mass destruc-tion should have those weapons denied to it.'[51] And he was confident Iraq now had them. 'I would have thought that the proposition that Iraq possesses weapons of mass destruction is beyond argument,' he told parliament.[52]

The bipartisan Australian political consensus on Afghanistan did not carry through to Iraq. The parliamentary Labor Party encompassed a variety of views on the possible war, but since Evatt's work on the UN Charter, Labor had been committed to the legitimising role of the Security Council in authorising the use of force. The different Labor approaches coalesced around that point. Simon Crean, who had replaced Kim Beazley as leader after the 2001 election loss, declared that 'no troops should be sent to war without a United Nations mandate'.[53]

Bush's main international supporter, Tony Blair, led a British Labour Party badly split over possible military action. In late 2002, prompted by Blair, Washington announced that it would take the Iraq issue back to the UN Security Council. The United States and Britain sought a new resolution outlining the consequences for Iraq if it failed to cooperate with the regime of UN inspections to which it had agreed in September. The resulting Resolution 1441 gave Iraq a 'final opportunity to comply with its disarmament obligations' and required it to allow arms inspectors unimpeded access to conduct their searches. France and Russia accepted the resolution on the understanding that further Security Council consideration would follow if Iraq failed to comply.

The weapons inspections of the United Nations Monitoring, Verification and Inspection Commission (UNMOVIC) failed to uncover evidence that Iraq possessed WMD, although they also pointed regularly to its government's failure to cooperate. In December 2002 Iraq submitted a 12,000-page declaration on its facilities to the UN, but the UNMOVIC chairman, Hans Blix, raised questions about the absence of supporting evidence. The US secretary of state, Colin Powell, said the declaration 'totally failed' to meet UN demands for full disclosure.

On 27 January 2003 Blix told the Security Council that UNMOVIC 'neither asserted nor excluded that weapons of mass destruction existed in Iraq', but concluded that 'Iraq appears not to have come to a genuine acceptance – not even today – of the disarmament which was demanded of it'.[54] There were, he said, question marks that needed to be resolved before the dossiers could be closed.

But the Bush administration had already moved on. In October 2002 Congress had authorised the president to use force in Iraq and by January 2003, 97,000 US troops had arrived in the Middle East. The arguments for war in Iraq marshalled by the administration's advisers ranged from revenge for claimed involvement in the 9/11 attacks to the prospect of democratising the Middle East, but as the deputy secretary of defense, Paul Wolfowitz, told a journalist in May 2003, WMD had been the 'bureaucratic reason' for the war, the one rationale on which all the proponents could agree.[55]

The Australian government was still insisting that it had taken no decision to commit troops to Iraq (although by now this was only true in the sense that no formal cabinet decision to do so had been taken) and that war could be avoided if Saddam implemented UN demands. But the Australian military headquarters in the Middle East had been moved in November to co-locate with the US Central Command, and on 10 January 2003 the government announced that it would deploy forces to the Gulf 'in support of diplomatic pressure on Iraq to disarm'.[56] By 25 February about 2000 ADF personnel were in the Middle East.[57]

On 4 February 2003 Howard outlined to parliament the case for war against Iraq. He offered three reasons for Australia to act: to ensure that Saddam did not possess WMD; to show that the United Nations enforced its own decisions; and the importance to Australia of the United States alliance, which 'has been and will remain an important element in the government's decision-making on the Iraqi issue'. Disarming Iraq would 'bring enormous benefits to the Middle East and will be widely welcomed', he said.[58] Absent from Howard's speeches was any of the moral universalism which informed Bush's language when he spoke to the American people: 'the power and appeal of human liberty is felt in every life and in every land.'[59]

By this time, Australian perspectives on the war were changing. The threat of terrorism was coming closer. Australia was specifically listed as a target in the first message bin Laden released to the media after the 11 September attacks. In December 2001 Singaporean authorities revealed they had foiled a plot for attacks on targets including the Australian High Commission by the al-Qaeda-affiliated Southeast Asian militant group Jemaah Islamiyah (JI). Then, in October 2002, the death of eighty-eight Australians in a JI terrorist attack in Bali gave the threat a new edge. The public debated the question of whether Australia's participation in war in Iraq would make it a bigger target for terrorists or whether, as the government said, Australia was already a target and needed to respond.

The war begins

On 18 March 2003 Bush issued an ultimatum to Saddam: unless he and his sons handed over power and left the country within forty-eight hours, the

United States would invade at the head of an international coalition. On the same day, following a telephone call from Bush, Howard finally sought cabinet agreement to commit Australia to the war. 'Disarming Iraq is necessary for the long-term security of the world and is therefore manifestly in the national interests of Australia,' he then told the House of Representatives.[60]

Operation Iraqi Freedom was launched on 20 March. Although forty-eight countries were named as partners in the international Coalition of the Willing, only four – the United States, the United Kingdom, Australia and Poland – took part in the initial military strikes.

Australian special forces conducted early raids across the Kuwaiti border to take out the sites of Iraqi missiles which the Americans feared might be pre-emptively launched against Israel. On 20 March Australia committed a special-forces task group, navy frigates and aircraft to the invasion. But, as had been the case in Vietnam, it was Australia's political rather than military contribution that mattered most to Washington. Other close allies, including Canada and New Zealand, declined to participate.

On the weekend of 14 to 16 February over 500,000 people across the country took part in rallies against the Iraq War. Opinion polls in early 2003 showed a sizeable majority of Australians opposed troops being sent to war without UN approval. But as Australian forces engaged in combat operations, public support increased.

The legality of the intervention under international law was a central point of contention in the Australian debate. Although Resolution 1441 had required Iraq to document its WMD programs and related facilities, it had not authorised the use of force. Indeed, that had been part of the price of its passage. The United States and United Kingdom argued, however, that a condition of the ceasefire that ended the first Gulf War in 1991 had been Iraq's agreement to eliminate its WMD. It had not done so, they contended, so that ceasefire no longer applied and the original UN resolution legitimising the use of force to remove Iraq from Kuwait continued to apply. Drawing on advice from its own lawyers, the Australian government followed suit. The UN secretary-general, a large number of international lawyers and the Labor Opposition disagreed.

The main body of American and British forces crossed from Kuwait and advanced rapidly on Baghdad. By 2 April US troops were on its outskirts. Saddam and senior regime figures fled. On 13 April Tikrit, Saddam's hometown, was taken and the war's initial phase was essentially over.

Speaking from the deck of an aircraft carrier in front of a banner reading 'Mission Accomplished', Bush declared on 1 May 2003: 'In the battle of Iraq, the United States and our allies have prevailed.' He was premature. The occupation, reconstruction and democratisation of the country were to prove far more difficult.

The government had already ruled out a major role for Australian ground forces in any post-war stabilisation and rebuilding, and the defence minister, Robert Hill, announced that most Australian soldiers would return to Australia in May and June 2003 because of commitments in East Timor and the Solomons. An embassy was re-established in Baghdad and Australian experts supported the Iraq Survey Group, the US-led effort to track down Saddam's WMD.

But although it scoured the Iraqi countryside, the Survey Group found no weapons. Neither were any clear links between Saddam and al-Qaeda discovered. It was becoming evident that the central rationale for war had no foundation. No matter what their position on the decision to go to war had been, almost all the key policy-makers, as well as the UN inspectors, were surprised by that result. Some of the intelligence on which the weapons claims were based had been false, but the greater failure had come with the analytical processes that drew the intelligence together and the policy decisions that followed. It was assumed that because Saddam had possessed the weapons in the past, had used them in the past and was reluctant to present all the evidence, he had them still. Howard noted in his autobiography that this 'gave a lethal political weapon to our opponents and they made the most of it'.[61]

Formal inquiries were launched into the work of the intelligence agencies in Washington and London, and Australia followed up with a parliamentary inquiry and a report by Philip Flood, a former head of DFAT and the Office of National Assessments. In March 2004, Flood found that the Australian intelligence agencies 'drew the most likely conclusions' from the available evidence but had made 'insufficient challenge both to the assumptions and sources'.[62] The much larger question, however, was whether Iraq's possible possession of WMD had been a sufficient reason to go to war in the first place. The unanticipated consequences of an ill-planned intervention were only beginning.

Violence in Iraq

The decision by the Coalition Provisional Authority to disband the Iraqi army in May 2003 unleashed old and bitter rivalries between the members of the Sunni sect of Islam, who dominated the power structure of Saddam's government, and the country's Shi'a majority. Between 2003 and 2005, as the American administrators organised the drafting of a new constitution and the transfer of power to an interim Iraqi administration, violence increased across the country. Criminal gangs, foreign terrorist fighters and insurgents targeted coalition forces, civilians and each other. Iraq descended into a civil war.

By June 2004 only 1000 ADF personnel remained in Iraq, half the number originally deployed. Howard resisted an American request for a significant increase in Australia's deployment. Australians, he declared in December 2003, had 'largely moved on' from the war in Iraq.[63]

Within Australia, public opinion continued to be divided on the war. A new Labor leader, Mark Latham, who replaced Simon Crean in December 2003, was promising to bring the remaining Australian forces home by Christmas. The government charged him with wanting to 'cut and run', notwithstanding the modest nature of its own contribution.

Latham's public hostility to the Bush administration was fuelling public doubts about his national security credentials. Despite the appointment of the moderate Kevin Rudd as shadow foreign minister, and the return to the front bench of Beazley as defence spokesperson, the polls swung strongly against Labor and Howard was returned easily in the election he called in September 2004. Voters had again been reminded of national security issues when, in the first week of the campaign, a suicide bomber in a car attacked the Australian embassy in Jakarta killing nine people, including local embassy staff.

The United States ratcheted up the pressure on Australia to do more in Iraq and in a significant reversal of policy the government sent 450 troops back in 2005 to help protect Japanese Self-Defense Force engineers operating in the southern (and largely violence-free) province of Al-Muthanna.

When, in January 2005, following ill health, frustration with his colleagues and criticism of his refusal to interrupt his holidays to respond to the Asian tsunami, Latham abandoned his job and politics, Beazley was returned to the ALP leadership. He and Rudd continued to oppose Australian involvement in Iraq but believed that 'whatever the argument about Iraq, Afghanistan needed to be effectively finished'.[64]

Return to Afghanistan

While international attention was focused on Iraq, the security situation in Afghanistan was also deteriorating. The Taliban clawed back influence in the southern and eastern provinces. Since the withdrawal of Australian forces in November 2002, the Australian presence in the country had been minimal – just two uniformed officers in Kabul and no Australian diplomatic presence. By mid-2005, however, Australia was coming under pressure from the United States to return to help the task of reconstruction and nation-building. There was little enthusiasm for the prospect within the government or its departments.

In June 2005, when the cabinet considered a submission from the defence minister, Robert Hill, to send a Provincial Reconstruction Team of engineers to assist the NATO forces in the nation-building task, Howard preferred to respond with an offer of special forces. When he announced their departure on a twelve-month deployment in July, however, he also kept open the option of providing forces to assist with reconstruction.[65]

Australia's agreement to expand its contribution was conditional: it would not take the lead role and would work only with a partner of its choice. That partner turned out to be the Netherlands, which was thinking of establishing a Provincial Reconstruction Team in Uruzgan province in the south. Thanks to the complexities of coalition politics in The Hague, it was not until February 2006 that Howard announced that an Australian Task Force would be sent to Afghanistan to join the Dutch team.[66] By the time the deployment to its new headquarters in Tarin Kowt finally began in August, a protection force of 150 had been added to guard the 270-member task reconstruction force. Australia also established an embassy in Kabul, a new indication of its diplomatic commitment. The original special forces deployment was also extended. In April 2007 Howard announced that a 300-strong Special Operations Task Group would also be sent to Uruzgan to help disrupt Taliban command and control supply routes.[67] So despite the government's original intentions, Australia now found itself engaged in the work of protecting civilians, holding territory and improving the economic and social conditions of the local people.

In 2004/05 the cost of Australian military operations in Afghanistan was $1 million. By 2010/11 it would be $1.6 billion.[68] In the five years after 2000, the defence budget grew by an average of 3 per cent per annum in real terms, in addition to the costs of funding counterterrorism measures and operations in Afghanistan.[69]

On 8 October 2007 Australia suffered its first combat death in Afghanistan in more than five years. Howard called an election in October. Another death, the second of many, followed on 25 October. By then any optimism

about the consequences of the intervention in Iraq or the speed with which
the new Afghan government could consolidate its control was fading. A
scandal in 2004 over the mistreatment of prisoners by American soldiers at
the Abu Ghraib prison, the growing violence in Iraq and an increasing sense
of military stalemate were changing the public mood. There was a particular
Australian angle, too. In November 2006 the Cole Royal Commission issued
its report on the Australian Wheat Board's sanctions-breaching payments of
$290 million in bribes to Saddam's regime between 1999 and 2003 in an
effort to protect Australia's large wheat market.

Consequences and lessons

The decision by the Bush administration to invade Iraq was a strategic disaster for the United States and for the region. None of the goals of the war,
except for the forced removal of Saddam, was met. Iraq did not become a
beacon for stability in the Middle East, the Iraqis did not embrace their lib-
erators and no weapons of mass destruction were found. Insufficient
attention had been paid to the question of what would happen after Saddam
was overthrown.

The Middle East wars generated a formal and long-term shift in the
nature of Australia's relationship with the United States. Australia had followed its ally, not blindly as some critics suggested but certainly
unthoughtfully, interpreting its contribution to the alliance in just one, limited, way. The shift began with the close friendship between Howard and
Bush (a challenge to scholars who downplay the importance of human
agency in foreign policy) but it was cemented by a much broader set of
events and experiences in the years between 2002 and 2008. The alliance
itself became subsumed within a larger War on Terror, which gave ANZUS
new global as well as regional dimensions.

The close collaboration between Australian and US forces in Afghanistan
and Iraq greatly deepened the intimacy of military cooperation. At all levels,
from planning to operations, from weapons systems to intelligence, Australia
became more closely integrated with the United States. The government's
2002 decision to commit Australia to join the Joint Strike Fighter development program was part of a larger drive to improve interoperability between
the armed forces.

The free trade agreement, to which this chapter will return, could not
have been secured without the Australian support for US actions in the

Middle East and was seen by the government as a parallel economic structure to balance and strengthen the security relationship.

Howard and Bush developed a genuinely warm and trusting relationship, but that dynamic had implications at times for the relationship between the two countries and for Howard's political judgement. His casual error in failing to rebut a journalist's assertion that Australia was acting as a sort of deputy sheriff to the United States was damaging only because it seemed to reflect an underlying reality. In February 2007 Howard declared that if he were running al-Qaeda he would pray for a victory by the Democratic presidential contender Barack Obama.[70] And there were other times during this period when the relationship seemed close to being claimed by one political alignment. In February 2003 Opposition leader Mark Latham told parliament that Bush was 'the most incompetent and dangerous president in living memory'.[71]

Finally, the Middle East assumed more importance in Australian strategic policy than at any time since the North African campaigns of World War II and the Gallipoli and Palestine campaigns of World War I. The Howard government's November 2005 update to its 2000 defence white paper declared that 'Australia's vital interests [are] inextricably linked to the achievement of peace and security in the Middle East'.[72] Vital interests, by definition, are those a country would go to war to defend. The 'achievement of peace and security' in the Middle East was a monumental aspiration. That judgement effectively extended Australia's primary area of strategic interest to West Asia. But the resource allocations and policy approaches of the Howard government never suggested for a moment that those 'vital interests' existed, or could exist, independently of America's presence in the region.

Opposition to the Iraq War on the part of some of the key members of the EU reinforced Howard's frustrations with Europe over agricultural trade and its demands for greater Australian action on climate change. The addition of ten new members from eastern and southern Europe to the Union in May 2004 made it even more unlikely that European attitudes on trade policy would change.

In the United Kingdom, however, Howard found a close international partner in Labour prime minister Tony Blair. As the two men became Bush's closest international allies on the Iraq War, a practical working relationship between Britain and Australia, absent for decades, developed. Annual meetings of the foreign and defence ministers of the two countries (known as AUKMIN in a direct parallel with AUSMIN) were established in 2006 and became over time an important fixture in the calendars of Australian ministers.

In the November 2007 election that brought Labor to power under Rudd just a year after he challenged and defeated Beazley for the ALP leadership, national security issues were secondary to domestic concerns – industrial relations, health, education and a sense that the government had been in power too long. Labor had maintained its opposition to the Iraq War while promising to do more in Afghanistan. So in June 2008 Australian combat forces were withdrawn from Iraq, although other forces remained in non-combat jobs and to provide embassy security. The new government continued to provide assistance for relief and rehabilitation.

Australia was not done with the Middle East. The questions of mission and means in Afghanistan would continue to preoccupy the government and its advisers. And further consequences of the interventions in Iraq and Afghanistan would reveal themselves over the following years in a destabilised region, deeper sectarian conflict, the emergence of new and more brutal terrorist groups, and vast numbers of new refugees.

The South Pacific: Tending 'our patch'

One of the arguments the Howard government had used to limit its initial commitments in Afghanistan and Iraq was the need to deploy ADF forces closer to home in East Timor and the Solomon Islands. This part of the world, Howard told reporters at the Pacific Islands Forum in Western Samoa in August 2004, 'is our patch'.[73] Most of his predecessors would have agreed with that sentiment in some form, but there was a new edge to the discussion now that it was feared that terrorists could use fragile states to prepare their attacks. If Australia was not a deputy sheriff, it certainly saw itself as having particular responsibilities for the South Pacific in an informal division of allied labour. Events in East Timor, the Solomons and Papua New Guinea played into this more proprietorial sense of Australian responsibility for 'our region'.[74]

The difficulty of dealing with PNG – Australia's closest neighbour, a former colony, a development challenge, a democracy with its own sometimes impenetrable logic – confronted every Australian government. Their objectives were easy enough to identify: all of them would at some time point to what Downer called Australia's 'real interest in a stable, prosperous, secure and well governed Papua New Guinea'.[75] But they would then encounter the challenge of translating that interest into effective policy. Each new government would seek ways of differentiating itself from the problems of its predecessors but would gradually accumulate its own set of problems. 'When I first became Foreign Minister … the bilateral relationship was not in great shape. There was a sense of fatigue and a lack of direction in the relationship which I wanted to dispel,' said Downer in 1998.[76] Ten years later, a new prime minister, Rudd, making an early visit to PNG in March 2008, saw the need for 'a new partnership that could be a model to the rest of the world'.[77]

Soon after he came to power, Howard faced an unprecedented problem in PNG. Unrest on the copper-rich island of Bougainville, then in its ninth year, continued to frustrate the government in Port Moresby. Its armed forces had been unable to subdue the rebels operating in the island's deep jungles under the banner of the Bougainville Revolutionary Army (BRA) and Australia was reluctant to help militarily. The lost revenue from the closed Panguna copper mine left a large hole in the PNG budget. The frustrated prime minister, Sir Julius Chan, sought help from a shadowy private military company, Sandline International, based in the UK, to recruit mercenary fighters from South Africa and provide weapons in order to defeat the BRA and reopen the mine. In February 1997 Australian intelligence agencies confirmed reports that a $36-million contract had been signed and the mercenaries had begun to arrive in the country. This was a serious policy challenge for the Australian government: PNG was an independent country and Australia needed to maintain close relations, but the introduction of mercenary fighters into weak South Pacific states was a terrible precedent which, in any case, in the view of the government's advisers, was only likely to increase the problems on Bougainville.

Howard and Downer acted as soon as they were briefed. Howard telephoned Chan, who dissembled: the contract was only for training PNG soldiers, he said. Downer flew to Port Moresby for more talks. He confirmed the story to journalists and it became public on 22 February. When they met in Sydney on 9 March, Howard warned Chan of 'consequences of a serious kind so far as the relationship between Australia and PNG was concerned' if the mercenaries were used.[78] Chan suggested that Australia buy out the Sandline contract, but this was not a precedent Howard would consider.[79] Behind the scenes, Australia coordinated international pressure on PNG as well, briefing friendly diplomats and international financial institutions.

Unhappy about the Sandline arrangements, the PNG Defence Force (PNGDF) commander, Brigadier General Jerry Singirok, had the company's chief in PNG, a British national, arrested on 17 March and demanded that the prime minister, the deputy prime minister and the defence minister resign. The police force decided to stand with the government, however. Singirok was dismissed but he continued to act as the de facto commander of the PNGDF and controlled loyal lieutenants throughout the crisis. Unrest spread and Parliament House in Port Moresby was surrounded by protesters. Facing what was in effect an attempted military coup in PNG, Howard sided with the elected government despite his opposition to the mercenaries. Up to 10,000 Australian citizens were based in PNG; evacuation plans were readied. Confronted on 19 March by the internal unrest, including tense stand-offs between army and police, and threats from visiting Australian envoys of 'dramatic and drastic measures that would harm PNG' if the contract went ahead, Chan capitulated. The contract was cancelled and the mercenary troops flown out to Hong Kong.[80]

The political unrest in PNG continued, however, forcing Chan to resign while a committee of inquiry examined the affair. He was eventually restored to office but lost his seat in the 1997 election. During the crisis Australia had, in its own interests, demonstrably interfered in the internal affairs of its neighbour, including by arranging for the diversion of a Russian transport plane delivering arms to Port Moresby and seizing its cargo of helicopter gunships and other weapons.

Some good came of the Sandline affair. It provided an important circuit-breaker for the Bougainville dispute. A series of meetings between most of the key players facilitated by New Zealand and Australia led finally, in January 1998, to a ceasefire agreement. From May 1998 Australia led a 300-strong Peace Monitoring Group (PMG), comprising unarmed military and civilian monitors from Australia and the region. Long and complex negotiations continued. Finally, in August 2001 a Bougainville Peace Agreement, brokered by Downer, was signed. It provided for elections to establish local autonomy with a referendum on full independence to follow between ten and fifteen years later. The constitution for the Autonomous Region of Bougainville was gazetted in December 2004 and elections followed. When the new Bougainville government was formed in June 2005, Australian policy and Downer's diplomacy could share a fair degree of the credit.

Alexander Downer

Downer was born into an established Liberal Party dynasty. His grandfather had been premier of South Australia twice, and a senator in the first federal parliament. His father was a minister in the Menzies government and later served as high commissioner in London. Downer spent some of his childhood in the same London residence into which he would later move as high commissioner in his own right, following his time in politics. He worked as a young diplomat in the Department of Foreign Affairs and Trade and as a political adviser to Fraser and Peacock before he was elected to the House of Representatives in 1984.

Downer had a brief and unsuccessful period as leader of the Opposition from May 1994 to January 1995, when he stepped down without a struggle to enable Howard to lead the Coalition to victory in the election the following year. He became foreign minister in the new government but, despite his experience in the area, had a shaky first year in office, coming close to misleading parliament over international reactions to cuts to an export financing aid program. His ministerial colleague, Peter Reith, recorded in his diary that 'at the end of our last parliamentary week of the opening session most people would be thinking that for Alexander it is only a matter of time'.[81] However, Howard felt an obligation to Downer for the way the leadership transition had been handled, and supported him through the difficulties. They differed over a handful of issues, including cuts to the aid budget and the handling of Hanson, but their overall approaches to the world were closely aligned – conservative, based on the national interest, supportive of old ties with traditional allies and suspicious of multilateral institutions and approaches. More than Howard, however, Downer was attracted by the universalist language of neo-conservatism. Castigating Labor for its caution about the Iraq War, he told an audience at the University of New England in May 2005 that while it was 'far too soon to reach triumphalist conclusions', developments in Afghanistan, Iraq, the Palestinian territories, Saudi Arabia, Egypt and Syria provided 'yet another powerful reminder that freedom is the most contagious idea in history'.[82]

Howard and Downer developed over time a closer relationship between prime minister and foreign minister than any in Australian history since the brief period Whitlam held the job himself. It is not possible to identify a Downer approach to foreign policy different from Howard's. And there was a broader political alliance at work as well: Downer was a strong supporter of Howard in the wider work of cabinet, in the government's overall political management and as one of its key political salesmen. A member of Downer's staff (and future minister), Greg Hunt, said, 'Nobody talked with Howard more at ministerial level over the life of the government than Alexander ... If the PM needed counsel, it would be more likely than not that he'd call Alexander.'[83]

Downer was partisan and tribal in his Liberal Party loyalties: 'I am born of the Liberal Party and I am a creature of the Liberal Party.'[84] Public servants and academics were tagged for their alleged political affiliations. He was gregarious, found gravitas difficult and often subverted himself by a tendency to joke. He was authentically his own person; not even the role of foreign minister could change that. He worked diligently and took the job seriously, but despite the very large increases in funding to defence and the intelligence agencies during these years there was no similar expansion in DFAT's diplomatic resources.

His own assessment of his achievements listed building the relationship with Indonesia, maintaining and improving relations with both China and the United States, '[giving] East Timor its freedom and its independence', ending the civil war on Bougainville and fixing the situation in the Solomons 'albeit at great expense'.[85]

PNG: The Enhanced Cooperation Program

Notwithstanding the political progress made in Bougainville, PNG's economic situation continued to deteriorate. 'None of us is in any doubt as to the serious and systemic nature of the problems PNG must tackle today as a result of the economic and social decline of the past decade,' Downer said bluntly in December 2004: 'High inflation, soaring budget deficits and public debt, outflows of foreign investment and rising unemployment.'[86] The prospect of the rapid spread of HIV/AIDS was adding to the problems.

Howard's relationship with Sir Michael Somare – PNG's most enduring political leader, who had returned to the prime ministership in 2002 – was uneasy in a number of ways. Australia's 'fragile state' and 'our patch' narratives grated with Somare's nationalism, and there were particular disagreements over Australia's successful push to have an Australian appointed as secretary-general of the Pacific Islands Forum, and Somare's helping a fugitive Solomon Islands politician escape Australian extradition efforts. Australia banned Somare's travel to Australia, to his indignation. Reflecting on the PNG relationship when he left office, Howard wrote carefully, 'there was a special bond, as well as the obligation of a former colonial power, but they constantly rubbed against corruption and governance issues throughout my entire prime ministership'.[87]

The longstanding debate about the effectiveness of Australian aid to PNG – $7.4 billion between independence and 2000 – continued. Like Bilney before him, Downer emphasised that 'Pacific countries themselves must recognise that [Australian] assistance is not a substitute for proper governance and management of their own affairs'.[88]

In early 2004 Australia's policy response to these serious problems came with the announcement of an $800-million Enhanced Cooperation Program (ECP), designed to directly address the declining law and order situation, improve governance and reduce corruption by bringing a higher level of hands-on Australian engagement to the aid program.[89] This approach was part of a recurring cycle in Australian aid policy that alternated between the view that as an independent country PNG should be left to learn from its own experience and a belief that only more active Australian involvement could make a difference. Under the ECP, 210 Australian police would be sent to work with the Royal Papua New Guinea Constabulary and sixty civilian public servants would be placed in central ministries to mentor local officials.[90] Downer described it as 'one of my government's most important and ambitious foreign policy initiatives'.[91]

The ECP proved difficult to implement, however, with disputes over the conditionality of aid and issues of immunity for the Australian police officers. An agreement on the ECP was finally signed in June 2004 but in May 2005 the PNG Supreme Court declared that the legislation providing immunity to Australian police was unconstitutional. The police departed, leaving about forty civil servants embedded in government departments.

Rudd visited PNG in early 2008, issuing with some fanfare a twenty-one-point Port Moresby Declaration committing Australia to work with Pacific Island nations 'on the basis of partnership, mutual respect and mutual responsibility' through a series of bilateral 'Pacific Partnerships for Development'.[92] The cycle had changed again.

Solomon Islands

Southeast of Bougainville and part of the same archipelago (the result of another random stroke of a European colonial administrator's pen) lay the Solomon Islands, encompassing over 900 islands and extending for more than 1500 kilometres across the Coral Sea from Queensland. A former British protectorate, it had been independent since 1978 but by 2000 it was in political and economic turmoil. Ethnic rivalry and conflicts over land and money were fuelling civil unrest on the two large islands of Guadalcanal and Malaita, where more than half the population of 500,000 lived. In 2000 police and Malaitan settlers living in the capital of Honiara, on Guadalcanal, seized the police armoury and forced the prime minister from office. Violence spread and more than 300,000 people were displaced from their homes. The Solomons economy shrank by 14 per cent in 2000 and by a further 9 per cent in 2001.[93] Australian diplomatic attempts to broker a ceasefire failed.

Requests to Canberra from the Solomons government for armed police and military assistance were rejected, however. Sending in Australian troops to occupy the Solomon Islands would be 'folly in the extreme', Downer wrote in a newspaper column in January 2003. 'It would be widely resented in the Pacific region. It would be difficult to justify to Australian taxpayers. And for how many years would such an occupation have to continue? And what would be the exit strategy? The real show-stopper, however, is that it would not work ... foreigners do not have answers for the deep-seated problems afflicting Solomon Islands.'[94]

But by the middle of that year, law and order had collapsed and any hopes for an internal solution had evaporated. The government commissioned a report from the Defence-funded think tank, the Australian Strategic Policy Institute (ASPI), which recommended a large-scale Australian intervention. Howard announced in June that Australia would provide assistance subject to formal requests from the Solomons government and parliament, changes in Solomons legislation to give legal cover to Australian police, military and civilian officials, and the endorsement of the other regional members of the Pacific Island Forum.

What had changed? Partly the circumstances on the ground in the Solomons had become intolerable, but more important was the government's new consciousness of the consequences of state failure. Regional instability was no longer being thought about in humanitarian and political terms alone, but as a security problem interlinked with terrorism and WMD. A failed state, Howard told parliament, 'would not only devastate the lives of the peoples of the Solomons but could also pose a significant security risk to the whole region', providing 'safe havens for transnational criminals and even terrorists'.[95]

The Solomons parliament unanimously requested the intervention and passed the necessary legislation. All sixteen members of the Pacific Islands Forum gave their support. The Regional Assistance Mission to Solomon Islands (RAMSI), which began operations in late July, was different from anything Australia had been involved in before. Unlike the mission in East Timor, Operation Helpem Fren was police-led, although it had strong logistic and force protection assistance from the military. Unlike in Bougainville, the peacekeepers were armed. The operation included troops from Fiji, PNG and Tonga. And it had broad development and reconstruction objectives beyond the restoration of law and order. Once the situation had stabilised, Howard told parliament, RAMSI could 'begin to implement the necessary governance and economic reforms and ensure that the Solomons has a firm foundation on which to build its future security and prosperity'.

Ten different Australian departments and agencies were involved and a senior Australian diplomat, Nick Warner, was appointed as Special Coordinator, to manage all these different elements. At its height, RAMSI comprised 2225 personnel including 1400 ADF troops, 134 Australian Federal Police (AFP) officers and more than 600 participants from other Pacific states. This demonstration of power was important. 'The size and capability of the RAMSI military force got [the attention of the militants] and helped convince them of the need to cooperate,' Warner reflected.[96]

The mission's first task was to seize weapons. One of the key militant leaders was persuaded to surrender and more than 3000 suspects were arrested, including senior government officials and politicians. Nearly 4000 firearms were collected and destroyed. But after the initial success in restoring order and providing financial stability, the other pillars of the intervention – improving economic governance and the machinery of government – were much harder to build. The Solomons political system proved resistant to change.

Elections in 2006 were followed by political unrest that forced the prime minister selected by the new parliament to step down. Anti-Chinese rioters destroyed parts of Honiara's Chinatown, and more police and troops were sent back in. The next prime minister was hostile to Australia and relations deteriorated, leading to the expulsion of the Australian high commissioner.

Rudd visited the Solomons in early 2008 following the election of a better-disposed Solomons leader. He made it clear that his government would continue the commitment to RAMSI for 'as long as it was welcome and as long as it had a job to do'.[97]

In 2014 the Lowy Institute's Jenny Hayward-Jones estimated that the real cost of spending on RAMSI between 2003 and 2013 was $2.6 billion.[98] The tiny Solomons was the third-largest recipient of Australian aid.[99] The initial intervention, well constructed and well managed, had an immediate and beneficial impact. Modest but real achievements with policing and governance were to follow. Despite these achievements, however, lasting improvements were more difficult to secure. Solomon Islands became the world's second most aid-dependent country.[100] And on many of the measures of social and economic development, nothing much changed. By 2015 the Solomons ranked 156th of 188 countries on the United Nations Human Development Index.

Downer's original questions – for how many years would such an occupation have to continue? What would be the exit strategy? – and his conclusion that 'foreigners do not have answers for the deep-seated problems afflicting Solomon Islands' turned out to have lasting relevance throughout the Pacific.

Fiji

Meeting in Kiribati in October 2000, members of the Pacific Islands Forum had declared that democratic processes and individual rights were regional norms. In their Biketawa Declaration they set out a framework for regional intervention to resolve conflict. The situation in the Solomons was one of the problems on their minds. The other was Fiji.

Communal divisions between indigenous Fijians and Indo-Fijians continued to simmer. After various constitutional reviews, a new multiethnic coalition government headed by Mahendra Chaudhry, the first Indo-Fijian prime minister, took office in 1999. Angered by the appointment and fearful of possible policy changes on land tenure, a group of armed men forced their way into the parliament building in Suva on 19 May 2000 and held the prime minister and most of the cabinet hostage for fifty-six days while they attempted to negotiate with the president to force political changes.

After a politically and legally confused period the president declared a state of emergency, handed power to a military administration led by the Commander of the Fiji Armed Forces, Commodore Frank Bainimarama, and resigned on 29 May. Bainimarama appointed a replacement prime minister, Laisenia Qarase. The hostages were released following a promise of immunity to the gunmen, on which the government promptly reneged. Further violence within the military followed in November.

The Qarase government was returned in new elections in 2001 and 2006 but when it proposed an amnesty for the earlier conspirators and legislation to strengthen the rights of indigenous Fijians, Bainimarama seized power again on 6 December 2006. Although he claimed to be acting in support of a modern, multiracial future for Fiji, he replaced officials with military officers; forced the removal of the Fiji police commissioner, an Australian; instituted fresh controls over the media; and began pressuring the established institutions of Fiji society, like the courts, the Methodist Church and the chiefly system, to conform.

Qarase asked New Zealand and Australia for military assistance but this was never an option. Fiji was in a different category from East Timor or the Solomon Islands. The policy options open to the Australian government were limited. Sanctions on tourists would harm Fijian workers (and Australian operators) more than the government, so the action was restricted to travel bans on members of the military and their families, and whatever diplomatic and moral force Australia could apply. There were, it turned out, clear limits to what Australian policy-makers were willing to do, and what they could achieve, in 'our patch'.

Other parts of the Pacific continued to deliver unexpected policy challenges. The region became a growing transit route for drugs and a place for money laundering. The role of the AFP in peacekeeping and training grew along with the broader definition of national security that Australian governments adopted.[101] Australia sent troops and police to Tonga in 2006 to assist the government after pro-democracy demonstrations (which led in 2010 to the country's first popularly elected government) and provided support to a nearly insolvent Nauru, whose last remaining aircraft had been seized by bankruptcy trustees, cutting it off from external contact. Concerns about the role of outside powers continued as China and Taiwan competed for regional influence. China's aid was increasingly visible in the form of high-profile construction projects.

But Australia by now had another set of its own much narrower national interests to pursue in the region. The growing and intractable problem of unauthorised boat arrivals seemed to demand a Pacific solution.

Asylum seekers

After the surge of Indochinese refugees in the 1970s, no 'boat people' reached Australian shores during the 1980s. A trickle of arrivals, mainly from Asia, came in the early 1990s. But then the numbers started to climb. Between 1996 and 1997 around 1200 people made it to Australian territory by boat. The figure rose to 3721 in 1999, with 2939 in the following year.[102]

These new asylum seekers were coming from Afghanistan, Iraq, Iran and Pakistan, part of a global movement of people. At the beginning of 2001, the United Nations High Commissioner for Refugees estimated the worldwide refugee population at 12 million. Unlike their European predecessors in the 1930s, these new refuge-seekers were the victims of state failure as much as state persecution. Their travel, often by air to Malaysia and then by boat from Indonesia to Australia, was facilitated by people smugglers, whose business was assisted by the technologies of the information revolution, such as mobile telephones.

The Howard government recognised that it had a problem. Temporary protection visas were introduced, limiting initial refugee visas to three years. People smuggling was made a crime. New detention centres were built but they were soon full. In the first five months of 2001, more than 1600 asylum seekers landed at Ashmore Reef, an Australian territory off the coast of Western Australia.

The issue came to a dramatic head on 26 August 2001 when a Norwegian freighter, the MV *Tampa*, rescued 433 asylum seekers from a sinking vessel inside the Indonesian maritime rescue zone and sought to deliver them to Christmas Island, about 140 kilometres away. Howard and his ministers decided to make the *Tampa* a test case: 'I believe it is in Australia's national interests that we draw a line on what is increasingly becoming an uncontrollable number of illegal arrivals in this country,' he told the press, declaring that those rescued would not be allowed to land in Australia.[103] The ship's captain was instructed not to enter Australian waters, but faced with a deteriorating situation on board he declared an emergency and did so anyway. An Australian special forces team was ordered to board the ship and take control.

The prime minister tabled the Border Protection Bill 2001, which sought to place beyond legal doubt, and with retrospective effect, the right of the government to use force to remove any ship from Australian territorial waters, to prevent asylum claims by people on such vessels and to remove all these activities from court control. The Labor Party voted against the bill in the Senate, where it was rejected.

There followed an intense week of activity as the government worked to shore up its legal position, find an offshore destination where the asylum seekers could be sent to have their refugee claims processed, and identify some sort of longer-term policy solutions to cope with the additional boats known to be setting out.

The government passed legislation excising some Australian territories, including Christmas Island, from the Australian migration zone for the purposes of asylum claims, forcing processing offshore. The immediate problem of finding a destination for the *Tampa* asylum seekers was settled when the New Zealand prime minister, Helen Clark, agreed to take 150 of them and the government of Nauru was persuaded to take the remainder after an urgent visit by defence minister Peter Reith and an offer of $13 million in aid.[104] PNG provided transit facilities for the Australian naval vessel to which the *Tampa* passengers were transferred.

Angered by what it saw as an Australian effort to shift the problem back to its neighbour, Indonesia was less responsive. The new Indonesian president, Megawati Sukarnoputri, refused to take a telephone call from Howard and cancelled a meeting with Downer, Reith and immigration minister Philip Ruddock when they arrived in Jakarta on 6 September.

The Australian Defence Force (ADF) was given a central role in the response. Under Operation Relex, ships and aircraft were sent out to identify and intercept vessels carrying asylum seekers between the Indonesian archipelago and Australia, with orders to board them if necessary and return them to international waters.

In the middle of all this, the September 11 terrorist attacks on New York and Washington added a new dimension to the debate. Downer and Howard began to use language suggesting that Islamist extremists and even terrorists could use people smugglers to penetrate Australia's borders.[105] No evidence of this emerged but the government's rhetoric, and the expanding role of the ADF, helped frame this immigration issue as a security threat. People smuggling joined terrorism on the lengthening list of what were being called 'non-traditional security challenges'.

Howard won the public over. An election was called on 5 October and the prime minister's campaign declaration that 'we decide who comes to this country and the circumstances in which they come' reflected a sentiment widely accepted by Australian voters. It was the arrivals by sea rather than those – more than twice as many – seeking protection visas after arriving by air who tested deep-seated Australian anxieties. The government successfully manoeuvred Labor into a position in which it looked both weak on national security and indecisive. Howard comfortably won a third term on 10 November 2001.

The government's response to the asylum seekers had significant foreign policy consequences. It engaged Australia's obligations under international law, especially the Refugee Convention and maritime conventions relating to the safety of life at sea. Australia's relations with multilateral bodies such as the United Nations High Commissioner for Refugees (UNHCR) were strained as a result, but those same agencies – UNHCR and the International Organization for Migration especially – would also be central to any successful response. The United Nations Convention against Transnational Organized Crime and its Protocol against the Smuggling of Migrants by Land, Sea and Air came into force in 2004 and were ratified by the government. An Ambassador for People Smuggling Issues was appointed in February 2002 to help develop international solutions to the problem.

In the South Pacific, Australia's power and money as the regional hegemon enabled it to develop the Pacific Solution. It persuaded PNG and impecunious Nauru to house new detention centres for asylum seekers in return for additional assistance ($30 million in Nauru's case).[106]

But it was Southeast Asia where the asylum seekers arrived, and the fishing villages of Indonesia from which the people smugglers dispatched them on their way.

Southeast Asia

It was not at all clear to Australian policy-makers in the early part of the century how Indonesia's democratic experiment was going to play out. Out of the complex political manoeuvring in Jakarta, Abdurrahman Wahid ('Gus Dur'), a partially blind Muslim cleric with a strong commitment to liberalism and a chaotic style, emerged in October 1999 as Habibie's successor. His vice president was Megawati, the daughter of the charismatic leader of Indonesia's independence, Sukarno.

Although the East Timor intervention had only been possible with Indonesia's agreement, an underlying sense of national humiliation over the result and anger at perceived Australian arrogance, as well as the uncertainty in the Indonesian political system itself, shadowed Australia–Indonesia relations for several years. Defence relations were largely frozen.

The Asian financial crisis had left Southeast Asian states with a deep feeling of resentment at the role of the IMF and the other international financial institutions. Malaysian prime minister Mahathir's calls for Asian solutions to Asian problems now found more receptive ears. Indonesia lined up beside Malaysia in efforts to sideline Australia from regional forums.

A version of Mahathir's Asia-only East Asian Economic Group was now established in the form of annual meetings of ASEAN states with China, Japan and South Korea – ASEAN Plus Three. Australia was excluded from a a new monetary swap arrangement called the Chiang Mai Initiative, which emerged from Japanese proposals (stymied by Washington) for an Asian Monetary Fund.[107] Australia's efforts to join the Asia-Europe Meeting (ASEM) as one of the Asian participants were blackballed by Mahathir in late 1998. In October 2000 longstanding negotiations to link the ASEAN Free Trade Area with the Australia New Zealand Closer Economic Relations were unexpectedly downgraded.

The government's political response to these setbacks was to downplay their importance by redefining the nature and form of Australian engagement with the region. Regionalism, Downer now asserted, could be divided into two sorts: 'what you might call a cultural regionalism, a regionalism which is built on common ties of history, of mutual cultural identity', and practical regionalism, which wasn't 'some sort of creed' but a way of achieving mutually agreed goals.[108]

Meanwhile, the agenda of issues in play between Australia and Indonesia was lengthening. Boat arrivals were a continuing problem. And even before September 11, terrorism was of growing concern. Since the loosening of the iron control of Suharto's New Order, terrorist incidents and general communal violence had been increasing in Indonesia. On Christmas Eve 2000, churches or priests in eleven cities were targeted in bombings which killed nineteen and injured 120. Jemaah Islamiyah's links to al-Qaeda and radical Islamist groups across Malaysia, Singapore and the southern Philippines were becoming clearer. In Aceh, at the tip of Sumatra, long-established Islamist separatist forces were fighting the Indonesian military.

So when Megawati, who had forced out Wahid as president in July 2001, invited Howard to visit Jakarta, he announced that 'positive realism' was to be the basis for rebuilding the Australia–Indonesia relationship.[109] One of the important effects of 9/11, a couple of months later, was to refocus the attention of policy-makers in Washington and Canberra on the importance of Southeast Asia in global terrorist networks.

When Howard next visited Jakarta in February 2002, the *Tampa* affair of August 2001 had rekindled irritations and the reception he received was much cooler. Even so, he and Megawati signed a new memorandum of understanding to cover counterterrorism cooperation, and laid the groundwork for the Bali conferences on people smuggling and human trafficking to come. These arrangements would bear fruit soon afterwards.

Their common concern about terrorism gave Australia and Indonesia a platform from which they could address broader areas of cooperation. As soon as the Australian election was over, some Indonesian agencies resumed giving tacit help to Australia on boat turn-backs. Police cooperation, based on agreements between the two forces dating back to 1995 and 2000, increased, including measures to disrupt people smugglers. As Howard acknowledged later, 'the success of our border protection policy from late 2001 onwards ... depended, in part, on Indonesia's willingness both to discourage people-smuggling from its shores and also to accept the return of boats intercepted by Australian naval vessels'.[110]

Indonesia always preferred multilateral to bilateral approaches. In February 2002 a more comfortable framework for dealing with Australia was established when Downer and his Indonesian counterpart, Dr Nur Hassan Wirajuda, co-hosted a Regional Ministerial Conference on People Smuggling, Trafficking in Persons and Related Transnational Crime in Bali. Thirty regional and source countries, as well as international organisations, took part. This was the first in a series of informal and non-binding ministerial meetings and officials' workshops that became known as the Bali Process. The advantage of this approach was that it placed Australia's interests in the context of broader issues of people movement – such as guest workers, trafficking in women, and child sex crimes – which were of more pressing concern to its regional neighbours. It also gave Indonesian agencies high-level political cover for the bilateral cooperation.

In the end, regional approaches proved critical to every subsequent Australian government's attempts to resolve the problem. The Bali Process helped in the development of more uniform laws to criminalise people smuggling and trafficking and it assisted in the sort of informal cooperation which led to the stationing of AFP officers in most regional capitals and to Australia providing extensive technical support on immigration services.

In 2002 just one person arrived in Australia by boat and, although the number increased slowly, by 2007 only 287 additional asylum seekers had done so.[111] The deterrent effect of the Pacific Solution, cooperation with Indonesia and other regional partners, and a steep reduction in the overall flow of asylum seekers from the Middle East to all OECD countries between

2002 and 2008[112] each had an impact. On coming to office, the Rudd government closed down the offshore detention centres and abandoned the threat of tow-backs to Indonesia.

The Bali bombings

Late in the evening of 12 October 2002, terrorist bombs placed in the crowded Sari nightclub and nearby Paddy's Bar in Kuta, Bali's main tourist area, killed 202 people, eighty-eight of them Australians. It was the largest terrorist action since September 2001 and the work, it soon became clear, of the Jemaah Islamiyah group.

The news reached Canberra in the early hours of the following morning, and the government found itself facing an unprecedented consular, security and political crisis. ADF and civilian relief teams, consular officials, police and intelligence officers were quickly dispatched to Bali.[113] A senior delegation of ministers and officials, led by Downer, left for Bali and Jakarta on the evening of 14 October. Howard, with the deputy prime minister and the Opposition leader, followed three days later to meet the injured and their families and the Indonesian officials dealing with the crisis.

By 21 October, 109 Australian law enforcement officers from every state and territory had arrived in Bali. Indonesia agreed to a joint three-year investigation of the bombing by the AFP and Indonesian police. In New York, Australia successfully pressed the UN Security Council to list Jemaah Islamiyah as an al-Qaeda-related entity, generating financial and other sanctions.

The Bali bombings brought the terrorist threat home to Australians. Almost everyone could identify with the ordinary tourists – sporting team members, family groups – who were the victims. The atrocity annealed the link between the global War on Terror and events in Australia's neighbourhood. 'In the light of this we have reappraised the way we view and deal with the threat of terrorism. We understand the danger of leaving threats unaddressed,' Howard told the House of Representatives in February 2003.[114]

The sense of threat was strengthened by further bombings at the Marriott Hotel in Jakarta in August 2003, outside the Australian embassy in September 2004 and then again in Bali in October 2005 – when four Australians were among the twenty people killed.

Across the Southeast Asian region, Australia stepped up its counterterrorism cooperation with regional states. In 2004 it committed $37 million to the Jakarta Centre for Law Enforcement Cooperation, a joint project with the Indonesian police to provide training for law-enforcement officials across Southeast Asia. This practical cooperation with Indonesia helped prepare the way for a restoration of the traditional defence relationship, which had been so strained by East Timor.

The election in September 2004 of Susilo Bambang Yudhoyono (known popularly as SBY) in Indonesia's first direct election for president brought a further improvement in relations. A former army general, Yudhoyono had worked closely with Australia in his previous position as Coordinating Minister for Political, Legal and Security Affairs under Megawati. Before his inauguration as president in October, and just shortly after Howard's own re-election, Howard decided 'on impulse ... that I would attend the inauguration',[115] although he had not received an invitation. This was well received. But within a much shorter time than he expected, Howard was back in Jakarta.

The Boxing Day tsunami

On Boxing Day 2004, a 9.1-magnitude earthquake off the coast of Sumatra generated one of the most powerful tsunamis ever recorded. Across fourteen countries around the Indian Ocean 230,000 people were killed, more than 150,000 of them in Indonesia. Another half-million people in Aceh and North Sumatra were made homeless. Sri Lanka, Thailand and the Maldives were also badly affected.

Howard took direct control of the Australian response. The government immediately offered $60 million in aid to Indonesia. Defence force, police and civilian aid teams were flown to the region to provide emergency assistance. Two weeks later, Howard visited Jakarta and announced with Yudhoyono a commitment of $1 billion over five years to an Australia–Indonesia Partnership for Reconstruction and Development, on top of the existing aid to Indonesia. This was the largest aid contribution ever made by Australia. A joint commission of ministers from both countries was to oversee its work.

With Japan and India, Australia became part of a 'core group' organised by Bush to deliver assistance to tsunami victims outside the framework of the United Nations, an extension to humanitarian relief of the idea of the Coalitions of the Willing.

In a range of bilateral and regional activities Downer and his Indonesian counterpart, Wirajuda, developed a close working relationship. When

Yudhoyono came to Australia in April 2005 he told a parliamentary lunch: 'it is not enough to be just neighbours. We have to be strong partners.'[116] Drawing on a proposal he had first raised in 2003, he announced that Australia and Indonesia had agreed to develop a 'Comprehensive Partnership', covering the increasing range of their bilateral activities. This became the Framework for Security Cooperation, known as the Lombok Treaty, which was signed in November 2006. Less ambitious than the earlier Agreement on Maintaining Security, it provided a structure for deepening and expanding bilateral cooperation and exchanges. At its heart it was a non-aggression pact, with both sides agreeing to 'refrain from the threat or the use of force against the territorial integrity or political independence of the other'. Australia agreed not to support either separatism or pre-emption.[117]

By then, two basic things had changed in Australia's relationship with Indonesia: the country had become a lively democracy, and the East Timor problem had been removed as a bilateral irritant. Yet the difficulties continued. At the level of public opinion, most Australians continued to see Indonesia as a problem – a source of terrorist threat, a facilitator of boat arrivals, the instigator of violence in Timor. In a poll by the Lowy Institute in 2006, only 50 per cent of Australian respondents expressed positive feelings about Indonesia, and just 51 per cent of Indonesians reciprocated. Indonesia was unambiguously the country most Australians saw as a threat, well ahead of China.[118]

The two countries came from very different foreign policy traditions. Modern Australia was founded as a European settler state; Indonesia had fought to escape European colonial control. Australia is a continent; Indonesia, a porous archipelago. Indonesia sought security by embedding itself in slow moving multilateral processes like the United Nations and ASEAN; Australia looked to a powerful external ally. Indonesia was low-profile and reactive internationally; Australia was, in Downer's words, 'irrepressibly activist'.[119] After learning in December 2004 that Australia had announced the establishment of a 1000-mile maritime exclusion zone to deal with asylum seekers, without consulting Jakarta, the Indonesian foreign minister, Wirajuda, remarked wearily to the Australian defence minister, Hill: 'You are blessed with a country that is rich in ideas and initiatives. Unfortunately, we seem to be on the receiving end of most of them.'[120]

Consular issues such as the jailing of a young Australian woman, Schapelle Corby and the death sentences imposed on some of the 'Bali Nine' drug smugglers captured the attention of the Australian popular media. On

Indonesia's side, the suspicion persisted that notwithstanding frequent official policy assertions of its strong support for Indonesia's unity and territorial
integrity, Australia sought to break up the Indonesian state, and that after
East Timor it would turn its attention to Papua.[121] Howard's loose comments
in December 2002 that Australia reserved the right to take pre-emptive action
in the region against terrorist threats reinforced the concerns.[122] The distrust
over Papua came to a head in early 2006 when forty-two Papuan asylum seekers who reached the Australian mainland near Cape York by boat were
granted refugee status. Indonesia reacted angrily and recalled its ambassador.
In response to a personal telephone call from Yudhoyono, Howard proposed
to introduce legislative changes that would ensure that in future any such
cases could only be considered offshore. He was concerned, he wrote later,
not to disturb cooperation against people smugglers and Indonesia's willingness to accept the return of boats intercepted by Australia.[123] Some of his own
party members reacted strongly against this, however, and, in the face of
inevitable Senate rejection, he withdrew the measure.

Like many Australian ministers before them and after, Howard and
Downer saw one of Australia's roles in the alliance as being to bring home to
an inattentive Washington the importance of Indonesia. A staple of Howard's
presentations to American interlocutors was a reminder that Indonesia was
the fourth-most populous country in the world, its third-largest democracy
and the largest Islamic-majority state. It showed how a successful moderate
Islamic democracy could operate.

By March 2010, speaking to a joint sitting of parliament, and to a new
Australian counterpart, Rudd, Yudhoyono recalled the Bali bombings and
the tsunami response as 'the emotional turning points of our bilateral relations'.[124] They were not quite that but they were important.

Partly propelled by changes in the relationship with Indonesia, partly
by the replacement of Mahathir as Malaysian prime minister in late 2003
by the more amenable Abdullah Ahmad Badawi, the trajectory
of Australian policy was moving back towards regional engagement.
Australia's exclusion from regional organisations always nagged its policy-
makers. The 2003 foreign and trade policy white paper, *Advancing the
National Interest*, declared that Australia would be pleased to be involved
in the ASEAN Plus Three process, the new forum involving the ASEAN
states and their main North Asian partners, China, Japan and South
Korea: 'We have registered our interest in joining the grouping if invited
at some later stage.'[125]

Conscious of China's growing power, ASEAN now decided that it should expand its range of high-level partners. With the prime ministers of New Zealand and India, Howard was invited to attend the ASEAN summit in Vientiane in November 2004, along with the Chinese, Japanese and South Korean leaders, and then to take part in an inaugural East Asia Summit (EAS) in December 2005.

Australia's price of admission to the EAS, however, was adherence to the ASEAN Treaty of Amity and Cooperation, which committed signatories to the peaceful settlement of disputes, noninterference in the internal affairs of other members and the renunciation of the threat or use of force. Howard was sceptical about regionalism in general, and high-flown declaratory language in particular, and uncomfortable with symbolism (at least of this worthy multilateral sort). Travelling to Laos, he was dismissive: 'I think we should not get hung up on whether or not we agree to a particular Treaty which was designed to come out of a period of time and an attitude of thinking which is not necessarily as relevant today as it was then.'[126] But by mid-2005, under pressure from Japan, Singapore and Vietnam, and with Downer converted to the benefits of compliance, Australia agreed to sign, provided it was entitled to full membership of the EAS beyond the initial meeting. When the summit met for the first time in December 2005 Australia was sitting at the regional table again.

Timor-Leste

The establishment of the new state of Timor-Leste on 20 March 2002 raised the question of its maritime boundaries with Australia, which divided an area rich in gas and petroleum. The 1989 Timor Gap Treaty between Indonesia and Australia had provided a regime for the exploitation of these seabed resources while putting off a final decision over a permanent seabed boundary. The Indonesians had wanted this drawn at the median point, halfway between the two countries, while Australia believed it should be measured from the outer edge of the continental shelf, which was closer to Timor.

In 2001 Australia and East Timor's transitional cabinet agreed to a similar arrangement for the Timor Sea Treaty, without prejudice to a final delimitation of the continental shelf between the two countries. Under this treaty, signed on 20 May 2002, East Timor was to receive 90 per cent of the hydrocarbon revenues generated in a jointly managed area called the Joint

Petroleum Development Area (JPDA). The new treaty was ratified by the East Timorese parliament in 2002, although not without significant internal dissent over the perceived unfairness of Australia's reluctance to negotiate new maritime boundaries. This would grow to become an important area of disagreement between the two countries. In March 2002 Australia withdrew from the compulsory procedures of the International Court of Justice and the International Tribunal for the Law of the Sea for the resolution of any maritime border disputes.

Despite Timor-Leste's successful transition to independence, the divisions within the society and its governing elite were not easily reconciled. More than thirty people were killed and tens of thousands driven from their homes when fighting broke out in Dili in April and May 2006 as 600 soldiers took to the streets protesting against perceived favouritism in the armed forces for people from the east of the country. The President, Xanana Gusmão sided with the dismissed soldiers against his political rival, the prime minister, Mari Alkatiri. But when the situation descended into chaos, Gusmão, Alkatiri and the foreign minister, José Ramos-Horta, jointly requested help from Australia, Portugal, Malaysia and New Zealand.[126]

Howard announced on 25 May that Australian forces would arrive back in Dili that day. They were soon joined by troops from New Zealand, Malaysia and Portugal. By the end of June Australia had 2650 defence personnel and some 200 police in the country. Downer visited in early June and proposed a new UN mandate, a large international police presence, and further international assistance with governance and political reconciliation.[127]

As a result, the new United Nations Integrated Mission in Timor-Leste (UNMIT) was established in August 2006 with 1600 police and a small complement of military liaison officers. Unwilling to place its own troops under UN command, the Australian government reached agreement for a separate International Stabilisation Force of Australian and New Zealand troops which would support, but not be part of, UNMIT.

Underlining the continuity in Australian support for East Timor, the new Australian prime minister, Kevin Rudd, made an early visit to Dili and returned there in February 2008, less than two months later, when Australian troop numbers were boosted after an attack on President Ramos-Horta by rebel soldiers.

China

The Howard government's early tensions with China had been resolved in a tacit agreement that the two countries would 'put aside ... differences and ... focus on those areas of common agreement ... and those common interests that can be pursued to great mutual benefit', as Howard put it.[128] Australia would not 'hector and lecture and moralise', he told a press conference in Beijing in April 1997.[129]

Around the turn of the century, the Australia–China relationship entered a period of much deeper engagement, driven overwhelmingly by the transformation of China's economy. China's entry into the WTO in 2001, which Australia had encouraged and facilitated, was the catalyst for major economic reforms driven by Premier Zhu Rongji. Australia's energy and mineral resources, its agriculture and its services became more central to the growth that those reforms unleashed.

These were the sunny uplands of globalisation for Australia. Between 1996 and 2006 Australian exports to China grew by 626 per cent, an average annual rate of 18 per cent.[130] From 2003 the commodity boom began and by 2007 China had displaced Japan as Australia's largest trading partner. Australia had to adapt to an important new reality: for the first time in its history, its major economic partner was not also part of the same alliance system.

In 1999 Jiang Zemin had been the first Chinese president to visit Australia. By the time his successor, Hu Jintao, came in 2003, every member of the powerful Politburo Standing Committee had done so, along with many senior party and government officials beneath them.[131] Howard, Downer and their federal and state government colleagues reciprocated. Howard noted that as prime minister he had visited China more frequently than any other country.

Australia became integrated into China's resources and energy security strategy, with the mines of Western Australia a frequent stop on the itineraries of Chinese political visitors. In 2002 Howard helped push through a 25-year $25-billion contract to sell China its first liquefied natural gas (LNG) imports for a consortium of North West Shelf producers. Australia became the largest destination for Chinese outbound direct investment in the mid-2000s, as BHP Billiton and Rio Tinto entered major joint iron-ore ventures with Chinese partners. And uranium exports began in 2008, following the negotiation of bilateral nuclear safeguards agreements.

Services exports grew too. By 2004 China had become Australia's largest source of overseas students and Australia was one of the first countries to become an approved destination for the wave of new members of the Chinese middle class now wanting to experience overseas travel.[132] In 2004 Australia and China agreed to negotiate a free trade agreement (FTA). This step required Australia to acknowledge China as a 'market economy', something the United States was unwilling to do.

Slowly but steadily political and defence links also grew. The first joint military exercise between the two countries was held in October 2004. During his Australian visit in 2007 for the APEC leaders' meeting, Hu Jintao announced that Australia and China would hold an annual strategic dialogue between the two foreign ministers, Beijing's first such arrangement with a Western country. By 2005 China was the third-largest source of immigrants to Australia after the United Kingdom and New Zealand. In Howard's own Sydney electorate, nearly 15 per cent of enrolled voters had an ethnic Chinese background. 'I count it as one of the greatest successes of this country's foreign relations that we have simultaneously been able to strengthen our longstanding ties with the United States of America, yet at the same time continue to build a very close relationship with China,' Howard said in August 2004.[133] Perhaps the symbolic high point of that effort came in October 2003 when Bush and Hu addressed joint sittings of the Australian parliament on successive days.

This 'great duality', as Howard called his policy,[134] worked effectively so long as American and Chinese interests in the world were broadly aligned, and while China's leaders adhered to Deng Xiaoping's foreign policy dictum that China should 'hide brightness, nourish capabilities' – in other words, keep its head down internationally while it built up its resources. With the exception of Japan, where relations continued to be weighed down by history, epitomised by Prime Minister Junichirō Koizumi's annual visits to the Yasukuni Shrine, where Japanese war dead, including Class A war criminals, were enshrined, China's regional diplomacy through the first decade of the century was marked by flexibility and pragmatism. Hu Jintao used the language of China's 'peaceful rise'. China's promised foreign policy approach of non-interference, multilateralism and 'win-win' solutions was attractive to regional states.

Its differences with ASEAN were eased by its agreement to a code of conduct in the South China Sea, its adherence to the Treaty of Amity and Cooperation and the signing of a framework for an FTA in November 2002. In June 2001 it helped establish the Shanghai Cooperation Organisation with four central Asian countries and Russia.

Most importantly for the relationship with the United States, the terrorist attacks of September 2001 refocused Washington's attention on a more urgent concern than China. With China's own Muslim community in the far-western province of Xinjiang becoming more fractious, the war against terrorism provided a common strategic objective in US–Chinese relations that had been missing since the dissolution of the anti-Soviet coalition at the end of the Cold War. Even more importantly, by hosting the six-party talks on the North Korean nuclear crisis in 2003, China offered a way of helping to manage one of the core members of Bush's 'axis of evil'.

Australia experienced differences from time to time with both Washington and Beijing as it adjusted its position within the framework of that larger relationship. Although the government subsequently backed away from his statement, Downer caused anxiety in Washington by noting, accurately enough, during a visit to China in August 2004 that the ANZUS Treaty would not automatically be invoked in the event of a crisis between the United States and China over the Taiwan Strait. In 2005 Australia failed to join Washington and Tokyo in opposing the European Union's proposal to lift its arms embargo against China. With a very different complexion to its economic relationship, it took a contrasting view to Washington's on the question of the revaluation of China's currency and over its recognition of China as a market economy. With China, consular and commercial problems and differences over Tibet and the Dalai Lama bubbled along.

Australians supported their government's approach. They saw China overwhelmingly as opportunity, not threat. A March 2005 Lowy Institute poll found 69 per cent of respondents had a favourable view of China, compared with 57 per cent for the United States. In the period after the Iraq War, more of them (57 per cent) thought that US foreign policy was a threat to Australia than were worried about China's growing power (35 per cent).[135]

Rudd came to office with a more ambitious objective: not simply to manage Australia's bilateral relationship with China but to help fashion the overarching relationship between China and the United States. He would seek to engage more actively with China in a multilateral context – on the global economy through the G20, on climate change through the United Nations Framework Convention, on regional security through the East Asia Summit and his proposed Asia Pacific Community.

He was the first Australian prime minister whose views of the world had been shaped by China's rise. As a student at the Australian National

University he studied Chinese history and language, and he served as an Australian diplomat in Beijing in the 1980s. The expectations were high – the Chinese believed that someone who knew them so well would sympathise; the Japanese worried about the same thing. He had startled and upstaged Howard by addressing Hu Jintao in fluent Mandarin when supporting the prime minister's speech of welcome at the official lunch during the APEC meeting in Sydney in 2007.

In Beijing in April 2008, on his first major overseas visit, Rudd's first stop was Peking University. To a packed auditorium of students, he delivered, in Chinese, a speech grandly titled 'A Conversation with China's Youth on the Future'. His objective was nothing less than to sketch a way in which Chinese and Western world views could be reconciled. The aims of the Chinese leadership for a 'harmonious world', he told the students, depended on China's 'being a participant in the world order and ... acting in accordance with the rules of that order'.[136] He spoke frankly about China's problems in Tibet and, using a particular Chinese expression for friendship – *zhengyou* – offered his hosts a 'true friendship which "offers unflinching advice and counsels restraint" to engage in principled dialogue about matters of contention'.[137] This contrasted with the Howard approach of declaring that differences existed but should be set aside. It was not at all clear the Chinese wanted Rudd's sort of friendship.

Japan

The steady deepening of Australia's security and defence ties with Japan continued under the Howard government. As usual, the pace of change was driven less by Australia's openness to it than by the progress in Japan's own search for a national consensus about its role in the world. Under the prime ministerships of Junichirō Koizumi (2001–06) and Shinzo Abe (2006–07), important shifts took place.

Howard met Koizumi, a Japanese political leader of unusual determination and political strength, on an official visit to Japan (his fourth) in August 2001. The September terrorist attacks provided both the reason and the political impetus needed for Koizumi to secure legislative changes permitting members of the Japanese Self-Defense Forces to be deployed overseas, albeit with a limited mandate and under United Nations auspices. So Japan sent military engineers to East Timor and then to southern Iraq, where ADF forces provided their security.

Over these years the foundations were laid in a series of declarations and communiqués for more substantial defence and security cooperation. Most strategically ambitious (and with China in mind) was the establishment of regular trilateral talks between the United States, Japan and Australia at senior officials' level from 2002 and at ministerial level after 2006. 'This quiet revolution in Japan's external policy – one which Australia has long encouraged – is a welcome sign of a more confident Japan assuming its rightful place in the world and in our region', Howard told the Lowy Institute in 2005.[138]

On Japan's side, its interest in developing the relationship with Australia was driven by its growing anxiety about China's rise. Tokyo's active support for Australian participation in the East Asia Summit was one manifestation of this. But Australia's long record as a secure supplier of energy and food, and the growing degree of trust in the security partnership, were also important.

Despite the years of economic stagnation and its ageing demographics, Japan's economic importance to Australia was still great. In 2005, when Howard visited China and Japan seeking free trade negotiations, Japan was still Australia's largest export market. But attempts to expand the economic relationship were constrained, in ways now very familiar to Australia, by the agricultural interest groups so influential in Japanese politics. Japanese responses to Australian approaches were cautious and incremental. In 2005 Koizumi agreed only to a two-year study on the feasibility of an FTA.

With Koizumi's departure in 2006, the long-term governing Liberal Democratic Party (LDP) entered a period of political decline. His successor, Abe, agreed in December 2006, at the peak of his authority, to launch FTA negotiations, although even then they had to be camouflaged under the euphemistic label of an Economic Partnership Agreement (EPA). Abe would hold on to power for only twelve months.

Japan's growing concern about China was evident in Tokyo's overanxious reaction to Rudd's political rise. Japanese officials worried that his experience of China and his knowledge of Mandarin would somehow translate into a pro-Beijing switch in Australian policies.

Whaling, the most obvious area where Australian and Japanese views diverged, had been an ongoing problem. Both the main Australian political parties opposed commercial whaling of any kind. The biennial meetings of the International Whaling Commission had always been forums for sharp disagreements between the two countries, although under Howard the issue was quarantined from the broader relationship. Rudd, however, had raised whaling as an issue during the election campaign, threatening to take Japan to the International Court of Justice. Just a week out from the election, the Japanese resumed the whaling hunt in the Southern Ocean. Rudd responded in January 2008 by dispatching a customs ship and surveillance aircraft to monitor the Japanese fleet. The omission of Japan in favour of China in the prime minister's first long overseas visit reinforced Japanese feelings of rejection.

The broad Australian objectives of the preceding years did not change, however. Rudd added new areas of cooperation on nuclear arms control and expanded defence ties. After paying the first visit by an Australian prime minister to Hiroshima, he announced the establishment of an International Commission on Nuclear Non-proliferation and Disarmament (ICNND), co-chaired by former Australian and Japanese foreign ministers Gareth Evans and Yoriko Kawaguchi. Its report *Towards a Nuclear-Weapons-Free World* was published in July 2010, but the response from both governments to its work was muted.

On his visit to Japan in June 2008, Rudd used words about the relationship that seemed indistinguishable from those of his predecessor: 'Australia and Japan have a comprehensive strategic security and economic partnership. It is not just based on common interest, it is also based on common values and an enduring friendship. We are both democracies. We are both open economies. We are both strong allies of the United States. We have so much in common that we can actually deliver great good to the world acting in partnership together.'[139]

India

Australia's relationship with India, still caught in what Howard described as the '"history and cricket" paradigm',[140] underwent a nuclear transformation in the late 1990s.

Despite its historical commitment to nuclear disarmament, dating back to Jawaharlal Nehru, India had refused to ratify the Nuclear Non-Proliferation Treaty (NPT), which it argued discriminated against the non-nuclear powers. Continuing strategic anxiety about both Pakistan and China drove its own nuclear research program. On 11 and 13 May 1998, under a right-wing nationalist government, India conducted its first nuclear weapons tests since 1974. Pakistan followed suit in the same month.

Perhaps with the recent example of the domestic politics of the French nuclear tests in mind, and conscious of his own successful efforts to have the

Comprehensive Nuclear-Test-Ban Treaty adopted, Downer reacted strongly. The tests, he said, showed 'wilful disregard for international opinion' and were a 'flagrant defiance of the international community's strong support for nuclear non-proliferation'.[141] Australia's high commissioner in New Delhi was recalled, defence ties and ministerial and official visits suspended and non-humanitarian aid cancelled. India's response was strong. Its foreign ministry would have virtually no dealings with the Australian mission for about a year.[142]

The broader framework within which the Australia–India relationship was conducted was changing, however, as the United States began to adjust its policies towards New Delhi. The relationship was slowly repaired as Downer, then Howard, visited India in 2000 and defence ties were resumed. 'It's time to move on,' Downer declared.[143]

Like so much else, the relationship with India was altered by the changing international security focus on terrorism and Afghanistan after the 9/11 attacks. The Bush administration wanted to incorporate India in its efforts to prevent nuclear proliferation and to engage it more closely on Afghanistan and Pakistan. It also saw India as a potential balance to China.

Perceptions of India's economic potential were also growing, after it instituted domestic reforms in the early 1990s. By 2003 it had become one of Australia's top ten export markets. Trade was dominated by non-monetary gold and coal, but the potential for services exports like tourism and education was becoming apparent. India was also a growing source of skilled migrants.

So when Howard visited India again in 2006 the atmosphere was very different. His visit overlapped with that of President Bush, who had announced a significant easing of restrictions on US nuclear cooperation with India. Howard found the Indians eager to purchase Australian uranium. This would require a major change in Australian policy, which had always insisted that uranium would only be sold to other signatories of the NPT. But the prime minister believed that a 'way around that policy would have to be found': it would not be sustainable, he believed, for Australia to sell uranium to China and Russia but not to India. In any case, it could always buy the uranium elsewhere.[144] Downer and his department were more concerned about the impact of such a decision on the nuclear non-proliferation regime,[145] but in August 2007 the government announced that the ban on selling uranium to India would be lifted.

India was re-entering Australian foreign policy for both economic and strategic reasons. The economic significance of the rise of the Indian middle class became a staple of Howard's speeches.[146] Strategically, India was, Howard wrote later, 'the perfect counterpoise to China'.[147] Downer began to talk about the need for Australians to think about 'the Indo-Asia-Pacific region'.[148]

Pakistan

Pakistan also became more significant to Australia as its role in Afghanistan and the influence there of radical Islamist groups with links to al-Qaeda grew. Howard had a good relationship with the president of Pakistan, Pervez Musharraf, an army man and fellow cricket tragic, whom he saw as being on Australia's side in Afghanistan. Howard also saw Australia playing a role in mediating Pakistan's sometimes difficult relations with Washington: 'I think it would be overstating it to say I was consciously a go-between', he told the journalist Karen Middleton, 'but I think I did provide a sort of alternative to the Americans' point of reference in the West which he felt comfortable with.'[149] In June 2005 Musharraf became the first president of Pakistan to visit Australia and signed a Memorandum of Understanding on Counter-Terrorism, which provided a basis for closer cooperation on intelligence and training. Australia maintained a limited avenue of training and contact with the Pakistan military leadership, even while Islamabad's relations with the United States and Britain were often strained.

Climate change and the environment

The debate over the environment was an early test of the Howard government's focus on the national interest. The Coalition said it accepted the importance of climate change – a 'critical issue' – and accepted the scientific evidence that human activity was responsible.[150] But Howard described his own position on the subject as 'agnostic',[151] and that tone kept resurfacing.

The objective of the Kyoto conference on climate change in December 1997 was to secure agreement on legally binding targets to limit greenhouse gas emissions to meet the objectives of the 1992 Rio United Nations Framework Convention on Climate Change (UNFCCC). Australia entered the negotiations in a weak position. The EU was demanding 15 per cent reductions by all industrialised countries from 1990 levels by 2015. The United States also wanted legally binding targets, but insisted that the large developing countries, which were overwhelmingly the fastest-growing source of new carbon emissions, should also play a part.

Australia's overall contribution to global emissions was small, but per capita it was among the highest emitters in the world. The government argued that there were special reasons for this – Australia's dependence on fossil fuel, its growing population, its geographic spread, the contribution of land use and forestry to its emissions and the important role its resources and food exports played in its neighbours' growth. These unique factors, it declared, should accord it special consideration.[152]

When the Kyoto conference ended, after a marathon 36-hour final session on 11 December 1997, Australia had secured, in a major diplomatic achievement, permission to increase its emissions by 8 per cent from its 1990 figures and to include reductions in land clearance as a part of its abatement totals. The government signed the protocol on 29 April 1998 but did not submit it to parliament for ratification.[153]

In March 2001 the Bush administration announced that it would not ratify the Kyoto Protocol (which was, in any case, highly unlikely to have passed the US Senate), especially because it did not include targets for developing countries. Australia followed the American lead in 2002, after claiming that it was incompatible with Australia's national interests and would be ineffective. It would impose economic costs on Australia that would not be shared by its competitors in greenhouse-intensive industries. Nevertheless, and to the surprise of many observers, Japan, Canada, Russia and Ukraine ratified the protocol, enabling it to come into effect in February 2005.

Public attitudes in Australia were changing, however. Drought across eastern Australia and bushfires in Victoria added a cyclical urgency to the long-term trend of climate change. Well-publicised visits to Australia by the environmental campaigner and former US vice president Al Gore and the British economist Nicholas Stern were shifting the public debate. The 2006 Lowy Institute poll on Australians' views of the world showed 68 per cent of respondents agreeing with this statement: 'Global warming is a serious and pressing problem. We should be taking steps now, even if this involves significant costs.'[154]

The government had been pursuing other options, such as a non-binding Asia Pacific Partnership on Clean Development and Climate (APP) involving China, India, Japan, South Korea and the United States, which it presented as a complement to Kyoto. But always alert to changes in the public mood, Howard decided to act: 'I concluded that the government would need to shift its position on climate change,' he recalled later.[155] The shift was more nominal than substantive. He announced in mid-2007 that the government would adopt by 2008 a long-term aspirational target for reducing emissions. This would be followed by a national carbon-trading scheme by 2012. He also established an inquiry into the processing of uranium and the use of nuclear energy in Australia as a way of reducing carbon intensity (and of complicating life for his political opponents).

Climate change issues were high on Rudd's foreign policy agenda. The issue, he had told an ALP climate change summit in March 2007, was 'the great moral challenge of our generation'. He appointed a Minister for Climate Change, Penny Wong, and the first official act of his new government on 3 December 2007 was the ratification of the Kyoto Protocol. He and Wong then led an Australian delegation to the Bali Climate Change Conference, where they received an enthusiastic international reception. For a time, at least, the Opposition followed suit. The new leader of the Liberal Party, Brendan Nelson, announced his support for ratification.

Global trade and the international economy

Although Australia had survived the Asian economic crisis well, the damage caused to its Asian neighbours was clear from the statistics: Australian exports to East Asia fell by 7 per cent in 1997/98 and by a further 9 per cent in 1998/99. By 2000, however, most of the countries of Asia were beginning to grow again, pulled along by Chinese growth. The Australian economy hitched a ride. By 2004, roughly 54 per cent of Australian exports were going to the East Asian region, compared with 11 per cent to Europe and 11 per cent to the Americas. Nearly half Australia's imports came from the same source.[156]

For several decades now, Australia had been a champion of multilateral trade liberalisation. Economists agreed that the benefits to any country of trade liberalisation came first from opening up its own economy, and then from the widest possible set of multilateral arrangements. Only in the special circumstances of New Zealand had Australia entered into a bilateral free trade agreement (FTA). But the global mood about trade was changing as the growing number of countries in the WTO and the increasing significance of the developing economies made the multilateral system harder to manage.

In 1999 the ministerial meeting of the WTO in Seattle was suspended in acrimony as 40,000 anti-globalisation protestors took to the streets in protest against further trade liberalisation. At the same time, APEC, the regional track Australia had used so energetically to pursue trade liberalisation, was also making heavy going. Hopes for an Early Voluntary Sectoral Liberalisation program were undone in 1998 as a result of Japanese backtracking, and any progress on other fronts was looking slow and small-scale.

As a result, the Australian government began to look again at preferential trade options. In 2000 it announced that it would begin negotiations on FTAs with South Korea and Singapore. And by the end of that year, the first discussions had begun over an agreement with the United States, an option that had been explored briefly by the Hawke government in the 1980s but rejected when economic modelling showed few benefits.

The incoming Bush administration promised more robust support for free trade than its Democratic opponents. The Australian ambassador in Washington, Michael Thawley, spoke during the presidential election campaign with Republican advisers about the idea of an FTA and discussed it with Howard. When cabinet agreed in principle to pursue the idea with the United States in November 2000, Thawley floated the idea in a speech in New York.

One of the major drivers of an FTA on the Australian side was defensive. The government was worried about the increasing protectionist mood in the US Congress, saw no signs of progress with multilateral negotiations and feared that Bush and his US trade representative, Robert Zoellick, would focus their trade agenda on Latin America, to the detriment of Australian agriculture. Australia needed greater leverage on trade issues in the United States but it had no natural political constituency that could be activated to support its interests. There was another potential benefit of an FTA: it would provide what the trade minister, Mark Vaile, called 'the commercial equivalent of the ANZUS treaty', a new economic support for the overall relationship which would stand alongside the security pillar.[157]

Howard proposed the agreement in an introductory letter to Bush in February 2002 (just as Keating had raised the idea of APEC leaders' meetings with Clinton), and Vaile quickly followed up with Zoellick. The administration responded positively in April and Australia worked to secure an announcement of the deal in time for Howard's proposed visit later that year. The communiqué Howard and Bush issued after their talks on 10 September 2001 referred to the possibility of an FTA. But nothing could be done until Congress granted the administration Trade Promotion Authority (an agreement, essential for any negotiations, that legislators would not try to unpick the final deal), which it did by the narrowest of margins in August 2002. Negotiations began in March 2003.[158]

The agreement – easily the most comprehensive bilateral negotiation Australia had entered into – covered a huge range of areas, such as intellectual property and competition policy, well beyond traditional trade in goods. There was opposition in both countries: from Americans worried about farm interests and agricultural subsidies; and from Australians concerned that the FTA would swamp their country with American culture or destroy the Pharmaceuticals Benefit Scheme.

The Americans were not easy negotiating partners – 'mercantilist, sectoral and legalistic', in the words of one Australian participant[161] – but the negotiations were intense and rapid. After just five rounds, remaining differences over the most sensitive issues of beef, sugar and pharmaceuticals were resolved in a final telephone call between Howard and Bush on 7 February 2004. Congress passed the Australia–United States FTA in July by one of the largest margins ever recorded for a free trade deal. There was no question that Australia's support for the United States in the Iraq War was an important element in the support the treaty received. Australian ratification followed in August after the longest debate in Senate history.

With much less publicity, Congress passed a related, but perhaps even more consequential, piece of legislation in May 2005, when it agreed to new immigration rules providing for a huge expansion in the number of working visas available for Australians in the United States, substantially improving the opportunities for Australians to work in the US and reinforcing the government's ambitions for greater economic integration.[160]

Ten years later, the economic evidence supported the views of the economic theorists about the effects of preferential arrangements. The best research suggested that in the face of competition from closer, growing and more competitive Asian economies, the agreement had only served to slow, but not prevent, an overall fall in the United States' share of Australian trade. The cost of its doing so, however, had been to reduce or divert about $53 billion of trade away from the rest of the world.[161]

Other preferential trade agreements followed. An agreement with Thailand was signed in 2004 and negotiations began with Malaysia, China and Japan. After the failure of Seattle, a new round of multilateral negotiations of the WTO – the Doha Round – was begun in 2001 with a special emphasis on the needs of developing countries, but progress proved glacially slow.

The main economic story, however, was that of the continuing growth of China and the direct and indirect effect that had on Australia. As China's demand for resources grew, Australia's terms of trade continued to improve.

The economy entered a boom period. Unemployment was at its lowest rate for three decades, the government delivered record budget surpluses and the nation's growth rate was above the OECD average.

The return of geo-economics

Perhaps the symbolic apotheosis of the national security decade in Australian policy-making came in December 2008, when Rudd made his first statement to parliament on national security. He defined national security in the broadest terms, as 'freedom from attack or the threat of attack, the maintenance of our territorial integrity, the maintenance of our political sovereignty, the preservation of our hard won freedoms and the maintenance of our fundamental capacity to advance economic prosperity for all Australians'.[162] Terrorism would be one ongoing challenge, but so would other non-traditional threats like trafficking in persons, drugs and arms; people smuggling; the illegal exploitation of resources; and serious and organised crime. The security of computer and information technology systems was an element of national security, as were pandemic disease and climate change, which 'over the long term ... represents a most fundamental national security challenge',[163] through irregular population movement, declining food production, the reduction in arable land and violent weather patterns. The Office of National Assessments was asked to coordinate an annual 'all-sources' national threat assessment involving government departments like health and transport, which had never before seen themselves as part of the national security community.

Almost all dimensions of the external environment were seen through this security lens. A national security adviser (NSA) located in the prime minister's department was appointed to advise him on 'all policy matters relating to the security of the nation'. But just as the events in East Timor and 9/11 had confounded the Howard government's expectations about its policy priorities, so the Rudd government found itself confronting new issues. Geo-economics swept back onto the global stage.

For a couple of years now, there had been unexpected signs that all was not right with the American economy, which for so long had been the smoothly firing engine of the international economy. As the US housing market had taken off early in the century, loans – delicately described as 'subprime' – had been provided promiscuously to high-risk borrowers who could not afford to repay them when house values began to fall after

2005. Shuffled and repackaged in ways newly devised by Wall Street's cleverest minds, they were then dispersed throughout the world's financial system.

First, the direct providers of such subprime loans were affected. By October 2007, 171 of them had collapsed. Then came larger firms that had taken such loans and their derivatives into their portfolios. Other countries were affected, too. A French bank, BNP Paribas, halted trading in asset-backed securities that were closely linked to the US market in August 2007. Northern Rock, a British bank, had to be rescued by the Bank of England in September. In March 2008 the American bank Bear Stearns collapsed and was taken over in a fire sale by its rival JP Morgan Chase.[164]

Rudd began to express concern about the implications of these developments for Australia soon after he came to office. At his request, calls on the head of the IMF and other financial institutions were added to the itinerary for his first extensive overseas visit in late March and April 2008. Two Treasury officials joined the travelling party, and part of the long trans-Pacific flight became a seminar on risks to the global financial system. 'A large part of my reason for being here,' he told reporters when he landed in Washington on 28 March 2008, was to discuss with the administration 'a coordinated global response to the current difficulties being experienced across global financial markets rolling through to the real economy'.[165]

9

A FRAGMENTING WORLD:

2008–2016

I n the twenty-four years after 1983 Australia had just three prime ministers and three foreign ministers, two of them the longest-serving in the country's history. But then came rapid change. Between the election of Kevin Rudd in 2007 and the elevation of Malcolm Turnbull eight years later, four prime ministers, one of them twice, and four foreign ministers held office. They included Australia's first female prime minister and foreign minister.

Rudd's first term was cut short in June 2010 as his early popularity faded; he was replaced by his deputy, Julia Gillard. After a close election in August she led a minority government in a hung parliament. Rudd's parliamentary colleagues returned him to the premiership before the end of Labor's term in June 2013, as they moved to shore up their position against looming electoral losses. Following a strong victory for the Coalition, led by Tony Abbott, in September 2013, he, too, was replaced by his own party in just two years. Turnbull took over.

The effect of these changes on Australian foreign policy was to refract it through a series of separate prisms. Rudd, Gillard, Abbott and Turnbull saw the world in quite distinct ways. On important issues like defence white papers, climate change, asylum seekers, trade and aid, policy veered and changed. And in contrast to those before them, prime ministers and ministers had little time to learn from their errors or shape their own views of the world before they found themselves out of a job.

These four different prime ministers were responsible for overseeing for-eign policy in a global situation that seemed to mirror Australia's political fragmentation. The worst global economic downturn since the Great Depression generated powerful counterforces to globalisation in the devel-oped world. Borders re-emerged. The European Union (EU) began to fracture and British voters chose to leave it. Multilateral institutions were fraying as established rules and norms were challenged. For all the efforts of Australia's major ally, the United States, to refocus on Asia, it kept being drawn back to the Middle East. In that region, hopes of democratic reform quickly faded and Islamist terrorist groups metastasised, generating new waves of asylum seekers and new terrorist threats. Most importantly for Australia, a more economically powerful China was shrugging aside the restraints of its past foreign policy and asserting a larger regional and inter-national role for itself. By the end of the period, the tension between Australia's economic and geo-strategic interests had never seemed greater.

Kevin Rudd

Foreign policy had played little part in the November 2007 election cam-paign that brought Rudd to power, but with university training in Asian studies and professional experience as a diplomat, he came to the prime minister's job with an established framework for thinking about Australia in the world.

He was the first Australian prime minister born after World War II and the first to speak Chinese. After graduating from the Australian National University, he joined the Department of Foreign Affairs and Trade (DFAT) and was posted to Stockholm and Beijing. He then returned to Queensland, where he worked as chief of staff to the premier, and as head of the cabinet office. Elected as the member for the Queensland seat of Griffith in 1998, he became Labor's foreign affairs spokesperson in 2001. From that position he successfully led an attack on the Howard government over the Australian Wheat Board's sanctions-breaching 'wheat for oil' deals with Iraq. In December 2006 he defeated Kim Beazley to become leader of the party and a year later won the election.

In his approach to Australia's role in the world, Rudd drew on Gareth Evans' activism and belief in 'good international citizenship', Bob Hawke's strategic realism and support for the US alliance, and Paul Keating's focus on Asia. He sought institutional responses to the world's problems. The government's first objective, he said, was 'to entrench our standing as a middle power with global interests and regional interests – committed to the principles of creative middle power diplomacy as we seek to enhance the global and regional rules-based order'.[1] In contrast to the Howard government, whose diplomatically parsimonious strategy had sought to advance Australia's interests by leveraging a few key relationships with large partners, Rudd's ambition required extensive coalition-building and a 'pervasive, formative and influential' Australian diplomacy to go with it.[2]

He wanted Australia to be 'a nation that, at the dawn of this Asian Century is the most Asia-literate country in the collective West for whom the language and civilisations of Asia are no longer foreign but familiar'.[3] He felt that he had a particular contribution to make in interpreting Asia to the West and acting as a bridge between them. His foreign minister, Stephen Smith, and defence minister, Joel Fitzgibbon, had no previous experience in their portfolios. Rudd's would be the dominant voice.

Rudd was a practising Anglican, and Christian values as well as interests shaped his policies on issues like foreign aid, climate change and the economy. They were evident in his moving parliamentary apology in February 2008 to the Stolen Generations – Indigenous children who had been removed from their parents as a result of earlier government policies to encourage assimilation. The apology would have foreign policy benefits during Australia's campaign for membership of the United Nations Security Council.

It was the method of his policy-making rather than its content that most distinguished Rudd from his predecessors. His mind was restless and analytical. He was prodigiously hard-working and ideas, initiatives, reviews and inquiries tumbled out: a homeland and border security review, a counterterrorism white paper, a National Science and Innovation Strategy, a National Energy Security Assessment, a cyber security review, a national brainstorming weekend called the 2020 Summit.

There was calculation in all this – he saw tactical political advantage in constant movement and in filling the news cycle – but it was also what most satisfied his personal needs. As Smith described it: 'Kevin thrived in the sense of crisis, the 24-hour media cycle, requests for immediate advice, urgent phone calls and briefings.'[4]

He was impatient, slept little, and in his personal dealings he could be testy and angry. He placed heavy demands on those around him. He could not easily delegate, however, nor lead a team. He wanted to master the detail of every issue himself and then to demonstrate that mastery. This meant that the system often became clogged around his personal office. Papers and reports were commissioned but lay unread or unacted upon. He preferred meetings as a mode of governing, but ministers as well as officials would frequently be kept waiting. Over time, his colleagues grew weary and resentful and the political consequences were not long coming.

The Global Financial Crisis and the establishment of the G20

As Rudd settled into office in 2008, nothing about the future was clear. Economic uncertainty had been an unexpected theme of his first visit to the United States as prime minister in March. But during the Australian winter and spring the dangers grew. Earlier than many of his advisers, Rudd saw that his domestic and foreign policy priorities would have to be adjusted to deal with the possibility of a global recession.

By November, following the September collapse of the huge Lehman Brothers bank and the bailing out by the US administration of the world's largest insurance company, AIG, the head of the International Monetary Fund (IMF), Dominique Strauss-Kahn, was describing the global financial system as on 'the brink of systemic meltdown'.[5] The world's major economies, the IMF predicted, were already in, or close to, recession.

The domestic economic policy challenges facing the government from the Global Financial Crisis were immediate and practical, but its foreign policy implications were longer-term and institutional.

It was clear that the G7, the established global steering group of industrialised countries, was no longer adequate to coordinate the international response to the crisis. China and the large developing countries were essential to charting a way out of the looming recession. Several alternative forums were being discussed. Some officials in Washington supported a limited expansion of the G7 to include Brazil, China, India, Mexico and South Africa. Another possibility, championed by the Canadian prime minister, Paul Martin, was to turn the G20 finance ministers' group, which had been established after the Asian financial crisis, into a leaders' group. This would add Australia, Indonesia and Korea, among others, to the membership list. Australia, with Peter Costello as treasurer, had played an active part in the G20's early work.

Australia's interest was in line with its long national search for a seat at the table. If there was to be an expanded global economic group, Australia wanted to be in it. In a speech to the UN General Assembly on 25 September, just after the Lehman Brothers collapse, Rudd pressed the case for the G20, which, he said, could provide the political authority needed to implement urgent reforms of the financial markets and regulatory systems which bodies like the IMF and the Financial Stability Forum – 'by their very nature bureaucratic' – lacked.[6]

Led by Rudd himself, Australian diplomats and officials began a major campaign to persuade President George W. Bush to adopt the G20 as the first point of response, and to see off counterproposals. Rudd hit the phones, speaking to ten world leaders in October. (A damaging newspaper leak of one of those conversations reported Rudd erroneously suggesting that Bush did not know what the G20 was.) He circulated a position paper to other leaders explaining why he thought the G20 should be the 'driving centre' for the global economy.[7]

In his last months as president, Bush opted for the G20 and convened its first leaders' meeting in Washington on 15 November 2008. But as Keating had found with Bill Clinton and APEC, if this was to advantage Australia over the longer term, the meetings needed to be institutionalised. Before the second meeting of the group in London in April 2009, Rudd spoke on the phone with sixteen of the twenty national leaders[8] and visited Washington to meet the new president, Barack Obama, and argue his case.

Obama proposed a follow-up meeting in Pittsburgh in September 2009, although some Europeans continued to resist its formalisation. Rudd's frenetic pace of advocacy continued – 'day and night', according to one of his staff.[9] At Obama's invitation, Rudd opened the discussion in Pittsburgh about the future of the G20. By the end of the meeting, leaders had designated the group as the 'premier forum for our international economic cooperation'.[10] They agreed to meet twice in 2010 and annually thereafter. Facing the worst global economic downturn since the Depression, the G20 Summits of 2008 and 2009 helped to secure joint action to promote growth, to improve regulatory systems and to reform global architecture.

As was the case during the Asian financial crisis, the underlying strengths in the Australian economy – a strong regulatory system, well-capitalised banks, a solid fiscal position which facilitated the stimulus response, and effective monetary policy – allowed Australia to maintain growth while many other industrialised countries were in trouble. Although economic activity dropped sharply in the December quarter of 2008, it then rebounded. Unemployment peaked at under 6 per cent and Australia was the only country in the OECD to avoid recession.[11] By late 2012, benefiting from China's huge stimulus to its own economy with infrastructure spending programs, it had become the twelfth largest economy in the world.

The establishment of the G20 leaders' meeting helped amplify Australia's voice in the global economic debate and expanded its international network of contacts with emerging powers outside Asia. Informal meetings of the foreign ministers of G20 'middle powers' – Mexico, Indonesia, Korea, Turkey and Australia – were instituted in 2013. Along with the establishment of the East Asia Summit, the G20 strengthened the long-term trend towards greater centralisation of Australian foreign policy-making around the prime minister. For Gillard, the G20 was one of Rudd's 'resounding successes as prime minister'.[12]

Gillard found when she became prime minister that the 'burning-platform desperation of the early days of the GFC ... had diminished'.[13] The focus shifted to the European sovereign debt crisis and the agenda became more diverse as issues like inequality, labour mobility and climate change were added. By the time Australia chaired the G20 meeting in 2014 (a hard-fought ambition of Gillard's), Abbott was prime minister.

The Global Financial Crisis had shown Rudd at his best: an indefatigable advocate, with a clear goal and a mastery of detail. But the management of the crisis established a pattern for adrenalin-fuelled crisis management in his office and his government which was to prove unsustainable. For Smith, 'The GFC decision-making format came to define the government permanently. We never reverted to orthodox decision-making.'[14]

Stephen Smith

Before his election to parliament for the seat of Perth in 1993, Smith had worked as a lawyer, as state secretary of the West Australian branch of the ALP and as a staffer for Paul Keating as treasurer. 'Stephen Smith is a cautious man,' wrote Julia Gillard, in the most common judgement made about him by both his colleagues and his officials.[15] But he was diligent, attentive to detail, and he travelled tirelessly. After the 2010 election, just at the time he was mastering the requirements of the portfolio, he moved, reluctantly but obligingly, to Defence when asked by Gillard to make room for Rudd. As with another West Australian foreign minister and fellow lawyer, Julie Bishop, it was difficult to distinguish the policies he pursued from those of the two prime ministers in whose cabinets he served. 'My operating principle,' he told the writer Paul Kelly, 'was to ensure there was not a crack of light between the Foreign Minister and the Prime Minister'.[16]

The US Alliance

As had been the case with the APEC leaders' meetings, American diplomatic support was critical to Australia's success in establishing the G20 as a permanent body. Despite the differences between all the Australian governments of the period, support for the US alliance remained central to Australian foreign policy. From Gillard on the left of her party to Abbott on the right of his, the language was unchanged, as was support for the US engagement in Afghanistan and eventually against ISIS.

With the return of the Democrats and the inauguration of Barack Obama in January 2009, foreign policies in Washington and Canberra aligned more closely than they had under Rudd and Bush, buttressed by new areas of cooperation in climate change and nuclear non-proliferation.

Obama, who was born in Hawaii and spent part of his childhood in Indonesia, brought an unusual Asia-Pacific perspective to US policies. Rudd's views on China, climate change, the G20 and US membership of the East Asia Summit were influential with Obama and his secretary of state, Hillary Clinton. 'Kevin is somebody [with whom] I probably share as much of a world view as any world leader out there,' the president told Kerry O'Brien in 2010.[17]

Gillard, too, established a warm level of personal engagement with Obama. 'The two of us clicked on several levels,'[18] she wrote. According to a leaked report, the US embassy in Canberra noted the significance of this: 'For decades, foreign policy, particularly the American Alliance, was a key point of difference between the [ALP] factions but today key figures in the Left like Gillard are as supportive of the Alliance as the Right.'[19]

Afghanistan

The most immediate manifestation of the alliance relationship was in Afghanistan. Australian forces left Iraq in 2008 but they continued to be heavily engaged in the NATO-led International Security Assistance Force (ISAF) in Afghanistan, most of them operating from the Dutch-run base of Tarin Kowt in southern Uruzgan province.

Obama had come to office supporting US military involvement in Afghanistan but sceptical about the strategy being followed. Following a review, in March 2009 he redefined America's aim in Afghanistan as 'to disrupt, dismantle and defeat Al Qaeda in Pakistan and Afghanistan and to prevent their return'. To achieve this, more troops would be committed to the conflict but also more civilian experts, part of a broader counterinsurgency strategy designed to address the causes of instability as well as their effect. He followed up with another surge of 33,000 troops in December 2009.

Like the Americans, the Australian government also began to describe Australia's objectives in these broader counterinsurgency terms. The month after Obama's statement, Rudd defined the Australian mission as preventing Afghanistan becoming a training ground and operating base for terrorism, stabilising the Afghanistan state to the extent necessary to achieve that, and training the army and police in Uruzgan province to a level sufficient to enable security responsibility to be handed to the Afghans.[20]

The focus on Uruzgan was designed to draw a clear boundary around Australian activities in Afghanistan, restricting the operations of Australian special forces to the province.[21] Largely to strengthen the training mission, the number of Australian personnel was increased from 1100 to 1550. Australian Federal Police trainers, development experts and diplomats were sent to Uruzgan, and the embassy in Kabul was increased in size.

After replacing Rudd, Gillard made her first visit to the troops in Afghanistan in October 2010. On her return, she opened the first parliamentary debate on Australia's participation in the war, the result of a deal the minority Labor government had reached with the independent members. Her message was sombre and similar to Rudd's. Australia had clear national interests in Afghanistan: there must be no safe haven for terrorists; Australia must stand firmly by its ally, the United States. She was blunt about the time it might take. Australia would be 'engaged through this decade at least' and good government in the country 'may be the work of an Afghan generation'.[22] Almost all the parliamentary speakers supported Australia's continuing commitment.

But Afghanistan continued to prove as intractable to foreign military intervention as it had for centuries. The insurgency led by the ousted Taliban was growing and local warlords fought to consolidate their power. For all the important signs of social progress in girls' education and health, corruption remained endemic and poverty entrenched. President Hamid Karzai was proving a difficult ally and clear signs of fraud had marked his re-election in 2009. More Australian soldiers were losing their lives: twenty-one of them by the time of the parliamentary debate, with a further eleven deaths in 2011.

Despite their words of commitment, all the Western partners in Afghanistan were now searching for the best way out. Following a change of government, the Dutch had withdrawn from Tarin Kowt in August 2010. At a series of international meetings that year, a policy of what the British called

'Afghanisation' had developed. This involved a more comprehensive international effort to coordinate military training and support governance and reconstruction in Afghanistan, coupled with diplomatic efforts to achieve reconciliation with those Afghan opposition forces that might be prised away from the hardest-line Taliban. The objective was to transfer responsibility for security to the Afghan authorities as soon as possible, but in response, its proponents insisted, to carefully measured conditions on the ground, rather than any artificial timetable.

The announcement by Obama on 1 May 2011 that US special forces had killed Osama bin Laden, hiding in a small town in Pakistan, was a symbolic and psychological watershed for the Americans. In June, the president announced a two-stage withdrawal of the 33,000 American surge troops by late 2012. The UK, too, announced a troop withdrawal. Gradually the commitment to a conditions-based transfer of power morphed into one that was time-based after all.

Just as Australia had gone into Afghanistan with the United States, its exit also reflected the pace and form of its ally's departure. In line with ISAF transition plans, Afghan forces took over the security lead in Uruzgan in July 2012. Later that year, forward operating and patrol bases were handed over. At the end of 2013 the centre of Australian operations, the base at Tarin Kowt, was closed. ISAF handed back security responsibility for the country as a whole to the Afghan government in January 2015.

Australia learnt again the lessons of the Bougainville and Solomons interventions: that most contemporary Australian overseas military operations were also likely to engage other government agencies, including the diplomatic service, the police, intelligence agencies and aid organisations. Over the course of the war, diplomacy and foreign policy were integrated more effectively into the Australian policy mix. In 2009 a former senior foreign affairs officer and defence department secretary, Ric Smith, was appointed as Special Envoy for Afghanistan and Pakistan to help coordinate the international diplomacy, and an informal and high-level coordination committee (colloquially known as the Shura) was established in Canberra to help smooth out inter-agency disagreements.

Through its participation in ISAF and its work with the Dutch, Australia developed a closer relationship with NATO and its European partners. This was not without friction: Australia frequently had to assert its right to a voice in decision-making, but the result was a new level of security cooperation with Europe.

Australia's involvement with Afghanistan was not finished. It continued to support NATO's follow-up support and training mission in Afghanistan. But combat operations, part of Australia's longest-ever military commitment, were over. More than 25,000 Australians had served in Afghanistan. Forty-one died and the lives of many more were permanently changed by the experience.

At a ceremony marking the closure of the Tarin Kowt base in October 2013, the assessment made by Abbott, the fourth of Australia's Afghanistan War prime ministers, was appropriately modest: 'Australia's longest war is ending, not with victory, not with defeat, but we hope an Afghanistan that's better for our presence here.' He repeated the consistent reasons all Australian governments had given for their involvement: 'The threat of global terrorism is reduced. Our reliability as an ally is confirmed.'[23]

The US pivot to the Asia-Pacific

As Australia reduced its commitments in Afghanistan and Iraq, a new test of that reliability was found closer to home. An early review of US global strategy and force disposition commissioned by Obama found that at a time when American predominance in Asia was being tested by China's rising power, its defence posture was unduly skewed towards Europe and the Middle East. In late 2011 and early 2012 Obama announced a shift – a pivot, or rebalancing – in US policy towards the Asia-Pacific region. His policy had political and economic as well as military dimensions, including the negotiation of a new trade agreement, the Trans-Pacific Partnership.

For policy-makers in Canberra the question was how Australia could support a continuing American military presence in practical terms, and how would this play out with China. Travelling to Washington in March 2011 for celebrations to mark the sixtieth anniversary of the ANZUS Treaty, Gillard told her staff she would 'do whatever she could with the voice she had to reinforce American self-belief'.[24] Even by the usual standards of Australian policy-makers on such occasions, her speech to a joint sitting of Congress was extravagant. Australia 'is an ally for all the years to come', she told her audience.[25] Quoting Ronald Reagan and recalling her memory of watching the moon landing as a girl, she played to all the patriotic feelings of Americans, their romantic self-image and their sentimental views of Australia. Her audience received the speech warmly.

In Canberra in November 2011 Obama gave his clearest exposition yet of the pivot: 'as a Pacific nation, the United States will play a larger and long-term role in shaping this region and its future', he told the Australian parliament.[26] He and Gillard announced new arrangements under which US marines – 250 at first, rising to 2500 over five years – would rotate every six months through Darwin for training and the US Air Force would make greater use of facilities in northern Australia. Additional cooperation in space activity and cyber issues was also announced.

Sounding like Howard, Gillard said she believed the Australian decision would 'send a self-confident message to our region that Australia was not succumbing to a dogma of false choices between valuing our alliance and our relationships in the region in which we live'.[27] Her confidence that 'the days of progressive Left protests against an American presence on Australian soil were behind us'[28] also seemed borne out by the general support for the decision. By the time of the 2012 Lowy Institute poll, a record 87 per cent of respondents saw the US alliance as 'very' (59 per cent) or 'fairly' important for Australia's security.[29]

The election of Abbott and the Coalition did not change the direction of policy towards the United States. The broader agenda of international coop-eration between the two countries (and the warmth at leadership level) moderated, however, with clear differences between the Obama and Abbott governments on issues such as climate change. But most importantly for a great power which was looking for allies that would share the burden of their own defence, actual defence expenditure, which had fallen under Labor to its lowest level as a percentage of GDP since 1938, increased. The 2016 defence white paper, begun under Abbott but issued after changes by Turnbull, committed the government to a new ten-year defence budget, reaching $42.4 billion in 2020/21, 2 per cent of Australia's estimated gross domestic product.

The United States, the white paper stated, would be Australia's most important strategic partner. Australia would seek to broaden and deepen its alliance, 'including by supporting its critical role in underpinning security in our region through the continued rebalance of United States military forces'.[30]

Australia and Asian regionalism

The wish to encourage high-level US security engagement in the Asia-Pacific was one of the objectives that drove Rudd's initiative to establish a new Asia-Pacific Community, launched in a speech in Sydney in June 2008. The Community he envisaged would engage the entire Asian region in a full spectrum of discussion about politics and security as well as economics. Incautious language about the European experience suggested to some (or enabled opponents to argue) that Australia was looking for an EU-type structure, and inadequate diplomatic preparation compounded the problem. Like Evans, with his Asian security forum proposals eighteen years earlier, and Whitlam before him, Rudd quickly ran into resistance from the ASEAN countries, led by Singapore, to anything that might derogate from their central role in the management of regional institutions. Still, he pressed on, giving greater emphasis in his speeches to ASEAN's importance. He repeated his central argument at the annual regional security conference, the Shangri-La Dialogue, in Singapore in May 2009: 'Managing major power relations, particularly in the context of the rise of China and India, will be crucial to our collective future ... Do we sit by and allow relations between states to be buffeted by economic and strategic shifts and shocks or do we seek to build institutions to provide anchorages of stability able to withstand the strategic stresses and strains of the future when they inevitably arise?'[31]

It was increasingly clear that the easiest way of doing this would be to include the United States, Russia and India in the existing, ASEAN-coordinated East Asia Summit (EAS). The Indonesian president, Susilo Bambang Yudhoyono, made that case to Rudd when he visited Australia in March 2010, and offered to talk to the Singaporeans and the Malaysians.[32]

The Americans were difficult to persuade. The Obama administration, the Australian ambassador, Kim Beazley, wrote later, had subjected him to 'a hostile full-court press'[33] over Rudd's original initiative, but he had responded that Rudd was trying to secure America's role in the region. The president's time is one of the most tenaciously fought-over commodities in Washington and some White House officials strongly opposed a commitment that would require another annual presidential trip to Asia. According to Beazley, Obama finally made a decision in June 2010, with strong support from the secretary of state, Hillary Clinton. Clinton would attend the EAS meeting in Hanoi that October, and the president's participation would begin the following year. Clinton acknowledged Rudd's role in securing this outcome. 'I was influenced by Kevin Rudd's very strong argument on behalf of an Asian-Pacific community,' she told journalists in September. 'I think he was absolutely on point.'[34]

Rudd decided to declare victory. He described the expanded EAS as an institution that 'brings to fruition the concept of Asia Pacific community ... A significant part of the product of more than three years of Australian diplomacy at the highest levels.'[35] But it was Gillard who represented Australia at the EAS in 2010, and in Bali the following year, when the United States and Russia joined the meeting for the first time.

Julia Gillard

From early 2010 Rudd's public popularity, the bulwark of his defence against colleagues who had never trusted him fully, began to slide. Political problems over climate change, a proposed mining tax and boat arrivals accumulated, and the processes of government became more frayed.[36] As internal party frustrations grew, the deputy prime minister, Julia Gillard, challenged and defeated him in a ballot for party leadership. She was sworn in as prime minister on 24 June 2010.

Gillard arrived in Australia as a child, the daughter of immigrants from Wales. She grew up and went to school in South Australia, then moved to Victoria, where she graduated in law and became a partner in a law firm. She was chief of staff to the leader of the state Opposition, before being elected to represent the western Melbourne seat of Lalor in 1998. In December 2006, she became deputy leader of the ALP in an alliance with Rudd when he defeated Beazley. As deputy prime minister after the 2007 election she had responsibility for a large portfolio of social issues including employment, workplace relations and education.

The suddenness of Gillard's political strike against Rudd and the opaqueness of the reasons for it unsettled public opinion. When she went to an election in her own right a couple of months later, in August 2010, the result was a hung parliament in which the balance of power was held by five members of minor parties and independents. Gillard secured the support of four of them and began her term as head of the first Commonwealth minority government since 1940.

She was hampered in her approach to foreign policy because, as she wrote later, after the 2010 election, 'I never had a Foreign Minister I could rely on.'[37] In order to bring Rudd, who had caused problems during the election campaign, back into government, she shifted Smith from Foreign Affairs to Defence. Her relationship with Rudd was always tense, however, and by late 2011 political mistrust had reached new lows. In February 2012 he resigned dramatically during a visit to Washington. Gillard won the subsequent leadership ballot by a large margin and announced her support for Bob Carr, a former New South Wales premier, to fill a casual vacancy in the

Senate and take up the foreign minister's job. But that didn't work for her either. The two had political differences over the Middle East, and Carr's support shifted towards Rudd. Facing catastrophic polling figures, the parliamentary party moved finally in June 2013 to remove her and reinstate Rudd as leader.

Gillard came to office with no deep experience or interest in foreign policy. 'I'm just going to be really upfront about this: foreign policy is not my passion,' she told a television interviewer at the end of her first overseas visit.[38] That was true, but she was comfortable and confident in a job she saw essentially as one of international advocacy. 'At the end of the day,' she wrote later, 'for all the machinery, doctrine, commentary and academic debate that swirls around foreign policy, in execution it is a tool for individuals, leaders of nations, coming together to see if they can find common accord.'[39] She mastered briefs and retained the details, but unlike Rudd she didn't want to 'sweat the small stuff', as she would say. The business of government was processed in an efficient and orderly way and she was unfailingly considerate to the staff and officials who worked with her. She was intelligent, hardworking and organised. Frequently under great political and personal pressure, she remained cool and controlled. She was 'a person with a hinterland', in the words of one of her staff.[40]

In her approach to international policy, Gillard was more like Howard than any other recent Australian prime minister. Her foreign policy worked outwards: that is, she began thinking about the world from a domestic perspective. Even her major foreign policy initiative was a way of linking domestic issues like education to the changing external environment. In September 2011, at the suggestion of the trade minister, Craig Emerson, she commissioned a new white paper, on Australia in the Asian Century. Prepared by a group of advisers inside and outside government, led by a former secretary of the Treasury, Ken Henry, its objective was to identify what Australia needed to do domestically to prepare for the changes in Asia. The 300-page report was released in October 2012. It contained rich research and useful case studies and a series of proposed national objectives and pathways to achieve them.[41] But by then the government's time was running out and no money was put into its proposed initiatives.

Gillard was sceptical of grand designs and content to achieve incremental change. But the policy future she sought was firmly in the Australian tradition: 'A peaceful, open, rules-based Asian system. Effective regional institutions, respect for all countries of the region, large and small. Space for a rising China. A robust alliance between Australia and the United States.'[42]

An effective advocate and diplomat, and a strong supporter of the alliance with the United States, she managed the core relationships with the United States, China, Japan and India skilfully, leaving solid policy legacies with each.

India

India was one of the focal countries identified in the Asian Century white paper, and also a member of the East Asia Summit. These were signs of an important change in the way Australia thought about its region. The term 'Indo-Pacific' was increasingly being used in official language as a way of describing Australia's strategic environment. Emerging first in academic and think-tank writing,[43] it made its first official appearance in the 2013 defence white paper ('over time, Australia's security environment will be significantly influenced by how the Indo-Pacific and its architecture evolves')[44] and achieved bipartisan consensus with its reappearance in the speeches of Bishop and in the 2016 defence white paper. In contrast to the more familiar 'Asia-Pacific', it was a framing device for Australian strategic policy that underlined the linkage between the two oceans around Australia and the increasingly critical energy, trade and security links between the Middle East though Southeast Asia to North Asia. It described a more central place for India on Australia's strategic map.

The new policy attention given to India was also a reflection of its growing economic weight – in 2012 it became the world's third-largest economy measured by purchasing power – and partly of its potential role in balancing a rising China. Change in the Australia–India relationship was not easily achieved, however.

When Rudd took office, ALP policy prevented him from proceeding with Howard's proposals to sell Australian uranium to India. For New Delhi the issue was symbolic as much as commercial. India wanted Australia to acknowledge its status as a nuclear power more than it needed uranium. For the Labor Party, the issue ran deep. The party's past internal struggles over nuclear policy and uranium had been resolved by an absolute commitment to restrict uranium exports to states that had signed the Nuclear Non-Proliferation Treaty.

When Rudd visited India in November 2009, however, a different problem was attracting Indian public interest. Reports of attacks, purportedly racist, on some of the estimated 95,000 Indian students now studying in Australia had been picked up by a competitive and sometimes reckless Indian media and blown up into a public relations crisis. This presented Australia with a major handling problem, involving state as well as federal authorities, before it was resolved.

Despite the differences over uranium and students, relations continued to expand. Rudd and his Indian counterpart, Manmohan Singh, agreed to establish a Strategic Partnership and signed a joint declaration laying out ways the two countries would work together on defence and security issues.

As part of the response to the attacks on students, Julia Gillard had visited India as education minister in 2009. When she became prime minister she decided that the best way of deepening the relationship was to clear away 'the biggest stumbling block of our refusal to export uranium to India'.[45] In a personal, and politically brave, decision, she took a proposal to amend policy to the ALP national conference in December 2011. It was not rational, she argued (as Howard had done), for Australia to sell uranium to China but not to democratic India. She secured change by a small margin after a tough debate. Although the policy shift took time to put in place, the psychological effect on the relationship was immediate. When she visited India again in October 2012, Gillard announced that the two countries would commence negotiations on a civil nuclear cooperation agreement. It was also agreed that there would be annual meetings between the two prime ministers.

Soon after Abbott's election in 2013, a new Indian prime minister, Narendra Modi, more pro-market and assertively nationalist than his Congress Party predecessor, took office. He and Abbott had similar worldviews and Abbott saw strategic opportunities for the relationship, including the balancing of China. The new Australian position on uranium mining under Gillard was given official form when the Australia–India Civil Nuclear Cooperation Agreement was signed during Abbott's visit to India in September 2014.

In November, Modi became the first Indian prime minister in twenty-eight years to make a bilateral visit to Australia. 'I see Australia as a major partner in every area of our national priority', he told a joint sitting of parliament, a claim that would have startled earlier generations of Indian politicians and officials.[46] In Sydney, Modi addressed an enthusiastic crowd of 16,000, mostly members of the Indian diaspora, a reflection of the impact of the 180,000 Indian migrants who arrived in Australia between 2010 and 2015.

By now there was an extensive structure for ministerial and official consultations between the two countries. Foreign, defence, trade and education ministers met regularly. During their meeting in Canberra, Modi and Abbot signed a Framework for Security Cooperation with an extensive action plan. Their statement pointedly noted the shared commitment of the two states to 'democracy, freedom, human rights and rule of law'. The first bilateral visit to Australia by an Indian defence minister took place in June 2013 and the first bilateral maritime exercise was held in September 2015. Progress was slower on trade, where India remained reluctant to liberalise, but the two countries began negotiation of a Comprehensive Economic Cooperation Agreement in 2011.

Southeast Asia

In these years after the Global Financial Crisis, Australia's policy towards Southeast Asia was being shaped by the ever-growing presence and weight of China and the pressures this placed on ASEAN's regional solidarity as maritime disputes in the South China Sea intensified. In Indonesia, democracy continued to embed itself through successful parliamentary and presidential elections but elsewhere in the region, in Thailand and Malaysia, political systems seemed increasingly stressed. Myanmar finally emerged from its decades of isolation

The Indonesian president for most of the period, Yudhoyono, understood Australia and believed in the importance of the relationship. Gillard found him 'wise and patient'.[47] Both characteristics would prove helpful to him in dealing with the increasing demands from his Australian counterparts over asylum seekers, the treatment of Australian prisoners and other domestic concerns.

In a well-crafted speech to a joint sitting of parliament during his visit to Australia in 2010, Yudhoyono described Australia and Indonesia as strategic partners: 'We are equal stakeholders in a common future with much to gain if we get this relationship right and much to lose if we get it wrong'.[48] The themes and sentiments would not have been unusual coming from the Australian side, but he was the first Indonesian president to put them that way.

By the end of the Howard government – after the Bali bombings, the response to the Boxing Day tsunami of 2004 and the election of Yudhoyono – Australia's relationship with Indonesia had entered a period of fruitful growth. Rudd continued these policies, supporting the expanded development assistance program and bringing into operation the Lombok Treaty, which Downer had negotiated. But he wanted to do more. He underlined his own commitment to the relationship in his immediate visit to Bali for the climate change conference and by agreeing to co-chair in December 2008 the new Bali Democracy Forum, established by Yudhoyono to promote regional democratic norms.

Rudd and Yudhoyono agreed to hold annual leaders' meetings and an annual '2+2' meeting between the foreign and defence ministers and to begin negotiating a Comprehensive Economic Partnership Agreement. Rudd also wanted the two countries to 'work in partnership in the world' on issues like climate change and responses to natural disasters,[49] as he put it in Jakarta. The continuing importance of counterterrorism cooperation was underlined by further bombings at Jakarta hotels in July 2009.

But as the flow of asylum seekers to Australia grew, most of them setting out from ports in Indonesia, the focus of the relationship changed. The stresses that accompanied Australia's unsuccessful efforts to return Sri Lankan asylum seekers to Indonesia on an Australian customs vessel, the MV *Oceanic Viking*, caused tension at working levels in Jakarta, and Australia stepped up efforts to secure more forceful Indonesian action against people smugglers.

Gillard had less invested in the Australia–Indonesia relationship than Rudd and held a less strategic view of it. She wanted Indonesia to move faster in dealing with people smuggling, changing visa-free travel for Iranians to Indonesia and acting on prisoner transfers.[50] Her government mishandled cattle exports after harrowing footage of animal cruelty was aired in a television documentary about the industry in June 2011. Without consulting Indonesia, ministers imposed a limited, then a full, provisional ban on all cattle exports.

This caused serious political problems for the Indonesian government. Almost all Indonesia's live cattle imports were from Australia and the ban threatened price rises and shortages during the sensitive period of Ramadan, especially affecting poor and lower-middle-class Indonesians who had no access to refrigeration. Jakarta responded by cutting Australia's beef quota and threatening to advance moves to self-sufficiency. Despite all this, Yudhoyono's response was patient and his strategic perspectives continued to be helpful as he offered Gillard assistance in managing any regional nervousness about Australia's commitment to help train US marines in the Northern Territory.[51]

Abbott's election promise to make Australian foreign policy 'more Jakarta, less Geneva' was less a policy prescription than a signal that under his government national and bilateral interests would trump multilateral aspirations. It was clear from the beginning that the new government's single-minded focus on 'stopping the boats' would take precedence over other policy objectives, including maintaining good relations with Indonesia.

Nevertheless, Abbott's first overseas visit was to Jakarta, again seeking help with people smuggling. Yudhoyono repeated his commitment to cooperation. The relationship was then derailed from an unexpected quarter. In November 2013, a former US intelligence contractor, Edward Snowden, claimed that Australian agencies had been involved in targeting the personal mobile telephones of the president and his wife. Yudhoyono reacted with uncharacteristic anger at the personal nature of the reported intrusion. Although any such activities would have pre-dated his government's election, Abbott chose to respond with a statement in parliament bluntly ruling out an apology and noting that all governments collected information and refusing to comment on intelligence operations. The Indonesian ambassador to Australia was recalled for several months to Jakarta. In Indonesia, cooperation on people smuggling ground to a halt.

Abbott sent a series of personal messages to Jakarta, mostly through former military officials, to try to calm the issue but it took until June 2014, when he met Yudhoyono on Indonesia's Batam Island, for the relationship to get fully back on track. This was formalised in August when the foreign minister, Julie Bishop, and her Indonesian counterpart signed a Joint Understanding declaring that neither country would 'use any of their intelligence, including surveillance capacities, or other resources, in ways that would harm the interests of the Parties'.[52]

By this time, Yudhoyono was in the last stages of his presidency. His successor, Joko Widodo, a businessman who had come to politics through local politics and outside the traditional Indonesian elites, took office in October 2014. Jokowi, as he was known, had little international experience and his priorities were determinedly domestic. As Howard had done with Yudhoyono, Abbott attended his inauguration.

The imminent execution of two Australian drug smugglers, Andrew Chan and Myuran Sukumaran, members of the Bali Nine group who had been arrested in 2005, caused new tensions in the relationship. Jokowi had campaigned on a strong anti-drug platform and ignored appeals for clemency from all sides of Australian politics. He declined to take Abbott's telephone calls. The death sentences on the two men were carried out in April 2015. This time it was the Australian ambassador who was recalled.

With Turnbull's accession to the prime ministership, another effort was made to put the relationship back on track. Turnbull visited Jakarta in November 2015 and established an easy relationship with Jokowi. Talks about the Comprehensive Economic Partnership Agreement, suspended after the intelligence disagreements, resumed. 'It is a personal foreign policy objective of mine to strengthen those ties with Indonesia,' Turnbull told the Lowy Institute in his first major foreign policy speech in March 2016, echoing the ambitions of Australian policy-makers before him.[53]

East Timor had ceased to be an issue in the Australia–Indonesia relationship, although resentment at Australia's actions still lingered in some nationalist circles in Indonesia. And despite the commitment of aid and support in the years after independence, Canberra's relations with the new government in Dili were not without strain. Australian and New Zealand forces supporting the UN Integrated Mission in Timor-Leste (UNMIT) were withdrawn in late 2013 and disagreements continued over the maritime boundaries issue. The 2006 Treaty on Certain Maritime Arrangements in the Timor Sea (CMATS) had set aside a final determination of the maritime boundaries for fifty years and provided for revenue from the rich Greater Sunrise oil and gas fields to be split equally. The East Timor government, with Australian supporters, wanted to annul the treaty and undertake a final negotiation of the boundaries, believing that this would deliver more resources and revenues to Dili. It noted that Australia had secured an unfair advantage in the earlier negotiations by spying on the East Timor delegation.

The Australian government's response was grounded in the longstanding Australian argument (which it had used in its earlier boundary negotiations with Indonesia) that, under the Law of the Sea Convention, maritime boundaries should be based on the 'natural prolongation of the continental shelf principle'. Canberra's withdrawal in 2002 from the compulsory jurisdiction of the International Court of Justice and the International Tribunal for the Law of the Sea for the resolution of any maritime boundary disputes frustrated Timorese efforts to secure a legal resolution of the dispute. In April 2016 Timor-Leste initiated compulsory conciliation under the United Nations Convention on the Law of the Sea 'with the aim of concluding an agreement on permanent maritime boundaries with Australia', although the report of a conciliation commission does not bind the parties.

In other areas of Southeast Asia, two of Australia's oldest partners, Malaysia and Thailand, were moving in a more authoritarian direction. In Malaysia, divisions deepened within the Malay community and the ruling United Malays National Organisation (UMNO) party. In Thailand, the army seized control in May 2014 after a period of deep social and political division. Nevertheless, the importance of each country to Australia's efforts to deal with people smugglers and terrorists, and the scale of the trade, education and people-to-people links, ensured a careful Australian government response in each case. Bishop was one of the most senior Western leaders to visit Bangkok after the Thai coup. With Malaysia, Australian cooperation deepened as the two countries worked together to respond to two tragedies, the search for Malaysian Airlines Flight MH370, lost over the Indian Ocean, and the recovery efforts after the shooting down of MH17 in Ukraine.

In Myanmar, the largest and poorest country in mainland Southeast Asia, the trajectory was more positive. After heavily circumscribed elections in November 2010, the ruling military regime released Opposition leader Aung San Suu Kyi, the internationally recognised symbol of Burma's democratic resistance, from house arrest. In 2011 and 2012 under Rudd and Carr, Australia moved quickly to resume trade and military ties. Suu Kyi's party took control of government in November 2015.

Links with Vietnam continued to grow. Trade expanded and Hanoi joined the negotiations for the Trans-Pacific Partnership Trade Agreement. 'Half a century ago,' Tony Abbott told the visiting Vietnamese prime minister, Nguyen Tan Dung, in 2015, 'we were on different sides of a savage conflict. But times change, attitudes mellow, perspectives shift and common ground emerges where none was once apparent.'[54] That common ground included a belief that closer relations between Australia and Vietnam could help balance growing Chinese power. Its diplomatic tokens included Agreements on a Comprehensive Partnership signed in 2009 and 2015 and the establishment in 2013 of regular defence ministers' meetings.

Among what sometimes seemed to be a promiscuous series of announcements of partnerships with any passing foreign minister, Abbott's Comprehensive Strategic Partnership (CSP) signed with Singapore in June 2015 stood out for its serious intent. For fifty years, Singapore had been an important regional partner for Australia. Defence cooperation was well established. With its limited hinterland, Singapore had been using facilities in northern Australia to train its armed forces since 1982. By 2016 it had become Australia's fifth-largest trading partner. High-level political and

official consultations were deep and regular. The interests of the two countries diverged from time to time, mostly over issues of regional architecture
or Indonesia, but with China's rise, their views on the importance of a continued United States presence in the region were increasingly aligned.
Singapore was not an American ally, but it provided valuable access for
American forces.

Abbott had a particularly strong commitment to the relationship, based
on 'the English language, the rule of law, a high and rising standard of living,
and support for the US-backed global order'.[54] He hoped that Australia's
relationship with Singapore could become 'as easy, close and familiar as it
has long been with New Zealand'.[55] In May 2016 Singapore agreed to spend
$2.25 billion on facilities and infrastructure at Australian defence bases at
Shoalwater Bay and Townsville as part of a 25-year deal under which it
would send 14,000 military personnel to Australia for training each year.[56]

Japan

For most of the period of the Rudd and Gillard governments, Japan was
going through a period of political turmoil, fuelled by deep-seated national
problems of declining growth, high government debt and an ageing population. In 2009 the opposition Democratic Party of Japan won an
unprecedented landslide victory over the Liberal Democratic Party, which
had governed almost continuously since World War II. The foreign policies
of the new government were focused on Asia and it was explicitly committed to a warmer relationship with China, although in the absence of a
response from Beijing the thawing did not last. It seemed less attached to the
US alliance than its predecessor. Despite these changes, the Australia–Japan
relationship continued on a consistent trajectory. Driven by a heightened
consciousness of China's rising power, governments of different political
outlook in both countries continued to build closer institutional links.

As prime minister and then foreign minister, Rudd had private doubts
about Japan's long-term prospects and the future of its economic model,
and he pushed the anti-whaling campaign forcefully, finally implementing
his promise to take the Japanese whaling program to the International
Court of Justice in 2010. (The Court ruled that the program was illegal in
2014 but Japan nevertheless resumed whaling in the Southern Ocean.)
Even so, Rudd worked effectively with the Democratic Party government
on non-proliferation issues and building Asian regionalism.

In March 2011 a magnitude-9 earthquake, the fourth most powerful ever recorded, hit eastern Japan, followed by a massive tsunami. Some 16,000 people were killed and hundreds of thousands forced from their homes. A nuclear power plant at Fukushima suffered a partial meltdown. With further precautionary cuts in nuclear power generation across the country, the cost to the Japanese economy was estimated at US$300 billion.

The government and the Australian public responded quickly. An Australian urban search and rescue team and a C17 aircraft for relief operations were quickly dispatched. Less than a month later, Gillard became the first foreign leader to visit the country after the disaster, travelling to the devastated region near the nuclear meltdown, a gesture that was greatly appreciated.

'I am committed to this most important security relationship ... one of the closest and most important that either of us has,' she told the National Press Club in Tokyo. Technical but important steps to facilitate closer security cooperation were being taken with the negotiation of a Japan–Australia Acquisition and Cross-Servicing Agreement, enabling transport, fuel and other logistical support between the defence forces, and a Security of Information Agreement, permitting the two countries to share classified information, 'so improving our inter-operability,' in Gillard's words.[57]

In December 2012, just three years after its rout, the Liberal Democratic Party swept back into office under the leadership of Shinzo Abe. Abe, who had served a short and unsuccessful stint as prime minister in 2007, hoped to recharge Japan's economic growth with an expansionist and reformist economic policy package known as 'Abenomics'. He wanted to revise Japan's pacifist security posture so it could provide greater military support to its US ally and to loosen legislative restrictions on its capacity to export weapons and military equipment. Japan's neighbours, China and South Korea, harboured deep suspicions of his policies. The grandson of Nobusuke Kishi, Japan's prime minister during the negotiation of the 1957 Commerce Agreement, Abe had a place for Australia in his plans.

Abbott, who came to power nine months later, was ready to respond. Closer practical engagement between Australia and Japan on security matters would, he believed, help strengthen the whole US alliance system in East Asia. Each of his predecessors since Menzies had seen Japan as an important regional partner, but Abbott's declaration in October 2013 that 'Japan is Australia's best friend in Asia'[58] shifted the language beyond the careful diplomatic locutions of Howard (Australia has 'no greater friend in Asia than Japan'[59]) or Gillard ('Japan is Australia's closest partner in Asia'[60]). He went further, describing Australia as 'a strong ally of Japan'[61] in the context of China's provocative declaration of an Air Defense Identification Zone over the East China Sea. 'Ally' is a specific term in international relations suggesting a treaty-level commitment to help in the case of military attack. Australia and Japan were each treaty partners of the United States, but the word exceeded any formal commitment they had made to each other.

The most practical outcome of Abbott's ambitions came in December 2013, when the defence minister, David Johnston, announced that Australia had asked Japan to consider sharing advanced submarine propulsion technology with Australia. Reports subsequently emerged that Australia was looking into the option of replacing its ageing Collins-class submarines with the Japanese Sōryū-class, some of the world's most sophisticated conventional submarines.[62] An agreement on the transfer of defence equipment and technology, which Abbott and Abe signed in Canberra in July 2014, would facilitate this.[63]

When the prime ministers signed the Japan–Australia Economic Partnership Agreement, which each had helped push through, Abe told members of the Australian parliament that 'Japan and Australia have deepened our economic ties. We will now join up in a scrum, just like in rugby, to nurture a regional and world order and safeguard peace'.[64] But that proved harder than he and Abbott had hoped. Domestic pressures to ensure that the next class of submarines was built in South Australia and concern among Abbott's colleagues about whether he had made a behind-closed-doors deal with Abe eventually forced the government to announce a competitive evaluation process for the procurement of twelve submarines. In the end, Abbott's successor, Turnbull, announced in April 2016, to the intense disappointment of the Japanese, that the French contender would be the preferred design partner for the $50-billion program.

The submarine debate had served an important purpose, however. It encouraged policy-makers in both Canberra and Tokyo to think beyond the conventional words of amity and shared values about the extent to which Australian and Japanese interests in the region were fully aligned, and the consequences for both countries of their security partnership as they grappled with a more complex regional strategic environment. That discussion would continue.

The South Pacific

In the South Pacific, as elsewhere, the relentless search for ways of dealing with asylum seekers and boat arrivals was an important driver of Australian foreign policy, offering greater leverage to some states. It was the two largest regional countries – Papua New Guinea and Fiji – which demanded most of Australia's policy attention.

Expectations had been growing that PNG's rich natural resources, symbolised by a new $15-billion gas project led by ExxonMobil which came into production in 2014, would fuel a transformative economic boom. The prime minister after 2011, Peter O'Neill, wanted PNG to move beyond its status as a developing country. In September 2013 he announced that PNG would establish its own aid program in the neighbouring Pacific.

But as global commodity prices began to fall, so did PNG's economic growth rate. With high deficits and rising debt, the government faced serious fiscal problems. PNG's great achievement of continuous democracy over forty years of independence was sustained, although it was being tested. A constitutional and political crisis in 2012 was resolved by an election for which Australia and New Zealand provided extensive civil and military support.

The country suffered from growing corruption in government and a sharp decline in the capacity of the public service. For the large majority of Papua New Guineans living outside the modern sector, the resource riches had done nothing to improve their lives. Health, education and social indicators all declined. In 2014 the United Nations Development Programme ranked PNG 158th of the 188 countries and territories on its Human Development Index.[65]

Through all this, Australia remained PNG's largest economic partner, with an aid program of around $500 million each year. But any leverage this might have provided was constrained by the political importance to the Rudd, Gillard, Abbott and Turnbull governments of the asylum-seeker detention and processing facilities on Manus Island, off the country's northern coast. The signing of the Regional Resettlement Arrangement in 2013 by the Rudd government changed the balance of dependence in the relationship. New aid flowed into areas nominated as priorities by the PNG government, such as infrastructure. Australian governments remained silent on issues of democracy and corruption on which they might otherwise have spoken out.

'Perhaps more than any other single relationship,' the secretary of DFAT, Peter Varghese, told the Lowy Institute in 2015, 'the state of our relationship with PNG is seen as a barometer of Australian foreign policy success'.[66] But it remained a complex connection: sensitive, intimate and co-dependent at the level of government, but increasingly distant from the perceptions of most Australians. That was unlikely to remain the case. Economic and social stresses in a population which by some estimates would grow from 7.4 million in 2016 to 18 to 24 million by 2050 would make it much more visible to its southern neighbours.

The difficulty of translating power into influence, even in Australia's own neighbourhood, was again demonstrated as Canberra struggled to respond to another challenge to the region's democratic norms in Fiji. In April 2009, the Fiji Court of Appeal found that the coup which had brought the former military commander, Frank Bainimarama, to power three years earlier, had been illegal. In response, the president, under the influence of Bainimarama, abrogated the constitution, declared a state of emergency and revoked judicial appointments. Controls were imposed on the media. Bainimarama continued to rule by decree.

Following what was by now a familiar playbook, Canberra condemned the actions, called for elections and imposed targeted travel sanctions on the regime's ministers, senior officials and military officers. Aid programs continued, although they were redirected through civil society groups and NGOs, and there was no attempt to interfere with tourism or other economic links.

Australian and New Zealand efforts to pressure the regime to adhere to the Court's ruling and restore the constitution were fruitless. Excluded from the Pacific Islands Forum, the first time the organisation had taken that step, and from the Commonwealth, Fiji simply responded by expanding its diplomacy in other directions. It worked within the subregional Melanesian Spearhead Group and established a new Pacific Island Development Forum, formally open to all countries except Australia and New Zealand. It became more active in the United Nations, chairing the Group of Seventy-Seven developing countries in 2012. It announced a 'Look North' foreign policy focused on China, which expanded its aid to Fiji.

After Bainimarama announced plans for a new constitution, which would fulfil his stated ambition to remove ethnic voting blocs (indigenous and Indo-Fijian) from Fijian politics, Australia began to re-engage. In September 2014 Bainimarama's Fiji First party won a convincing majority in elections international observers found 'broadly represented the will of the Fijian voters'.[67] Australia restored full relations, including in defence, and

Fiji was invited back into the Commonwealth and the Pacific Islands Forum. Nevertheless, Bainimarama declined to attend the forum personally while Australia and New Zealand remained as members.

Region-wide negotiations to achieve free trade in goods and services and harmonised quarantine arrangements, which began in 2009, made slow progress. The small island states baulked at anything that seemed to them like a reduction in their sovereignty, and for small economies with few resources, tariffs were an important revenue source. One potentially important economic change, however, lay in labour mobility – schemes to permit Pacific Island guest workers to come to Australia for short periods. In August 2008 the Rudd government announced a trial scheme for workers in the horticulture industry, and this was extended by the Gillard government. The scheme was complex to administer, competition from backpacker labour turned out to be extensive, and take-up was much lower than with a similar scheme in New Zealand. But the Coalition, and Bishop, who saw the Pacific as 'central to Australia's foreign policy',[68] supported it strongly. By September 2015 more than 6000 Pacific Islanders had begun work in Australia under the scheme.

As usual, Australia paid close attention to the activities of outside powers in the region. China's growing aid, investment and diplomatic activity was evident and high-profile. Partly in response to China's activity, Washington restored its own regional aid program after a sixteen-year gap and stepped up its diplomacy.[69] Nevertheless, despite worries in some quarters of Canberra and Washington, there was little evidence that the South Pacific was an area of the world to which Beijing accorded much priority.

Through all this, New Zealand remained Australia's key partner in the Pacific. Differences of interest and emphasis emerged from time to time but it was clear that any successful Australian policy in the region had to be pursued in a coordinated and cooperative way with Wellington.

Aid

Rudd had committed his government to raise Australia's official development assistance (ODA) to 0.5 per cent of its gross national income (GNI) – the most commonly used measure of aid generosity – by 2015/16. This was twice the average level during the Howard years. By 2011 the aid program had doubled in just five years. But as budget constraints began to bite, the government pushed out the 0.5 per cent target date and, where it could count it as aid, redirected some of the money into the increasing costs of the refugee program.

Although the Coalition was formally committed to a similar 0.5 per cent goal, it sliced Labor's aid budget by $700 million when it came to office and continued to cut it in subsequent budgets. In total, Australian aid fell from $5 billion in 2013/14 to $3.8 billion in 2016/17, bringing it to an historic low of 0.23 per cent of GNI.[70] The Australian Agency for International Development (AusAID) was brought back into DFAT in order, the government said, to align more closely the aid and diplomatic arms of Australian international policy. Despite these heavy cuts, however, the scale of Australia's development assistance in the Pacific ($124.7 million in 2015/16) remained largely unchanged.

The Middle East

The heightened policy focus on the Middle East that had developed during the previous decade was reinforced for all the Australian governments of this period by the bitter sectarian war between Sunni and Shi'a Arabs revived by the US invasion of Iraq. On the longstanding dispute between Israel and the Palestinians, both Labor and the Coalition continued to support Israel's right, like that of every state in the region, to 'live in peace within secure and recognised boundaries' as UN Resolution 242 had affirmed in 1967. But the level of Palestinian representation in the United Nations became an important source of tension within the Gillard government. Gillard, who held a strongly pro-Israel position, disagreed with Rudd[71] and then Carr on whether Australia should alter its voting position on the Palestinian question in the United Nations General Assembly, partly, at least, to shore up Arab support for Australia's UN Security Council campaign.

Australia won that vote without foreshadowing a change in its position but by then the Palestinian issue was also caught up in the internal power struggle underway within the parliamentary Labor Party. The Victorian Right faction (close to the Australian Jewish community) and its New South Wales counterparts (where growing Muslim immigration was shifting electoral views) were on different sides. When Gillard decided that Australia would vote against a resolution for increased formal recognition of Palestine in the General Assembly, she was faced with the highly unusual prospect of being overruled by a caucus revolt and was forced to shift Australia's vote to an abstention. Her third foreign minister, Bob Carr, was central to this.

Bob Carr

The appointment in March 2012 of Carr, a successful state premier, with a broad range of interests and superb communication skills, to replace Rudd in a position he had made his own was widely welcomed. Gillard was to be disappointed in her choice, however. 'It is one thing to chat knowledgeably and engagingly about world affairs at a dinner party. It is quite another to methodically pursue Australia's interests in carefully calibrated diplomatic exchanges all around the world,' she wrote when it had all gone sour.[72]

Unlike Rudd, it was difficult to identify a distinct framework which Carr brought to the foreign affairs portfolio. 'There is a relentlessly pragmatic cast to Bob's approach to the world which . . . I don't completely share', one of his predecessors, Gareth Evans, noted in studied understatement.[73] His diaries, published after his period as minister, record his ambivalence about some of the core questions of Australian foreign policy. He is torn, he recounts several times, between the different advice about the US alliance he has been given by two senior Australian diplomats: whether Australia should be 'a different kind of ally' to the United States, supporting it reliably under all conditions or whether 'our interests are different from a great power's'.[74]

Like Rudd before him, Carr found himself having to respond to the consequences of the widespread public demonstrations which had broken out in late 2010 and early 2011 in Tunisia, Egypt, Libya, Syria and elsewhere against the oppressive regimes which governed much of the Middle East. These had seemed to many to herald a new Arab Spring. With an eye on its candidacy for election to the UN Security Council, the Gillard government responded to the changes supportively. As protests spread, Rudd declared that Australia needed to 'commit ourselves to decades of support for the long-term process of building democracy'.[75]

But short of warm words, modest aid and a diplomatic helping hand, there was little Australia could do to shape the changes. Little by little the early hopes for democratic reform were disappointed. In Egypt, the most populous Arab state, the army seized back control from a democratically elected Muslim Brotherhood government in July 2013.

Protests in Damascus and other Syrian cities had begun in March 2011. The regime of Bashar al-Assad, centred around his Alawite supporters (members of a schismatic branch of Shi'a Islam), had responded not with capitulation but heavy force to opponents ranging from moderate democrats to violent jihadists. As the bloodshed worsened through 2012 and 2013, Rudd and Carr were clear in their condemnation of the regime and their efforts to secure international action, including by expelling Syrian diplomats in Canberra and seeking to refer al-Assad to the International Criminal Court. Australia provided more than $230 million in humanitarian assistance.[76] But 4.8 million Syrian refugees were now living outside their country, mostly in overcrowded camps in Lebanon, Jordan and Turkey, in despair and biding their time.

Tony Abbott

Most political observers agreed that the Labor Party's decision to return Rudd to the leadership in June 2013 managed to limit the scale of Labor's defeat in the September election, but the result was a decisive victory for the Coalition and Tony Abbott. Abbott had studied at the University of Sydney and as a Rhodes scholar at Oxford. He spent time preparing for the priesthood before becoming a journalist and a political staffer. Elected to the North Sydney seat of Warringah in 1994, he served in senior ministries, including employment and health, in Howard's government.

Abbott had been a participant in Australian public debate since his time at university. The core beliefs of his social conservatism were constant: 'Awareness of the limitations of government and the imperfectability of man, consciousness of the shades of grey which are part and parcel of the human condition, respect for values and institutions which have stood the test of time, a sense of the importance of family and cultural bonds, a belief in the value of ritual and tradition.'[77]

His book *Battlelines*, published in 2009, before he became leader, set out his views on many issues of public policy. It had little to say about foreign policy, however, apart from its emphasis on the ongoing importance to global order of the 'Anglosphere', the English-speaking countries like the United Kingdom, the United States, Canada, Australia and, potentially, India, whose 'civic culture' emphasised fairness, democracy and the rule of law. 'Overwhelmingly', he believed, 'the modern world is one that's been made in English.'[78]

The core responsibility of government, he said in many different venues and forms, was to 'keep our borders secure and our country safe'.[79] National security rather than foreign policy was his dominant concern and where he found his closest relationships. He wanted, he said later, 'to make a difference, not just to strike a pose or indulge in gesture'.[80] He was driven less than most Australian prime ministers by a dispassionate calculation of the national interest and moved more readily by a view of the country's role in a great global conflict between right and wrong. He was 'a Romantic ... [who] grew up on the romance of the army and battle', in the words of Greg Sheridan, the Australian journalist who was closest to him.[81]

The new government was soon confronted by a series of international crises: the revelations about Australian intelligence that followed disclosures by former US intelligence contractor Edward Snowden and the mysterious disappearance of Malaysian Airlines Flight MH370, lost over the Indian Ocean in Australia's search and rescue zone.

Then, on 17 July 2014, another Malaysian Airlines flight, MH17, was shot down over Ukraine on its way from Amsterdam to Kuala Lumpur. Conflict had broken out in Ukraine after Russian troops seized the Crimean Peninsula in March and President Putin began supporting rebel forces in eastern Ukraine. Thirty-eight Australian citizens and residents were among the 298 people killed by those rebels using a Russian-supplied missile. Abbott quickly labelled the shooting a crime not an accident, condemned Russia and promised to 'shirtfront' Putin when they next met. (The encounter, less dramatic than the language promised, eventually took place in November at the APEC meeting in Beijing.)

For Abbott, the tragedy was also a national security crisis. He convened the National Security Committee of Cabinet seventeen times in the three weeks after the shooting.[82] AFP officers were dispatched to work with the Dutch in Ukraine. It took the combined opposition of all the defence and national security agencies, and the former chief of the defence force, Angus Houston, who had been sent to Kiev as a special envoy, to dissuade the prime minister from sending 1000 Australian troops to the disputed territory in Ukraine to secure the site so bodies could be removed.[83]

The prime minister's relationship with his foreign minister, Julie Bishop, who was also deputy leader, was polite but not intimate. The highly disciplined and tightly managed political operation that had marked Abbott's period as Opposition leader continued in government. As with Rudd, the centralising tendencies of Abbott's office would help generate the internal dissent within his own party that would eventually contribute to his replacement.[84]

However, Abbott's national security concerns were predominantly shaped by events in the Middle East. Out of the chaos of Sunni resistance to the American invasion of Iraq and the new Shi'a-led government in Baghdad, an extremist millenarian force had emerged in the Sunni heartland between Iraq and Syria. Its origins lay in al-Qaeda, but its operating style was different.

It used the sophisticated tools of social media to mobilise individuals and small autonomous groups with a message of violent jihadism.

Known variously as Daesh, the Islamic State of Iraq and the Levant (ISIL), the Islamic State of Iraq and al-Sham (ISIS) or simply Islamic State, its power spread rapidly across large areas of Iraq and Syria. In June 2014 it captured the important Iraqi city of Mosul and declared the establishment of a new caliphate. By late that year, fighters under its banner appeared in Libya and Pakistan. Thousands of foreign fighters, many of them disaffected young Muslims from the West, travelled to Syria to join it. At least 110 Australians were among them.[85] The role in the Bali bombings of the earlier generation of jihadists who had trained in Afghanistan weighed heavily on the minds of the Australian government and its officials.

Inside Australia, Islamic State propaganda was influencing a small number of Australian Muslims. In 2014, police officers in Melbourne were attacked and a police worker murdered in Sydney. A disturbed gunman seized hostages in a coffee shop in the middle of Sydney in December. Abbott announced that $630 million would be invested in a range of new counterterrorism measures. Polls showed that the Australian public saw Islamic extremism as the largest threat facing the country.[86]

The prime minister warned the Australian public of a dark world that was becoming more dangerous. 'In proclaiming a caliphate, the Islamist death-cult has declared war on the world,' he told the Australian people in his National Security Statement of February 2015.[87]

Despite President Obama's caution about military intervention, he decided in August 2014 to use limited air strikes and special forces to counter the ISIS advance in Iraq. Despite its withdrawal from Iraq, Australia had retained an operational hub at Al Minhad Air Base in the United Arab Emirates, and Abbott quickly offered the United States a 600-strong force of Super Hornet aircraft and special forces.[88] The air-force mission soon expanded from humanitarian support to air strikes on ISIS targets, first inside Iraq and later across the Syrian border. The special forces were deployed in headquarters and training roles.

With Abbott's replacement by Turnbull in September 2015, the government's language changed, initially at least. After terrorist attacks in Paris in June 2015 Abbott had warned Australians: 'As far as the Daesh death cult is concerned, it is coming after us.'[89] Following further strikes in the same city in November, Turnbull's response was much calmer. He told Australians that 'by most measures ... ISIL is in a fundamentally weak position ... [It] has many more smart phones than guns, more Twitter accounts than fighters'. He made it clear that he did not see any reason to increase Australian military involvement.[90]

Iran

Australia also had to respond during these years to growing concern about Iran's nuclear weapons potential, as Tehran's civil nuclear program steadily accumulated supplies of enriched uranium. Taken together with its separate ballistic missile ambitions, this potential worried all Western governments and Israel, and alarmed suspicious Sunni neighbours like Saudi Arabia which feared Tehran's support for Shi'ite groups throughout the Middle East. All Australian governments of the period supported a growing regime of economic sanctions designed to force Iranian compliance with United Nations Security Council resolutions. Australia had its own direct interests at stake in Iran, as a market for Australian wheat and the source of a growing number of asylum seekers. Almost alone of the Western countries, it had maintained a diplomatic presence in Tehran since 1985.

Despite these tensions, tentative signs were emerging under President Obama that United States policy was changing. In addition to the negotiations already underway with the permanent five members of the United Nations Security Council plus Germany (P5+1), Washington was conducting its own efforts to reach out to Iran.

The election of a reformist candidate, Hassan Rouhani, in the 2013 presidential election led almost immediately to movement in the negotiations with the P5+1 as the Iranians sought relief from biting economic sanctions. (Ultimate power, however, still resided with the theocratic leadership of the Supreme Leader, backed by the elite Revolutionary Guard force.) Obama faced opposition to any deal from Israel and his own Republican-dominated Congress, but finally, in July 2015, a comprehensive agreement, freezing key elements of the nuclear program for ten to fifteen years under inspection from the International Atomic Energy Agency, was announced. Australian economic sanctions were lifted in January 2016.

In April 2015, Bishop became the first senior Australian politician to visit Tehran for twelve years, and one of the first Western leaders to visit after Rouhani's victory. She was seeking, above all, agreement from the Iranian authorities to accept the repatriation from Nauru and Manus Island of Iranians whose asylum claims had been rejected.

Asylum seekers

The question of how to respond to asylum seekers arriving in Australia by boat preoccupied all Australian governments during this period. It was framed in many different contexts: as an immigration matter, a national security threat, a humanitarian obligation, a question of regional order-building, and an effort to counter international criminal enterprises. Each of these elements had implications for Australia's foreign policy in the Middle East, South Asia, Southeast Asia and the Pacific.

When Labor returned to office in 2007, irregular maritime arrivals (IMAs), as official language described them, seemed to be less of a problem for most Australians. Only 288 asylum seekers had arrived by boat in the six years from 2002.[91] The Howard government's Pacific Solution – the excision of Christmas Island and other territories from Australia's immigration zone, the introduction of offshore processing on Christmas Island, Manus Island and Nauru, and boat 'turn-backs', was part of the reason, but so were issues quite outside the control of Australian policy, like a reduced outflow of refugees from Afghanistan.

The Rudd government was caught between a desire to take a more humanitarian approach towards refugees and concern to show it could control the border. It abolished temporary protection visas (which required holders to reapply after three years), closed offshore processing on Nauru and Manus Island, and returned to Australia the last twenty-one asylum seekers held on Nauru. But it retained the principle of detention and the excision of overseas territories from the migration zone.

The overall message, however, was one of a more accommodating Australian policy and it was received just as international developments were generating new sources of refugees. The security situation in Afghanistan and Iraq deteriorated and members of the Afghan Hazara minority began to leave in greater numbers. In Sri Lanka a bitter civil war came to an end with the defeat of the Tamil resistance forces in May 2009, displacing 200,000 people. The relationship between 'push' and 'pull' factors in migration is complex and difficult to disentangle, but the pull factors – stability, employment or education prospects, established refugee determination systems and the likelihood of success in refugee applications – are all important in determining secondary movements beyond the neighbouring countries of first asylum.[92] The numbers of asylum seekers reaching Australia with the help of people smugglers in Indonesia began to pick up. Sixty boats carrying 2767 irregular migrants arrived in 2009.[93]

In October 2009, without consulting either his foreign or immigration ministers,[94] Rudd secured President Yudhoyono's agreement to transfer to Indonesia for detention seventy-eight Sri Lankan asylum seekers who had been taken aboard an Australian customs vessel, the *Oceanic Viking*. What was planned as a neat demonstration of the government's resolve turned farcical when the Sri Lankans refused to leave the boat. They threatened self-harm unless they were sent to Australia, and the Indonesians declined to remove them forcibly. The four-week-long standoff that followed, Gillard said later, 'moved the asylum seeker issue from a drum beat in the background to being flashpoint centre-stage'.[95] It was resolved only when Rudd agreed to rapid processing of the asylum seekers' claims. By the end of April 2010, over 2000 asylum seekers were held in detention on Christmas Island. The government began to harden its response, suspending the processing of new asylum applications from Sri Lanka and Afghanistan.

The asylum seeker issue was increasingly being presented as a humanitarian response to the loss of life at sea and the criminal actions of people smugglers. The 2009/10 budget included provision for a $654 million 'whole-of-government strategy to combat people smuggling and enhance border protection'. Rudd's language on the subject became increasingly strident. People smugglers, he said, 'represent the absolute scum of the earth ... The vilest form of human life'.[96]

Boat arrivals were one of several issues playing into the loss of public support for the prime minister that led the parliamentary Labor Party to replace Rudd with Gillard in June 2010. Gillard immediately emphasised the ·need to build a sustainable regional protection framework as 'the most effective way to address irregular migration, including to Australia'.[97]

But the political desire for a quick fix led her to announce prematurely in early July that Australia would establish a regional processing centre for irregular migrants in Timor-Leste. Beyond a telephone call to the president, Ramos-Horta, however, she had not consulted the East Timorese government. The deal fell apart.[98] Despite this, Australian efforts to build a broad regional response to the problem continued. Australia and Indonesia had signed an agreement in 2010 to cooperate on people smuggling. The members of the Bali Process agreed in early 2011 to a Regional Cooperation Framework (RCF) to address refugees and asylum seekers. In it, ministers from around the region acknowledged the 'collective responsibility of source, transit and destination countries in responding to complex migratory movements'.[99]

Desperate for a deal, Gillard announced in May 2011 a new arrangement with Malaysia. Australia would accept 4000 refugees from camps in Malaysia. In return, the first 800 irregular migrants to arrive in Australia would be sent to Malaysia for processing by the United Nations High Commissioner for Refugees (UNHCR). People returned in this way would have the right to live in the community with health and education services. Other countries in the region, including Thailand, expressed interest in similar arrangements. In August 2011, however, the High Court declared the agreement invalid. The Opposition (citing unexpected concerns about human rights in Malaysia, which was not a signatory to the Refugee Convention) and the Greens refused to support the necessary legislation to authorise the deal in parliament. Labor had no alternative but to restore onshore processing.

The numbers kept growing. In the twelve months to July 2012, 7120 asylum seekers, mostly Afghans, Iranians and Sri Lankans, had reached Australia.[100] Twenty-five thousand would arrive over the following year.[101] The deaths continued, too. Six hundred and four asylum seekers and crew were lost at sea in known incidents between October 2009 and July 2012.[102] The public mood was hardening. A 2012 Scanlon Foundation survey found fewer than one in four respondents agreeing that asylum seekers arriving in Australia by boat should be eligible for permanent settlement. Just 6 per cent thought the government was doing a good job in handling the issue.[103]

Searching for any circuit breaker, the government appointed an expert panel, chaired by the former chief of the defence force, Angus Houston, to report on the options available. Acknowledging that there 'were no quick or simple solutions', the panel recommended in August 2012 that the government should institute a 'no advantage' principle, ensuring that asylum seekers who tried to circumvent regular processing arrangements received no benefit. This meant returning them for offshore processing in Nauru or PNG. The panel also recommended a parallel and immediate increase in Australia's humanitarian intake to 20,000 and a major effort to build regional cooperation with source countries and regional governments.[104] The government accepted all its recommendations.

By the time Rudd returned to the prime ministership in June 2013, refugee policy was virtually back where it had been when he replaced Howard. He made a deal with Port Moresby: in return for substantial new aid, PNG would reopen the processing facility on Manus Island and accept for resettlement those who were found to be genuine refugees. 'As of today,' Rudd announced, 'asylum seekers who come here by boat without a visa will never be settled in Australia.'[105] The number of new arrivals began to fall immediately from 4236 in July to 1585 in August.[106]

The Abbott government was elected easily in September 2013, campaigning strongly on a promise to 'stop the boats'. It immediately established a new operational framework, Operation Sovereign Borders, under the control of a very senior ADF officer. Naval patrols intercepted boats heading towards Australia and towed them back, or transferred their passengers to specially designed emergency vessels that were then returned to Indonesian waters. All new boat arrivals were to be transferred to facilities in PNG or Nauru within forty-eight hours of their arrival. Strict secrecy was imposed over what were now called 'on-water operations'. Immigration, customs and border protection responsibilities were later combined in a new Department of Immigration and Border Protection.

Together with Rudd's arrangements with PNG, these measures had an immediate and lasting effect. By late March 2014, the prime minister was able to say that after one hundred days no asylum-seeker boats had reached Australia. For Abbott, this success rested on strong national actions: 'a unified chain of command through Operation Sovereign Borders to cut through the different priorities of the different Australian government agencies; the refusal to discuss operational matters on the water to deny people smugglers the oxygen of publicity; and, most important, the availability of big orange lifeboats to make turnarounds work, when people-smugglers scuttled their boats'.[107]

Regional cooperative approaches ranked lower. Relations with Indonesia were strained by turn-backs and other policy disagreements. In 2015 a $55-million deal was reached with Cambodia to resettle from Nauru people found to be refugees, but by 2016 there had been few takers.[108] When, in May 2015, Southeast Asian countries faced an immediate problem with boats carrying Rohingya Muslim refugees fleeing from Burma and Bangladesh, Abbott quickly ruled out any prospect of resettling some in Australia: 'Nope, nope, nope,' he told a press conference.[109] The size of the humanitarian program was smaller than under the previous government.

The issue affected other dimensions of Australian foreign policy. There was no international leader with whom Abbott was more closely aligned than Canada's Conservative prime minister, Stephen Harper, but the policies of the two governments towards Sri Lanka diverged markedly. Keen to ensure the continuing cooperation of the Sinhalese-dominated government in preventing boats setting out, Australia provided patrol boats to the Sri Lankan navy and Abbott attended the Commonwealth Heads of Government

Meeting in Colombo in November 2013. Harper, conscious of the large Canadian Tamil population, boycotted it on human rights grounds.

Aware of the continuing public hard line on boat arrivals, the two major Australian political parties were locked in agreement on the broad parameters of policy. There were new uncertainties on the horizon, however. The annual cost of maintaining the offshore processing centres on Manus Island and Nauru, according to the 2015/16 budget papers, was around $1 billion a year; the future of Manus was in doubt as a result of a ruling of the PNG Supreme Court in April 2016 that the detention there of asylum seekers and refugees was unlawful, and the long-term consequences of detentions on Nauru were being increasingly debated.

By 2016 the mass movement of people was a growing global issue, given new focus by the flood of Syrian and other Middle Eastern refugees moving to Europe, and by Central American immigrants entering the United States. In many Western countries longstanding approaches to dealing with refugees were coming under new pressure.

This was just one of the many issues on the global agenda where established norms were being challenged and rules becoming harder to establish. The most difficult and consequential of these was climate change.

Climate change

The urgent need to address the problem of climate change was one of the issues on which Rudd had distinguished the Labor Party from the Coalition in his 2007 election victory.

The key policy question now facing the parties to the United Nations Framework Convention on Climate Change (UNFCCC) was what would replace the Kyoto Protocol commitments when they expired in 2012, and whether developing countries would also be required to make legally binding commitments to reduce their carbon emissions. In December 2009, ninety world leaders and 45,000 accredited officials, media and NGO representatives descended on Copenhagen to try to find an answer. There was a clear split in the negotiations between the developed world, particularly the United States, and the major industrialising countries, Brazil, South Africa, India and China, which would be responsible for much of the world's future carbon emissions. President Obama had more ambitious climate change goals than his predecessor, but he had not been long in office and there were deep divisions between the Congress and the administration.

Throughout 2009, the Australian government had been pressing the climate change cause in its multilateral and bilateral diplomacy, including in the Commonwealth, APEC and the Pacific Islands Forum, which Rudd was chairing that year. The small Pacific island states like Tuvalu, less than five metres above sea level at its highest point, were particularly vulnerable to sea-level rises, and more immediately to more intense weather patterns and tidal surges.

One of the principal issues in the Australian debate was whether the country should move ahead of the rest of the world, encouraging movement, or wait and respond to others. Rudd had hoped to go to Copenhagen with a model Australian emissions trading scheme in place, but his ambition was thwarted in mid-2009 when the Opposition and the Greens combined in the Senate to defeat legislation proposing an overall cap on Australia's carbon emissions and a 'cap and trade' system in which the market would determine the cost of carbon. The Greens complained that the proposals did not go far enough, while the Opposition, which had supported a scheme of this sort during the previous election, split on the issue. Turnbull, who had agreed as Opposition leader to back a compromise deal, was replaced by Abbott, who was deeply opposed.

Despite the setback to his domestic plans, Rudd went to Copenhagen intending that Australia, and he personally, should play an active part in the negotiations. At the request of the chair of the conference, the Danish prime minister, he had already taken part in preparatory video-conferences with a small group of other leaders and by the time he arrived he understood more of the technical detail than most of the other leaders. In the meeting rooms and corridors of the conference, he was indefatigable in his search for an outcome.

Possibly concerned that they would be blamed for their own reluctance to commit to binding targets, the Chinese resisted allowing others to make them. In the end, consensus failed, and the parties could agree to do no more than 'take note of' the accord and its aspirations to restrict global temperature increases to below 2°C. The Chinese premier sent a more junior official to attend the final session in his place.

The result of Copenhagen devastated (and exhausted) Rudd. 'Kevin went into meltdown,' his treasurer, Wayne Swan, wrote. 'It was hard for anyone in the government to properly communicate with him for a period.'[110] There were many reasons for the conference's failure, but Rudd blamed the Chinese particularly.

In Australia, the politics of climate change were shifting again and the abandoned hopes of Copenhagen played into them. The Global Financial Crisis dramatically altered the government's fiscal situation and the retail politics shifted as Abbott recast the debate from the science of climate change to a 'giant new tax' on everything.[111] And slowly, between 2008 and 2010, the eleven-year-long drought in Australia broke. With his bills blocked in the Senate, Rudd decided against holding a double dissolution election over the issue. In late April 2010, facing new political pressures, he announced a delay in the introduction of an emissions trading system for three years. This reversal on an issue about which he had spoken so passionately was part of the reason for a rapid decline in his public support, and his replacement by Gillard. She proposed in February 2011 a phased carbon pricing policy beginning with a fixed price on carbon for 500 of Australia's biggest emitters, but her concession to a television interviewer that a fixed price was the same as a tax was politically devastating. Abbott pounced and support for the ALP hit new lows.

During Abbott's two-year term as prime minister, his government's scepticism about climate change was clear. No Australian government minister represented Australia at UNFCCC negotiations in Warsaw in November 2013 and Abbott declined to attend a climate change summit for world leaders organised by the UN secretary-general in September 2014.

But gradually, internationally and domestically, the science of climate change and the politics began to realign. The work which had been undertaken for Copenhagen was dusted off. By November 2011, when UNFCCC members next met, China had shifted its position and agreed with India, Europe and the United States to negotiate a replacement for Kyoto by 2015.

A 2014 report summarising the conclusions of more than 800 scientists working with the Intergovernmental Panel on Climate Change underlined the scientific consensus that 'the atmosphere and oceans have warmed, the amount of snow and ice has diminished, sea level has risen and the concentration of carbon dioxide has increased to a level unprecedented in at least the last 800,000 years'.[112] In 2015 global surface temperatures on the land and in the oceans were the highest on record. Extreme weather events were becoming more common in Australia's region: Vanuatu and Fiji were hit by unusually damaging tropical cyclones in 2015 and 2016. In the Arctic and Antarctica, ice sheets were melting and contributing to sea-level rises.

The Australian government was looking increasingly out of touch with international trends. The principal international players, the European

Union, the United States and China, were all shifting their policies. Australian representatives downplayed the need for climate change to be discussed at the G20 Summit in Brisbane in November 2014, but other members effectively forced it onto the agenda.[113] Just before the meeting the United States and China announced that they would work together to ensure an ambitious agreement when the UNFCCC parties met again in Paris in December 2015.

Australian public views were turning, too. The number of respondents to the annual Lowy poll who agreed that Australia should act on climate change now 'even if this involves significant costs' began climbing again in 2013. By 2016 it had risen to 53 per cent, up from 36 per cent four years earlier.[114]

By the time of the Paris meeting, Turnbull was back in charge. He and Bishop attended the conference and Bishop chaired the Umbrella Group of non-EU developed countries. The 'abiding ambivalence'[115] of the Abbott government towards international climate change negotiations seemed to be over. An agreement was reached on annual carbon emissions targets which would keep global warming 'well below' 2°C. By then, however, the target was looking increasingly out of reach.

The United Nations and the multilateral order

On 28 March 2008, to the scepticism of most of his public service advisers, Rudd announced that Australia would seek election as one of the non-permanent members of the United Nations Security Council for the 2013/14 term. This would be the first occasion on which Australia had held a seat since 1985/86. Finland and Luxembourg, two other members of the Western European and Others Group (WEOG), to which Australia belonged, were already in the race. The Opposition declared the bid a waste of money and threatened to withdraw if it won the 2010 election. But both the Rudd and Gillard governments committed substantial human and financial resources (an estimated $25 million) to the campaign. Special envoys were dispatched to various parts of the world to support the candidacy. Aid and other forms of engagement with Africa and the Caribbean were stepped up.

The result, in October 2012, was a strong victory for Australia, which attracted 140 of the 193 votes. It reflected the diplomatic effort, including by Rudd and Gillard, which had gone into the campaign, and Australia's commitment to the UN and the multilateral system generally.

The period of Australia's term, which began on 1 January 2013, was marked by the deteriorating situation in Syria, the rise of ISIS, the transfer of security responsibility in Afghanistan and the crisis in Ukraine. Australia made well-regarded diplomatic contributions in all these areas, helping to secure the passage of humanitarian relief in Syria, counterterrorism measures against ISIS and new measures on the illicit transfer of small arms and light weapons, and drawing attention to human rights abuses in North Korea.

Despite scepticism about multilateral institutions in some areas of the Coalition and its initial opposition to the bid, the Abbott government played an active part in the Council's diplomacy when it took over halfway through the term. In particular, Julie Bishop made effective use of the Council after the shooting down of Flight MH17, co-sponsoring with the Netherlands a resolution, eventually passed unanimously, condemning the attack, requiring unfettered access to the crash site and calling for an investigation.

Julie Bishop

Bishop became Australia's first female foreign minister with the election of the Abbott government in September 2013. A lawyer by training, she was elected to the West Australian seat of Curtin in 1998. She served as Minister for Education in the Howard government and after the Coalition's defeat in 2007 became Deputy Leader of the Liberal Party, a position she held under four leaders.

By the time she became minister, she had already spent four years in the shadow portfolio and had used the time effectively, paying particular attention to challenging low-profile issues like those in the Pacific. As minister she was hardworking, efficient and popular with the department's staff, who felt they had experienced more than their share of difficult ministers. She was an effective diplomat: warm and sociable as she made her way around the endless reception rooms of the international circuit, but tough when this was needed. She showed this most effectively when she pressed Australian interests in Kiev and in the UN Security Council during the MH17 crisis.

She was not, however, a conceptual thinker. She did not gravitate to grand initiatives, and the achievements she listed in foreign policy debates during the 2016 election campaign[116] – 'economic diplomacy' (which meant requiring diplomatic posts to pay more attention to trade and investment), the addition of eight new posts to the diplomatic network, the New Colombo

Plan offering Australian students opportunities to study in Asia, and a DFAT InnovationXchange 'to catalyse and support innovation across the Australian aid program' – were practical and operational.

Bishop's relationship with Abbott and his office, polite but not intimate, grew strained over time, but it was not easy to identify the points of foreign policy on which they disagreed.

The experience of Security Council membership tempered the Coalition's views of the United Nations. Bishop declared that Australia's term on the Council had been 'one of the finest manifestations of Australian values on the global stage and the prosecution of those values for the betterment of all'.[117] She announced that Australia would stand again for election to the Council for the 2029/30 term and that it would seek election to the UN Human Rights Council.[118]

When Turnbull addressed a reception in honour of the seventieth anniversary of the United Nations in Sydney in September 2015, it was hard to see partisan division about the issue. 'Australia plays a very committed role in the United Nations system,' he said. 'We were there at the foundation and we have been an enthusiastic partner, member of the United Nations ever since.'[119] It was the UN's role in establishing and sustaining the rules-based order that mattered to Turnbull. When he spoke of the 'challenge that nations working collectively can say to the great and powerful, there are rules, the weak must be protected, the rule of law must be obeyed, not just domestically but internationally',[120] he sounded very like Rudd talking of Australia's interests in 'the building of a rules-based order which protects the interests of small and middle powers as much as it does the great powers'.[121]

Africa

The search for votes for the UN Security Council campaign was one of the reasons Africa's importance in Australian foreign policy increased during the period to the highest level since the struggle over apartheid and Zimbabwe. But more durable reasons were Africa's growing importance to the global mining industry and the prospects for Australian investment and services, and the emergence of new security threats from Salafi jihadist terrorist groups in Nigeria and East Africa.

A new Australian embassy was established in Addis Ababa. From 2011 Australian forces were deployed in headquarters roles in the United Nations Mission in South Sudan (UMNISS). The coincidence of the long service by two Perth-based ministers in Smith and Bishop encouraged this westward focus of policy.

Carr also successfully drew on the residual instrumental value of the oldest of Australia's multilateral institutional associations, the Commonwealth, as he pursued African and Caribbean votes for the UN campaign. Frequently attacked for time- and money-wasting irrelevance and a fundamental lack of purpose, the Commonwealth had long proved impervious to its critics. Yet again, as Gillard hosted a Commonwealth Heads of Government Meeting in Perth in October 2011, an Australian prime minister set out on the quixotic task of trying to modernise the organisation and make it more relevant. Finding himself in the middle of all this, Carr may have been the Australian leader with the highest hopes for the body since Malcolm Fraser. 'Hey, I think we can elevate this drowsy old outfit into a community of democracies based on the rule of law, separation of power and respect for human rights,' he mused dreamily in his diary after chairing a meeting of Commonwealth foreign ministers in London.[122]

Europe

By 2016 the 'European project', the noble strategic enterprise to build peace in Europe after World War II by embedding its nations in an integrated market, and later a political union, was coming under intense pressure. As the Global Financial Crisis unrolled, first Greece in 2009 then other Eurozone economies needed substantial bailouts to enable them to repay rapidly expanding sovereign debt. The domestic austerity measures demanded in response by Germany and the IMF fuelled deep popular resistance to the dictates of Brussels and Frankfurt. Then, in 2015, more than one million asylum seekers and economic migrants crossed into Europe, mostly by sea from North Africa and the Middle East. This generated new anger about EU rules on the free movement of people. Far-right nationalism grew across the continent. Hostility to immigration was a large element in the shock decision by British voters in June 2016 to leave the Union.

In 2007, when Rudd came to office, he placed an unusual degree of foreign policy emphasis on the importance of the EU. He visited Brussels on his first major overseas trip and called for 'a new positive partnership with Europe'.[128] Taken together, EU members represented Australia's second-largest trading partner and its largest investment source. Growing consciousness of Asia's economic weight rekindled European interest in Australia.

The partnership Rudd called for came in several different ways in the following years. The establishment of the G20 provided a new global economic forum in which Australia leaders could engage Europe, as did the Asia-Europe Meeting, which Australia joined in 2010. And out of the joint operations with the Netherlands in Afghanistan, and later the anti-ISIS campaign in Iraq, came closer military cooperation with NATO and some of its individual partners.

The thrust of Australian foreign policy towards Europe under all Australian governments of the period was privately summarised by Australian diplomats as 'The EU Plus 3': a solid institutional relationship with Brussels buttressed by deeper bilateral relations with the Union's three largest states, the United Kingdom, France and Germany.

In most areas of foreign and national security policy, from the sharing of intelligence and diplomatic reporting to joint work on international development, Australia's relationship with the United Kingdom continued to be more intimate and easy than with almost any of Australia's other international partners. Two of Australia's prime ministers during the period, Gillard and Abbott, were born in Britain. The annual Australia–United Kingdom Ministerial Consultations (AUKMIN) meeting between foreign and defence ministers and their key officials became a regular fixture on the diplomatic calendar.

But the most important foreign policy changes with Europe came in the relationship with France. The security and military relationship deepened, and was registered formally in a Joint Statement of Strategic Partnership signed in January 2012. François Hollande paid the first official visit to Australia by a French president in November 2014 after the G20 Summit. In Iraq, RAAF tankers provided air-to-air refuelling to French aircraft in the anti-ISIL coalition.[124] Then, in May 2016, the Turnbull government announced that the French company DCNS would be the preferred design partner for the $50 billion Australian submarine project. Turnbull was expansive: 'This partnership will frame a 50-year alliance of collaboration which will transform our strategic relationship', he told a press conference with the French prime minister in Canberra.[125] In the South Pacific, long and important area of engagement and disagreement between Australia and France, political and military cooperation continued.

At the institutional level, Rudd had signed a European Union–Australia Partnership Framework agreement in 2008, which captured the various forms of cooperation between Europe and Australia. Under Gillard, both sides agreed to raise this to treaty level. An official framework of this sort was an essential precursor to the negotiation of a free trade agreement, an objective that Abbott announced at the G20 leaders' summit in Brisbane, although that would be made more difficult by the United Kingdom's decision to withdraw from the EU.

Trade

Despite the optimistic hopes of Simon Crean, Rudd's first trade minister, that Australia could help revitalise the multilateral trade negotiations being conducted by the WTO, the Doha Round continued to drown in its own complexity. Crean's successor, Emerson, pushed the idea of 'new pathways' that would break the global negotiations into smaller portions and secure outcomes where they could be found. WTO ministers accepted this approach, which delivered some early reforms in agriculture and customs facilitation, but it was a sign that the whole idea of grand global trade negotiations requiring agreement from all parties – the single undertaking deal – was no longer workable. In 2015, ministers finally conceded that there was no consensus to continue with the original mandate of the Doha Round. The multilateral trading system, at least in the way it had operated since World War II, had reached the end of that particular track towards liberalisation.

In Asia and the Pacific, regional trade negotiations continued, but along a divided path. Three of the small and open APEC economies, Singapore, New Zealand and Chile (later joined by Brunei), had begun discussing a more ambitious economic agreement in 2002 that would move beyond tariffs on goods to address barriers to services and investment by seeking common rules and greater transparency. In 2008 the Bush administration signalled an interest in joining these negotiations. The Obama administration eventually signed up in 2009. Japan, Mexico, Canada, Peru, Vietnam and Australia also joined the negotiations on the Trans-Pacific Partnership (TPP).

Australia's major trading partner, China, was not part of this deal, however, and because the agreement deliberately included provisions on state-owned enterprises, transparency and data flows, it would find it difficult to join. The TPP became the economic leg of the Obama administration's declared pivot back to Asia. In selling the agreement to an increasingly sceptical Congress, administration officials underlined its strategic objective in helping to contest China's growing influence. 'In terms of our rebalance in the broadest sense, passing TPP is as important to me as another aircraft carrier,' the US defence secretary Ash Carter, said.[126]

Whatever strategic impact the TPP might have on regional perceptions of continuing American engagement in Asia, the economic implications for Australia were slight. According to a World Bank report, the TPP would boost Australia's economy by just 0.7 per cent by the year 2030.[127] One reason for this limited result was that China and the large Southeast Asian economies were not part of it. The negotiations were concluded in October 2015, but within a year the agreement foundered on the political rocks of the US presidential election and an increasingly protectionist Congress.

A parallel process of negotiations for a Regional Comprehensive Economic Partnership centred on ASEAN, had begun in November 2012. This track included the ASEAN countries, China, Japan, Korea, India, Australia and New Zealand but not the United States. It took a more traditional approach to trade negotiations and was less ambitious in its 'behind the borders' reform ambitions. It would build on the ASEAN-Australia-New Zealand Free Trade Agreement, covering nearly two-thirds of Australia's trade with ASEAN countries, which had been signed in February 2009. With the collapse of the TPP in 2016, the clear and difficult challenge for Australian trade policy-makers was to find some new way of pursuing the old APEC goal of maintaining open trade links across the Pacific.

Breakthroughs in bilateral preferential trade agreements with Japan, South Korea and China finally came under the Abbott government. A good deal of the basic work had already been done but the Coalition gave them a high priority and the trade and investment minister, Andrew Robb, was a skilful and tenacious negotiator.

In the case of the Japan–Australia Economic Partnership Agreement, signed in Canberra in June 2014, progress was assisted by the coincidence of strategic views between Abbott and the Japanese prime minister, Shinzo Abe. Australian trade with Japan, still the country's second-largest export market and trading partner, was substantially liberalised, even, for the first time, in limited agricultural areas such as beef. As the first major agricultural exporter to conclude such an agreement with Japan, Australia secured potential advantages over its competitors. The Korea-Australia Free Trade Agreement entered into force in December 2014, giving Australian exporters some modest additional access to the Korean market and levelling the playing field with US and European competitors. But the one that mattered most was the China–Australia Free Trade Agreement (ChAFTA).

The rise of China

The happy period in which Australian policy-makers from all sides of politics could insist that the ANZUS alliance was not in any way directed against China, that Australia did not have to choose between its alliance and its economic interests, and that there was nothing inevitable about escalating strategic competition between China and the United States was fast drawing to a close.

Australia's challenge with China, Rudd told the Brookings Institution in 2007 before becoming prime minister, was 'to maximise our common economic interests ... while robustly asserting, both publicly and privately, our continuing points of difference and disagreement'.[128] He was 'a brutal realist' about China, he told Clinton, according to a leaked US state department report of 2009. He believed Australia should speak frankly about its differences, and engage where possible 'while also preparing to deploy force if everything goes wrong'.[129]

A series of political and economic differences during 2008 and 2009 tested the relationship. The organised arrival in Canberra of thousands of patriotic students and others to 'protect' the Olympic torch as it was run through the capital in early 2008 was a reminder of a growing Chinese nationalism. China protested when Australia gave a visa to an activist from the Uyghur community in China's west, and about Rudd's criticisms of the human rights situation.

In May 2009, with Rudd personally involved in its drafting, Australia released its first defence white paper since 2000. China was central to it. Behind its careful language – 'The pace, scope and structure of China's military modernisation have the potential to give its neighbours cause for concern if not carefully explained'[130] – lay a clear hedging strategy against a more assertive China. The government promised a large investment in submarines and sea and air power to respond to the challenge.

As national defence and economic systems became increasingly dependent on information networks, governments were paying more attention to the need to protect them. In 2009 the Rudd government released Australia's first Cyber Security Strategy and a second followed under Turnbull in 2016.[131] Suspicions of China's involvement in state-sponsored cyber intelligence collection activities grew. The Labor government banned a Chinese manufacturer from a role in supplying certain equipment to the National Broadband Network, and Beijing was accused of intrusions into Australian government systems including the Bureau of Meteorology and the Parliament House network.[132]

To prop up the Australian housing market when the financial crisis hit in 2008, the Rudd government had liberalised the rules governing foreign investment in residential property, including new apartments. As Chinese buyers moved into the market, public concern about Chinese investment in residential property and agricultural land rose. In 2010, 57 per cent of the Lowy poll respondents believed Australia was allowing too much Chinese investment.[133]

China's growing dependence on Australian resources caused anxiety in both countries. To protect themselves, Chinese companies began to seek larger stakes in their Australian suppliers. The Foreign Investment Review Board reviewed Chinese investment proposals valued at $6.8 billion in 2008/09. The amount doubled the following year.[134]

Nearly 40 per cent of China's iron ore was now supplied by BHP Billiton and Rio Tinto and price increases were worrying Beijing.[135] In February 2008, the large state-owned Chinese mining company Chinalco, fearing that Rio might take over BHP and raise prices, launched its own bid for a 9 per cent stake in Rio. It followed this in February 2009 with an even more ambitious proposal for a joint venture that would give Chinalco two seats on Rio's board. These developments and others highlighted the increasingly pressing issue of investments in Australian companies by Chinese state-owned enterprises (SOEs). The government, and Rudd particularly, was concerned that SOEs might act according to the broader interests of the Chinese government rather than in response to commercial imperatives. By April 2009 it was clear that the Chinalco proposal was unlikely to secure approval on national interest grounds, but by then the deal had fallen victim to the Global Financial Crisis.

In late 2009, strains were evident across the Australia–China relationship. 'Australia has made itself the champion leader of an anti-Chinese chorus,' declared the *China Daily* in August.[136]

Rio's chief iron-ore negotiator, Stern Hu, and three Chinese members of Rio's negotiating team, were arrested in July 2009 on charges of theft of state secrets and bribery. The Australian government expressed its concern and recalled the ambassador for consultations. Hu was eventually convicted of receiving bribes from smaller iron-ore companies in China to secure them access to the lower benchmark prices.[137]

But by mid-October, the Chinese government was ready to move the relationship forward and Australia was willing to reciprocate. Foreign minister Smith signalled this in a conciliatory speech on Australia–China relations in the presence of the Chinese ambassador at the Australian National University on 26 October. While not backing away from differing views which 'could not be denied or wished away', he expressed Australia's intention to be 'constructive, patient and forward-looking' towards China in its policies.[138] With just one week's notice, the Chinese announced that the vice-premier (and premier-in-waiting), Li Keqiang, would like to visit Australia. He brought with him a soothing message: bilateral relations should not be diverted 'from the main track of growth because of a particular incident at a particular time'. A joint communiqué was drawn up, the first the two countries had issued since Whitlam's visit to China in 1972. Australia restated its support for the One-China Policy and, explicitly, for Chinese sovereignty in Tibet and Xinjiang. In return, China offered support to Australia's role in East Asia and to Rudd's Asia-Pacific community initiative.[140] Something like the Howard policy of underlining interests and setting aside differences had been resumed.

In June 2010 Xi Jinping, seen by then as one of the most likely candidates to succeed Hu Jintao as China's president, visited Australia. Rudd devoted considerable time and effort to the visit, hosting a dinner for him at the Prime Minister's Lodge. In Darwin, on the way out of the country, a surprised Xi learnt from his ambassador that his host had lost his job and that Australia had a new prime minister.

The legacy of the difficulties of 2009 had not been forgotten when Gillard made her first visit to Beijing in April 2011. One of her objectives was to ensure that 'focusing China's attention on Australia was no longer a question of grace and favour but a standing part of the diplomatic calendar'.[141] She told the Chinese that she would come back to them with a formal proposal to put in place regular meetings between Australian and Chinese leaders.

This obscure structural question became part of a power struggle between Rudd as foreign minister and Swan as treasurer. Rudd wanted a single meeting of foreign and economic ministers in which he could participate; Swan was determined to keep them separate. Gillard sided with Swan. She wrote to Beijing with proposals and, as China's leadership transition went through its ritual form, slow negotiations followed.

By the time of her second visit to China in April 2013, the new leadership team was in place. Xi Jinping had become president and party secretary and Li Keqiang was premier. Gillard and Li announced the establishment of a 'Strategic Partnership' between Australia and China. There would be annual meetings of prime ministers supported by two cabinet-level strategic dialogues, one between the foreign ministers, and a Strategic Economic Dialogue with economic and trade ministers. Just three other countries – the United Kingdom, Germany and Russia – had the same commitment to annual premiers' meetings with China. Gillard also secured agreement to direct trading between the Chinese renminbi and the Australian dollar, a useful step forward in reducing transaction costs for business.

As Xi consolidated his power as the dominant figure in the leadership, China's defence spending and capability grew. Its navy was now the largest in Asia and it was more explicitly asserting its claims to disputed maritime territories in the East and South China Seas. In the South China Sea, a rich fishing ground and prospective source of energy, it was building up its presence on small reefs and islands within a large and contested area bounded by a vague and expansive 'nine-dash line'.

China's approach was causing divisions within ASEAN, especially between Vietnam and the Philippines, claimants to some of the disputed islands, and Cambodia, which acted as China's proxy in the group. In June 2012, for the first time in the Association's history, ASEAN leaders were unable to issue a consensus post-summit statement. Further examples would follow of China's ability to divide ASEAN.

The Gillard government released another defence white paper in 2013, by which time a clear gulf had emerged between the optimistic funding promises of its 2009 predecessor and the capacity of the government, struggling for an elusive budget surplus after the Global Financial Crisis, to meet them. Its ambitious acquisition plans for submarines and fighter aircraft were not matched by the necessary financial commitments.

The strategic analysis in the new paper was not greatly different from 2009, but the language on China was calmer. 'The Government does not approach China as an adversary,' it stated.[142] Indeed, Australia continued to pursue defence engagement opportunities with the Chinese, including by hosting, in September 2010, the first joint war games China had conducted with a Western state.

Gillard's successor, Abbott, was privately suspicious of China's ambitions. Two emotions drove Australian policy towards China, he reportedly told the German chancellor, Angela Merkel, 'fear and greed'.[143] When, in November 2013, China declared an Air Defense Identification Zone over the East China Sea, including the territorial airspace over the disputed Senkaku/Diaoyu Islands, Bishop described the decision as 'coercive'. She was dressed down by her Chinese counterpart when they met in Beijing a couple of weeks later. Australia had 'jeopardised bilateral mutual trust and affected the sound growth of bilateral relations', he told her in front of reporters.[144] Abbott's strategic objective was to build Australia's security relationship with the United States, Japan and India as a counter to China's growth, but his public language was more measured. He drew heavily on Howard's model of a relationship in which economic partnership could be pursued along a separate track from the political relationship.

By then, talks about a free trade agreement had been grinding on for eight years, through twenty-one rounds of difficult negotiations. From mid-2007 the discussions were largely stalemated as Australia sought preferential market access in agriculture and services and China looked for greater investment access and short-term working visas. But when Abbott and Xi met at the APEC summit in October 2013 they agreed that the FTA was a priority.

When he visited China in April 2014 Abbott's focus was all on 'economic diplomacy'. He was accompanied by a delegation of 600 businesspeople. 'Team Australia is here in China to help build the Asian century,' he told his audience.[145] Australia's cooperation with China in coordinating the Indian Ocean search for Flight MH370, which disappeared in March, and on which many Chinese nationals had been travelling, was received gratefully.

Robb and his trade negotiators became regular visitors to China during 2014 and when Xi returned to Australia in November he was able to sign the ChAFTA. The agreement was more comprehensive and ambitious than any China had previously negotiated with a developed country. China provided unprecedented access to Australian agricultural exports and, particularly, services. Australia shifted its position on investment and the provision of specialist workers for large projects. The agreement was to be regularly reviewed and updated.

Robb thought the reason the Chinese had been willing to agree to this ambitious outcome was to send a signal that that 'they're ready and able to engage in a 21st-century, open way with the developed world. And it was ... easier to do it with the smaller economy.'[146]

In Canberra, Xi made a reassuring speech to a joint sitting of parliament: 'We are not burdened by historical problems between us, nor do we have any conflict of fundamental interests ... We have every reason to go beyond a commercial partnership to become strategic partners who have a shared vision and pursue common goals.'[147]

Both countries were entering important economic transitions. China could no longer rely on infrastructure investment and export-oriented manufacturing for its growth. It needed a new model built on domestic demand and services. For Australia, the resources boom was over and it needed to develop new markets in services, agriculture and high-end manufacturing.

By 2016 China was Australia's largest source of imported goods, the largest destination for its goods exports and the biggest purchaser of Australian services. More than one million Chinese tourists visited Australia in 2015 and more than 170,000 Chinese students were studying at its educational institutions, one-quarter of all international enrolments. China was also the fifth-largest source of foreign direct investment into Australia. Australia, in turn, was the second-largest destination for Chinese global outbound direct investment after the United States between 2005 and 2014.[148]

A debate of central relevance to Australian foreign policy was now developing about what China's role should be in the changing global order. It was clear after the Global Financial Crisis that China would be critical to any collective economic effort to avoid a depression. China's growth rate may have slowed, but at 6.9 per cent, it was still adding an economy the size of Turkey's to the global market each year. By 2016 its economy was close to US$12 trillion in size. It was the top-ranked trading partner of more than one hundred countries.

Did being a 'responsible international stakeholder', as Robert Zoellick, the US president of the World Bank, had asked of China, mean that it should accept the existing institutions and rules or did those need to be adjusted? Should new institutions and rules be created? Was the 'global order' the same thing as the status quo? These questions were increasingly urgent. The US Congress's refusal to agree to changes in the governance of the World Bank and the IMF made those institutions look increasingly anachronistic.

In speeches in September and October 2013, Xi had proposed the development of a 'New Silk Road Economic Belt' from China through Central Asia to Europe and a '21st-century Maritime Silk Road' through Southeast Asia. These were to be new transport corridors that, by helping to fill a gap in regional infrastructure needs estimated at US$8 trillion, would address an important constraint on intra-regional economic growth.[149] Some of the funding would come from the Asian Infrastructure Investment Bank (AIIB), which China would establish, a new multilateral institution in a system China was itself shaping. 'One Belt, One Road', as the Chinese branded it, had clear economic objectives, but it offered strategic and soft power benefits as well.

Any large increase in regional infrastructure spending of this sort seemed likely to offer great opportunities for Australian resources and services exports. When China solicited Australian support for its new bank, promising a senior position in the new institution, the treasurer, Joe Hockey, indicated interest. But divisions soon emerged within the government. Washington and Tokyo saw the bank as a further step in Chinese ambitions to dominate the region economically and strategically. They feared it would compete with the established forums of the World Bank and the Asian Development Bank, driving down lending standards and loosening human rights and environmental requirements. Obama and Abe asked Abbott not to join.[150] At the same time, other close partners like New Zealand, Indonesia and Singapore, which had agreed to become members, were urging Australian participation.

Canberra policy-makers were confronted with the choice they had so long wanted to avoid between their country's economic and strategic interests; between its principal trading partner and its long-time ally. The National Security Committee of Cabinet split between the foreign minister and the prime minister on the one hand and the treasurer and the trade minister on the other. Abbott told the Chinese that Australia would not join the board unless there were improvements, especially around board responsibilities. In August 2014 Australia put a series of proposals for governance and transparency improvements to China, some of which were adopted.[151] By December 2014 Robb was saying publicly that it was 'the wish of everyone in the Cabinet, from the prime minister down'[152] that Australia would join the bank. Yet no action had been taken.

In March 2015 the United Kingdom, without warning Australia and contrary to Washington's wishes, announced that it would become a foundation member of the AIIB. Germany, France and others quickly followed. Australia applied for membership too, but by that time it appeared to be playing catch-up. On 24 June 2015 Hockey announced that Australia would join the bank, contributing around $930 million as paid-in capital to the AIIB over five years and becoming the sixth-largest stakeholder.[153] The debate inside the government, Robb said, was whether to enter conditionally, or to await the conditions being met first: 'No one will ever know which was right.'[154]

It was just one of the challenges facing all Australian governments of the period as they tried to find ways of integrating and balancing the complex economic, strategic and political interests with China that were now in play.

Malcolm Turnbull

As with Rudd, the centralising tendencies of Tony Abbott's office helped generate the internal dissent within his own party that eventually contributed to his replacement. In September 2015, just two years after he took office, and as a series of opinion polls pointed to a likely loss in the next election, the Liberal Party turned back to Malcolm Turnbull. Turnbull was a former journalist, lawyer and businessman who had come relatively late to politics. He was elected to the eastern Sydney seat of Wentworth in 2004, and promoted to cabinet as Minister for the Environment in 2007. Following the Coalition's election loss, he served as shadow treasurer, then leader, until his replacement by Abbott in 2009.

Unlike Abbott, Turnbull was a social liberal. He supported a multicultural Australia and marriage equality. His belief in anthropogenic climate change, and his support for Australian action on it, was one of the issues on which he had lost his leadership. In contrast to the royalist Abbott, he had led the case for an Australian republic during the 1999 referendum campaign.

The new prime minister had travelled widely and worked internationally. He knew the world well. The tonal differences with Abbott were clear immediately, especially on climate change and national security. The language of optimism returned – 'These … extraordinary times, these exciting times.'[155]

Turnbull saw the country's future intimately engaged with Asia. His innovation agenda picked up some of the themes from Gillard's Asian Century white paper, arguing that domestic transformation was central to Australia's economic and strategic future. 'It is here in our Asian region,' he told the Lowy Institute, 'that the opportunities are most abundant … But if we are to make the most of these exciting new opportunities in Asia, we first need to ensure we are resilient and agile at home.'[156] But by the time of the 2016 election, the framework of his foreign policy was still unfinished.

The defence white paper he released in 2016 with Marise Payne, Australia's first female defence minister, declared that Australia would, 'seek to deepen and broaden our important defence relationship with China while recognising that our strategic interests may differ in relation to some regional and global security issues.'[157] The force capabilities and budget projections it included clearly anticipated the latter.

Australian public views about China were becoming increasingly complex. In the 2016 Lowy Institute poll, respondents were divided equally on whether the relationship with China or the United States was more important to Australia.[158] Thirty per cent of them saw China as Australia's 'best friend in Asia', compared with 25 per cent for Japan, a six-point increase from 2014. Most respondents (52 per cent) disagreed that 'Australia should join with other countries to limit China's influence', although 66 per cent thought that 'Australia should do more to resist China's military aggression in our region, even if this affects our economic relationship'.[159]

Separate polling from the United States Studies Centre in Sydney showed that almost 69 per cent of Australians thought that China had replaced, or would replace, the United States as the world's leading superpower. This was much higher than in the other Asian countries polled at the same time.[160] Forty per cent of Australian respondents thought the US alliance hindered Australia's relationships in Asia, twice the number who thought it helped.[161]

As the country went into the 2016 election, the bipartisan national consensus on foreign policy was holding firm. It was impossible to detect serious differences between the two major parties on the centrality of the alliance, the importance of the rules-based order, policies towards Australia's major partners in Asia, or the core elements of national security policy. The election campaign came and went without any sign that foreign policy was much on the minds of voters or their representatives.

But at the political margins, increasingly insistent, the sounds could be heard of more fundamental disagreements about the liberal international order and the globalised world it had delivered.

10

WHAT AUSTRALIAN FOREIGN POLICY?

T he story this book tells began in 1942, as Australia faced a future more uncertain than at any time since European settlement. The parliamentarians listening with half an ear to the debate about the ratification of the Statute of Westminster would be astonished by the world their successors in the second decade of the twenty-first century are dealing with.

The British Empire, so central to Australia's sense of identity and security, has faded away, its lingering echoes in the Commonwealth weaker with each passing year. The alliance with the United States which replaced it has expanded greatly in ambition: from a reassurance about a resurgent Japan to an integrated global partnership that has most recently taken Australian forces not to the Pacific core of the ANZUS Treaty but back to the Middle East. Japan itself has become a 'close friend and bedrock economic partner'.[1]

The European colonies which then stretched across Australia's north and east from India to the South Pacific are now independent states. For half a century, the sometimes violent process and consequences of decolonisation in Indonesia, Malaysia, Vietnam, Cambodia and East Timor consumed much of Australia's foreign policy – and often military – attention. Elsewhere in the world that same shift, coupled with the challenges of modernisation, generated unrest across the Middle East and Africa. Support for the struggle against racist postcolonial regimes in southern Africa helped the Whitlam,

Fraser and Hawke governments recast Australia's view of itself and reshape its reputation in the world.

China – and who would have expected this in 1942? – has become Australia's largest trading partner and by some measurements the largest economy in the world, challenging US dominance in Asia.

To the surprise of all the combatants, a dangerous Cold War that threatened nuclear annihilation ended quickly and peacefully, to be replaced by a more multipolar order. But globalisation has changed the way states and economies work. Governments have found themselves challenged by terrorist groups, computer hackers and organised criminals, empowered by the technologies of the information revolution, operating across national borders.

It would be just as hard for the legislators of 1942 to recognise the country itself. Australia's recorded population in the 1940s was only seven million, of whom the overwhelming majority were European – 99.7 per cent, according to the 1947 census, which did not register Indigenous Australians at all. By 2016, in a nation of 24 million, the largest groups of new immigrants came from China and India. Nearly one in ten Australians claimed some Asian ancestry.[2]

The economy has been transformed. Agriculture's share of GDP has declined steadily; manufacturing peaked in the early 1960s, then fell; the share of mining fluctuated; and services have become the largest part of the economy and the biggest employer. The direction of trade, overwhelmingly to Britain in 1942, now points by an even greater margin to Asia. Exports of services such as tourism and education have boomed. By the time of the 2016 federal election Australia's economy had been growing continuously for twenty-five years, an achievement unmatched by any other OECD economy. In terms of nominal GDP, it was the twelfth-largest economy in the world.

The way Australia understands its interests and values has changed too. An interest in an open, global and multilateral trading system has edged out the belief that the country was best served by preserving imperial trade preferences. A deep bipartisan effort to restrain Japan's capacity to act independently in the world has been replaced by an interest in encouraging it to do so. Values have also shifted. Opposition to racial discrimination overcame the conviction that Australia had a sovereign right to a race-based immigration policy. And new values, like the preservation of the global environment through sustainable development, have emerged to shape policies. Issues of gender have become more central. 'There is an inescapable truth,' the Coalition foreign minister Julie Bishop told the UN General Assembly in September 2015: 'we cannot transform our world unless the place of women within it is transformed.'[3] Australia has had its first female prime minister, foreign minister and defence minister.

How successful has Australian foreign policy been over those seventy-five years? The primary function of foreign policy is to expand the international space within which the nation-state can operate; to increase its options and maximise its choices. One way of measuring success is to ask how well, given the circumstances of the time and the resources available, the interests of the country (defined in a democracy by the elected government and judged by the voters) have been advanced, and the values and norms in which it believes promoted.

By these criteria, Australia's policy-makers have surely succeeded. In the second decade of the twenty-first century Australia is peaceful, prosperous, well-regarded. Notwithstanding occasional clumsiness and insensitivity, it has developed close and wide-ranging relations with its Asian and Pacific neighbours.

From its early participation at Bretton Woods and San Francisco, Australia has been an active, sometimes creative, partner in the building of global and regional organisations. APEC, the East Asia Summit, the World Trade Organization and the G20 all owe something to Australian energy and ideas. Australia has contributed to international rule-setting in trade, disarmament and arms control, the law of the sea and the environment. Thanks in part to its own carpentry, it has successfully secured a seat at the regional and global tables.

What Gareth Evans defined as Australia's instincts for good international citizenship, and even Tony Abbott, one of the more sceptical multilateralists among Australian policy-makers, called being a 'good global citizen',[4] has motivated it to make significant contributions to peacekeeping and development.

There were certainly blunders – the slowness to recognise the changing world of the 1950s and '60s, the miscalculation of Suez, the incoherent response to the Indonesian takeover of East Timor, and an overabundance of enthusiasm to support its major ally as it made self-defeating choices, among others. Some prime ministers and ministers drove policy in new directions; some were persuasive and skilful advocates. Others hardly made a mark. But at their best – Spender on ANZUS and the Colombo Plan, Hawke and Keating on APEC and its leaders' meetings, Hayden and Evans on Cambodia,

Howard and Downer on East Timor and Solomon Islands, Rudd on the G20 – Australian policy-makers have shown that they possess the skill to recognise the moment when it is possible to drive new paths through the international landscape and have the creative tools to forge them. On both sides of politics, difficult and complex relationships like those with Indonesia and China have been managed well through storms of occasionally self-inflicted problems. A capable public service, skilful diplomats and efficient decision-making processes have contributed to the success.

But, some people ask, when you think about it, how much of an accomplishment is this? Australia begins, after all, with the strategic security of a continent, a rich endowment of natural and human resources that are complementary to the growth of Asian economies, and it is allied with the world's most powerful state. The degree of difficulty is not large. The question to be asked is not what has been done, but what might have been.

For some critics on the right, too little focus has been paid to the national interest and there has been too much woolly do-goodism. For some on the left, Australia has failed – in areas such as the treatment of refugees and provision of aid – to live up to its own highest values. Others, on both sides of politics, believe that dependence on the United States alliance has inhibited Australia from pursuing its best strategic interests.[5]

A deeper, more structural, criticism can be made of Australia's occasional lack of ambition and reluctance to wield the power available to it; its preference for hunkering down in the company of allies, its diplomatic caution. 'Australia has . . . shied away from the exercise of power,' argued the secretary of DFAT, Peter Varghese, in 2015. 'We have tended to see power as belonging to others. And when we have engaged with the projection of power we have traditionally been more comfortable in the slipstream than in the lead.'[6]

But in a world whose largest components are propelling themselves erratically in uncertain directions, the slipstream will be a dangerous place for Australia to linger. The country's diplomatic capabilities are about to be tested again.

Throughout its modern history Australia has known only a globalising world. The ambitions of European imperialism drove its British settlement. Its sovereign foreign policy emerged against the background of the Allied war aims, globalising in their mission, set out in the Atlantic Charter of 1941. Those aims shaped the great post-war institutions of Bretton Woods and the United Nations. Throughout the period covered by this history, the rules the international community has worked towards in trade, investment, arms control, maritime law and environmental protection, and the visions of the future which underpinned them, were global in scope. Even the great strategic struggle of the Cold War was global in its purposes and dimensions.

Now a push-back against globalisation is gathering strength across the world, from Indiana to Indonesia. Identities are becoming more atomised and the evidence of slowing globalisation is mounting in trade and investment data, migration trends and rates of treaty-making.[7] The counter-globalising mood fuels a new protectionism that could have calamitous economic consequences, and a new nationalism that might spark fresh military conflict.

Each of the three strands that has been woven through the foreign policies of every Australian government after World War II – alliance with a powerful friend, engagement with the Asian region, and support for a global order based on recognised and negotiated rules – now needs to be reconceived. China is at the centre of this. Every Australian strategic planning document of the twenty-first century has come to the same conclusion: 'the roles of the United States and China and the relationship between them' are the most important factors shaping Australia's future.[8]

Australia's principal trading partner and its main ally are no longer part of the same strategic system. As Paul Keating discovered in the 1990s, not even that alignment was sufficient to prevent tensions emerging between Australia's economic interests in Japan and the objectives of the United States. The debate about whether to join the Asian Infrastructure Investment Bank and Australia's response to China's assertion of its interests in the South China Sea point to the difficulties that might now arise.

The United States remains, as it has been since 1942, the world's most powerful state, and the only one with global reach. Its flexible economy, favourable demographics and deep democracy give it many advantages, but its relative weight in the world is declining. As the strategic and financial costs of the Iraq intervention become clearer, and as some of the consequences of globalisation bear down, American citizens are asking new questions about the economic and social price they are willing to pay for their pre-eminence. Their bracing first answer came with the election as president of a political outsider, Donald Trump, in November 2016. Every recent Australian government has declared that the foundation on which the ANZUS alliance rests is one of shared interests and common values. The interests, as we have seen, have diverged at times, but not the support for the values of a rules-based international order, an open international trading system, democracy and the rule of law, however imperfectly implemented these may have been. The inchoate and contradictory statements made by Trump as a candidate during the US election campaign promised to test the shared understanding of those values.

As during World War II and the Cold War, great power competition is playing itself out in Southeast Asia and its maritime surrounds. For the first time since Deng Xiaoping's reforms began to transform China's economy and the Cold War ended, the idea of 'Asia' in Australian foreign policy is beginning to fragment. The Asia with which Hawke wanted to enmesh and Keating to engage is becoming a more complex region. Australian foreign policy faces not just a binary choice between Washington and Beijing, but a series of increasingly complex choices involving Japan, India and the ASEAN countries.

Finally, the rules-based order Australia has known from the beginning of its modern history, one in which the rules have mostly been set with its friends and allies, is also changing. The purpose of that order has always been to constrain the untrammelled exercise of power by great states, but it also, inevitably, reflects their power, just as American dominance shaped the structure and location of the new global institutions at the end of the 1940s.

The emerging countries now have a greater interest in moulding the system in which they are stakeholders. Norms and standards in new areas like cyberspace, genetic engineering and lethal autonomous weapons can only be set with their participation. Multilateralism is in flux: it is unclear which organisations will continue, which will emerge, and which will atrophy. And it is not just the institutions of global economic governance that China and the other developing economies want to influence. Other foundational elements of the rules-based order, such as the UN Convention on the Law of the Sea, are being tested.

This shift in the prevailing order means that if Australia is to secure its future, it will have to become even more directly and deeply engaged in the international diplomacy necessary to shore up the system and establish new rules.

That will test its resources. In a series of reports and surveys, the Lowy Institute has identified the extent of Australia's diplomatic deficit, including the underinvestment in the instruments of foreign policy – the network of overseas posts and people necessary to shape and persuade – compared with defence, intelligence and other dimensions of national security.[9] In 2016

Australia ranked just twenty-seventh among G20 and OECD countries in the number of its diplomatic missions.[10]

I have argued in this book that the motivating force of Australia's international engagement has been fear of abandonment. For some, that will seem too timid and unheroic a motivation for a great country's foreign policy. But it has also been the driver of one of the most consistent and commendable aspects of Australia's worldview – its rejection of isolationism; its conviction that Australia needs to be active in the world in order to shape it, and that gathering combinations of allies, friends and ad hoc partners is the best way of doing this. That will be a tradition worth defending in the years ahead.

Yet in the second decade of the twenty-first century it is no longer an adequate story for Australians to tell themselves about their place in the world. No new narrative is evident, however. Speaking of the limited role of foreign policy during the 2016 election campaign, the former Labor leader Kim Beazley thought this was 'not a product of irrelevance but mutual neutralisation'.[11]

With few exceptions (mostly when citizens felt their security threatened by war or terrorists or uncontrolled arrivals by boat), Australian foreign policy has been the preserve and preoccupation of a small elite of politicians, officials, commentators and academics. That seems unlikely to last. As in other parts of the world, Australian voters show signs of questioning the benefits of globalisation in their lives. Opinion polling is beginning to register public attitudes to Australia's role in Asia and the relationships with the United States and China that differ from those of the foreign policy establishment.[12] New Australian citizens from the Middle East, China and India are expressing a fresh set of interests in Australia's role in the world and bringing to the debate a different, less Anglo-centric, understanding of the past.

Like all history, this book has been prologue, not prediction. The question is: what comes next? Everything Australia wants to accomplish as a nation depends on its capacity to understand the world outside its borders and respond effectively to it.

ACKNOWLEDGEMENTS

In writing this book I have drawn on primary sources and on the work of fine Australian historians acknowledged in the text who have shaped my own views over many decades, but this is the work of a practitioner, not a scholar. From positions inside and outside the Australian public service, I was familiar with much of the latter part of this story and close to some of it. Nevertheless, my early training was in history, and in some ways my thinking for this book began with an undergraduate honours essay on Australian foreign policy in the 1920s. I also spent a happy part of my career as an analyst in the Office of National Assessments and I have tried to bring those values of accuracy, dispassion and balance to my conclusions. Whether I have succeeded is for others to judge.

DFAT's continuing investment in its historical section and in the publication of documents on Australian foreign policy has been a great national asset. So, too, has been the work for so many years of the Australian Institute for International Affairs, especially its Australia in World Affairs series. James Cotton, who edited a number of those volumes, also made invaluable comments on this book.

My views of the world have been shaped by my professional experiences in the Australian Public Service. But I thank in particular my colleagues from the Department of External Affairs Class of 1969, with whom I have enjoyed a nearly fifty-year-long floating international seminar on the objectives of Australian foreign policy. Bill Farmer, Sandy Hollway, Graeme Lawless, Colin Heseltine and Dennis Richardson have made particular contributions to this book. Ric Smith has my special thanks, however. He has been there from the beginning of this project and has been a penetrating critic and editor of each of the chapters as I produced them.

I thank, too, other friends from the Australian Public Service, among them John Bowan, Justine Braithwaite, Scott Dewar, David Irvine, David Lee, Richard Maude, Margot McCarthy, Bruce Miller, Greg Moriaty, Gary Quinlan, Richard Rowe, Andrew Shearer, Heather Smith, Michael Thawley, Margaret Twomey, Peter Varghese, Ian Watt and Justin Whyatt for their help.

The Australian National University was created around the time this story begins and its scholars were important to the outcome. I am grateful to its Chancellor, Gareth Evans, who features in the story, for his help in this in and his earlier life, and to my ANU colleagues Shiro Armstrong, Howard Bamsey, Peter Drysdale, Rory Medcalf, Bob McMullan, Michael L'Estrange, Richard Rigby and Michael Wesley.

Derek Abbott was also a reader from the beginning. He brought an invaluable outside perspective, sympathetic but critical, to the story, rescuing me from errors of fact and interpretation. Thanks as well to Dan Flitton, who at an earlier stage of both our careers in the Lowy Institute, as well as more recently, helped me with what would become a couple of these chapters. Belinda Lawton's professional skills with citations helped me when I needed them most.

I want to acknowledge the role of two great Australians, Paul Keating and Frank Lowy, with whom I have been privileged to work. Paul Keating provided me with a masterclass in politics and economics and helped me understand Australian foreign policy in the round. The contribution Frank Lowy and his family continue to make through the Lowy Institute for International Policy to deepening the debate in this country about Australia and the world is reflected in these pages. I'm grateful for the faith he had in me.

It was Hugh White who forced my hand when I told him I was thinking about writing a history of Australian foreign policy by immediately texting Chris Feik at Black Inc. I'm grateful to him for that, as well as to Chris who has been a wonderfully kind and patient publisher and to my great editor, Kirstie Innes-Will. The book is much better because of her help.

My thanks to my children, Toby, Dominic, Joe and Chris, for their love and support. But the final, and greatest, thanks go to my wife, Catherine, who has been there throughout this long journey. She was the first reader of this book and for that, but so much more, she has, always, my deep love and gratitude.

ENDNOTES

Note:

CPD, HR   *indicates*   Commonwealth Parliamentary Debates, House of
Representatives, Hansard, Canberra: AGPS

CPD, Senate *indicates* Commonwealth Parliamentary Debates, Senate, Hansard,
Canberra: AGPS

1   FEAR OF ABANDONMENT

1   Watkin Tench, *A Complete Account of the Settlement at Port Jackson*, Sydney:
University of Sydney Library, 1998.

2   David Goldsworthy, *Losing the Blanket: Australia and the End of Britain's Empire*,
Melbourne: Melbourne University Press, 2002, p. 21.

3   Shannon C. Smith, 'Towards Diplomatic Recognition' in David Goldsworthy
(ed.), *Facing North: A Century of Australian Engagement with Asia*, Vol. 1, Carlton
South, Vic.: Melbourne University Press, 2002, p. 72.

4   ibid.

5   Peter Edwards, *Prime Ministers and Diplomats*, Melbourne: Oxford University
Press, 1983, p. 90.

6   Percy Claude Spender, *Exercises in Diplomacy: The Anzus Treaty and the Colombo
Plan*, Sydney: Sydney University Press, 1969, p. 26.

7   John D. Legge, *Australian Outlook: A History of the Australian Institute of
International Affairs*, St Leonards: Allen & Unwin, 1999, p. 62.

8   Smith, 'Towards Diplomatic Recognition', p. 93.

9   ibid., p. 94.

10 CPD, HR, 1 October 1942, p. 1327.

11 ibid., p. 1433.

12 ibid., p. 1399.

13 Hedley Bull, *The Anarchical Society: A Study of Order in World Politics*, third edn,
Basingstoke: Palgrave, 2002 (originally published 1977).

14 CPD, HR, 20 April 1955, p. 44.

2   ASIA AND DECOLONISATION: THE 1940s TO 1960s

1   Paul Hasluck, *Diplomatic Witness: Australian Foreign Affairs 1941–1947*, Carlton,
Vic.: Melbourne University Press, 1980, p. 3.

2   Paul Hasluck and Nicholas P. Hasluck, *The Chance of Politics*, Melbourne: Text
Publishing, 1997, p. 82.

3   John Burton, 'Herbert Vere Evatt: A Man out of His Time', in David Day (ed.),
Brave New World: Dr H.V. Evatt and Australian Foreign Policy, St. Lucia, Qld:
University of Queensland Press, 1996.

4   Edwards, *Prime Ministers and Diplomats*, p. 180.

5   Hasluck, *Diplomatic Witness*, p. 41.

6   ibid., p. 106.

7   Christopher Waters, 'War, Colonisation and Postwar Security' in David
     Goldsworthy (ed.), *Facing North: A Century of Australian Engagement with Asia*,
     Vol. 1, Carlton South, Vic.: Melbourne University Press, 2002, p. 113.

8   ibid.

9   CPD, HR, 14 October 1943, p. 572.

10   David Lee, 'Indonesia's Independence', in David Goldsworthy (ed.), *Facing
     North: A Century of Australian Engagement with Asia*, Vol. 1, Carlton South, Vic.:
     Melbourne University Press, 2002, p. 144.

11   David Fettling, 'J.B. Chifley and the Indonesian Revolution, 1945–1949', *Australian
     Journal of Politics and History*, vol. 59, no. 4, December 2013, pp. 517–31.

12   Lee, 'Indonesia's Independence', p. 146.

13   ibid., p. 147.

14   Philip Dorling (ed.), *Diplomasi: Australia & Indonesia's Independence: Documents
     1947*, Canberra: AGPS, 1994, p. xix.

15   ibid., p. xxi.

16   Lee, 'Indonesia's Independence', p. 152.

17   CPD, HR, 24 September 1947, p. 74

18   Fettling, 'J.B. Chifley and the Indonesian Revolution, 1945–1949'.

19   Memorandum from Ball to Burton, in Philip Dorling and David Lee (eds),
     Australia and Indonesia's Independence: The Renville Agreement: Documents 1948,
     Canberra: AGPS, 1996, p. 194.

20   Lee, 'Indonesia's Independence', p. 166.

21   Edwards, *Prime Ministers and Diplomats*, p. 186.

22   Peter Gifford, 'The Cold War Across Asia' in David Goldsworthy (ed.), *Facing
     North: A Century of Australian Engagement with Asia*, Vol. 1, Carlton South, Vic.:
     Melbourne University Press, 2002, p. 173.

23   CPD, HR, 2 September 1948 p. 58; Gifford, 'The Cold War Across Asia', p. 195.

24   Edwards, *Prime Ministers and Diplomats*, p. 86.

25   Gifford, 'The Cold War Across Asia', p. 194.

26   CPD, HR, 31 May 1950, p. 3464.

27   C.P. Fitzgerald, 'Australia and Asia' in Gordon Greenwood and Norman Harper
     (eds), *Australia in World Affairs 1950–1955*, Melbourne: F.W. Cheshire, 1957, p. 238.

28   Norman Harper, 'Australia and the United States' in Gordon Greenwood and
     Norman Harper (eds), *Australia in World Affairs 1950–1955*, Melbourne: F.W.
     Cheshire, 1957, p. 191.

29   Alan Stewart Watt, *The Evolution of Australian Foreign Policy, 1938–1965*,
     London: Cambridge University Press, 1967, p. 168.

30   Richard Casey and T.B. Millar, *Australian Foreign Minister: The Diaries of
     R.G. Casey, 1951–60*, London: Collins, 1972, p. 33.

31   W.J. Hudson, *Casey*, Melbourne: Oxford University Press, 1986, p. 227.

32   Casey and Millar, *Australian Foreign Minister*, p. 312.

33   Hasluck and Hasluck, *The Chance of Politics*, p. 86.

34   CPD, HR, 27 September 1951, p. 151

35   Casey and Millar, *Australian Foreign Minister*, p. 82.

36   Gifford, 'The Cold War Across Asia', p. 211.

37   ibid.

38   Goldsworthy, *Losing the Blanket*, p. 47

39   Gifford, 'The Cold War across Asia', p. 214.

40   ibid.

41   ibid, p. 215.

42 ibid.
43 ibid.
44 Garry Woodard, 'A "Radical Tory": Sir Garfield Barwick, 1961–64' in Joan Beaumont, *Ministers, Mandarins and Diplomats: Australian Foreign Policy Making, 1941–1969*, Melbourne: Melbourne University Press, 2003, p. 115.
45 ibid.
46 David Lee and Moreen Dee, 'Southeast Asia Conflicts' in David Goldsworthy (ed.), *Facing North: A Century of Australian Engagement with Asia*, Vol. 1, Carlton South, Vic.: Melbourne University Press, 2002, p. 266.
47 Woodard 'A "Radical Tory"', p. 118.
48 Lee and Dee, 'Southeast Asian Conflicts', p. 267.
49 Manila Accord between the Philippines, the Federation of Malaya and Indonesia, signed in Manila, 31 July 1963.
50 Lee and Dee, 'Southeast Asian Conflicts', p. 269.
51 ibid., p. 270.
52 ibid.
53 ibid.
54 ibid.
55 ibid., p. 275.
56 Gordon Greenwood, 'Australian Foreign Policy in Action', in Gordon Greenwood and Norman Harper (eds), *Australia in World Affairs 1961–1965*, Melbourne: F.W. Cheshire, 1968, p. 109.
57 CPD, HR, 14 August 1969, p. 316.
58 Neville Meaney, *Australia and World Crisis 1914–1923: A History of Australian Defence and Foreign Policy 1901–23*, Sydney: Sydney University Press, 2009, p. 361.
59 Department of Foreign Affairs and Trade, *Australia–New Zealand Agreement 1944*, Canberra, 21 June 1944.
60 R.G Neale, 'India' in Gordon Greenwood and Norman Harper (eds), *Australia in World Affairs 1950–1955*, Melbourne: F.W. Cheshire, 1957, p. 261.
61 Francis J. West, 'Papua New Guinea' in Gordon Greenwood and Norman Harper (eds), *Australia in World Affairs 1961–1965*, Melbourne: F.W. Cheshire, 1968, p. 445.
62 T.B. Millar, *Australia in Peace and War: External Relations, 1788–1977*, Canberra: Australian National University Press, 1978, p. 310.
63 CPD, HR, 23 August 1960, p. 262
64 R.S. Parker, 'Papua New Guinea' in Gordon Greenwood and Norman Harper (eds), *Australia in World Affairs 1966–1970*, Melbourne: F.W. Cheshire, 1974, p. 393.
65 ibid., p. 404.
66 ibid., p. 393.
67 ibid., p. 394.
68 W.D. Forsyth, 'The South Pacific Commission' in Gordon Greenwood and Norman Harper (eds), *Australia in World Affairs 1961–1965*, Melbourne: F.W. Cheshire, 1968, p. 481.
69 CPD, HR, 26 February 1947, p. 173
70 Gifford, 'The Cold War in Asia', p. 190.
71 'Message from Attlee to Menzies', 17 December 1949, in Stuart Doran and David Lee (eds), *Australia and the Recognition of the People's Republic of China 1949–1972*, DFAT, 2002, p. 2.
72 Menzies, Cablegram to Fadden and Spender, 30 December 1950, ibid., p. 42.
73 Casey and Millar, *Australian Foreign Minister*, p. 189.
74 Hudson, *Casey*, p. 252.

75 Odd Arne Westad, *Restless Empire: China and the World Since 1750*, New York: Basic Books, 2012, p. 303.

76 Harper, 'Australia and the United States', p. 271.

77 Hedley Bull, 'Australia and the Great Powers in Asia' in Gordon Greenwood and Norman Harper (eds), *Australia in World Affairs 1966–1970*, Melbourne: F.W. Cheshire, 1974, p. 335.

78 Goldsworthy, *Losing the Blanket*, p. 132.

79 David Goldsworthy, David Dutton, Peter Gifford and Roderic Pitty, 'Reorientation' in David Goldsworthy (ed.), *Facing North: A Century of Australian Engagement with Asia*, Vol. 1, Carlton South, Vic.: Melbourne University Press, 2002, p. 333.

80 ibid, p. 334.

81 Meaney, *Australia and World Crisis 1914–1923*, p. 353.

82 James Cotton, 'R.G. Casey's Writings on Australia's Place in the World', in Melissa Conley Tyler, John Robbins and Adrian March (eds), *R.G. Casey: Minister for External Affairs 1951–1960*, Canberra: Australian Institute of International Affairs, 2012.

83 Charles Price, 'Immigration' in Gordon Greenwood and Norman Harper (eds), *Australia in World Affairs 1966–1970*, Melbourne: F.W. Cheshire, 1974, p. 181.

84 Waters, 'War, Decolonisation and Post-War Security', p. 130.

85 ibid.

86 CPD, HR, 4 April 1957, p. 357.

87 Casey and Millar, *Australian Foreign Minister*, p. 93.

88 Neale, 'India', p. 335.

89 A.C. Palfreyman, 'Immigration' in W.J. Hudson, *Australia in World Affairs 1971–1975*, Sydney: George Allen & Unwin and Australian Institute of International Affairs, 1980, p. 99.

90 Goldsworthy, Dutton, Gifford and Pitty, 'Reorientation', p. 323.

3 GREAT AND POWERFUL FRIENDS: THE 1940s TO THE 1960s

1 Norman Harper, *A Great and Powerful Friend: A Study of Australian American Relations between 1900 and 1975*, St Lucia, Qld: University of Queensland Press, 1987, p. 12.

2 ibid., p. 11.

3 John Curtin, 'The Task Ahead', Melbourne *Herald*, 27 December 1941.

4 James Curran, *Curtin's Empire*, Port Melbourne, Vic.: Cambridge University Press, 2011, p. 14.

5 Hasluck, *Diplomatic Witness*, p. 168.

6 ibid., p. 81.

7 ibid., p. 84.

8 Neville Meaney, 'Dr HV Evatt and the United Nations: The Problem of Collective Security and Liberal Internationalism', in James Cotton and David Lee (eds), *Australia and the United Nations*, DFAT: Canberra, 2012, p. 52.

9 Edwards, *Prime Ministers and Diplomats*, p. 162.

10 Spender, *Exercises in Diplomacy*, p. 23.

11 Harry S. Truman, Address to Joint Session of Congress, 12 March 1947.

12 John Lewis Gaddis, *The Cold War: A New History*, New York: Penguin, 2005, p. 29.

13 Meaney, 'Dr HV Evatt and the United Nations', p. 58.

14 David Horner, *The Spy Catchers: The Official History of ASIO 1949–1963*, Sydney: Allen & Unwin, 2014, p. 56.
15 ibid.
16 Spender, *Exercises in Diplomacy*, p. 15.
17 ibid., p. 16.
18 ibid., p. 14.
19 ibid., p. 39; P.J. Boyce and J.R. Angel (eds), *Independence and Alliance: Australia in World Affairs 1976–80*, Sydney: Allen & Unwin and the Australian Institute of International Affairs, 1983.
20 Spender, *Exercises in Diplomacy*, p. 54.
21 Gifford, 'The Cold War in Asia', p. 179.
22 ibid. p. 182.
23 ibid., p. 183.
24 Alan Stewart Watt, *Australian Diplomat: Memoirs of Sir Alan Watt*, Sydney: Angus and Robertson in association with the Australian Institute of International Affairs, 1972, p. 174.
25 ibid., p. 175.
26 Watt, *The Evolution of Australian Foreign Policy, 1938–1965*, p. 124.
27 Harper, *A Great and Powerful Friend*, p. 242.
28 Sandra Penrose, 'Percy Spender and the Origins of ANZUS: An Australian Intiative', Australian Political Studies Association Conference, University of Adelaide, 2004, p. 9.
29 Spender, *Exercises in Diplomacy*, p. 61.
30 ibid., p. 65.
31 CPD, HR, 28 November 1950, p. 3170.
32 Watt, *Australian Diplomat*, p. 184.
33 Beaumont, *Ministers, Mandarins and Diplomats*, p. 75.
34 CPD, HR, 21 February 1952, p. 233.
35 Watt, *The Evolution of Australian Foreign Policy, 1938–1965*, p. 124.
36 Casey and Millar, *Australian Foreign Minister*, p. 214.
37 ibid., p. 88.
38 ibid., p. 104.
39 Hudson, *Casey*, p. 268.
40 ibid.
41 Harper, *A Great and Powerful Friend*, p. 270.
42 Casey and Millar, *Australian Foreign Minister*, p. 244.
43 W.J. Hudson, *Blind Loyalty: Australia and the Suez Crisis, 1956*, Carlton, Vic.: Melbourne University Press, 1989, p. 57.
44 ibid., p. 63.
45 ibid., p. 27.
46 ibid., p. 95.
47 Norman Harper, 'Australia and Suez' in Gordon Greenwood and Norman Harper (eds), *Australia in World Affairs 1950–1955*, Melbourne: F.W. Cheshire, 1957, p. 346.
48 Hudson, *Blind Loyalty*, p. 105.
49 ibid., p. 113.
50 Gaddis, *The Cold War*, p. 127.
51 Hudson, *Blind Loyalty*, p. 118.
52 Harper, 'Australia and Suez', p. 355.
53 Stan Correy, 'The Suez Crisis 1956', *Background Briefing*, ABC Radio National, 2006.

54   Goldsworthy, *Losing the Blanket*, p. 99.
55   Andrea Benvenuti, *Anglo-Australian Relations and the 'Turn to Europe',*
      1961–1972, Woodbridge, UK: Royal Historical Society/Boydell Press, 2008, p. 19.
56   Andrea Benvenuti, *Anglo-Australian Relations and the 'Turn to Europe',*
      1961–1972, Woodbridge, UK: Royal Historical Society/Boydell Press, 2008, p. 21.
57   ibid., p. 40.
58   Woodard, *Asian Alternatives*, p. 60.
59   Watt, *The Evolution of Australian Foreign Policy, 1938–1965*, p. 167.
60   ibid., p. 283.
61   Benvenuti, *Anglo-Australian Relations and the 'Turn to Europe', 1961–1972*, p. 146.
62   Goldsworthy, *Losing the Blanket*, p. 157.
63   Benvenuti, *Anglo-Australian Relations and the 'Turn to Europe', 1961–1972*, p. 97.
64   J.L Richardson, 'Australian Strategic and Defence Policies' in Gordon Greenwood
      and Norman Harper (eds), *Australia in World Affairs 1966–1970*, Melbourne:
      F.W. Cheshire, 1974, p. 242.
65   Benvenuti, *Anglo-Australian Relations and the 'Turn to Europe', 1961–1972*, p. 101.
66   ibid., p. 104.
67   Goldsworthy, *Losing the Blanket*, p. 141.
68   Richardson, 'Australian Strategic and Defence Policies', p. 239.
69   Benvenuti, *Anglo-Australian Relations and the 'Turn to Europe', 1961–1972*, p. 24.
70   Casey and Millar, *Australian Foreign Minister*, p. 125.
71   ibid., p. 133.
72   David Marr, *Barwick*, Sydney: George Allen & Unwin, 1980, p. 176.
73   Greenwood, 'Australian Foreign Policy in Action', p. 113.
74   Woodard, *Asian Alternatives*, p. 62.
75   Marr, *Barwick*, p. 176.
76   Woodard, *Asian Alternatives*, p. 50.
77   Lee and Dee, 'Southeast Asian Conflicts', p. 282.
78   Marr, *Barwick*, p. 176.
79   Harper, *A Great and Powerful Friend*, p. 267
80   ibid. p. 268.
81   Peter Edwards, *Permanent Friends?: Historical Reflections on the Australian-*
      American Alliance, Lowy Institute Paper, Sydney: Lowy Institute of International
      Policy, 2005, p. 23.
82   CPD, HR, 23 March 1965, p. 230.
83   CPD, HR, 11 September 1968, p. 239.
84   ibid., p. 234.
85   Beaumont, *Ministers, Mandarins and Diplomats*, p. 140.
86   Woodard, *Asian Alternatives*, p. 199.
87   Philip Flood, *Dancing with Warriors*, Melbourne: Arcadia, 2011, p. 48.
88   Geoffrey Bolton, *Paul Hasluck*, Perth: UWA Publishing, 2014, p. 374.
89   Waters, 'War, Decolonisation and Post-War Security', p. 288.
90   ibid., p. 291.
91   Robert Menzies, *The Measure of the Years*, London: Cassell, 1970, p. 217.
92   Woodard, *Asian Alternatives*, p. 196.
93   Benvenuti, *Anglo-Australian Relations and the 'Turn to Europe', 1961–1972*, p. 89.
94   CPD, HR, 4 May 1965, p. 1102.
95   Gordon Greenwood, 'The Political Debate in Australia' in Gordon Greenwood
      and Norman Harper (eds), *Australia in World Affairs 1966–1970*, Melbourne:
      F.W. Cheshire, 1974, p. 44.

96   Benvenuti, *Anglo-Australian Relations and the 'Turn to Europe', 1961–1972*, p. 103.
97   Richard Nixon, *US Foreign Policy for the 1970s: A New Strategy for Peace*, Report to the Congress, 18 February 1970.
98   Neville Meaney, 'The United States' in W.J. Hudson, *Australia in World Affairs 1971–1975*, Sydney: George Allen & Unwin and Australian Institute of International Affairs, 1980, p. 164.
99   Greenwood, 'The Political Debate in Australia', p. 88.
100 CIA, Memorandum for the Director, 'Would the Loss of South Vietnam and Laois Precipitate the Domino Effect in the Far East?', 9 June 1956.

4   ORGANISING THE WORLD: THE 1940s TO THE 1960s

1   CPD, HR, 14 October 1943, p. 571.
2   H.C. Coombs, *Trial Balance*, Melbourne: Macmillan, 1986, p. 3.
3   Hasluck, *Diplomatic Witness*, p. 58.
4   ibid., p. 194.
5   CPD, HR, 8 September 1944, p. 603.
6   Meaney, 'Dr HV Evatt and the United Nations', p. 45.
7   Gareth Evans, 'Herbert Vere Evatt: Australia's First Internationalist', 1995 Daniel Mannix Memorial Lecture.
8   Edwards, *Prime Ministers and Diplomats*, p. 158.
9   Bolton, *Paul Hasluck*, p. 148.
10   Hasluck and Hasluck, *The Chance of Politics*, p. 80.
11   Coombs, *Trial Balance*, p. 35.
12   ibid., p. 91.
13   CPD, HR, 18 March 1947, p. 593.
14   CPD, HR, 26 February 1948, p. 224.
15   CPD, HR, 3 March 1948, p. 353.
16   Arthur Tange, 'Political Objectives of the Colombo Plan', 19 March 1952, in David Lowe and Daniel Oakman (eds), *Australia and the Colombo Plan, 1949–1957*, Canberra: DFAT, 2004, p. 463.
17   Spender, *Exercises in Diplomacy*, p. 215.
18   Gifford, 'The Cold War Across Asia', p. 175.
19   Casey and Millar, *Australian Foreign Minister*, p. 17; Hudson, *Casey*, p. 249.
20   Greenwood, 'Australian Foreign Policy in Action', p. 119.
21   Greenwood, 'The Commonwealth', p. 44.
22   CPD, HR, 7 March 1951, p. 73.
23   ibid., p. 74.
24   CPD, HR, 11 April 1961, p. 669.
25   CPD, HR, 31 March 1960, p. 790.
26   Greenwood, 'Australian Foreign Policy in Action', p. 63.
27   Goldsworthy, *Losing the Blanket*, p. 104.
28   Woodard, *Asian Alternatives*, p. 83.
29   W.J. Hudson, 'The United Nations' in Gordon Greenwood and Norman Harper (eds), *Australia in World Affairs 1966–1970*, Melbourne: F.W. Cheshire, 1974, p. 218.
30   Robert Menzies, *Rhodesian Statement by the Prime Minister*, Press statement, Canberra, 6 January 1966.
31   Hudson, 'The United Nations', p. 218.
32   ibid.

33 Matthew Jordan, 'Arms Control and Disarmament' in James Cotton and David Lee (eds), *Australia and the United Nations*, DFAT: Canberra, 2012, p. 269.
34 ibid., p. 273.
35 ibid., p. 275.
36 ibid., p. 278.
37 Dean Rusk, Secretary of State, US Embassy Canberra cable 4842 to Department of State, 6 April 1968, Secret Nodis, National Security Archive.
38 Jordan, 'Arms Control and Disarmament', p. 278.
39 ibid., p. 279.
40 ibid.
41 Harper, 'Australia and the United States'.
42 Roderic Pitty, 'The Postwar Expansion of Trade with East Asia' in David Goldsworthy (ed.), *Facing North: A Century of Australian Engagement with Asia*, Vol. 1, Carlton South, Vic.: Melbourne University Press, 2002, p. 221.
43 Richard Pomfret (ed.), *Australia's Trade Policies*, Melbourne: Oxford University Press, 1995, p. 194.
44 Pitty, 'The Postwar Expansion of Trade with East Asia', p. 228.
45 ibid., p. 229.
46 ibid., p. 231.
47 ibid., p. 232.
48 ibid., p. 242.
49 CPD, HR, 29 August 1957, p. 151.
50 Hedley Bull, 'Australia and the Great Powers in Asia', p. 338.
51 Nancy Anderson and John Crawford, 'Foreign Payments' in Gordon Greenwood and Norman Harper (eds), *Australia in World Affairs 1966–1970*, Melbourne: F.W. Cheshire, 1974, p. 126.
52 Pitty, 'The Postwar Expansion of Trade with East Asia', p. 247.
53 Bull, 'Australia and the Great Powers in Asia', p. 339.
54 Benvenuti, *Anglo-Australian Relations and the 'Turn to Europe', 1961–1972*, p. 173.
55 ibid.
56 H.W. Arndt, 'Foreign Payments' in Gordon Greenwood and Norman Harper (eds), *Australia in World Affairs 1966–1970*, Melbourne: F.W. Cheshire, 1974, p. 142.
57 Flood, *Dancing with Warriors*, p. 55.
58 James Cotton, 'Barwick, Hasluck and the Management of Foreign Policy Towards Northeast Asia: The Limits of Australian "Realism"' in Melissa Conley Tyler, John Robbins and Adrian March (eds), *Ministers for Foreign Affairs, 1961–1972*, Deakin: Australian Institute of Foreign Affairs, 2014, p. 13.
59 Watt, *Australian Diplomat*, p. 255.

5 TRANSITIONS: THE 1970S

1 Henry S. Albinski, *Australian External Policy under Labor*, St Lucia: University of Queensland Press, 1977, p. 1.
2 E.G. Whitlam, Opening Address to the AIPS Summer School, 27 January 1973.
3 CPD, HR, 1 June 1976, p. 2734.
4 ibid.
5 CPD, HR, 12 April 1971, p. 1928.
6 Whitlam, Opening Address to the AIPS Summer School, 27 January 1973.
7 Graham Freudenberg, *A Certain Grandeur: Gough Whitlam in Politics*, South Melbourne, Vic.: Macmillan, 1977, p. 64.

8 Richard Woolcott, *The Hot Seat*, Sydney: HarperCollins, 2003, p. 112.

9 A.C. Palfreyman, 'Immigration', p. 99.

10 E.G. Whitlam, Election Policy Speech, 13 November 1972.

11 Moreen Dee and Frank Frost, 'Indochina' in David Goldsworthy and Peter Edwards (eds), *Facing North: A Century of Australian Engagement with Asia*, Vol. 2., Melbourne: Melbourne University Press, 2003, p. 181

12 CPD, HR, 8 April 1974, p.1260.

13 Dee and Frost, 'Indochina', p. 184.

14 ibid., p. 192.

15 ibid.

16 UNHCR, 'Flight from Indochina', *The State of the World's Refugees*, UNHCR, 2000, accessed at <www.unhcr.org/3ebf9bad0.pdf>.

17 Bruce Grant, *The Boat People: An Age Investigation*, Ringwood: Penguin, 1979, p. 7.

18 Nancy Viviani, 'Refugees – the End of Splendid Isolation' in P.J. Boyce and J.R Angel, *Independence and Alliance, Australia in World Affairs 1976–1980*, Sydney: Allen & Unwin and Australian Institute for International Affairs, 1983, p. 134.

19 Dee and Frost, 'Indochina', p. 195.

20 Grant, *The Boat People*, p. 180.

21 Glen Barclay, 'Australia and North America' in P.J. Boyce and J.R. Angel (eds), *Independence and Alliance: Australia in World Affairs 1976–80*, Sydney: Allen & Unwin and the Australian Institute of International Affairs, 1983, p. 151.

22 CPD, HR, 7 March 1974, p. 205.

23 Whitlam, Opening Address to the AIPS Summer School, 27 January 1973.

24 John Ingleson, 'South-East Asia' in W.J. Hudson, *Australia in World Affairs 1971–1975*, Sydney: George Allen & Unwin and Australian Institute of International Affairs, 1980, p. 302.

25 CPD, HR, 24 May, 1973, p. 2646.

26 'Cablegram Evatt to Curtin', 1 July 1943, in Department of Foreign Affairs and Trade, *Documents on Australian Foreign Policy*, Volume 6, July 1942–December Canberra: DFAT, 1943 .

27 Wayne Reynolds, 'Labor Tradition, Foreign Shifts and the Foreign Policy of the Whitlam Government' in David Lee and Christopher Waters, *Evatt to Evans: The Labor Tradition in Australian Foreign Policy*, Sydney: Allen & Unwin, 1997, p. 117.

28 'Record of Conversation Between Whitlam and Soeharto', 4 April 1975, in Wendy Way (ed.), *Australia and the Indonesian Incorporation of Portuguese Timor 1974–1976*, Canberra: Melbourne University Press, 2000, p. 245.

29 'Record of Meeting Between Whitlam and Soeharto', 6 September 1974, in Wendy Way (ed.), *Australia and the Indonesian Incorporation of Portuguese Timor 1974–1976*, Canberra: Melbourne University Press, 2000, p. 95.

30 ibid., p. 96.

31 'Submission to McMahon: Australian Consulate: Dili', 1 December 1970, in Wendy Way (ed.), *Australia and the Indonesian Incorporation of Portuguese Timor 1974–1976*, Canberra: Melbourne University Press, 2000, p. 42.

32 Senate Foreign Affairs Defence and Trade Reference Committee, East Timor, Canberra: 2000.

33 'Letter from Barnard to Willesee', 11 February 1975, in Wendy Way (ed.), *Australia and the Indonesian Incorporation of Portuguese Timor 1974–1976*, Canberra: Melbourne University Press, 2000, p. 177.

34 ibid., p. 179.

35 'Minute from Woolcott to Renouf', 24 September 1974', in Wendy Way (ed.), *Australia and the Indonesian Incorporation of Portuguese Timor 1974–1976*, Canberra: Melbourne University Press, 2000, p. 111.

36 'Letter from Whitlam to Soeharto', 28 February 1975, in Wendy Way (ed.), *Australia and the Indonesian Incorporation of Portuguese Timor 1974–1976*, Canberra: Melbourne University Press, 2000, p. 201.

37 'Cablegram to Canberra: Discussion with President Soeharto', 8 March 1975, in Wendy Way (ed.), *Australia and the Indonesian Incorporation of Portuguese Timor 1974–1976*, Canberra: Melbourne University Press, 2000, p. 219.

38 ibid., p. 218.

39 'Record of Conversation Between Whitlam and Soeharto', 4 April 1975, in Wendy Way (ed.), *Australia and the Indonesian Incorporation of Portuguese Timor 1974–1976*, Canberra: Melbourne University Press, 2000, p. 246.

40 'Cablegram to Canberra from Jakarta: Portuguese Timor', 16 August 1975, in Wendy Way (ed.), *Australia and the Indonesian Incorporation of Portuguese Timor 1974–1976*, Canberra: Melbourne University Press, 2000, p. 313.

41 'Cablegram to Canberra from Lisbon: Portuguese Timor', 21 August 1975, in Wendy Way (ed.), *Australia and the Indonesian Incorporation of Portuguese Timor 1974–1976*, Canberra: Melbourne University Press, 2000, p. 326.

42 'Cablegram to Jakarta: Portuguese Timor', 25 August 1975, in Wendy Way (ed.), *Australia and the Indonesian Incorporation of Portuguese Timor 1974–1976*, Canberra: Melbourne University Press, 2000, p. 340.

43 CPD, HR, 26 August 1975, p. 492.

44 Woolcott, *The Hot Seat*, p. 153.

45 ibid., p. 154.

46 'Cablegram to Jakarta', 20 November 1975, in Wendy Way (ed.), *Australia and the Indonesian Incorporation of Portuguese Timor 1974–1976*, Canberra: Melbourne University Press, 2000, p. 579.

47 'Statement by the Foreign Minister, Mr. Andrew Peacock', 7 Decemer 1975, in Wendy Way (ed.), *Australia and the Indonesian Incorporation of Portuguese Timor 1974–1976*, Canberra: Melbourne University Press, 2000, p. 604.

48 'Developments in the UN General Assembly After the Invasion', in Wendy Way (ed.), *Australia and the Indonesian Incorporation of Portuguese Timor 1974–1976*, Canberra: Melbourne University Press, 2000, p. 625.

49 'Cabinet Decisions on Timor', in Wendy Way (ed.), *Australia and the Indonesian Incorporation of Portuguese Timor 1974–1976*, Canberra: Melbourne University Press, 2000, p. 711.

50 'Record of Conversation Between Peacock and Panggabean', 14 April 1976, in Wendy Way (ed.), *Australia and the Indonesian Incorporation of Portuguese Timor 1974–1976*, Canberra: Melbourne University Press, 2000, p. 741.

51 David Goldsworthy, 'East Timor' in David Goldsworthy and Peter Edwards (eds), *Facing North: A Century of Australian Engagement with Asia*, Vol. 2., Melbourne: Melbourne University Press, 2003, p. 370.

52 Ross Terril, *Facing the Dragon: China Policy in a New Era*, Canberra: Australian Strategic Policy Institute, 2013, p. 8.

53 'Minute from McMahon to Shann', 17 December 1970, in Stuart Doran and David Lee (eds), *Australia and the Recognition of the People's Republic of China 1949–1972*, DFAT, 2002, p. 357.

54 'Cabinet Decision no. 678: Australia's Policy Towards China', 23 February 1971, in Stuart Doran and David Lee (eds), *Australia and the Recognition of the People's*

Republic of China 1949–1972, Canberra: DFAT, 2002, p. 395.

55 'Cablegram to Paris', 22 May 1971, in Stuart Doran and David Lee (eds), *Australia and the Recognition of the People's Republic of China 1949–1972*, Canberra: DFAT, 2002, p. 453.

56 I.F.H. Wilson, 'China' in Gordon Greenwood and Norman Harper (eds), *Australia in World Affairs 1966–1970*, Melbourne: F.W. Cheshire, 1974, p. 338.

57 Stephen Fitzgerald, 'The Coup That Laid the Fear of China: Gough Whitlam in Beijing, 1971', The Whitlam Legacy: A Series of Occasional Papers Published by the Whitlam Institute, Vol. 2, September 2012, p. 14.

58 'Cablegram To Canberra from Washington', 15 July 1971, in Stuart Doran and David Lee (eds), *Australia and the Recognition of the People's Republic of China 1949–1972*, Canberra: DFAT, 2002, p. 502.

59 ibid., p. 510.

60 'Letter from Anderson to Renouf' in Stuart Doran and David Lee (eds), *Australia and the Recognition of the People's Republic of China 1949–1972*, Canberra: DFAT, 2002, p. 753.

61 Goldsworthy, Dutton, Gifford and Pitty, 'Reorientation', p. 337.

62 CPD, HR, 1 June 1976, p. 2740.

63 Philip Ayres, *Malcolm Fraser: A Biography*, Melbourne: William Heinemann, 1987, p. 331.

64 ibid., p. 336.

65 ibid., p. 338.

66 D.C.S. Sissons, 'Japan' in W.J. Hudson (ed.), *Australia in World Affairs 1971–1975*, Sydney: George Allen & Unwin and Australian Institute of International Affairs, 1980, p. 258.

67 Moreen Dee, *Friendship and Cooperation: The 1976 Basic Treaty between Australia and Japan*, Canberra: DFAT, 2006, p. 6.

68 ibid., p. 8.

69 Goldsworthy, Dutton, Gifford and Pitty, 'Reorientation', p. 339.

70 ibid.

71 Sissons, 'Japan', p. 240.

72 Alan Rix, 'Australia and East Asia: Japan' in P.J. Boyce and J.R. Angel (eds), *Independence and Alliance: Australia in World Affairs 1976–80*, Sydney: Allen & Unwin and the Australian Institute of International Affairs, 1983, p. 194.

73 ibid., p. 196.

74 Sissons, 'Japan', p. 254.

75 Dee, *Friendship and Cooperation*, p. 37.

76 Rix, 'Australia and East Asia: Japan', p. 191.

77 ibid., p. 193.

78 ibid., p. 200.

79 James Griffin, 'Papua New Guinea' in W.J. Hudson (ed.), *Australia in World Affairs 1971–1975*, Sydney: George Allen & Unwin and Australian Institute of International Affairs, 1980, p. 347.

80 Nancy Viviani, 'Aid Policies and Programmes' in P.J. Boyce and J.R. Angel (eds), *Independence and Alliance: Australia in World Affairs 1976–80*, Sydney: Allen & Unwin and the Australian Institute of International Affairs, 1983, p. 125.

81 Richard Herr, Australia and the Southwest Pacific' P.J. Boyce and J.R. Angel (eds), *Independence and Alliance: Australia in World Affairs 1976–80*, Sydney: Allen & Unwin and the Australian Institute of International Affairs, 1983, p. 283.

82 ibid., p. 279.

83 ibid., p. 285.

84 E.G. Whitlam, *The Whitlam Government 1972–1975*, Ringwood: Penguin, 1985, p. 36.

85 E.G. Whitlam, Address to National Press Club, Washington, 30 July 1973.

86 ibid.

87 James Curran, 'The Dilemmas of Divergence: The Crisis in American-Australian Relations, 1972–1975', *Diplomatic History*, vol. 38, no. 2, 2014.

88 James Curran, *Unholy Fury: Whitlam and Nixon at War*, Melbourne: Melbourne University Press, 2015, p. 163.

89 Albinski, *Australian External Policy under Labor*, p. 125.

90 Curran, 'The Dilemmas of Divergence', p. 390.

91 Reynolds, 'The Labor Tradition, Global Shifts and the Foreign Policy of the Whitlam Government', p. 123.

92 E.G. Whitlam, *The Whitlam Government 1972–1975*, Ringwood: Penguin, 1985, p. 30.

93 CPD, HR, 24 May 1973, p. 2648.

94 Albinski, *Australian External Policy under Labor*, p. 168.

95 Curran, *Unholy Fury*, p. 268.

96 Albinski, *Australian External Policy under Labor*, p. 260.

97 ibid.

98 CPD, HR, 1 June 1976, p. 2738.

99 Ayres, *Malcolm Fraser*, p. 338.

100 CPD, HR, 1 June 1976, p. 2738.

101 CPD, HR, 10 March 1970, p. 235.

102 Ian Clark, 'Indian Ocean' in W.J. Hudson, *Australia in World Affairs 1971–1975*, Sydney: George Allen & Unwin and Australian Institute of International Affairs, 1980, p. 313.

103 CPD, HR, 1 June 1976, p.2737.

104 Senate Committee on Foreign Affairs and Defence, *Australia and the Indian Ocean Region*, November 1976.

105 Meg Gurry, *Australia and India: Mapping the Journey*, Melbourne: Melbourne University Press, 2015, p. 129.

106 Albinski, *Australian External Policy under Labor*, p. 116.

107 ibid., p. 117.

108 Ayres, *Malcolm Fraser*, p. 345.

109 Richard Higgott, 'Australia and Africa' in P.J. Boyce and J.R. Angel (eds), *Independence and Alliance: Australia in World Affairs 1976–80*, Sydney: Allen & Unwin and the Australian Institute of International Affairs, 1983, p. 248.

110 Ayres, *Malcolm Fraser*, p. 349.

111 ibid., p. 380.

112 Richard Higgott, 'Australia and Africa', p. 250.

113 ibid., p. 259.

114 CPD, HR, 9 May 1972, p. 2224.

115 Claire Clark, 'The United Nations' in W.J. Hudson, *Australia in World Affairs 1971–1975*, Sydney: George Allen & Unwin and Australian Institute of International Affairs, 1980, p. 154.

116 ibid., p. 157.

117 ibid., p. 156.

118 Albinski, *Australian External Policy under Labor*, p. 142

119 CPD, HR, 1 June 1976, p. 2741.

120 Marty Harris, *Australia and the Middle East Conflict: A History of Key Government Statements (1947–2007)*, Canberra: Parliamentary Library, 2012.

121 ibid.
122 CPD, HR, 27 February 1979, p. 365.
123 Richard Leaver, 'Australia and the Indian Ocean Region' in P.J. Boyce and
     J.R. Angel (eds), *Independence and Alliance: Australia in World Affairs 1976–80*,
     Sydney: Allen & Unwin and the Australian Institute of International Affairs,
     1983, p. 270.
124 Goldsworthy, Dutton, Gifford and Pitty, 'Reorientation', p. 349.
125 General Assembly Declaration on the Establishment of a New International
     Economic Order, 1 May 1974.
126 Albinski, *Australian External Policy under Labor*, p. 205.
127 ibid., p. 186.
128 Millar, *Australia in Peace and War*, p. 430.
129 CPD, HR, 1 June 1976, p. 2742.
130 Malcolm Fraser, Speech to University of South Carolina Columbia, 8 July 1981.
131 Owen Harries, *Australia and the Third World*, Report of the Committee on
     Australia's Relations with the Third World, Canberra: AGPS, 1979, p. 179.
132 Gregory Pemberton, 'Whitlam and the Labor Tradition' in David Lee and
     Christopher Waters (eds), *Evatt to Evans: The Labor Tradition in Australian
     Foreign Policy*, Sydney: Allen & Unwin, 1997, p. 147.
133 CPD, HR, 1 June 1976, p. 2741.
134 Ralph Harry, 'Australian Multilateral Diplomacy' in P.J. Boyce and J.R. Angel
     (eds), *Independence and Alliance: Australia in World Affairs 1976–80*, Sydney:
     Allen & Unwin and the Australian Institute of International Affairs, 1983, p. 97.
135 Kevin Ryan, 'International Law' in W.J. Hudson (ed.), *Australia in World Affairs
     1971–1975*, Sydney: George Allen & Unwin and Australian Institute of
     International Affairs, 1980, p. 113.
136 ibid.
137 Gerard A. Brennan, 'Australia and International Law' in P.J. Boyce and J.R. Angel
     (eds), *Independence and Alliance: Australia in World Affairs 1976–80*, Sydney:
     Allen & Unwin and the Australian Institute of International Affairs, 1983, p. 65.
138 ibid., p. 77.
139 Albinski, *Australian External Policy under Labor*, p. 252.
140 Ryan, 'International Law', p. 112.
141 ibid.
142 ibid., p. 122.
143 J.D.B. Miller, 'Australia and Western Europe' in P.J. Boyce and J.R. Angel (eds),
     Independence and Alliance: Australia in World Affairs 1976–80, Sydney: Allen &
     Unwin and the Australian Institute of International Affairs, 1983, p. 167.
144 CPD, HR, 27 February 1979, p. 361.
145 Hugh Smith, 'Defence Policy' in P.J. Boyce and J.R. Angel (eds), *Independence
     and Alliance: Australia in World Affairs 1976–80*, Sydney: Allen & Unwin and the
     Australian Institute of International Affairs, 1983, p. 41.
146 Peter Edwards, *Robert Marsden Hope and Australian Public Policy*, Canberra:
     Office of National Assessments, 2011, p. 18.
147 Leaver, 'Australia and the Indian Ocean Region', p. 263.
148 Odd Arne Westad, *The Global Cold War*, Cambridge University Press, 2007, p. 3218.
149 Gaddis, *The Cold War*, p. 211.
150 Malcolm Fraser, Address to Luncheon in Honour of Prime Minister of Japan,
     17 January 1980.

6 OPENING UP: THE 1980s

1 CPD, HR, 19 February 1980, p. 17.

2 ibid., p. 23.

3 ibid., p. 20.

4 ibid., p. 27.

5 ibid.

6 Ayres, *Malcolm Fraser*, p. 435.

7 Morgan Gallup Poll, 'Russia Is Now Seen as the Chief Threat to Australia's Security', Roy Morgan Research, 1982.

8 Bill Hayden, *Hayden*, Angus and Robertson, 1996, p. 357.

9 Bob Hawke, 1983 ALP Election Policy Speech, 16 February 1983.

10 Bob Hawke, Speech to the Washington Press Club, 15 June 1983.

11 Hayden, *Hayden*, p. 475.

12 Stephen Mills, *The Hawke Years*, Ringwood: Viking, 1993, p. 157.

13 Blanche d'Alpuget, *Hawke: The Prime Minister*, Melbourne: Melbourne University Press, 2010, p. 180.

14 Hayden, *Hayden*, p. 370.

15 ibid., p. 311.

16 ibid., p. 370.

17 ibid., p. 386.

18 ibid.

19 Flood, *Dancing with Warriors*, p. 133.

20 Gareth Evans, *Inside the Hawke Keating Government: A Cabinet Diary*, Melbourne: Melbourne University Press, 2014, p. 339.

21 ibid., p. 253.

22 Hayden, *Hayden*, p. 477.

23 Mills, *The Hawke Years*, p. 159.

24 Hayden, *Hayden*, p. 379.

25 CPD, HR, 7 December 1983, p. 3409.

26 Dee and Frost, 'Indochina', p. 197.

27 ibid., p. 199.

28 ibid.

29 d'Alpuget, *Hawke*, p. 184.

30 Hayden, *Hayden*, p. 396.

31 Goldsworthy, 'Regional Relations', p. 155.

32 Gareth Evans, 'Tributes Flow for the Former Face of Indonesia', Kirrin Mckechnie, *The World Today*, 12 December 2008.

33 Graeme Gill, 'Australia and the Eastern Bloc' in P.J. Boyce and J.R. Angel (eds), *Diplomacy in the Marketplace: Australia in World Affairs 1981–90*, Australia in World Affairs, Vol. 7, Melbourne: Longman Cheshire, 1992, p. 234.

34 Hayden, *Hayden*, p. 470.

35 Peter Fitzsimons, *Beazley: A Biography*, Sydney: HarperCollins, 1998, p. 265.

36 'Sitiveni Rabuka's Coups Prompted Cautious Reaction', *The Australian*, 1 January 2014.

37 Hayden, *Hayden*, p. 432.

38 Joint Declaration of Principles Guiding Relations between Australia and Papua New Guinea, 1987.

39 Gareth Evans and Bruce Grant, *Australia's Foreign Relations in the World of the 1990s*, 2nd edn, Melbourne: Melbourne University Press, 1995, p. 176.

40 Jonathan Shultz, 'Overseeing and Overlooking: Australian Engagement with the Pacific Islands 1988–2007', University of Melbourne, 2012, p. 106.

41 Greg Fry, 'Australia in the South Pacific', in P.J. Boyce and J.R. Angel, *Diplomacy in the Marketplace: Australia in World Affairs 1981–90*, Australia in World Affairs, Vol. 7, Melbourne: Longman Cheshire, 1992, p. 190.

42 Fry, 'Australia in the South Pacific', p. 189.

43 Ann Capling, *Australia and the Global Trade System: From Havana to Seattle*, Cambridge: Cambridge University Press, 2001, p. 95.

44 Richardson, 'Australia and Western Europe', p. 214.

45 Bob Hawke, *The Hawke Memoirs*, Australia: Mandarin, 1996, p. 422.

46 Capling, *Australia and the Global Trade System*, p. 95.

47 ibid., p. 104.

48 ibid., p. 108.

49 ibid., p. 104.

50 Mary Quilty and David Goldsworthy, 'Social and Cultural Engagement', in David Goldsworthy and Peter Edwards (eds), *Facing North: A Century of Australian Engagement with Asia*, Vol. 2., Melbourne: Melbourne University Press, 2003, p. 276.

51 Edmund S.K. Fung, 'Australia and China' in P.J. Boyce and J.R. Angel (eds), *Diplomacy in the Marketplace: Australia in World Affairs 1981–90*, Australia in World Affairs, Vol. 7, Melbourne: Longman Cheshire, 1992, p. 280.

52 Mills, *The Hawke Years*, p. 180.

53 Fung, 'Australia and China', p. 277.

54 Mills, *The Hawke Years*, p. 181.

55 Hawke, *The Hawke Memoirs*, p. 345.

56 ibid., p. 343.

57 Fung, 'Australia and China', p. 285.

58 Goldsworthy, 'Regional Relations', p. 142.

59 Ezra F. Vogel, *Deng Xiaoping and the Transformation of China*, Harvard: Belknap, 2011, p. 631.

60 d'Alpuget, *Hawke*, p. 239.

61 Mills, *The Hawke Years*, p. 182.

62 Hawke, *The Hawke Memoirs*, p. 367.

63 John Welfield, 'Australia's Relations with Japan and the Korean Peninsula' in P.J. Boyce and J.R. Angel (eds), *Diplomacy in the Marketplace: Australia in World Affairs 1981–90*, Australia in World Affairs, Vol. 7, Melbourne: Longman Cheshire, 1992, p. 256.

64 ibid., p. 255.

65 ibid., p. 263.

66 ibid., p. 264.

67 ibid., p. 248.

68 ibid.

69 ibid., p. 250.

70 ibid., p. 251.

71 ibid., p. 268.

72 ibid., p. 270.

73 Evans and Grant, *Australia's Foreign Relations in the World of the 1990s*, p. 131.

74 Mills, *The Hawke Years*, p. 194.

75 Bob Hawke, 'Regional Cooperation: Challenges for Korea and Australia', Speech at Luncheon of Korean Business Associations, 31 January 1989.

76   Gareth Evans, 'APEC: A Blueprint for Asia's Long-Term Growth', Address to World Economic Forum, Singapore, 22 September 1995.

77   Hawke, *The Hawke Memoirs*, p. 424.

78   Keith Scott, *Gareth Evans*, Sydney: Allen & Unwin, 1999, p. 272.

79   ibid.

80   Woolcott, *The Hot Seat*, p. 238.

81   Evans, 'Apec: A Blueprint for Asia's Long-Term Growth'.

82   Gregory Pemberton, 'Australia and the United States' in P.J. Boyce and J.R. Angel (eds), *Diplomacy in the Marketplace: Australia in World Affairs 1981–90*, Australia in World Affairs, Vol. 7, Melbourne: Longman Cheshire, 1992, p. 128.

83   Evans, *Inside the Hawke Keating Government*, p. 49.

84   Pemberton, 'Australia and the United States', p. 133.

85   Hayden, *Hayden*, p. 391.

86   ibid., p. 434.

87   Hawke, *The Hawke Memoirs*, p. 212.

88   Hayden, *Hayden*, p. 384.

89   CPD, HR, 6 June 1984, p. 2987.

90   d'Alpuget, Hawke.

91   Hawke, *The Hawke Memoirs*, p. 288.

92   Hayden, *Hayden*, p. 460.

93   Bob Hawke, 'Reflections on the Australia–United States Alliance', Discussion with Paul Kelly at the United States Studies Centre, University of Sydney, 3 May 2011.

94   Pemberton, 'Australia and the United States', p. 135.

95   Hawke, *The Hawke Memoirs*, p. 487.

96   Paul Dibb, *Review of Australia's Defence Capabilities*, Canberra: AGPS, 1986.

97   ibid.

98   Graeme Cheeseman, 'Defence Policy and Organisation: The Search for Self-Reliance' in P.J. Boyce and J.R. Angel (eds), *Diplomacy in the Marketplace: Australia in World Affairs 1981–90*, Australia in World Affairs, Vol. 7, Melbourne: Longman Cheshire, 1992, p. 68.

99   ibid., p. 76.

100   Hayden, *Hayden*, p. 384.

101   Boyce and Angel, *Diplomacy in the Marketplace*, p. 128.

102   David O'Reilly, *The Australian*, 9 August 1985.

103   Hayden, *Hayden*.

104   Paul Kelly, *The End of Certainty*, Sydney: Allen & Unwin, 1992, p. 528.

105   Hawke, *The Hawke Memoirs*, p. 468.

106   Kelly, *The End of Certainty*, p. 538.

107   ibid., p. 533.

108   Hawke, *The Hawke Memoirs*, p. 470.

109   ibid., p. 354.

110   Sam Lipski and Suzanne D. Rutland, *Let My People Go: The Untold Story of Australia and the Soviet Jews 1959–89*, Melbourne: Hybrid Publishers, 2015.

111   Mills, *The Hawke Years*, p. 165.

112   ibid., p. 167.

113   Lipski and Rutland, *Let My People Go*.

114   ibid.

115   d'Alpuget, *Hawke*, p. 203.

116   Gareth Evans, 'Interview with the Hon. Gareth Evans' by Dr Sue Onslow, 15 June

2015, accessed at <www.commonwealthoralhistories.org/2015/interview-with-the-hon-gareth-evans/>.

117 Gareth Evans, 'Australia, Nelson Mandela and the End of Apatheid', Speech at Government House, Sydney, 17 July 2012.

118 ibid.

119 Hawke, *The Hawke Memoirs*, p. 322.

120 T.B. Millar, 'Australia and the United Kingdom' in P.J. Boyce and J.R. Angel (eds), *Diplomacy in the Marketplace: Australia in World Affairs 1981–90*, Australia in World Affairs, Vol. 7, Melbourne: Longman Cheshire, 1992, p. 203.

121 J.l. Richardson, 'Australia and Western Europe' in P.J. Boyce and J.R. Angel (eds), *Diplomacy in the Marketplace: Australia in World Affairs 1981–90*, Australia in World Affairs, Vol. 7, Melbourne: Longman Cheshire, 1992, p. 220.

122 Kelly, *The End of Certainty*, p. 128.

123 Hawke, *The Hawke Memoirs*, p. 364.

124 ibid., p. 359.

125 Bob Hawke, Remarks by the President upon the Departure of Prime Minister Hawke of Australia, Washington, 1988.

7 A 'POST-' WORLD: THE 1990s

1   Scott, *Gareth Evans*, p. 229.

2   Department of Defence, *Strategic Review 1993*, Canberra: AGPS, 1993.

3   Paul J. Keating, *Engagement: Australia Faces the Asia-Pacific*, Sydney: Macmillan, 2000, p. 40.

4   Graeme Dobell, *Australia Finds Home*, Sydney: ABC Books, 2000, p. 189.

5   CPD, Senate, 6 December 1989, p. 4022.

6   Keating, *Engagement*, p. 4.

7   ibid.

8   George H.W. Bush, Address before a Joint Session of the Congress on State of the Union, 29 January 1991.

9   CPD, HR, 21 August 1990, p. 1119.

10 ibid., p. 1121.

11 d'Alpuget, *Hawke*, p. 293.

12 Mills, *The Hawke Years*, p. 145.

13 d'Alpuget, *Hawke*, p. 296.

14 ibid., p. 314.

15 CPD, HR, 18 October 1977, p. 2083.

16 Paul J. Keating, *Advancing Australia: The Speeches of Paul Keating, Prime Minister*, selected and edited by Mark Ryan, Sydney: Big Picture Publications, 1995, p. 190.

17 CPD, HR, 27 February 1992. p. 374 .

18 Paul Keating, Personal note.

19 Keating, *Engagement*, p. 20.

20 ibid., p. 32.

21 Paul J. Keating, Letter to President Clinton, 1993.

22 Keating, *Engagement*, p. 90.

23 APEC Leaders Economic Vision Statement, Blake Island, Seattle, 20 November 1993.

24 Keating, *Engagement*, p. 100.

25 ibid., p. 109.

26 ibid., p. 116.

27 ibid., p. 122.

28 John Ravenhill, 'Australia and the World Economy 1991–95: Closer Economic Integration with Asia?' in James Cotton and John Ravenhill (eds), *Seeking Asian Engagement: Australia in World Affairs, 1991–95*, Melbourne: Oxford University Press, 1997, p. 107.

29 CPD, Senate, 24 November 1989, p. 3300.

30 Evans and Grant, Australia's *Foreign Relations in the World of the 1990s*, p. 230.

31 Scott, *Gareth Evans*, p. 268.

32 Evans and Grant, *Australia's Foreign Relations in the World of the 1990s*, p. 230.

33 Scott, *Gareth Evans*, p. 270.

34 Evans and Grant, *Australia's Foreign Relations in the World of the 1990s*, p. 234.

35 ibid., p. 2354.

36 Paul Keating, 'Australia and Asia: Knowing who we are', 7 April 1992, in Paul Keating, *Advancing Australia: The Speeches of Paul Keating, Prime Minister*, selected and edited by Mark Ryan, Sydney: Big Picture Publications, 1995, p. 196.

37 Keating, *Engagement*, p. 136.

38 Scott, Gareth Evans, p. 260.

39 Keating, *Engagement*, p. 130.

40 ibid., p. 176.

41 Paul J. Keating, Speech Launching 'Australia Today Indonesia '94", Sydney, 16 March 1994.

42 Keating, *Engagetment*, p. 136.

43 Department of Defence, *Strategic Review 1993*.

44 Keating, *Engagement*, p. 141.

45 Paul J. Keating, Conversation between the Prime Minister and President Soeharto, Bali Cliff Resort, 17 September 1995.

46 Allan Gyngell, 'Australia and Indonesia', in Brendan Taylor (ed.), *Australia as an Asia Pacific Regional Power*, Routledge, 2007, p. 102.

47 Peter Hartcher, 'Indonesian Deal – an Act of Faith', *Australian Financial Review*, 5 July 1996.

48 Gyngell, 'Australia and Indonesia', p. 103.

49 Paul J. Keating, Interview, Boeing Factory, Seattle, 21 November 1993.

50 Keating, *Engagement*, p. 170.

51 ibid., p. 172.

52 ibid., p. 173.

53 ibid., p. 176.

54 ibid., p. 178.

55 ibid., p. 190.

56 ibid., p. 191.

57 Department of Defence, *Strategic Review 1993*.

58 Allan Gyngell and Michael Wesley, *Making Australian Foreign Policy*, 2nd edn, Melbourne: Cambridge University Press, 2007, p. 10.

59 CPD, Senate: 6 December 1989, p. 4022.

60 Scott, *Gareth Evans*, p. 294.

61 ibid., p. 285.

62 Rodolfo C. Severino, *The Asean Regional Forum*, Singapore: ISEAS, 2009, p. 16.

63 Department of Defence, *Strategic Review 1993*, p. 22.

64 Keating, *Engagement*, p. 41.

65 Evans and Grant, *Australia's Foreign Relations in the World of the 1990s*, p. 260.

66 Keating, *Engagement*, p. 194.

67 Gareth Evans, *The Responsibility to Protect: Ending Mass Atrocity Crimes Once and for All*, Washington: Brookings Institution Press, 2008.

68 Scott, *Gareth Evans*, p. 262.

69 ibid., p. 263.

70 Gareth Evans, 'The Style of Australian Foreign Policy', Address to the Fabian Society, 10 November 1989.

71 Gareth Evans, 'Cooperating for Peace', Award Lecture, University of Louisville, 24 October 1995.

72 ibid.

73 Gareth Evans, 'The United Nations: New Opportunities, New Challenges', Address to the 47th Session of the United Nations General Assembly, 28 September 1992.

74 ibid.

75 Gareth Evans, 'Arms Control and Disarmament: A Chance for Progress', Address to United Nations Conference on Disarmament Issues, Kyoto, 27 May 1991.

76 Scott, *Gareth Evans*, p. 349.

77 Keating, *Engagement*, p. 224.

78 ibid., p. 223.

79 ibid., p. 226.

80 Department of Foreign Affairs Trade, *Report of the Canberra Commission on the Elimination of Nuclear Weapons*, Canberra: DFAT, 1996.

81 Alexander Downer, 'Approaches to Disarmament, the Peaceful Settlement of Disputes and International Humanitarian Law', in Timothy Mccormack, Michael Tilbury and Gillian D. Triggs, (eds), *A Century of War and Peace: Asia-Pacific Perspectives on the Centenary of the 1899 Hague Peace Conference*, The Hague: Kluwer Law International, 2001, p. 18.

82 ibid., p. 20.

83 Andrew Carr, *Winning the Peace: Australia's Campaign to Change the Asia-Pacific*, Melbourne: Melbourne University Press, 2015, p. 176.

84 Gareth Evans, 'Australia's Human Rights Diplomacy', Melbourne, 8 September 1994.

85 Gareth Evans, 'The New Australia in Asia', Address to the Asia Society, Hong Kong, 1994.

86 Evans, 'Australia's Human Rights Diplomacy', Melbourne, 8 September 1994.

87 Stuart Harris, 'Australia and the International Environment', in James Cotton and John Ravenhill (eds), *Seeking Asian Engagement: Australia in World Affairs, 1991–95*, Melbourne: Oxford University Press, 1997.

88 ibid., p. 128.

89 Keating, *Engagement*, p. 47.

90 ibid., p. 56.

91 Greg Sheridan, 'Keating's Touch of Madness on Indonesia', *The Australian*, 18 July 1994.

92 Keating, *Engagement*, p. 60.

93 ibid., p. 61.

94 Yoichi Funabashi and Barak Kushner (eds), *Examining Japan's Lost Decades*, Routledge, 20145, p. xxvi.

95 Record of Conversation between Keating and Murayama, September 1994.

96 Keating, *Engagement*, p. 34.

97 ibid., p. 70.

98   Alan Rix, 'Australia and Japan', in James Cotton and John Ravenhill (eds), *Seeking Asian Engagement: Australia in World Affairs, 1991–95*, Melbourne: Oxford University Press, 1997, p. 145.

99   Joint Declaration on the Australia-Japan Partnership, 26 May 1995.

100 Alexander Downer, 'Australia and Japan: A Long-Standing Relationship', Speech at Japan's National Press Club, Tokyo, 6 June 1996.

101 Paul J. Keating, Press Conference, Australian Embassy Washington, 14 September 1993.

102 ibid.

103 Department of Defence, *Strategic Review 1993*, p. 35.

104 Evans and Grant, *Australia's Foreign Relations in the World of the 1990s*.

105 Keating, *Engagement*, p. 28.

106 Dobell, *Australia Finds Home*, p. 260.

107 Keating, *Engagement*, p. 145.

108 Ravenhill, 'Australia and the World Economy 1991–95', p. 109.

109 David Goldsworthy, 'An Overview' in James Cotton and John Ravenhill (eds), *The National Interest in a Global Era: Australia in World Affairs 1996–2000*, Melbourne: Oxford University Press, 2002, p. 26.

110 Keating, *Engagement*, p. 205.

111 Keating, *Engagement*, p. 200.

112 Gordon Bilney, 'Australia's Relations with the South Pacific – Challenge and Change', Australian Development Studies Network, Briefing Paper No. 34, July 1994.

113 Keating, *Engagement*, p. 201.

114 ibid., p. 197.

115 Bilney, 'Australia's Relations with the South Pacific'.

116 ibid.

117 ibid.

118 Keating, *Engagement*, p. 206.

119 ibid., p. 217.

120 Evans and Grant, *Australia's Foreign Relations in the World of the 1990s*, p. 123.

121 Paul J. Keating, Press Conference, Parliament House, 15 December 1993.

122 Capling, *Australia and the Global Trade System*, p. 146.

123 Department of Foreign Affairs and Trade, *In the National Interest: Australia's Foreign and Trade Policy White Paper*, Canberra, 1997, p. vi.

124 Alexander Downer, 'Australia and Asia: Taking the Long View', Address to the Foreign Correspondents' Association, Sydney, 11 April 1996.

125 DFAT, *In the National Interest*.

126 Rawdon Dalrymple, 'Perspectives on Australian Foreign Policy 1996', *Australian Journal of International Affairs*, vol. 51, no. 2, 1997.

127 John Howard, *Lazarus Rising*, Australia: HarperCollins, 2010, p. 321.

128 DFAT, *In the National Interest*.

129 Howard, *Lazarus Rising*, p. 258.

130 CPD, HR, 10 September 1996, p. 3859.

131 Paul Kelly, *The March of Patriots: The Struggle for Modern Australia*, Melbourne: Melbourne University Press, 2009, p. 368.

132 Quilty, 'Immigration and Multiculturalism', p. 319.

133 Howard, Lazarus Rising, p. 260.

134 Kelly, *The March of Patriots*, p. 455.

135 Kelly, *The March of Patriots*, p. 365.

136 Dobell, *Australia Finds Home*, p. 319.

137 CPD, HR, 10 September 1996, p. 3859.
138 John Howard, 'Australia's Defence Policy: Lessons from the Past, Principles for the Future', Speech to Australia Defence Association, 5 October 1995.
139 Australia–United States Ministerial Consultations, Joint Security Declaration, Sydney, 1996.
140 Howard, *Lazarus Rising*, p. 501.
141 Kelly, *The March of Patriots*, p. 452.
142 ibid., p. 455.
143 Howard, *Lazarus Rising*, p. 502.
144 ibid.
145 ibid., p. 503.
146 ibid., p. 501.
147 Kelly, *The March of Patriots*, p. 457.
148 ibid., p. 457.
149 ibid., p. 459.
150 DFAT, *In the National Interest*.
151 Glenn Stevens, 'The Asian Crisis: A Retrospective', Address to the Anika Foundation Luncheon, Sydney, 18 July 2007.
152 ibid.
153 ibid.
152 Keating, *Engagement*, p. 238.
153 Paul Blustein, *The Chastening: Inside the Crisis That Rocked the Global Financial System and Humbled the IMF*, New York: Public Affairs, 2001.
154 Stevens, 'The Asian Crisis: A Retrospective'.
155 Alexander Downer, 'The East Asian Economic Crisis and Our Place in the Region', Speech at Australian Stock Exchange, Sydney, 4 November 1998.
156 Alexander Downer, 'Australia and Asia – A New Paradigm for the Relationship', Speech to the Foreign Correspondents' Association', Sydney, 16 April 1999.
157 Kelly, *The March of Patriots*, p. 467.
158 Peter Costello, 'Australia's Role in Asia', Speech to the Asia Society, 16 October 2002.
159 Downer, 'Australia and Asia – a New Paradigm for the Relationship'.
160 Alexander Downer, 'Australia's Future in the Asia Pacific: Cooperation, Economic Reform and Liberalisation', Speech at the University of Melbourne, 8 May 1998.
161 Downer, 'The East Asian Economic Crisis and Our Place in the Region'.

8 THE NATIONAL SECURITY DECADE: 1998–2007

1 Department of Foreign Affairs and Trade, *East Timor in Transition 1998–2000: An Australian Policy Challenge*, Canberra: DFAT, 2001, p. 17.
2 Howard, *Lazarus Rising*, p. 338.
3 ibid., p. 341.
4 DFAT, *East Timor in Transition 1998–2000*, p. 181.
5 David Goldsworthy, 'East Timor' in David Goldsworthy and Peter Edwards (eds), *Facing North: A Century of Australian Engagement with Asia*, Vol. 2., Melbourne: Melbourne University Press, 2003, p. 228.
6 DFAT, *East Timor in Transition 1998–2000*, p. 183.
7 Goldsworthy, 'East Timor', p. 228.
8 ibid., p. 231.
9 ibid., p. 237.

10   DFAT, *East Timor in Transition 1998–2000*, p. 52.
11   Howard, *Lazarus Rising*, p. 343.
12   ibid.
13   Goldsworthy, 'East Timor', p. 239.
14   ibid., p. 245.
15   Howard, *Lazarus Rising*, p. 245.
16   Goldsworthy, 'East Timor', p. 248.
17   Howard, *Lazarus Rising*, p. 345.
18   ibid.
19   ibid., p. 346.
20   Goldsworthy, 'East Timor', p. 248.
21   Howard, *Lazarus Rising*, p. 347.
22   Goldsworthy, 'East Timor', p. 245.
23   Geoffrey Robinson, *East Timor 1999: Crimes Against Humanity*, Report
      Commissioned by the United Nations Office of the High Commissioner for
      Human Rights, 2003.
24   Goldsworthy, 'East Timor', p. 252.
25   Peter Cosgrove, *General Peter Cosgrove: My Story*, Sydney: HarperCollins, 2006,
      p. 313.
26   Kelly, *The March of Patriots*, p. 515.
27   James Cotton, 'The East Timor Commitment and Its Consequences', in James
      Cotton and David Goldsworthy (eds), *Trading on Alliance Security: Australia in
      World Affairs 2001–2005*, Melbourne: Oxford University Press, 2007, p. 226.
28   David Connery, *Crisis Policymaking: Australia and the East Timor Crisis of 1999*,
      Canberra: ANU E-press, 2010, p. 138.
29   Connery, *Crisis Policymaking*, p. 53.
30   Howard, *Lazarus Rising*, p. 357.
31   CPD, HR, 21 September 1999, pp. 10025–31.
32   M.C. Ricklefs, 'Australia and Indonesia', in Robert Manne (ed.), *The Howard
      Years*, Melbourne: Black Inc., 2004, p. 276.
33   CPD, HR, 21 September 1999, p. 10025.
34   DFAT, *East Timor in Transition 1998–2000*, p. 142.
35   Paul Kelly, *Howard's Decade: An Australian Foreign Policy Reappraisal*, Sydney:
      Lowy Institute for International Policy, 2006, p. 11.
36   John Howard, 'Australia in the World', Address to the Lowy Institute for
      International Policy, Sydney, 31 March 2005.
37   Paul Kelly, *The March of Patriots*, p. 569.
38   Downer, 'The East Asian Economic Crisis and Our Place in the Region'.
39   Roger Bell, 'Extreme Allies: Australia and the USA', in James Cotton and David
      Goldsworthy (eds), *Trading on Alliance Security: Australia in World Affairs
      2001–2005*, Melbourne: Oxford University Press, 2007, p. 25.
40   John Howard, Press Conference, Australian Embassy, Washington, DC,
      11 September 2001.
41   Howard, *Lazarus Rising*, p. 424.
42   Karen Middleton, *An Unwinnable War: Australia in Afghanistan*, Melbourne:
      Melbourne University Press, 2011, p. 29.
43   Kelly, *The March of Patriots*, p. 583.
44   Middleton, *An Unwinnable War*, p. 38.
45   Howard, *Lazarus Rising*, p. 425.
46   *The National Security Strategy of the United States of America*, Washington:

United States Government, 2002, p. 15.

47   Condoleezza Rice, Interview with Wolf Blitzer, CNN Late Edition, 8 September 2002.

48   Howard, *Lazarus Rising*, p. 430.

49   Department of Defence, *The War in Iraq: ADF Operations in the Middle East in 2003*, Canberra: Department of Defence, 2004.

50   CPD, HR, 17 September 2002, p. 6378.

51   John Howard, 'Strategic Leadership for Australia: Policy Directions in a Complex World', Address to Committee for Economic Development of Australia, Sydney, 20 November 2002.

52   CPD,HR: 16 September 2002, p. 6244.

53   CPD, HR, 4 February 2003, p. 10652.

54   Hans Blix, Statement to the UN Security Council on Inspection, 27 January 2003, <www.un.org/Depts/unmovic/Bx27.htm>.

55   'WMDS only "Bureaucratic Reason for War": Wolfowitz', *Sydney Morning Herald*, 29 May 2003.

56   Defence, 'The War in Iraq'.

57   ibid.

58   CPD, HR, 4 February 2003, p. 10644.

59   George W. Bush, Address to the Nation, 17 March 2003.

60   CPD, HR, 18 March 2003, p. 12506.

61   Howard, *Lazarus Rising*, p. 452.

62   Philip Flood, *Report of the Inquiry into Australian Intelligence Agencies*, Canberra, 2004.

63   Bell, 'Extreme Allies', p. 40.

64   Middleton, *An Unwinnable War*, p. 158.

65   ibid., p. 161.

66   ibid., p. 181.

67   ibid., p. 199.

68   ibid., p. 162.

69   Hugh White, 'Security, Defence and Terrorism', in James Cotton and David Goldsworthy (eds), *Trading on Alliance Security: Australia in World Affairs 2001–2005*, Melbourne: Oxford University Press, 2002, p. 189.

70   'Howard Blasts Obama', *Sydney Morning Herald*, 11 February 2007.

71   CPD, HR, 5 February 2003 p. 10926.

72   Anthony Bubalo, 'Perfect Strangers: Australia and West Asia', in James Cotton and John Ravenhill (eds), *Trading on Alliance Security: Australia in World Affairs 2001–2005*, Melbourne: Oxford University Press, 2007, p. 167.

73   'Howard Sees Pacific Involvement Growing', *The Age*, 8 April 2004.

74   ibid.

75   Alexander Downer, 'Papua New Guinea: The Road Ahead', Speech at the Launch of DFAT Economic Analytical Unit Report, Canberra, 2004.

76   ibid.

77   Kevin Rudd, Address to the PNG Business and Alumni Breakfast, Port Moresby, Papua New Guinea, 7 March 2008.

78   CPD, HR, 18 March 1997, p. 2263.

79   Gyngell and Wesley, *Making Australian Foreign Policy*, p. 3.

80   ibid., p. 5.

81   Peter Reith, *The Reith Papers*, Melbourne: Melbourne University Press, 2015.

82   Alexander Downer, 'The Earle Page College's Annual Politics Dinner', University of New England, Armidale, 2005.

83   Graeme Dobell, 'The Downer Legacy: Howard and Downer', *The Interpreter*, Sydney: Lowy Institute for International Policy, 2008.

84   Alexander Downer, 'The More Things Change Part 1', *Australian Story*, ABC TV, 2007.

85   Alexander Downer, Interview with Monica Attard, *Sunday Profile*, ABC TV, 30 March 2008.

86   Downer, 'Papua New Guinea: The Road Ahead'.

87   Howard, *Lazarus Rising*, p. 527.

88   Alexander Downer, 'Development in the Pacific', Speech to ANU Seminar, Canberra, 14 October 2003.

89   Downer, 'Papua New Guinea: The Road Ahead'.

90   Michael O'Keefe, 'Australia and Fragile States in the Pacific', in James Cotton and John Ravenhill (eds), *Trading on Alliance Security: Australia in World Affairs 2001–2005*, Melbourne: Oxford University Press, 2007, p. 137.

91   Downer, 'Papua New Guinea: The Road Ahead'.

92   Kevin Rudd, 'Port Moresby Declaration', Media release, 6 March 2008

93   Gyngell and Wesley, *Making Australian Foreign Policy*, p. 227.

94   Alexander Downer, 'Neighbours Cannot Be Recolonised', *The Australian*, 8 January 2003.

95   John Howard, Ministerial Statement to Parliament on the Regional Assistance Mission to the Solomon Islands, 12 August 2003.

96   Gyngell and Wesley, *Making Australian Foreign Policy*, p. 229.

97   Nautilus Institute, 'Australian Government Policy on Solomon Islands', accessed 6 December 2016 at: <http://nautilus.org/publications/books/australian-forces-abroad/solomon-islands/australian-government-policy-on-solomon-islands/>

98   Jenny Hayward-Jones, *Australia's Costly Investment in Solomon Islands: The Lessons of RAMSI*, Sydney: Lowy Institute for International Policy, 2014, p. 2.

99   ibid., p. 6.

100   ibid., p. 6.

101   Stewart Firth, 'Australia, the Pacific Islands and Timor Leste', in James Cotton and John Ravenhill (eds), *Middle Power Dreaming: Australia in World Affairs 2006–2010*, Melbourne: Oxford University Press, 2011, p. 151.

102   Janet Phillips and Harriet Spinks, *Boat Arrivals in Australian Since 1976*, Canberra: Parliament of Australia, 2013, p. 22.

103   John Howard, Interview on Radio 3AW, with Neil Mitchell, 31 August 2001.

104   Reith, *The Reith Papers*.

105   Carr, *Winning the Peace*, p. 107.

106   O'Keefe, 'Australia and Fragile States in the Pacific', p. 139.

107   Ravenhill, 'Australia and the Global Economy', p. 293.

108   Alexander Downer, Speech at the Opening of the Asia Leaders' Forum, Beijing, 23 April 2000.

109   John Howard, 'Australia's International Relations – Ready for the Future', Address to Menzies Research Centre, Canberra, 2001a).

110   Howard, *Lazarus Rising*, p. 521.

111   Phillips and Harriet Spinks, *Boat Arrivals in Australia since 1976*, p. 22.

112   John Menadue, 'The Pacific Solution Didn't Work before and It Won't Work Now', Centre for Policy Development (online), 8 March 2012.

113   Howard, *Lazarus Rising*. p. 413.

114   CPD, HR, 4 February 2003, p. 10647.

115   Howard, *Lazarus Rising*, p. 519.

116 Susilo Bambang Yudhoyono, Speech at the Great Hall, Parliament House, Canberra, 4 April 2005.

117 Gyngell, 'Australia and Indonesia', p. 109.

118 Ivan Cook, *Lowy Institute Poll 2006: Australia, Indonesia and the World*, Sydney: Lowy Institute for International Policy, 2006.

119 Gyngell and Wesley, *Making Australian Foreign Policy*, p. 10.

120 Ric Smith, Interview with author, 2016.

121 Ricklefs, 'Australia and Indonesia', p. 286.

122 Cotton, *East Timor, Australia and Regional Order*, p. 143.

123 Howard, *Lazarus Rising*, p. 521.

124 Susilo Bambang Yudhoyono, Address to Joint Sitting of Parliament, Canberra, 10 March 2010.

125 Department of Foreign Affairs and Trade, *Advancing the National Interest: Australia's Foreign and Trade Policy White Paper*, Canberra: DFAT, 2003.

126 Firth, *Australia, the Pacific Islands and Timor-Leste*, p. 151.

127 James Cotton and John Ravenhill, *Trading on Alliance Security: Australia in World Affairs 2001–2005*, Melbourne: Oxford University Press, 2007, p. 10.

128 John Howard, Address at the Reception to Mark the 25th Anniversary of Diplomatic Relations between Australian and China. Sheraton on the Park, Sydney', Canberra, 17 December 1997.

129 Kelly, *Howard's Decade*, p. 67.

130 Howard, *Lazarus Rising*, p. 505.

131 Alexander Downer, 'China's Industrial Rise: East Asia's Challenge', Speech at the Launch of Economic Analytical Unit Report, Hotel Intercontinental, Sydney, 29 October 2003.

132 Alexander Downer, 'Australia and China's Shared Interests – Security and Strategic Dimensions', Speech to Australia-China Free Trade Agreement Conference, Sydney, 13 August 2004.

133 John Howard, 'Australia's Engagement with Asia: A New Paradigm', Address to the AsiaLink-ANU National Forum, Canberra, 13 August 2004.

134 John Howard, '2007 Election Campaign Speech', Brisbane, 12 November 2007.

135 Ivan Cook, *Australians Speak 2005: Public Opinion and Foreign Policy*, Sydney: Lowy Institute for International Affairs, 2005.

136 Kevin Rudd, 'A Conversation with China's Youth on the Future', Peking University, 12 June 2008.

137 ibid.

138 Howard, 'Australia in the World', Address to the Lowy Institute for International Policy, Sydney, 31 March 2005.

139 Kevin Rudd, 'Remarks Following a Meeting with Prime Minister Fukuda, Tokyo', 12 June 2008.

140 Howard, *Lazarus Rising*, p. 529.

141 Alexander Downer, 'Australian Response to Indian Nuclear Tests', Media release, Canberra, 14 May 1998.

142 Gurry, *Australia and India*, p. 169.

143 Alexander Downer, 'Australia Backs Down over Indian Nuclear Program', *AM*, ABC Radio National, 24 March 2000.

144 Howard, *Lazarus Rising*, p. 530.

145 Kelly, *Howard's Decade*, p. 66.

146 Gurry, *Australia and India*.

147 Howard, *Lazarus Rising*, p. 530.

148 Alexander Downer, 'Australia, Asia and Drivers for Global Change', Speech to Davos Future Summit, Brisbane, 12 May 2006.

149 Middleton, *An Unwinnable War*, p. 165.

150 John Howard, 'Safeguarding the Future: Australia's Response to Climate Change', Statement by the Prime Minister of Australia, Canberra: AGPS, 1997.

151 Howard, *Lazarus Rising*, p. 553.

152 Howard, 'Safeguarding the Future'.

153 Lorraine Elliot, 'Australia in World Environmental Affairs', in James Cotton and Ravenhill (eds), *The National Interest in a Global Era: Australia in World Affairs 1996–2000*, Melbourne: Oxford University Press, 2002, p. 250.

154 Ivan Cook, *Lowy Institute Poll 2006: Australia, Indonesia and the World*, Sydney: Lowy Institute for International Policy, 2006.

155 Howard, *Lazarus Rising*, p. 551.

156 Mark P. Thirlwell, *The New Terms of Trade*, Sydney: Lowy Institute for International Policy, 2005, p. 105.

157 Bell, 'Extreme Allies', p. 46.

158 Gyngell and Wesley, *Making Australian Foreign Policy*, p. 268.

159 ibid., p. 270.

160 ibid., p. 271.

161 Shiro Armstrong, 'The Economic Impact of the Australia–United States Free Trade Agreement', *Australian Journal of International Affairs*, vol. 69, no. 5, 2015.

162 Kevin Rudd, Prime Ministerial Statement on National Security, Hansard, Canberra: AGPS, 4 December 2008, p. 12549.

163 ibid.

164 Martin Wolf, *The Shifts and the Shocks: What Weve Learned – and Have Still to Learn from the Financial Crisis*, London: Allen Lane, 2014, p. 19ff.

165 Kevin Rudd, Press Conference, Blair House, Washington, 28 March 2008.

9 A FRAGMENTING WORLD: 2008–2017

1 Kevin Rudd, 'The Australia We Can All Be Proud of', Charteris Lecture, Australian Institute of International Affairs, Sydney, 24 November 2011.

2 Kevin Rudd, Prime Minister's Statement on National Security, CPD, HR, 4 December 2008, p. 12549.

3 Rudd, 'The Australia We Can All Be Proud of'.

4 Paul Kelly, *Triumph and Demise: The Broken Promise of a Labor Generation*, Melbourne: Melbourne University Press, 2014, p. 151.

5 BBC News, 'IMF in Global "Meltdown" Warning', 12 November 2008.

6 Kevin Rudd, Address to the United Nations General Assembly, New York, 25 September 2008.

7 Patrick Weller, *Kevin Rudd: Twice Prime Minister*, Melbourne: Melbourne University Press, 2014, p. 371.

8 ibid., p. 234.

9 Personal interview.

10 G-20 Leaders Statement: The Pittsburgh Summit, 25 September 2009.

11 Tony Mcdonald and Steve Morling, 'The Australian Economy and the Global Downturn Part 1: Reasons for Resilience', Treasury Economic Roundup, Issue 2, 2011.

12 Julia Gillard, *Julia Gillard: My Story*, Sydney: Knopf, 2014, p. 196.

13 ibid., p. 203.

14 Kelly, *Triumph and Demise*, p. 151.
15 Gillard, *Julia Gillard: My Story*, p. 158.
16 Kelly, *Triumph and Demise*, p. 149.
17 Barack Obama, 'Face to Face with Obama', *7.30 Report*, ABC TV, 14 April 2010.
18 Gillard, *Julia Gillard: My Story*, p. 155.
19 'The Age Publishes Wikileaks Cables from US Embassy', *The Age*, 15 December 2010.
20 Kevin Rudd, Press Conference, Parliament House, Canberra, 29 April 2009.
21 Middleton, *An Unwinnable War*, p. 219.
22 CPD, HR, 19 October 2010, p. 692.
23 Tony Abbott, Address at Recognition Ceremony, Tarin Kot, 23 October 2013.
24 Michael Cooney, *The Gillard Project: My Thousand Days of Despair and Hope*, Penguin Viking, 2015, p. 82.
25 Julia Gillard, Address to Congress of the United States, 10 March 2011.
26 Barack Obama, 'Remarks by President Obama to the Australian Parliament', 17 November 2011.
27 Gillard, *Julia Gillard: My Story*, p. 158.
28 ibid.
29 Lowy Institute for International Policy, *The Lowy Institute Poll – Understanding Australian Attitudes to the World*, Sydney: Lowy Institute for International Policy, 2016.
30 Department of Defence, *2016 Defence White Paper*, Canberra, 2016.
31 Kevin Rudd, Keynote Address, Shangri-La Dialogue, Singapore, 29 May 2009.
32 Greg Sheridan, 'Indonesia Shows New Sympathy in Politics and Human Grief', *The Australian*, 13 March 2010.
33 Kim Beazley, 'The US Pivot and Australia's Role, Part 2', *The Strategist*, Canberra: Australian Security Policy Institute, 2016.
34 Hillary Clinton, Joint Press Conference between Foreign Minister Kevin Rudd and US Secretary of State Hillary Clinton, Washington, 17 September 2010.
35 Rudd, 'The Australia We Can All Be Proud of', Charteris Lecture, Australian Institute of International Affairs, Sydney, 24 November 2011.
36 Kelly, *Triumph and Demise*, p. 314.
37 Gillard, *Julia Gillard: My Story*, p. 169.
38 Middleton, *An Unwinnable War*, p. 268.
39 Gillard, *Julia Gillard: My Story*, p. 164.
40 Cooney, *The Gillard Project*, p. 238.
41 Australian Government, *Australia in the Asian Century White Paper*, Canberra, 2012.
42 Julia Gillard, Speech to the Asialink and Asia Society Lunch, Melbourne, 28 September 2011.
43 Rory Medcalf, 'The Indo-Pacific: What's in a Name?', *The National Interest*, vol. 9, no. 2, October 2013.
44 Department of Defence, 2013 *Defence White Paper*, Canberra, 2013.
45 Gillard, *Julia Gillard: My Story*, p. 187.
46 Narendra Modi, Address to Joint Session of the Australian Parliament, CPD, HR, 18 November 2014, p. 12730.
47 Gillard, *Julia Gillard: My Story*, p. 181.
48 Yudhoyono, Address to Joint Session of the Australian Parliament, CPD, HR, 10 March 2010, p. 2136.
49 Kevin Rudd, 'Australia and Indonesia – Inseparable Partners Working Together and Working Together in the World, Jakarta', 2008.
50 Gillard, *Julia Gillard: My Story*, p. 181.

51   ibid.

52   Australian Government, Joint Understanding on a Code of Conduct between the Republic of Indonesia and Australia in Implementation of the Agreement between the Republic of Indonesia and Australia on the Framework for Security Cooperation, completed at Bali, 28 August 2014.

53   Malcolm Turnbull, 2016 Lowy Lecture, Lowy Institute, Canberra, 23 March 2016.

54   Tony Abbott, Address at State Dinner Welcoming Prime Minister Nguyen Tan Dung, 18 March 2015.

55   Tony Abbott, Address to the 35th Singapore Lecture, Singapore, 29 June 2015.

56   James Massola and David Wroe, 'Australia Seals Trade Expansion and $2.25b Defence Deal with Singapore', *Sydney Morning Herald*, 6 May 2016.

57   Julia Gillard, Keynote Address to the Japan National Press Club, 22 April 2011.

58   AAP, 'Tony Abbott Reaches out to Australia's "Best Friend in Asia", Japan', *The Australian*, 10 October 2013.

59   Quoted in Warren Truss, 'Australia and Japan, Realising Our Potential', Speech to the Australia New Zealand Chamber of Commerce, Tokyo, 2006.

60   Gillard, Keynote Address to the Japan National Press Club.

61   Mark Kenny and Philip Wen, 'Tony Abbott Refuses to Back Down over China Comments', *Sydney Morning Herald*, 29 November 2013.

62   David Johnston, 'Defence Minister David Johnston Hails Defence Science and Technology Accord with Japan', 8 July 2014, accessed at: <www.minister.defence.gov.au/2014/07/08/minister-for-defence-defence-minister-david-johnston-hails-defence-science-and-technology-accord-with-japan>.

63   Agreement between the Government of Australia and the Government of Japan Concerning the Transfer of Defence Equipment and Technology, 8 July 2014.

64   Shinzo Abe, Address to Joint Session of the Australian Parliament, CPD, HR, 8 July 2014, p. 7645.

65   UNDP, *Human Development Index*, UNDP, 2015.

66   Peter Varghese, 'An Australian World View: A Practitioner's Perspective', Address to Lowy Institute, 20 August 2015.

67   Tim Meisburger, 'Groundbreaking Observer Group Certifies Fiji Elections', *Asia Foundation* (online), 22 April 2015.

68   Julie Bishop, Address to State of the Pacific Conference, Australian National University, 18 June 2014.

69   Firth, 'Australia, the Pacific Islands and Timor-Leste', p. 163.

70   Stephen Howes, 'Scaled Down. The Last of the Aid Cuts?', *DevPolicy*, Canberra: Development Policy Centre, 2016.

71   Daniel Flitton, 'Rudd Says Abstain on Palestine Vote; Gillard Backs Israel', *Sydney Morning Herald*, 8 August 2011.

72   Gillard, *Julia Gillard: My Story*, p. 171.

73   Gareth Evans, 'Gareth Evans: "Bob Learned Early Self-Deprecation Is for Dummies"', *The Conversation*, 14 April 2014.

74   Bob Carr, *Diary of a Foreign Minister*, Sydney: NewSouth Publishing, 2014.

75   Kevin Rudd, 'Keep the Faith with the Arab Spring', *The Australian*, 20 May 2011.

76   Malcolm Turnbull, National Security Statement, CPD, HR, 24 November 2015, p. 13483.

77   Tony Abbott, 'The Moral Case for the Howard Government', Speech to Young Liberal Convention, 23 January 2004.

78 Tony Abbott, *Battlelines*, Melbourne: Melbourne University Press, 2013, p. 161.

79 Michelle Grattan, 'Grattan on Friday: In Conversation with Tony Abbott', *The Conversation*, 2016.

80 Tony Abbott, 'The National Security Case for the Abbott Government', *The Australian*, 26 March 2016.

81 Jessica Tapp, 'Greg Sheridan: Tony Abbott Is a Romantic', *The Drum*, ABC News online, 29 July 2015, accessed at <www.abc.net.au/news/2015-07-28/sheridan-greg-sheridan:-the-pm-is-a-romantic/66528047>.

82 Peter Hartcher, 'Shirtfronted: The Story of the Abbott Government', *Sydney Morning Herald*, 29 November to 3 December 2015.

83 Emma Griffith, 'MH17: Prime Minister Tony Abbott Confirms "There Was Talk" About Sending Australian Troops into Ukraine after Plane Shot Down', ABC, 23 February 2015.

84 Niki Savva, *The Road to Ruin: How Tony Abbott and Peta Credlin Destroyed Their Own Government*, Melbourne: Scribe, 2016.

85 Tony Abbott, National Security Statement, Canberra, 22 February 2015.

86 James Brown, *Australia: Asian Research Network Survey on America's Role in the Asia-Pacific*, Sydney: United States Studies Centre, University of Sydney, 2016.

87 Abbott, 'National Security Statement'.

88 Tony Abbott, 'Paris Attacks: We Must Boost Military Role in the Middle East', *The Australian*, 17 November 2015.

89 Tony Abbott, Doorstop Interview, Melbourne, 27 June 2015.

90 Turnbull, National Security Statement, Canberra, 24 November 2015.

91 Phillips and Spinks, *Boat Arrivals in Australia since 1976*, p. 22.

92 Angus Houston, Paris Aristotle, and Michael L'Estrange, *Report of the Expert Panel on Asylum Seekers*, Australian Government, August 2012, p. 161.

93 Phillips and Spinks, *Boat Arrivals in Australia since 1976*, p. 22.

94 Gillard, *Julia Gillard: My Story*, p. 451.

95 Kelly, *Triumph and Demise*, p. 176.

96 Kevin Rudd, Doorstop Interview, Government House, Sydney, 17 April 2009.

97 Julia Gillard, 'Moving Australia Forward', Address to the Lowy Institute for International Policy', Sydney, 6 July 2010.

98 Paul Toohey, *That Sinking Feeling: Asylum Seekers and the Search for the Indonesian Solution*, Quarterly Essay 53, Melbourne: Black Inc., 2014.

99 Carr, *Winning the Peace*, p. 129.

100 Houston, Aristotle and L'Estrange, *Report of the Expert Panel on Asylum Seekers*.

101 Janet Phillips, 'Boat Arrivals in Australia: A Quick Guide to the Statistics', *Parliamentary Library Research Paper Series 2013–14*, Canberra: Australian Parliament, 2014.

102 Houston, Aristotle and L'Estrange, *Report of the Expert Panel on Asylum Seekers*.

103 Andrew Markus, *Mapping Social Cohesion: The Scanlon Foundation Surveys 2012*, Melbourne: Monash University, 2012, p. 3.

104 Houston, Aristotle and L'Estrange, *Report of the Expert Panel on Asylum Seekers*.

105 Bianca Hall and Jonathan Swan, 'Kevin Rudd to Send Asylum Seekers Who Arrive by Boat to Papua New Guinea', *Sydney Morning Herald*, 19 July 2013.

106 Kelly, *Triumph and Demise*, p. 483.

107 Abbott, 'The National Security Case for the Abbott Government'.

108 Dan Confier, 'First Refugees Sent to Cambodia under $55m Deal Have Left', ABC News online, 26 May 2016.

109   George Roberts and James Bennett, 'Tony Abbott Rules out Resettling Rohingyas in Australia, Indonesia Says It Is Obliged to', ABC News online, 21 May 2015.

110   Wayne Swan, *The Good Fight: Six Years, Two Prime Ministers and Staring Down the Great Recession*, Sydney: Allen & Unwin, 2014, p. 185.

111   Tony Abbott 'Abbott Discusses New Leadership Role', Interview with Tony Jones, ABC *Lateline*, 8 December 2009.

112   Intergovernmental Panel on Climate Change, *Concluding Instalment of the Fifth Assessment Report: Climate Change Threatens Irreversible and Dangerous Impacts, but Options Exist to Limit Its Effects*, Press release, 2 November 2014.

113   Howard Bamsey and Kath Rowley, *Australia and Climate Change Negotiations: At the Table, or on the Menu?*, Lowy Institute Analysis, Sydney: Lowy Institute for International Policy, 2015.

114   Alex Oliver, *The Lowy Institute Poll 2016*, Sydney: Lowy Institute for International Policy, 2016.

115   Bamsey and Rowley, 'Australia and Climate Change Negotiations'.

116   Julie Bishop and Tanya Plibersek, Debate at the National Press Club, 21 June 2016.

117   Julie Bishop, Address to the United Nations Association of Australia, National Press Club, Canberra, 2015.

118   Julie Bishop, National Statement, United Nations General Assembly 70th Session, 2015.

119   Malcolm Turnbull, Remarks at UN 70th Anniversary Reception, Sydney, 23 October 2015.

120   ibid.

121   Rudd, 'The Australia We Can All Be Proud of', Charteris Lecture, Australian Institute of International Affairs, Sydney, 24 November 2011.

122   Carr, *Diary of a Foreign Minister*, p. 79.

123   Kevin Rudd, 'A Change of Climate – A New Approach to Australia–Europe Relations', European Policy Centre Briefing, Brussels, 2 April 2008.

124   David Johnston, 'French and Australian Defence Ministers Meet in Perth, 2 November 2014, accessed at: <www.minister.defence.gov.au/2014/11/02/french-and-australian-defence-ministers-meet-in-perth>.

125   Malcolm Turnbull, Joint Press Conference with Prime Minister of France, 2 May 2016.

126   Prashanth Parameswan, 'TPP as Important as Another Aircraft Carrier: US Defense Secretary', *The Diplomat*, 8 April 2015.

127   Peter Martin, 'Trans-Pacific Partnership Will Barely Benefit Australia, Says World Bank Report', *The Age*, 13 January 2016.

128   Kevin Rudd, 'The Rise of China and the Strategic Implications for US-Australia Relations', Speech to The Brookings Institution, Washington DC, 31 March 2008.

129   Daniel Flitton, 'Rudd the Butt of WikiLeaks Exposé', *Sydney Morning Herald*, 6 December 2010.

130   Department of Defence, *Defending Australia in the Asia-Pacific Century: Force 2030*, Canberra, 2009.

131   Malcolm Turnbull, Launch of Australia's Cyber Security Strategy, Sydney, 21 April 2016.

132   Primrose Riordan and Paul Smith, 'Bureau of Meteorology Hit by Major Chinese Cyber Attack: Reports', *Australian Financial Review*, 2 December 2015.

133   Fergus Hanson, *The Lowy Institute Poll 2010*, Sydney: Lowy Institute for International Policy, 2010.

134 David Uren, *The Kingdom and the Quarry: China, Australia, Fear and Greed*, Melbourne: Black Inc., 2012, p. 67.

135 ibid., p. 80.

136 'Australia's Relations with China: Different Approaches', *The Economist*, 20 August 2009.

137 Uren, *The Kingdom and the Quarry*, p. 172.

138 Stephen Smith, 'Australia-China Relations: A Long-Term View', 26 October 2009.

139 Luke Santow, *Chinese Leader Mends Fences on Australian Visit*, ABC PM, 30 October 2009.

140 Australia–China Joint Statement, Canberra, 30 October 2009.

141 Gillard, *Julia Gillard: My Story*, p. 173.

142 Department of Defence, *2013 Defence White Paper*.

143 John Garnaut, '"Fear and Greed" Drive Australia's China Policy, Tony Abbott Tells Angela Merkel', *Sydney Morning Herald*, 16 April 2015.

144 Stephen Mcdonnell, 'East China Sea Row Escalates, as Wang Yi Tells Julie Bishop that Australia Has "Jeopardised Trust"', ABC online, 7 December 2013.

145 Mark Kenny and Philip Wen, 'Tony Abbott Lauds Wealth and Friendship in Speech at Business Forum in China', *Sydney Morning Herald*, 10 April 2014.

146 Andrew Robb, 'The China-Australia Free Trade Agreement', Speech, Sydney, 20 November 2014.

147 Xi Jinping, Address to Joint Session of the Australian Parliament, CPD, HR, 17 November 2014, p. 1272.

148 Australia Centre on China in the World, 'Chinese Investment in Australia', *The Australia-China Story*, accessed 7 July 2016 at: <http://aus.thechinastory.org/archive/chinese-investment-in-australia/>.

149 Joe Hockey and Julie Bishop, 'Australia to join the Asian Infrastructure Investment Bank', Joint media release, 24 June 2015.

150 Phil Coorey and Greg Earl, 'Tony Abbott Held Talks with Shinzo Abe before Decision on China Bank', *Australian Financial Review*, 1 November 2014.

151 Rowan Callick, 'Australia Will Join Asian Infrastructure Investment Bank', *The Australian*, 8 December 2014.

152 ibid.

153 Hockey and Bishop, 'Australia to Join the Asian Infrastructure Investment Bank'.

154 Callick, 'Australia Will Join Asian Infrastructure Investment Bank'.

155 Turnbull, 2016 Lowy Lecture.

156 ibid.

157 Department of Defence, *2016 Defence White Paper*.

158 Oliver, *The Lowy Institute Poll 2016*.

159 ibid.

160 Brown, *Australia: Asian Research Network Survey*.

161 ibid.

10 WHAT AUSTRALIAN FOREIGN POLICY?

1 Malcolm Turnbull, Remarks at bilateral meeting with Mr Shinzo Abe, Prime Minister of Japan, 14 January 2017.

2 Australian Government, *Australia in the Asian Century White Paper*, p. 98.

3 Julie Bishop, National Statement, United Nations General Assembly 70th Session, 29 September 2015.

4 Tony Abbott, Address to the UN General Assembly, 25 September 2014.

5   Malcolm Fraser, *Dangerous Allies*, Melbourne: Melbourne University Press, 2014; John McCarthy, 'Australian Foreign Policy', Speech to Australian Institute of International Affairs National Conference, 27 October 2014.

6   Varghese, 'An Australian World View'.

7   Ruchir Sharma, 'When Borders Close', *The New York Times*, 12 November 2016.

8   Department of Defence, *2016 Defence White Paper*.

9   Lowy Institute for International Policy, Submission to the Joint Standing Committee on Foreign Affairs, Defence and Trade Inquiry into Australia's Overseas Representation, 2011.

10   Lowy Institute for International Policy, *Global Diplomacy Index 2016*, Sydney: The Institute for International Policy, 2016.

11   Kim Beazley, 'Should Foreign Policy Play a Part in the Election Campaign?', Australian Institute of International Affairs website, updated 12 May 2016, accessed 5 December 2016 at: <www.internationalaffairs.org.au/australian_outlook/should-foreign-policy-play-a-part-in-the-election-campaign>.

12   Greg Earl, 'Opinion Poll Reveals Australians Split over What to Do About the US and China', *Australian Financial Review*, 10 June 2016.

INDEX